PREFACE

Thecla, believed to have been a disciple and colleague of the apostle Paul, became perhaps the most celebrated female saint and 'martyr' among Christians in late antiquity. She was recognized for her example of chastity, and honoured as an apostle and protomartyr, the first female martyr, of the early church. Thecla's example was associated with the piety of women—in particular, with issues of women's empowerment and ministry. Because of the patriarchal social customs of the time, these associations lent an air of controversy and 'transgressiveness' to her sanctity.

Thecla's fame can be traced quite early in written records, starting at least in the second century CE with the *Acts of Paul and Thecla*. This work served as the basis for later biographical legends about Thecla, and for the many references to her in ascetic treatises and miracle stories from late antiquity. Thecla also became a popular subject for Christian artists: her image is painted on walls, stamped on clay flasks and oil lamps, engraved on bronze crosses, wooden combs, and stone reliefs, etched onto golden glass medallions, and even woven into a textile curtain.

By the fourth and fifth centuries, devotion to Saint Thecla was widespread in the Mediterranean world; from Gaul (modern France) to Palestine, writers and artists extolled her as an exemplary virgin and martyr. However, it is not my task here to survey the geographical range of Thecla devotion, or to catalogue all the literary and artistic evidence related to the figure of Thecla. Much of this work has in fact already been done by other scholars.[1] Instead, I am more interested in reconstructing the *cult*

---

[1] Carl Holzhey, *Die Thekla-Akten: Ihre Verbreitung und Beurteilung in der Kirche*, Veröffentlichungen aus dem kirchengeschichtlichen Seminar München, 2/7 (Munich: J. J. Lentner, 1905); Claudia Nauerth and Rüdiger Warns, *Thekla: Ihre Bilder in der frühchristlichen Kunst* (Wiesbaden: O. Harrassowitz, 1981); Claudia Nauerth, 'Nachlese von Thekla-Darstellungen', in *Studien zur spätantiken und frühchristlichen Kunst und Kultur des Orients*, ed. G. Koch, Göttinger Orientforschungen, series 2, Studien zur spätantiken und frühchristlichen Kunst, vi (Wiesbaden: Otto Harrassowitz, 1982), 14–18, pl. 4–9.

of Saint Thecla—that is, the complex set of social practices (such as asceticism, pilgrimage, burial), institutions (such as churches, martyr shrines, monasteries), and material artefacts (such as texts, relics, sacred souvenirs) that marked the lives of actual devotees.

In this book, I focus my attention specifically on the cult of Saint Thecla in Asia Minor (modern Turkey) and Egypt: only in these regions does archaeological, artistic, and literary evidence provide enough context for a 'thick' description of communities and practices connected with Thecla devotion. Asia Minor has been the subject of previous study—its well-known shrine of Saint Thecla at Seleucia was the hub of her cult in late antiquity.[2] In contrast, the diverse but scattered evidence from Egypt has up till now been largely neglected. I bring this evidence together for the first time in order to reconstruct the Egyptian cult of Saint Thecla. I will argue that in both Egypt and Asia Minor, the cult of Saint Thecla remained closely linked with communities of women among whom Thecla's example was a source of empowerment and a cause of controversy.

---

[2] E. Herzfeld and S. Guyer, *Meriamlik und Korykos: Zwei christliche Ruinenstätte des Rauhen Kilikiens*, Monumenta Asiae Minoris Antique, ii (Manchester: Manchester University Press, 1930); G. Dagron (ed.), *Vie et miracles de Sainte Thècle* (Brussels: Société des Bollandistes, 1978).

OXFORD EARLY CHRISTIAN STUDIES

General Editors
Gillian Clark   Andrew Louth

THE OXFORD EARLY CHRISTIAN STUDIES series includes scholarly volumes on the thought and history of the early Christian centuries. Covering a wide range of Greek, Latin, and Oriental sources, the books are of interest to theologians, ancient historians, and specialists in the classical and Jewish worlds.

Athanasius and the Politics of Asceticism
David Brakke (1995)

Jerome's *Hebrew Questions on Genesis*
Translated with an introduction and commentary by
C. T. R. Hayward (1995)

Ambrose of Milan and the
End of the Nicene-Arian Conflicts
Daniel H. Williams (1995)

Arnobius of Sicca
Religious Conflict and Competition in the Age of Diocletian
Michael Bland Simmons (1995)

Gregory of Nyssa's Treatise
on the Inscriptions of the Psalms
Ronald E. Heine (1995)

Ascetics and Ambassadors of Christ
The Monasteries of Palestine 314–631
John Binns (1994) paperback (1996)

Titles in the series include:

John of Scythopolis and the Dionysian Corpus
Annotating the Areopagite
Paul Rorem and John Lamoreaux (1998)

Eusebius of Caesarea's
Commentary on Isaiah
M. J. Hollerich (1999)

Ascetic Eucharists
Food and Drink in Early Christian Ritual Meals
Andrew McGowan (1999)

The Cult
of Saint Thecla:

A Tradition of Women's Piety in Late Antiquity

Stephen J. Davis

OXFORD
UNIVERSITY PRESS

UNIVERSITY LIBRARY

*This book has been printed digitally and produced in a standard specification
in order to ensure its continuing availability*

OXFORD
UNIVERSITY PRESS

Great Clarendon Street, Oxford OX2 6DP

Oxford University Press is a department of the University of Oxford.
It furthers the University's objective of excellence in research, scholarship,
and education by publishing worldwide in

Oxford New York

Auckland Bangkok Buenos Aires Cape Town Chennai
Dar es Salaam Delhi Hong Kong Istanbul Karachi Kolkata
Kuala Lumpur Madrid Melbourne Mexico City Mumbai Nairobi
São Paulo Shanghai Taipei Tokyo Toronto

Oxford is a registered trade mark of Oxford University Press
in the UK and in certain other countries

Published in the United States
by Oxford University Press Inc., New York

© Stephen J. Davis 2001

ISBN 0-19-827019-4

Printed in Great Britain by
Antony Rowe Ltd., Eastbourne

ACKNOWLEDGEMENTS

While writing this book, I have been sustained by a family and by a community of scholars and friends whose support and counsel are difficult to measure. Above all, I owe a huge debt of gratitude to my wife Jennifer for her love, patience, and willingness to share me with 'that other woman', Thecla. Jenny, this work is dedicated to you and our children Evanleigh, Harrison, and Rowyn.

Among those who have assisted me directly in my research and writing, I especially want to thank Bentley Layton for his critical eye and his cogent advice as I prepared my manuscript for publication. I owe special thanks as well to Maria Georgopoulou, who instilled in me a passion for early Christian and Byzantine art: εὐχαριστῶ γιά αὐτό τό πολύτιμο δῶρον. I also have had the pleasure of working closely with Rowan Greer and Wayne Meeks; both read large portions of my manuscript and were charitable with their time and suggestions. In addition, other colleagues have provided invaluable help, criticism, and encouragement: among them, Roger Bagnall, Paul-Alain Beaulieu, Betsy Bolman, David Brakke, Elizabeth Clark, Jaime Clark-Soles, Scott Cormode, Andrew Crislip, Stephen Emmel, Georgia Frank, David Frankfurter, Todd Hickey, Theo Joppe, Rebecca Krawiec, Susan Matheson, Timothy Poncé, Stephen Shoemaker, Warren Smith, Donald Spanel, Heinrich von Staden, and Terry Wilfong. In the summer of 1995, Henry Maguire and the staff at Dumbarton Oaks in Washington, DC, showed me great hospitality and helped facilitate my research into early Byzantine pilgrimage. Opportunities to lecture at Harvard University and at the American Research Center in Egypt allowed me to refine my interpretation of Egyptian wall paintings of Saint Thecla in Chapter 5. I also want to recognize those institutions and persons who have facilitated my research in Egypt: Yale University, the American Research Center in Egypt (ARCE), the Dar Comboni Arabic Study Centre, the Evangelical Theological Seminary in Cairo (ETSC), the Société d'archéologie copte, the

Deutsches Archäologisches Institute in Cairo, Peter and Eleni Grossmann, Josef Engelmann, Monsour Osman and Abd el Aziz at El Bagawat, his Eminence Archbishop Damianos, and the gracious monks at the Monastery of Saint Catherine. Finally, I want to thank Hilary O'Shea, Gillian Clark, Andrew Louth, Georga Godwin, John Callow, and the other editors associated with Oxford University Press for their fine work in preparing my book for publication.

Stephen J. Davis

Cairo, Egypt
14 November 1999

CONTENTS

LIST OF FIGURES

ABBREVIATIONS

For bibliographic abbreviations, I use those found in the *Society of Biblical Literature: Membership Directory and Handbook* (Decatur, Ga.: Society of Biblical Literature, 1994), 231–40; for Greek patristic works, those in G. H. W. Lampe, *Patristic Greek Lexicon* (Oxford: Clarendon Press, 1961), pp. ix–xliii; for classical Greek works, those in H. G. Liddell and R. Scott, *A Greek-English Lexicon*, 9th edn. (Oxford: Clarendon Press, 1990), pp. xvi–xlv; for Greek papyrological sources, those in *Checklist of Editions of Greek and Latin Papyri, Ostraca and Tablets*, 4th edn., ed. John F. Oates, Roger S. Bagnall, William H. Willis, and Klaas A. Worp (Bulletin of the American Society of Papyrologists, Supplements 7 (Atlanta: Scholars Press, 1992). However, note the following exceptions:

AA	*Acts of Andrew* (*Acta Andrae*), ed. Jean-Marc Prieur, CCSA 6 (1989).
ATh	*Acts of Paul and Thecla*, in *Acta Apostolorum Apocrypha*, ed. Richard A, Lipsius and M. Bonnet (Leipzig: Hermann Mendelssohn, 1891) 235–72.
Apa Mêna	*Apa Mêna: A Selection of Coptic Texts Relating to St. Menas*, ed. James Drescher (Cairo: Société d'archéologie copte, 1946).
CCSA	Corpus Christianorum, Series Apocryphorum (Turnhout: Brepols, 1983–).
CCSL	Corpus Christianorum, Series Latina (Turnhout: Brepols, 1953–).
CSEL	Corpus Scriptorum ecclesiasticorum latinorum (Vienna: Geroldi, 1866–).

Casey
 'Der dem Athanasius
zugeschriebene Traktat Περὶ
παρθενίας', ed. R. P. Casey,
SPAW 33 (1935), 1026–45.

Conybeare
 *The Apology and Acts of
Apollonius and Other Monuments
of Early Christianity*, ed. F. C.
Conybeare (London: Swan
Sonnenschein; New York:
Macmillan, 1894).

Dag.
 Vie et Miracles de Sainte Thècle,
ed. Gilbert Dagron (Brussels:
Société des Bollandistes, 1978).

Francheschini
 Egeria, *Itinerarium*, ed. E.
Francheschini and R. Weber,
CCSL 175 (1958), 27–90.

Hennecke-Schneemelcher
 New Testament Apocrypha, 2
vols., rev. edn., ed. E. Hennecke
and W. Schneemelcher, trans.
R. McL. Wilson (Cambridge:
James Clarke & Co.; Louisville,
Ky.: Westminster, 1992).

Lefort
 Athanasius, *Lettres festales et
pastorales*, i, ed. L. Th. Lefort
(CSCO 150; Louvain:
L. Durbecq, 1955).

Reymond and Barns
 *Four Martyrdoms from the
Pierpont Morgan Coptic Codices*,
ed. E. A. E. Reymond and J. W.
B. Barns (Oxford: Clarendon
Press, 1973).

PART I

The Cult of Saint Thecla in Asia Minor

I

Origins of the Thecla Cult

INTRODUCTION

For Christians living in the late Roman Empire, holiness was by
no means simply a private matter. Not only were holy virtues
preached to the laity from public pulpits, but 'holy persons'
—especially heroic monks and martyrs—were understood by
many to be conduits of both spiritual and social power. In the
eyes of the faithful, such figures played important civic roles as
healers, exorcists, patrons, counsellors, and arbiters of disputes.[1]
During life, their personal sanctity attracted cadres of adherents and onlookers; after death, their exploits were retold (and
multiplied) in hagiographical narratives. The lives of these
saints were presented in such texts as models for pious imitation:[2]

---

[1] Peter Brown, 'The Rise and Function of the Holy Man in Late Antiquity',
Journal of Roman Studies, 61 (1971), 80–101; I use the reprinted version of this
article (with updated notes) that appears in his book *Society and the Holy in Late
Antiquity* (Berkeley: University of California Press, 1982), 103–52. In a more
recent assessment, Brown recognizes how the civic role of such holy persons
was a function of their *representation* in hagiographical literature (P. Brown,
'Arbiters of the Holy: The Christian Holy Man in Late Antiquity', in *Authority
and the Sacred: Aspects of the Christianization of the Roman World* (Cambridge:
Cambridge University Press, 1995), 55–78, 85–7).

[2] In such lives, Christian writers 'could present an image not only of the
perfect Christian life, but also of the life in imitation of Christ, the life that
becomes an icon' (A. Cameron, *Christianity and the Rhetoric of Empire: The
Development of Christian Discourse* (Berkeley: University of California Press, 1991),
143). Richard Valantasis characterizes the lives of early Christian ascetics as 'tex-
tualized performances' that constructed an 'imitable subject' (R. Valantasis,
'Constructions of Power in Asceticism', *Journal of the American Academy of
Religion* 63/4 (1995) 799). On the presentation of saints as models for imitation,
see also Peter Brown, 'The Saint as Exemplar in Late Antiquity', in J. S. Hawley
(ed.), *Saints and Virtues* (Berkeley: University of California Press, 1987), 3–14;
this article originally appeared in *Representations*, 1/2 (1983), 1–25.

by imitating the saints, ordinary Christians believed that they could gain access to the power of Christ manifest in the saints' lives.

Devotion to the saints could take many forms—from radical acts of asceticism and long pilgrimage journeys to more mundane activities like the decoration of a grave, the reading of sacred texts at a local martyr shrine, or private veneration of images in the home. This diverse array of social practices, and the institutions that accompanied them, is commonly referred to as the *cult of the saints*. For the historian of late antiquity, the literature and arte-facts connected with the cult of a saint can serve as vital evidence for assessing the values and even the social practices of devotees who participated in the life of the cult.[3] In this book, I focus on evidence related to the cult of Saint Thecla—a female saint whose popularity rivalled that of Mary in the early church—in an attempt to reconstruct traditions of women's piety associated with her cult.

The cult of Saint Thecla originated and flourished in Asia Minor (modern Turkey). During the fourth and fifth centuries of our era, she was lauded in literature as an exemplary virgin and martyr by ascetic writers and theologians such as Methodius, Gregory of Nyssa, and Gregory of Nazianzus, and her burial place became a vibrant centre for international pilgrimage.

The saint's reputation for virginity impressed itself deeply on ascetic admirers in the fourth century. Methodius, in his *Symposium* written *c*.300 CE, establishes Thecla as the 'chief' among a choir of virgins who present speeches in the work glorifying virginity.[4] Her speech extols the virtue of those who think little of 'wealth, glory, birth, and (earthly) marriage',[5] and at the end of the discourses, she is given the honour of leading the other virgins in a hymn celebrating their spiritual marriage to Christ.[6] The learned theologians Gregory of Nazianzus and Gregory of Nyssa (late fourth century CE) describe Thecla in similar terms. Gregory of Nazianzus presents Thecla as one who had escaped

---

[3] Recently it has been recognized how the life of a holy person or saint func-tioned as a 'validator of practices that were widespread within Christian com-munities of the time' (P. Brown, 'Arbiters of the Holy', 60).

[4] Methodius, *Symp.* 11. 1; ed. H. Musurillo, SC 95 (1963), 308. 57.

[5] Methodius, *Symp.* 8. 2; ed. H. Musurillo, SC 95 (1963), 204. 12.

[6] Methodius, *Symp.* 11. 2; ed. H. Musurillo, SC 95 (1963), 308 ff.

marriage and the 'tyranny' of her betrothed.[7] Gregory of Nyssa calls her the apostle Paul's virgin disciple, and as one 'whose story was considered of great importance among the virgins'.[8]

Thecla also was given a place among the pantheon of martyrs celebrated by Christian writers in late-antique Asia Minor. Gregory of Nazianzus includes Thecla as the only female witness in a list of early Christian apostolic martyrs including John, Peter, Paul, James, Stephen, Luke, and Andrew.[9] Elsewhere, she is honoured as the first female martyr and ranked alongside her counterpart Stephen, the first male martyr (Acts 6: 8–7: 60).[10]

Thecla's popularity in the region extended from Constantinople to Syria, but the focal point of Thecla devotion was her martyr shrine, Hagia Thekla, near the city of Seleucia (modern Silifke, Turkey) in south-central Asia Minor (see map of Asia Minor, Fig. 1). In 374, Gregory of Nazianzus himself withdrew to the shrine of 'the highly praised young maid Thecla'[11] at Seleucia in order to evade an undesirable episcopal post. About a decade later (*c*.384 CE) the female pilgrim Egeria, whose *Itinerarium* provides us with valuable information about early Christian pilgrimage and the Jerusalem liturgy, made a special trip to Hagia Thekla on her way back home from visiting the Holy Land.

Only three nights from Tarsus, in Isauria, is the martyr shrine of Saint Thecla. Since it was so close we were pleased to travel there.[12]

In the early fifth century Marana and Cyra, two ascetic women from Beroea in Syria, made a pilgrimage to 'the shrine of the triumphant Thecla in Isauria', journeying the entire way there and back without any food.[13] Even from this cursory survey of well-known, early visitors to Hagia Thekla, it is evident that by the fifth century the shrine of Thecla at Seleucia accommodated

---

[7] Gregory of Nazianzus, *Or.* 24. 10 (PG 35. 1180D–1181A).
[8] Gregory of Nyssa, *In Cantica Canticorum, Homily* 14 (PG 44. 1068A); *V. Macr.* 2, ed. Pierre Maraval (SC 178), 148; PG 46. 961B.
[9] Gregory of Nazianzus, *Or.* 4. 69 (*Contra Julianum* i); PG 35. 589B.
[10] *Life* 1. 12–15 (5th cent. CE), ed. G. Dagron, *Vie et miracles de Sainte Thècle* (Brussels: Société des Bollandistes, 1978), 172 (= 172 Dag.).
[11] Gregory of Nazianzus, *De vita sua*, 548–9 (PG 37. 1067).
[12] Egeria, *Itin.* 22. 2, ed. E. Francheschini and R. Weber, CCSL 175. 65–6 (= 65–6 Francheschini).
[13] Theodoret of Cyrrhus, *H. rel. 29* (PG 82. 1283–496).

a visible, international pilgrimage clientele. Excavations this century have uncovered the fifth-century remains of three basilicas, a large public bath, and a number of cisterns (Fig. 2).[14] The main basilica at the site measured over 80 metres in length. These remains attest to the large number of pilgrims who visited Hagia Thekla and the rapid physical development of her cultic centre in the fifth century.

Who was Saint Thecla, and why did her life inspire such a cultic following? Thecla's story first appears in the late-second century *Acts of Paul and Thecla* (*ATh*).[15] The text, which narrates events set in Asia Minor, served as a foundation for the development of later legends and practices associated with Thecla the saint. It became both a source of hagiographic information and a narrative prototype for later literary and artistic adaptations of her legend. The protagonist of the story is not Paul, but Thecla, a young woman allegedly from the city of Iconium[16] in Asia Minor. The plot can be summarized briefly. It consists of two acts.

Thecla, a young woman of Iconium, is betrothed to a man named Thamyris, when the apostle Paul comes preaching a message of chastity. Enamoured of his teaching, Thecla leaves her fiancé and follows Paul. Enraged, the fiancé and Thecla's mother Theocleia petition the governor of Iconium to have Paul exiled[17] and Thecla burned at the stake for disrupting marital convention. However, when Thecla is brought to the stake, a miraculous storm of rain and hail quenches the flames. Afterward, Thecla is reunited with Paul in a cave at Daphne by Antioch; there she asks to be baptized, offering to cut her hair short as a sign of commitment. But fearing that she might succumb to future temptation, Paul puts her off her request.

---

[14] E. Herzfeld and S. Guyer, *Meriamlik und Korykos: Zwei christliche Ruinenstätten des Rauhen Kilikiens*, Monumenta Asiae Minoris Antique, ii. (Manchester: Manchester University Press, 1930), 1–89.

[15] The fullest critical edition is still to be found in *Acta Apostolorum Apocrypha*, ed. R. A. Lipsius and M. Bonnet (Leipzig: Hermann Mendelssohn, 1891); Coptic version (fragmentary), *Acta Pauli: Aus der heidelberger koptischen Papyrushandscrift*, no. 1, ed. Carl Schmidt (Leipzig: Hinrichs, 1904).

[16] The city also figures in Luke's biography of Paul: Acts 13: 51–14: 6; 16: 2.

[17] Iconium is mentioned as a place where Paul taught and suffered persecution in 2 Tim. 3: 11.

Thecla then travels with Paul to Antioch, and on the road a man named Alexander attempts to rape her. Thecla resists by tearing his clothes and publicly humiliating him. In anger, Alexander arranges to have Thecla thrown to the beasts. In the arena, attacked by lions, bears, and raging bulls, she dives into a pool filled with ravenous seals and thus baptizes herself. She is preserved from harm by a bolt of lightning that strikes the seals dead, and, awestruck by her power, the governor releases her. Thecla then dresses like a man to travel to Myra, where she finds Paul preaching. With his blessing, she returns to Iconium and begins to teach where Paul had taught. A short epilogue relates that her life ends near Seleucia—there she 'slept with a noble sleep' (μετὰ καλοῦ ὕπνου ἐκοιμήθη).[18]

While Thecla's story probably had roots in oral legend (I shall give the reasons for this assumption later in this chapter), the *ATh* was originally published as a chapter of the larger *Acts of Paul*, a collection of stories that report the apostle Paul's travels, teaching, and working of wonders throughout Asia Minor.[19] Tertullian, writing in North Africa around the year 200 CE, provides the first known external reference to the *Acts of Paul* and the story of Thecla. In his treatise *On Baptism*, he remarks on the 'example of Thecla' (*exemplum Theclae*) in 'the falsely written Acts of Paul' (*Acta Pauli quae perperam scripta sunt*) as a common source of appeal for those who mistakenly 'defend the liberty of women to teach and to baptize' (*ad licentiam mulierum docendi tinguendique defendere*).[20] Tertullian's reference to the *Acts of Paul* corroborates the provenance of the work by identifying its author as a 'presbyter in Asia [Asia Minor]'.[21] Tertullian also

---

[18] *ATh* 43.

[19] The genre of the Apostolic Acts was a popular one in the second and third centuries CE—Acts of Peter, Andrew, John, and Thomas were also produced. Such works share with the *Acts of Paul* a similar ascetic outlook and affinity for the miraculous.

[20] *De bapt.* 17 (CSEL 20. 215). There are some important textual problems with this passage. In the manuscript tradition of Tertullian's *On Baptism*, there are two extant Latin versions and they differ at this point, while Thecla's name appears in both Latin versions, some editors have questioned whether it was part of Tertullian's original text (T. Mackay, 'Response', *Semeia*, 38 (1986), 145–6).

[21] The author's acquaintance with the roadways of Paul's travels perhaps offers further confirmation of this geographical background (W. M. Ramsay, 'The Acta of Paul and Thekla,' in *The Church in the Roman Empire Before A.D. 170* (New York and London: Putnam, 1893), 375–428).

provides a *terminus ante quem* for dating the *Acts of Paul*: the Asian presbyter had to have completed the work before the end of the second century. The *terminus post quem* is less certain.[22] Finally, in addition to provenance and dating, Tertullian also offers a clue as to the social context of the work's reception. Specifically, Tertullian's polemic against those who 'defend the liberty of women to teach and to baptize' confirms Thecla's early association with the social and religious empowerment of women.

WOMEN'S CULTURE IN THE *ACTS OF PAUL* AND *THECLA*

In recent scholarship, much attention has been given not only to the literary role of women in the *ATh*, but also to the reconstructed role and place of real women in the ancient author's environment. The prominence of female characters in the *ATh* (and in other apocryphal Acts of the apostles) has prompted a considerable amount of speculation about the relation of women's communities to the composition of the *ATh*.

Beyond the fact that the heroine is a woman, the role of women in the *ATh* is underscored by numerous references to female supporters of Thecla during her imprisonment and her trials in the arena. For example (*ATh* 27), an anonymous group of women appears before governor's judgement seat in Antioch. After the governor condemns Thecla to the beasts for resisting the advances of Alexander, these women cry out, 'An evil judgement! An unholy judgement!'[23] The advocacy of this group of women becomes a consistent motif throughout the rest of the story. As Thecla is being led with the beasts in procession, the women with their children cry out again along the route, saying: 'O God, an unholy judgement is occurring in this city!'[24] During Thecla's contest with the beasts in the arena, the group

---

[22] The *Acts of Paul* has generally been assigned to the late second century, with its apparent dependence upon the *Acts of Peter* cited as a factor in this dating (Hennecke-Schneemelcher, 235; on the priority of the *Acts of Peter*, see Πράξεις Παύλου: *Acta Pauli nach dem Papyrus der hamburger Staats- und Universitätsbibliothek* ed. C. Schmidt (Glückstadt and Hamburg: J. J. Augustin, 1936), 127 ff.). However, the dating of the *Acts of Peter* itself is also tenuous.

[23] *ATh* 27.   [24] *ATh* 28.

of women appears again. First, when Thecla indicates her intention to baptize herself in the pool of seals, the women weep and implore Thecla not to cast herself into the water.[25] Then later, after Thecla emerges unscathed from the water and other beasts are set loose upon her, the women again voice their protest and throw leaves, nard, cassia, and amomum, so that 'an abundance of perfumes' ($\pi\lambda\hat{\eta}\theta os\ \mu\acute{v}\rho\omega v$) fills the arena.[26] At crucial times throughout the second half of the narrative, this faceless group of women functions almost like the chorus in a Greek tragedy, reappearing and voicing their commentary of support or lamentation over the heroine's predicament.

In particular, Thecla enjoys the support of 'a certain rich woman named Tryphaena, whose daughter had died'.[27] Thecla quickly becomes a proxy for her late daughter. Tryphaena's dead daughter Falconilla appears to Tryphaena in a dream and validates Thecla's role as her surrogate: 'Mother, you will have in my place the stranger, the desolate one, Thecla, in order that she may pray for me and that I may be translated to the place of the righteous.'[28] Tryphaena actively embraces Thecla as her own, taking her into her home and loving her 'like her own daughter Falconilla'.[29] By providing safe haven for Thecla on the eve of her battle with the beasts, Tryphaena effectively protects Thecla from further sexual assault.[30] Finally, when Thecla is taken away to the beasts, Tryphaena mourns again just as she had for Falconilla: 'A second mourning for my Falconilla comes upon my house . . .'[31] Tryphaena's public fainting during the tortures of Thecla in the arena finally has the fortuitous effect of bringing Thecla's trials to an end. The governor stops the proceedings abruptly because he becomes dismayed at the thought that he may reap the punishment for so distressing a 'kinswoman' of

---

[25] *ATh* 34.

[26] *ATh* 35. Perfumes were used to anoint bodies for burial in antiquity; the implication in this scene is that the women feel that Thecla's death is imminent.

[27] *ATh* 27.   [28] *ATh* 28.   [29] *ATh* 29.

[30] Thecla is taken under Tryphaena's wing immediately after 'Thecla asked the governor that she might remain pure until she was to fight with the beasts' (*ATh* 27). After Tryphaena escorts Thecla to the arena, Thecla gives thanks to God and asks that Tryphaena might receive a reward 'because she has kept me pure' (*ATh* 31).

[31] *ATh* 30.

Caesar.[32] In the end, Tryphaena not only becomes Thecla's first convert, but also ushers in the conversion of 'a great many of the female servants' under her charge.[33]

Thecla's association with female characters extends even to her confrontation with the wild animals in the arena. Among all the beasts Thecla faces, a 'fierce lioness' befriends her, licking her feet during the procession before the games.[34] Later in the arena, that same lioness defends Thecla against two male animals, a bear and a lion.[35] The lioness's battle with the bear and lion serves as a metaphor for Thecla's own struggles against the opposition and antagonism of male characters in the story. By punctuating the battle between the lioness and the male beasts with the supportive responses of the anonymous 'crowd of women,' the story incorporates the lioness into that community of female supporters, and portrays the animal herself as a martyr for Thecla's cause.

Thecla's consistent association with women throughout the narrative prompts important questions from those interested in the social-historical study of women's roles in early Christianity. First, for whom was the *ATh* written? Several scholars have suggested that the favourable characterization of women in the *ATh* would have especially resonated with female readers or listeners.[36] Within the story Thecla becomes sympathetically linked with other women—a chorus of female spectators, the patroness Tryphaena along with the women in her household, and even a lioness in the arena.

The devaluing of men in the *ATh*, uncharacteristic for ancient literature, also raises the possibility that the work would have attracted a female audience. Even a cursory reading of the *ATh* reveals a stark contrast of moral characterization along gender

---

[32] *ATh* 36.   [33] *ATh* 39.   [34] *ATh* 28.   [35] *ATh* 33.

[36] Stevan L. Davies, *The Revolt of the Widows: The Social World of the Apocryphal Acts* (Carbondale, Ill.: Southern Illinois University Press, 1980); Dennis Ronald MacDonald, *The Legend and the Apostle: The Battle for Paul in Story and Canon* (Philadelphia: Westminster Press, 1983); id., 'The Role of Women in the Production of the Apocryphal Acts of Apostles', *Iliff Review*, 41 (1984), 21–38; Virginia Burrus, *Chastity as Autonomy: Women in the Stories of the Apocryphal Acts*, Studies in Women and Religion, 23 (Lewiston; Queenston: Edwin Mellon Press, 1987); Ross Shepard Kraemer, *Her Share of the Blessings: Women's Religions Among Pagans, Jews, and Christians in the Greco-Roman World* (New York and Oxford: Oxford University Press, 1992), 153.

lines. While the women in the story (with the exception of Thecla's mother Theocleia) are portrayed favourably, the men in the story almost without exception are not. Thecla's fiancé Thamyris, Paul's disloyal companions Demas and Hermogenes, the sexual offender Alexander, the governors of Iconium and Antioch, and finally the male lions, bears, and bulls in the arena all conspire against Thecla and her commitment to chastity. Even the apostle Paul himself often comes across as obtuse or ambivalent. When Thecla, having been miraculously rescued from the fire, comes to him seeking baptism, he simply puts her off with the assumption that her (female) beauty would make her weak in the face of future temptations: 'The timing is bad; you are beautiful. Do not let another temptation take hold of you, worse than the first one, for fear that you not endure [it] and act as a coward.'[37] Later, when the suitor Alexander approaches him with the intent of seducing Thecla, Paul denies even knowing her, 'I do not know the woman you are talking about. And she is not mine.'[38] Finally, Paul disappears from the scene altogether just as Alexander attempts to rape Thecla. While this diametrical portrayal of male and female characters in the *ATh* is striking, it is impossible to draw any definitive conclusions about the work's audience from this internal evidence alone.

Comparative literary approaches have been used both to support and to counter claims of a female audience. As a case in point, early this century scholars began recognizing the various formal and thematic correspondences between the apocryphal Acts and Hellenistic romance novels.[39] These correspondences were originally thought to be significant for the issue of a female audience inasmuch as it was assumed that ancient romances were directed

---

[37] *ATh* 25.   [38] *ATh* 26.

[39] In 1902, Ernst von Dobschütz proposed that the apocryphal Acts displayed characteristics of the literary genre of the Hellenistic romantic novel (Ernst von Dobschütz, 'Der Roman in der alt-christlichen Literatur', *Deutsche Rundschau*, 111 (1902), 87–106). Rosa Söder later broadened the scope of this comparison to include a range of common thematic elements: 1. the element of travel; 2. the aretological element; 3. the teratological element; 4. the tendentious element; and 5. the erotic element (Rosa Söder, *Die apokryphen Apostelgeschichten und die romanhafte Literatur der Antike* (Stuttgart: S. Kohlhammer, 1932)). For a review of scholarship on the literary (and folkloric) background of the apocryphal Acts, see Burrus, *Chastity as Autonomy*, ch. 1.

primarily toward literate women.[40] Thus, it was argued that
the apocryphal Acts shared with Hellenistic fiction the character
of popular stories designed both to instruct and to entertain a
largely female clientele.[41]

However, scholars of late antiquity no longer accept the
assumption that the Hellenistic novels were composed exclusively for a female audience.[42] It is now evident that this assumption reflected latent Victorian biases about a literature 'thought
beneath the notice of serious men'.[43] As a result, the hypothesis
of a female audience for the apocryphal Acts has likewise been
called into question: one scholar has recently argued that the
Hellenistic novels were actually directed toward the civic concerns
of literate men, and that the Christian apocryphal Acts (the *ATh*
included) presented the same demographic group with an alternative vision of civic renewal.[44]

While the *ATh* may very well have had this kind of social function for male readers,[45] Tertullian provides solid external evidence
indicating that the *ATh* did in fact have an early audience
among women for whom the work had a very different public
function. When he remarks in his treatise *On Baptism* on the fact

---

[40] Erwin Rohde, in his classic work, *Der griechische Roman*, writes, 'Indeed
the character of just that part of Hellenistic fiction with which we are deal-
ing here can only be completely explained if we take it as being first and fore-
most *intended for women*' (Rohde's emphasis), *Der griechische Roman und seine
Vorläufer*, 3rd ed. (Leipzig: Breitkopf & Hartel, 1914), 67). See also the work
of F. F. Abbott who supports a similar conclusion by pointing to 'lady pupils'
in Horace and the literary women of Juvenal's diatribe (F. F. Abbott, *Society
and Politics in Ancient Rome* (New York: Scribner's Sons, 1909), 87).

[41] Söder, *Die apokryphen Apostelgeschichten*, 216.

[42] Kate Cooper, *The Virgin and the Bride: Idealized Womanhood in Late
Antiquity* (Cambridge, Mass. and London: Harvard University Press, 1996), 23;
see also Susan A. Stephens, 'Who Read the Ancient Novels?' and Ewen Bowie,
'The Readership of Greek Novels in the Ancient World', in James Tatum (ed.),
The Search for the Ancient Novel (Baltimore: Johns Hopkins University Press,
1994), 405–18, 435–59.

[43] Wayne Meeks, *per litt.*, 23 November 1996.

[44] Cooper, *The Virgin and the Bride*, 20–67; see also Simon Goldhill
(*Foucault's Virginity: Ancient Erotic Fiction and the History of Sexuality* (Cambridge: Cambridge University Press, 1995), 112 ff.), who argues that the representation of women in ancient novels largely reflects the concerns of 'men of a
particular class and education'.

[45] Cooper, *The Virgin and the Bride*, 50 ff.

that the *ATh* was being used to justify women's teaching and ministry,[46] he provides important contemporaneous evidence as to the social context of the work's reception among certain communities of women. The characterization of Thecla in the story indeed seems to have inspired women who read or heard it to embrace new roles of leadership in the early Christian mission.

The empowered role of Thecla and other female figures in the *ATh* has also raised significant questions about the background and social milieu of the text itself. The speculation of one scholar[47] that a woman may have been the *author* of the work has no basis in the evidence: it is contradicted directly by Tertullian's testimony that it was a '(male) presbyter in Asia who put together the book' (*in Asia presbyterum qui eam scripturam construxit*).[48] However, other scholars have sought alternative ways to account for the empowerment of women in the story. In particular, folkloric studies of the apocryphal Acts have recently shifted the focus away from *literary* origins and toward antecedent *oral* traditions of the apocryphal Acts. This approach has provided a more workable theoretical framework for discussing the possible role of women's communities in shaping the story of Thecla—for understanding women's contributions not only as *hearers* but as *tellers* of the story as well.[49] In this context, it has been argued that while a presbyter in Asia Minor was probably the editor of the text itself, his literary work may be the crystallization of oral traditions handed down earlier by communities of women.[50]

---

[46] *De bapt.* 17 (CSEL 20. 215).

[47] Davies, *Revolt of the Widows*, 95–109.

[48] Tertullian, *De bapt.* 17 (CSEL 20. 215). For a refutation of Davies' hypothesis of female authorship, see MacDonald, 'The Role of Women', 21–38.

[49] MacDonald, *Legend*, 17–53; id., 'The Role of Women', 26 ff.; Burrus, *Chastity as Autonomy*, 88 ff.

[50] MacDonald (*Legend*, 35) collects examples in ancient Christianity where male authors recorded the oral communications of women in Asia Minor: 1. Papias of Hierapolis' incorporation of two stories he heard from the daughters of Philip the evangelist in his *Expositions of the Oracles of the Lord* (Eusebius, *H.E.* 3. 39. 9); 2. the Marcionite Apelles' book of the oracles of the prophetess Philoumene (Tertullian, *De praes. haer.* 30; Hippolytus, *Haer.* 7. 26; and Theodoret, *Haer.* 1. 25); and 3. the Montanist Asterius Urbanus' account of the oracles of the prophetess Maximilla (Eusebius, *H.E.* 5. 16. 17).

The hypothesis that the *ATh* was composed from earlier traditions is supported by both external and internal evidence. Tertullian's account seems to confirm that the unnamed presbyter was involved in editing materials already at his disposal: the man 'put together (*contruere*) that book, amassing (*cumulare*) it from his own materials as if it were in the name of Paul'.[51] The *Acts of Paul and Thecla* itself also exhibits standard marks of oral form, including features of plot movement, characterization, and the presentation of typical scenarios.[52] It has proven possible to discern the oral background of the *ATh* by means of a more formal structural analysis of its plot in comparison with other Hellenistic 'chastity stories' about women.[53] In addition, the

[51] Tertullian, *De bapt.* 17 (CSEL 20. 215).

[52] MacDonald (*Legend*, 27–33) has evaluated the narrative technique of the *Acts of Paul*, discovering how the stories conform to a list of folk narrative 'laws' derived primarily from the work of folklorists Alex Olrick and A. B. Lord. Features of plot movement that indicate orality include Olrick's laws of opening and closing (an initial movement 'from calm to excitement' balanced by a concluding movement 'from excitement to calm'), and Lord's principle of narrative inconsistencies. Oral features of characterization include Olrick's laws of concentration on a leading character, contrast, and twins. Finally, Olrick's laws of doubling and tableaux scenes involve the oral formulation of narrative scenarios. Alex Olrick, 'Epic Laws of Folk Narrative,' in Alan Dundes (ed.), *The Study of Folklore* (Englewood Cliffs, NJ: Prentice-Hall, 1965), 131–41; A. B. Lord, *The Singer of Tales* (Cambridge, Mass.: Harvard University Press, 1960).

[53] Burrus (*Chastity*, 34–5) compares the story of Thecla to a group of these chastity stories—1. *The Story of Agrippina, Nicaria, Euphemia, Doris and Xanthippe*; 2. *The Story of Maximilla*; 3. *The Story of Drusiana*; 4. *The Story of Artemilla and Eubula*; 5. *The Story of the 'Princess Bride'*; and 6. *The Story of Mygdonia and Tertia*. She then identifies a common sequence of plot elements that suggests an oral background:

Apostle arrives in town—woman goes to hear apostle preach—woman vows chastity—husband attempts to violate vow—apostle encourages woman—woman resists husband—husband/governor imprisons apostle—woman visits apostle in prison (encouragement; baptism)—husband/governor attempts to kill apostle—apostle dies or is rescued (leaves the scene)—husband/governor persecutes woman—woman is rescued—woman defeats husband/governor (who may be converted or punished, and never succeeds in persuading the woman)—woman is freed (allowed to remain chaste).

The story of Thecla presents two consecutive sequences (the events in Iconium and the events in Antioch), each corresponding to this plot framework. For an earlier (less successful) attempt to classify the Thecla legend in terms of an ancient tale type, see Ludwig Radermacher, *Hippolytus und Thekla: Studien zur Geschichte von Legende und Kultus*, Kaiserliche Akademie der Wissenschaften in Wien, Philosophisch-historische Klasse, Proceedings 182, 3 (Vienna: Alfred Hölder, 1916).

story of Thecla suggests intriguing parallels to tale types in which the heroine is abandoned by the hero and ends up pursuing him in male clothing in order to reunite with him.[54] Whether the *ATh* represents a chastity story, a transvestite legend, or a merging of the two types, its formal features strongly suggest orality.

Could women have had a hand in shaping this legend?[55] The evidence for women's storytelling in antiquity is not lacking. While the private and public roles of ancient women varied considerably depending on their specific time period, region, wealth, and social status, there are indications that in some domestic contexts the act of storytelling may have taken on a sex-specific character.[56] About the same time the *ATh* was

[54] This motif of transvestitism appears in two episodes of the *ATh* that go beyond the basic structural framework of the chastity story—namely, Thecla's search for Paul in chapters 23–5 (when she finds Paul she offers to cut her hair short) and in chapters 40–3 (when she disguises herself in male clothing) (Burrus, *Chastity*, 37–8). These scenes share elements with A. Aarne/Stith Thompson tale types 881, 882, and 891A (*The Types of the Folk-tale* (Helsinki: Academia Scientiarum Fennica, 1928/61), 298, 299, 306).

[55] It should be noted that the theme of female-to-male transvestitism itself is not necessarily an indicator of the sex of the original storytellers. In a study of transvestite motifs in twentieth-century Afghani folklore, male storytellers actually employed the motif with greater frequency than did female storytellers, although '[w]omen in male dress and masculine activist roles are universally heroic in both men's and women's tales' (Margaret Mills, 'Sex Role Reversals, Sex Changes, and Transvestite Disguise in the Oral Tradition of a Conservative Muslim Community in Afghanistan', in R. A. Jordan and S. J. Kalcik (eds.), *Women's Folklore, Women's Culture* (Philadelphia: University of Pennsylvania Press, 1985), 193–5). Mills herself notes that her data sampling and quantitative analysis are only preliminary: a broader study of transvestite disguise in men's and women's folklore is needed to determine to what extent her observations apply in other cultural contexts (op. cit., 190, 211–12).

[56] MacDonald, *Legend*, 13–14; Burrus, *Chastity*, 68–9. The anthropologist Helen Watson (*Women in the City of the Dead* (London: Hurst, 1992), 12–16) has documented the practice of storytelling among contemporary Egyptian women. She shows how the women's gatherings are determined not only by spatial factors, but also by temporal factors related to household life: the women meet most evenings from late afternoon until nightfall (the hour when dinner has to be prepared) in a small back room sectioned off by a heavy curtain. Archaeological evidence from Roman antiquity does not indicate a strict separation of domestic space into male and female spheres (A. Wallace-Hadrill, 'Engendering the Roman House', in Diana E. E. Kleiner and Susan B. Matheson (eds.), *I Claudia: Women in Ancient Rome* (New Haven: Yale University Art Gallery, 1996), 104–15). While available space would have been

composed, the writers Apuleius and Lucian each associate storytelling with women. In Apuleius, for instance, an old woman offers to console a younger woman who had been kidnapped from her wedding by telling her 'pleasant stories and old women's tales' (*narrationes lepidae anilesque fabulae*).[57] This association of women's storytelling with superstition and banal amusement appears in the writing of second-century Christian (male) authors as well. The author of 1 Timothy enjoins his reader to 'avoid the profane tales of old women', and later criticizes widows who 'learn to be idlers, going around from house to house, and not only idlers but meddlers and babblers of nonsense, speaking about things they should not'.[58] In fact, it has been argued that the Pastoral Epistles (1 and 2 Timothy, and Titus) are criticizing here the oral traditions about Paul that lay behind the formation of the *ATh*.[59] A similar social context is reflected in the writings of the late second-century theologian Clement of Alexandria, who warns against those who spend the day with women, 'idly telling erotic legends'.[60]

The role of women as storytellers was documented from a patriarchal, misogynist perspective for centuries before the time of our text. 'Mythic legends and marvellous accounts' were regarded by Strabo (64/3 BCE–*c*.21 CE) as the only effective teaching tool for

an important consideration for gatherings of female storytellers, the organization of time within ancient households may have been even more determinative for such gatherings. That is, women's privacy in the home could have been secured during hours in which men were not present. On the importance of temporal factors in the organization of ancient households, see Wallace-Hadrill, op. cit., 106; Lisa Nevett, 'Perceptions of Domestic Space in Roman Italy', in B. Rawson and P. Weaver (eds.), *The Roman Family in Italy: Status, Sentiment, Space* (Oxford: Clarendon Press, 1997), 281–98; and L. M. Meskell, 'An Archaeology of Social Relations in an Egyptian Village', *Journal of Archaeological Method and Theory*, 5/3 (1998), 209–43.

[57] Apuleius, *Metamorphoses* 4. 27; Lucian, *Philopseudes* (*The Lover of Lies*), 9.

[58] 1 Timothy 4: 7; 5: 13.

[59] MacDonald, *Legend*, 54–77. In addition to the allusions to women's storytelling in the Pastoral Epistles, MacDonald also notes that the Epistles and the *Acts of Paul* share a common set of references to the names of Paul's associates and to events from Paul's life. In order to account for this shared material, he argues that the Pastoral Epistles were written specifically to contend for the legacy of Paul over against the picture of the apostle presented in the oral legends behind the *Acts of Paul*.

[60] *Paed.* 3. 4. 27. 2.

'a crowd of women'.[61] Eratosthenes, as paraphrased by Strabo, speaks of the 'highly learned, creative storytelling ($\mu\nu\theta\circ\lambda\circ\gamma\iota\alpha$) of an old woman, who has been given the opportunity to fabricate . . . whatever seems appropriate to her for persuasion'. (Eratosthenes was head of the Alexandrian Library at the beginning of the second century BCE).[62] Long before Strabo's day, Plato had voiced a concern to monitor the education of children by censoring the stories told by women in the home: 'We shall persuade the nurses and the mothers to tell the children (only) the stories we have chosen . . . Many of the stories they are telling now must be thrown out.'[63]

These references to women's storytelling in antiquity consistently betray the misogynistic prejudices of their authors—women tell stories either because they are incapable of rational studies (Strabo) or because they have grown lazy in their household routines (1 Timothy). Yet, beneath these distorting biases, these male writers may offer us a rare glimpse into the domestic activities of certain women in late antiquity. While these writers would have us believe that this storytelling merely enlivened women's 'private' lives, it also would have been an important means by which social (public) traditions were preserved, transmitted, and shaped.

Matched with the consistent and pervasive characterization of women's community in the *ATh*, this evidence for the practice of women's storytelling (and storylistening) in the ancient world provides a possible scenario for the social origins of Thecla's story.

In what setting might this storytelling have taken place? Some scholars have suggested that it may be possible to discern traces of social relations within the communities that hypothetically sponsored this literature in Tryphaena's 'adoption' of Thecla.[64] With her mother, fiancé, and even Paul virtually absent from the second half of the narrative, Thecla enters into a new familial relationship with a community of women organized in the context of a household. Tryphaena's status as a widow corresponds to an identifiable order of women in the early Church (Acts 6: 1–6; 9: 36–42; 1 Timothy 5: 3–16). By the second century in Asia Minor, widows were increasingly associated with virgins in their

---

[61] *Geog.* 1. 2. 8.   [62] *Geog.* 1. 2. 3.   [63] Plato, *Rep.* 2. 377C.
[64] MacDonald, *Legend*, 71–7; cf. Davies, *Revolt of the Widows*, 70–94.

mutual commitment to a life of continence. In fact, Ignatius of Antioch even refers to virgins who have attained the status of 'widow', presumably without even having been married.[65] Tertullian notes, and disparages, a similar situation where an unmarried virgin was included in the order of widows.[66] The storytellers behind the *ATh* may have been found among such communities of celibate widows.

SOCIAL PRACTICE IN THE *ACTS OF PAUL AND THECLA*: ASCETICISM AND ITINERANCY

In the preceding section I have synthesized the work of recent scholars who have argued that communities of women had a hand in transmitting the oral legend of Thecla. Based on a social-historical reading of the *ATh*, is it possible to press the reconstruction of these hypothetical communities a little further? For instance, what might the text tell us about the values espoused or encouraged in the telling of this tale? What themes in the *ATh* infused the promotion of Thecla as a model for women's piety? What (if anything) does the story suggest about the social world of the communities that promulgated it?

It should be noted that in the last few years certain epistemological concerns have been raised about whether one can reconstruct real women's experience from ancient literature like the apocryphal Acts.[67] One scholar has argued that the role of female characters in the Acts is a thoroughgoing literary construct that reflects not the social experience of women at all, but rather male preoccupation with authority and civic order.[68] This new approach to the study of ancient narrative has properly emphasized the role of rhetoric in shaping (and distorting) social realities, and has helpfully redirected our attention to the ways in which texts were used to negotiate power between social groups. At the same time, however, this approach may be a bit too pessimistic

---

[65] Ignatius of Antioch, *Smyrn.* 13. 1.   [66] Tertullian, *De virg. vel.* 9. 2.

[67] Elizabeth Clark, 'The Lady Vanishes: Dilemmas of a Feminist Historian after the "Linguistic Turn" ', *Church History*, 67/1 (March 1998), 1–31; Cooper, *The Virgin and the Bride*, esp. 45–67.

[68] Cooper, *The Virgin and the Bride*, op. cit.

about the historian's ability to read ancient narratives for insight
into the social roles of early Christian women.

In the study of ancient narrative, the relationship between
'fiction' and social 'reality' is anything but straightforward; even
realistic details may be understood as part of an attempt to
'make the reader believe the truth of the illusion that was being
constructed'.[69] Yet, at the same time such details would only have
been believable (i.e. realistic) insofar as they bore some relation
to the social world of their audience. Thus, while it is not possible to read ancient narrative as direct evidence for women's
experience, it may be possible to infer from this literature something of the social context of ancient women's experience—at the
very least, the roles and values thought to be available to women
by the dominant (male) culture. With narratives composed of
folkloric elements, the potential may be even greater for drawing conclusions about social context: recent ethnographic studies have shown how folktales, especially women's folktales, often
reflect the social world of the storytellers themselves.[70] In the case
of the *ATh*, to view the characterization of Thecla merely as
a stereotype of ancient romance is to neglect several aspects of
her story that at least potentially suggest verisimilitude with
the social concerns of ancient Christian women—especially the
concerns of women's asceticism and travel, and the relation of
charismatic wandering women to settled, local communities. In
these areas, the characterization of Thecla may offer the historian insight into the social values of the early communities who
promoted her legend.

Asceticism

The ascetic tenor of the *ATh* suggests that the communities who
told Thecla's story would have valued and practised chastity as

---

[69] Clark, 'The Lady Vanishes', 18–20.

[70] Helen Watson (*Women in the City of the Dead*, 14–16, *et passim*) documents
the intimate relation between the tales told by contemporary Egyptian women
and the personal details of their own life histories. Rosan Jordan ('The Vaginal
Serpent and Other Themes from Mexican-American Women's Lore', in
Women's Folklore, Women's Culture, 26–44) analyses a body of lore that reflects
their female storytellers' sense of sexual vulnerability and fear of rape. On methods
of relating folk narratives to their historical and social background, see Burrus,
Chastity as Autonomy, 81 ff.

a central manifestation of the gospel. The pervading emphasis on sexual purity in the *ATh* manifests itself in the character of Paul's preaching and its effect upon his female listeners in the story. Thecla's commitment to chastity therefore is validated in the text by the authority of apostolic teaching. Paul's gospel in the *ATh* is specifically defined in terms of sexual continence and a flight from the bonds of matrimony. In the house of Onesiphorus (in Iconium), Paul preaches a series of Beatitudes that are modelled after those of Jesus in the Gospel of Matthew but that diverge noticeably from Matthew in their emphasis upon chastity as the pre-eminent virtue.[71]

Blessed are the pure in heart, for they will see God.[72]
Blessed are they who have kept the flesh pure, for they will become a temple of God.
Blessed are the continent, for to them will God speak.
Blessed are they who have renounced this world, for they will be well pleasing to God.
Blessed are they who have wives as if they did not have them, for they shall be heirs to God . . .

The final line of Paul's ascetic Beatitudes reiterates the concept of purity and forms an *inclusio* with the opening lines quoted above.

Blessed are the bodies of the virgins, for they will be well pleasing to God, and will not lose the reward of their purity.[73]

This final phrase of the *inclusio* suggests that these ascetic beatitudes, in part, were directed to the 'bodies' and physical-emotional experience of women ('virgins') who sought to emulate the 'virgin named Thecla', and who embraced with her the 'word concerning the virgin life' that Paul was preaching.[74]

Although Paul's disruptive gospel applies equally to both men and women—'he deprives young men of their wives and young women of their husbands'—the *ATh* describes a societal backlash against Paul that focuses (patriarchally) especially on Paul's

---

[71] *ATh* 5; cf. Matthew 5: 1–11.   [72] Matthew 5: 8.
[73] *ATh* 6.   [74] *ATh* 7.

influence over young women like Thecla.[75] As one might expect, Thamyris, bitter over his loss of Thecla, claims that Paul 'does not allow young women to marry'.[76] But the personal resentment spills quickly over into broader accusations concerning Paul's widespread influence: 'And the whole crowd said: "Away with the sorcerer! For he has corrupted all of our wives!" '[77] Even Theocleia's desperate and damning betrayal of her own daughter ('Burn the lawless woman! Burn the unmarried woman in the middle of the assembly, so that all the women who have been taught by this man may be afraid!'[78]) describes Thecla's rebellion against social mores and family expectations as emblematic for the experience of other women influenced by Paul's gospel. As a response to Paul's preaching, Thecla's flight from marriage and family becomes the governing metaphor for her life of chastity.

In subsequent centuries, the value placed on remaining continent in the *ATh* and the characterization of Thecla as the virgin *par excellence* would serve as inspiration for women who sought to enter the monastic life. While the second-century communities who told Thecla's story would likewise have valued continence, historians know much less about how women at that time put ascetic values into practice. Some, like the early Christian prophetesses Priscilla and Maximilla (*c.*160 CE), seem to have left their husbands and lived independently as ecstatic 'virgins'—the New Prophecy movement they helped found was especially active in Phrygia, a region of Asia Minor not far from Thecla's putative hometown of Iconium.[79] Others lived in home-based

---

[75] *ATh* 12. The makarism, 'Blessed are the ones who have wives as if they did not have them . . .' (*ATh* 5), is the only instance where an enjoinder to chastity seems to apply only to men. However, the statement could just as easily be interpreted in light of the story's preponderant concern for the ascetic freedom of women—in this case, the husband, as paterfamilias, would be urged to 'have his wife as if he had her not' in order to provide the social opportunity for a mutual commitment to chastity.

[76] *ATh* 16.   [77] *ATh* 15.   [78] *ATh* 20.

[79] On the role of women in the New Prophecy (also known as Montanism), see Christine Trevett, *Montanism: Gender, Authority and the New Prophecy* (Cambridge: Cambridge University Press, 1996); and Kraemer, *Her Share of the Blessings*, 157–71.

communities of widows or consecrated virgins: these groups were characterized by their commitment to continence and prayer, although apparently some may also have claimed the right to teach and baptize.[80] In any case, regardless of the specific form of piety it inspired, the emphasis on continence in the *ATh* tells us something about the ascetic concerns of the earliest communities who preserved the legend of Thecla.

Itinerancy

The *Acts of Paul and Thecla* also places a high value on freedom of travel, because it is by definition associated with apostolic ministry. Paul's missionary travels serve as a model for the shape of Thecla's discipleship: Thecla leaves her fiancé and family in order to follow after Paul and become a teacher of chastity like him.[81] When Thecla is separated from Paul after each of her martyr trials, she wanders about in search of Paul. After surviving the pyre, she searches for Paul and is encountered by one of Onesiphorus' sons, who asks her, 'Thecla, where are you walking (πορεύεσθαι)?'[82] Later, after her liberation from the beasts, Thecla again 'yearned for Paul and sought after him, sending round in every direction'.[83] In each situation, Thecla's search seems to be conspicuously without direction—her movement conforms more to aimless wandering than to a purposeful journey.

[80] A third-century church manual from northern Syria, the *Didascalia Apostolorum*, criticizes widows who teach and perform baptisms (*Didascalia Apostolorum*, 15; *Constitutiones Apostolorum*, 3. 5–9). The original Greek of the *Didascalia* is lost; the work is preserved in a Syriac version (ed. A. Vööbus; CSCO 401, 402, 407, 408 (1979)) and as part of the fourth-century church manual, the *Constitutiones Apostolorum* (ed. F. X. Funk (Paderborn: Schoeningh 1905)). For recent treatments of this work as a source of information about early Christian widows, see Susanna Elm, *'Virgins of God': The Making of Asceticism in Late Antiquity* (Oxford: Clarendon Press, 1994), 168–74; and Karen Jo Torjesen, *When Women Were Priests: Women's Leadership in the Early Church and the Scandal of their Subordination in the Rise of Christianity* (San Francisco: Harper, 1993). On the social location of widow communities in separate households, see MacDonald, *Legend*, 50, 75.

[81] Paul's travels also provide the literary framework for the story of Thecla. Paul's mission in Iconium and his intermittent travel to Antioch with Thecla form a narrative bridge between his earlier work in Antioch and his later work in Myra in the larger *Acts of Paul*.

[82] *ATh* 23.   [83] *ATh* 40.

Paul and Thecla's identity as 'strangers' (ξένοι) in the *ATh* also subtly bespeaks their social station as wanderers.[84] In Hellenic antiquity, the term 'stranger' was intimately associated with the social function of itinerancy. This social function was widespread and long lasting in the Greek-speaking world, and was exemplified by the characterization of Odysseus in the *Odyssey*, a work that was widely read in the second century CE.[85] In the *Odyssey*, the wandering Odysseus is frequently described as a *xeinos* (i.e. ξένος). For example, when Odysseus visits the Cyclops' cave, the one-eyed beast spies him and his companions, and questions them:

Strangers [ξεῖνοι], who are you? From where do you sail over the watery ways? Are you on some trading voyage, or do you wander at random [μαψιδίως ἀλάλησθαι] over the sea like pirates? Behold, they wander [ἀλάσθαι], risking their lives and bringing evil to people living in other lands.

Odysseus responds by specifically requesting the hospitality due to travellers:

Respect the gods, brave sir; we are your suppliants. Zeus is the avenger of suppliants and strangers [ξεῖνοι], the protector of strangers, [the one] who accompanies reverend strangers.[86]

Here, the designation *xenos* appears in connection with the verb 'to wander' (ἀλᾶσθαι), and with the idea of Zeus as the benefactor and protector of itinerants.[87]

---

[84] The term's primary definition of 'stranger' is frequently qualified by the sense of 'wanderer' or 'refugee'.

[85] The papyrological record illustrates the enduring popularity of Homer in late antiquity: around 400 papyrus fragments of the *Odyssey* have been published from the first to the sixth century CE, over twice as many as there are of the Old and New Testaments combined (Stephens, 'Who Read Ancient Novels?', 411, 415–16). D. R. MacDonald (*Christianizing Homer: The Odyssey, Plato, and the Acts of Andrew* (New York: Oxford University Press, 1994)) argues that the second-century author of the *Acts of Andrew* modelled his work after Homer's *Odyssey*.

[86] *Od.* 9. 252–5, 269–71.

[87] *Od.* 6. 206–9. Nausicaa, the daughter of King Alcinous, instructs her handmaids to welcome Odysseus, as an unfortunate 'wanderer' (ἀλώμενος) and a 'stranger' (ξεῖνος); see also *Od.* 8. 572–6, where the 'stranger' (ξένος) is again associated with wandering (ἀποπλάζειν), hospitality, and reverence for the gods.

Similar uses of the word *xenos* appear in the Septuagint (first century BCE) and in Christian literature from the first and second centuries CE. In Job 31: 32, the author of the Septuagint translates the Hebrew *ger* (גֵּר 'sojourner') with the Greek *xenos*. Insisting that he has fulfilled his obligation of hospitality to the traveller, Job declares: 'A stranger was not accustomed to spend the night outside; my doors had been opened to all who came.' The virtue of hospitality to strangers seeking lodging is enjoined frequently in the New Testament literature—e.g. the Gospel of Matthew (25: 31–46), where Jesus promises that only those who welcome the stranger (ξένος) will inherit the kingdom.[88] In the second century, Clement of Alexandria speaks metaphorically about the Christian as 'one who lives on earth as a stranger (ξένος) . . . as someone who sets out on a long journey (ἀποδημία), stopping at inns and dwellings along the road'.[89] Finally, in the *Acts of Peter*, another of the non-canonical Acts from the late second century, the term 'strangers' is expressly used as a synonym for 'pilgrims and poor people' (*peregrinantes et pauperes*) who seek shelter at the home of a prominent Roman Christian.[90] Thus, in *ATh*, when Theocleia designates Paul as a 'stranger (ξένος) teaching deceitful and subtle discourses', she is not simply expressing her ignorance about his identity and origin; she is also marking the apostle's social station as an itinerant—namely, one who, as an unknown outsider, was disrupting the civil fabric of Iconium.[91] One finds the same charge levelled by the proconsul of Patras against the apostle Andrew in the *Acts of Andrew*: 'The final judgement concerning you has drawn near, you stranger

---

[88] See also Hebrews 13: 2, where the writer enjoins his readers to demonstrate hospitality (φιλοξενία) at all times, in case they entertain angels unawares.

[89] *Strom.* 4. 26. 165–6.

[90] *A. Petr.* 8 (*Acta Apostolorum Apocrypha*, ed. Lipsius-Bonnet, 55). As noted above, the author of the *Acts of Paul* may actually have borrowed material from the *Acts of Peter* (Carl Schmidt (ed.), Πράξεις Παύλου, 127 ff.).

[91] *ATh* 8; cf. 13. In the *ATh*, there is considerable uncertainty about Paul's identity among his enemies: even his (hostile) companions Demas and Hermogenes admit, 'Who this man is, we do not know . . .' (*ATh* 12). However, it is Paul's itinerancy as an apostle that occasions their ignorance. Paul's constant travels obscure his origins and thereby make him more suspicious to the governing authorities. Thus, Thamyris draws attention to Paul's mysterious origins in order to raise suspicion about him before the proconsul: 'Proconsul, we do not know where this person is from . . .' (*ATh* 16).

(ξένος ἄνθρωπος), alien to the present life, enemy of my household, and destroyer of my entire family. Why did it seem good to you to burst into alien places and secretly corrupt a woman . . . ?'[92]

While in the *ATh* it is Paul's enemies who accuse him of being a 'stranger' in their midst, Thecla describes her own self by the feminine form *xenê*. When Alexander, 'a powerful man', tries to seduce her forcibly on the open street, Thecla searches in vain for Paul and cries out, 'Do not force the stranger [ξένη], do not force the handmaid [δούλη] of God.'[93] This scene takes place as Thecla is walking on the road into Antioch—the designation ξένη is again immediately informed by her activity of travel, as well as the danger of sexual violence for women on the road. Her protest places her identity as 'stranger' and as 'handmaid of God' in syntactic parallel, suggesting a connection between her itinerant status as a follower of Paul and her vocation as a virgin ('handmaid of God'). This connection between itinerancy and the ascetic life seems to be confirmed two chapters later by Falconilla who, in a vision to her mother Tryphaena, refers to Thecla as 'the stranger, the desolate one' (ἡ ξένη ἡ ἔρημος).[94]

At the end of the *ATh*, Paul's formal commissioning of Thecla as a teacher implicitly recognizes that she has in fact already claimed the right to travel freely. It is only after she declares outright, 'I am going to Iconium', that Paul responds, 'Go and teach the word of God.' This characterization of Thecla as an itinerant teacher, as a ξένη, may suggest something about the social options available to women in the communities who transmitted her legend. We already know that the public ministries of Montanist women in second- and third-century Asia Minor was the source of considerable controversy.[95] The women who, according to Tertullian, claimed that they inherited the right

[92] *AA* 51, ed. J.-M. Prieur, *Acta Andrae*, CCSA 6 (Brepols: Turnhout, 1989), 507–9.

[93] *ATh* 26.

[94] *ATh* 28. A study by Hans Campenhausen has disclosed an enduring link between ascetic piety, itinerancy, and the language of 'strangerhood' through the Middle Ages (*Die asketische Heimatlosigkeit im altkirchlichen und frühmittelal-terlichen Mönchtum*, Sammlung gemeinverständlicher Vorträge und Schriften aus dem Gebiet der Theologie und Religionsgeschichte, 149 (Tübingen: J. C. B. Mohr, 1930).

[95] C. Trevett, *Montanism*, 174–5.

to teach from Thecla, would also have claimed the right to travel freely in order to enable themselves in that calling.

THECLA AS A SOCIAL TYPE: CHARISMATICS AND COMMUNITIES OF FEMALE SUPPORT IN SECOND-CENTURY ASIA MINOR

In early Christian culture, there was a standard social type which we know as the wandering charismatic; the salient characteristics of this social type were persons who spurned home, family, possessions, and protection for the sake of teaching the Gospel.[96] Thecla's asceticism and itinerancy mark her as a clear example of this type in early Christianity. In the first two centuries CE, apostles and other itinerant miracle workers enjoyed considerable authority in local Christian communities—an authority not dependent on institutional structures, but instead on persuasive demonstrations of *charisma* or spiritual power. The rest of this chapter will be devoted to the ways in which Thecla is presented as a charismatic figure in the *ATh*, and to what this emphasis on *charisma* might suggest about the communities behind the *Acts*.

In the *ATh*, Thecla's commitment to chastity seems to lie at the root of her charismatic power; her physical purity is presented as the source of her divine favour. Her power comes to bodily expression in her invulnerability to torture, both on the fiery pyre and in the arena. When she is stripped and brought in naked to the pyre in Iconium, the governor weeps and marvels 'at the power in her'.[97] At the stake, the 'fire did not touch her'; she remains completely impervious to the threatening elements around her.[98] When a violent hailstorm quenches the fire, 'many were endangered and died', but Thecla was saved.[99] Later in the arena, when Thecla baptizes herself in the pool of ravenous seals, the seals are all struck dead at the sight of a lightning flash, but Thecla emerges unscathed. Significantly, her action was also

---

[96] For a concise, sociological description of the wandering charismatic, see Gerd Thiessen, *Sociology of Early Palestinian Christianity* (Philadelphia: Fortress Press, 1978), 8–16; and id., *The Social Setting of Pauline Christianity* (Philadelphia, Fortress Press, 1982), 28–35.
[97] *ATh* 22.   [98] Ibid.   [99] Ibid.

accompanied by a cloud of fire that formed about her, 'so that neither could the beasts touch her nor could she be seen naked'.[100] (Here, even the probing eyes of the spectators are considered potential threats to her physical purity.) Thus, at her baptism, Thecla's purity of body is once again preserved and highlighted in a demonstration of miraculous power.[101]

As one who is imprisoned and undergoes torture, Thecla assumes the charismatic authority of a *confessor*. In the early church, martyrs who awaited death in prison after having publicly confessed their faith (hence, 'confessors') were often thought to have earned the power to forgive sins. In the second and third centuries, the power to grant forgiveness or restore communion was contested by bishops and presbyters, as being their own exclusive privilege.[102] However, early Christian martyr-confessors attained a similar authority within communities by virtue of their willingness to endure suffering and death in the name of Christ. In the second century, Irenaeus writes of the confessor-martyrs in Gaul (modern-day France):

Through their endurance the immeasurable mercy of Christ was shown forth, for through the living the dead were being made alive and martyrs were giving grace to those who had not been martyred [i.e. those who had denied the faith] . . . At that time they defended everyone; they accused none. They released all and bound none; and they prayed for those who had arranged the tortures . . .[103]

The authority of such confessors often resulted in political conflict with local bishops. The career of the bishop Cyprian in third-century North Africa serves as a prime example. Cyprian's short tenure as bishop of Carthage (*c*.248–53 CE) was plagued by conflict over whose authority it was to forgive those who had denied the faith during the persecution under the emperor Decius. North African confessors had begun claiming that

---

[100] *ATh* 34.

[101] Thecla's earlier request for baptism reflects this view that baptism safeguarded the baptized against temptation: 'Only give me the seal in Christ, and temptation shall not touch me' (*ATh* 25). A commitment to chastity was thought to accompany baptism in some early churches.

[102] e.g. Hippolytus, *Trad. ap.* 3. 5.

[103] *Letter of the Churches of Vienne and Lyons* to the churches of Asia and Phrygia; in Eusebius, *H.E.* 5. 1. 45; 5. 2. 5.

authority, and Cyprian was hard-pressed to reassert his own institutional authority as bishop.[104]

Given the authority granted to confessors in the early Church,
the path to martyrdom may have provided an access to 'priestly'
authority for early Christian women who were otherwise ex-
cluded from the office. The New Prophecy (Montanist) movement in second-century Asia Minor provides contemporaneous
evidence of female confessors acquiring this kind of status.[105] In
the *Martyrdom of Saints Perpetua and Felicitas*, a North African
work based on Perpetua's first-hand diary account of her imprisonment and martyr trials (*c*.203 CE), Perpetua describes her successful intercession for her dead brother Dinocrates, who had
'died horribly of cancer of the face when he was seven years old'.[106]
Having recalled Dinocrates' suffering during her imprisonment,
Perpetua has a vision in which she sees her brother 'very hot and
thirsty, pale and dirty', a pool of water just beyond his reach, his
face still marred by the tumour.[107] After awakening, feeling
'confident that [she] could help him in his trouble', she again
begins to pray for her brother 'day and night with tears and sighs
that this favour might be granted [her]'.[108] A few days later, when

---

[104] On Cyprian's social and political means of consolidating his authority
as bishop over against the opposition of local confessors, see C. A. Bobertz,
'Cyprian of Carthage as Patron: A Social Historical Study of the Role of Bishop
in the Ancient Christian Community of North Africa' (Ph.D. diss.; Yale
University, 1988).

[105] Frederick C. Klawiter, 'The Role of Martyrdom and Persecution in
Developing the Priestly Authority of Women in Early Christianity: A Case
Study of Montanism', *Church History*, 49 (1980), 251–61. Christine Trevett
(*Montanism*, 195–6) argues that the clericalization of women was primarily the
product of the movement's belief in 'the in-breaking of a Spirit-guided,
covenantally promised, Christian order', but admits that it is right to assume
'that a New Prophet or later Montanist woman could become "priestly" by virtue
of having suffered as a confessor'.

[106] *Mart. Perp.* 7. 5, ed. H. Musurillo, *Acts of the Christian Martyrs* (Oxford:
Clarendon Press, 1972), 114–15.

[107] *Mart. Perp.* 7. 4, 7; Musurillo, *Acts*, 114–15.

[108] *Mart. Perp.* 7. 9–10; Musurillo, *Acts*, 114–17. Klawiter offers an interesting, alternative translation of the phrase *et feci pro illo orationem die et nocte gemens
et lacrimans ut mihi donaretur*—'I prayed for him day and night, sighing and shed-
ding tears, *that he might be pardoned for me*' (my italics). His translation 'seeks
to bring out the sense of "to pardon" in the verb *donare* and assumes that the
subject of the third person *donaretur* is *he*, which refers back to *illo*' (Klawiter,
'The Role of Martyrdom', 258, n. 24.).

she has another vision, she sees Dinocrates 'clean, well dressed, and refreshed', his cancerous wound now healed, drinking water freely from a golden bowl. On account of Perpetua's prayers, her brother 'had been delivered from his suffering'.

Perpetua's visions and intercessions for her dead brother illuminate Tryphaena's request for Thecla to pray for the salvation of her dead daughter Falconilla. After her daughter appears to her in a dream, Tryphaena approaches Thecla in the hope that, through Thecla's prayers, Falconilla might be 'translated to the place of the righteous'.[109] Tryphaena's petition reflects the belief that Thecla, as an expectant martyr like Perpetua, had been granted the power to forgive sins during her imprisonment and martyr trials. By interceding for the salvation of Tryphaena's daughter—'My God, the Son of the Most High who is in heaven, give her what she desires, that her daughter Falconilla may live in eternity'[110]—Thecla is simply exercising the charismatic authority invested in her as an imprisoned confessor of the Church.

The power that Thecla later displays in the arena confirms for Tryphaena the efficacy of Thecla's prayer on behalf of Falconilla. Awaking from a faint to hear that Thecla has escaped death, Tryphaena proclaims, 'Now I believe that the dead are raised! Now I believe that my child lives!'[111] The reader is left to wonder which 'child' Tryphaena is referring to—her biological daughter Falconilla, or her adopted daughter Thecla. In fact, Tryphaena's words probably have a double meaning. Tryphaena celebrates both the fact that Thecla is still alive, and the knowledge that eternal life has been guaranteed for Falconilla by Thecla's demonstration of her power as a confessor.

The *charisma* of confessors in the early Church also helps explain Thecla's authority to baptize herself in the arena. In light of her subsequent release from her martyr trial, Thecla's self-baptism functions as a seal of her confession (in the place of physical martyrdom), and as the confirmation of her authority to travel and teach as a surviving 'confessor'.

Numerous conflicts arose in the early Church over the status of confessors who were released from prison before suffering a martyr's fate. Normally, martyrdom was expected to be the final

---

[109] *ATh* 28.   [110] *ATh* 29.   [111] *ATh* 39.

seal of their public confession—the confessors' 'irregular' priestly function would thereby neatly culminate with their death.[112] However, questions quickly arose over the role and place of confessors who had been released from prison and remained active in Christian communities. Did these persons retain the power to forgive sins they were thought to have earned in prison, or did they automatically relinquish that power upon their release?

There is evidence to suggest that some confessors could, and did, retain their charismatic status even after discharge from prison.[113] In Phrygia of Asia Minor, two released confessors named Themiso and Alexander, leaders of the New Prophecy movement (late second, early third century CE), each 'boasted that he was a martyr'.[114] As a self-proclaimed martyr, Alexander (along with the female prophetesses of the New Prophecy) claimed the right to forgive sins.[115] In other cases, the charisma of surviving confessors was channeled into institutional forms of authority. For example, in late second-century Rome (c.190), the confessor Callistus, who would later become bishop, rose initially to the rank of presbyter after having been set free from a Roman jail.[116] The *Apostolic Tradition*, written by Hippolytus, presumes a similar

---

[112] Later, the rise of the cult of martyrs in the fourth century eventually provided a means for conceptualizing and realizing the ongoing power of the martyrs in the life of the church: see Ch. 2, especially on the portrayal of Thecla's power in competition with other cults in fourth- and fifth-century Asia Minor.

[113] Klawiter, 'The Role of Martyrdom', 254–6.

[114] Apollonius, in Eusebius, *H.E.* 5. 18. 5–6.

[115] This claim draws the sarcastic ire of Apollonius: 'Which then forgives the other's sins? Does the prophet forgive the martyr's robberies or does the martyr forgive the prophet's covetous acts?' (Eusebius, *H.E.* 5. 18. 6–7). In an interesting parallel to the argumentation of Hippolytus, Apollonius goes on to argue against Alexander's status as a martyr by revealing the actual, criminal cause of Alexander's imprisonment: he was judged 'not because of the Name, but because of the robberies he dared to commit' (Eusebius, *H.E.* 5. 18. 9). When Irenaeus, in his *Letter of the Churches of Vienne and Lyons* to the churches of Asia and Phrygia, sharply underscores the distinction between a confessor and a martyr, he may have been waging an implicit polemic against such claims to ecclesiastical authority by surviving 'martyrs' of the New Prophecy (Klawiter, 'The Role of Martyrdom', 256).

[116] Hippolytus, *Haer.* 9. 12. 1–13. Hippolytus' account of his bitter rival's promotion is telling. He never questions the propriety of conferring the status of presbyter on released confessors. Instead, he attacks Callistus by accusing him of never actually having been a true confessor in the first place. Hippolytus claims that Callistus was arrested not because of his confession as a Christian, but on a criminal charge of embezzlement.

situation for Roman confessors in the early third century: '[A] confessor [who] has been in chains in prison for the Name . . . has the office of the presbyterate by his confession.'[117] Seen in the context of these examples, Thecla's authority to travel and teach the Gospel at the end of the *ATh* may reflect similar social assumptions about the protracted authority of confessors who have survived martyr trials.[118]

Finally, Thecla's transvestitism serves as a final marker of her status as a wandering, charismatic teacher. Thecla's change of dress has often been interpreted as an androgynous gesture, a physical expression of the baptismal dissolution of gender distinctions mentioned in Galatians 3: 28: 'There is no longer Jew or Greek, there is no longer slave or free, there is no longer male and female.'[119] In the *ATh*, both of Thecla's androgynous gestures in fact seem to relate closely to the theme of baptism— Thecla's offer to cut her hair short occurs at her initial request for baptism, and her change into male garb follows on the heels of her self-baptism in the arena. In the context of an ancient society that held fast to misogynistic assumptions about women's weakness, the act of dressing 'like a man' would have signified a radical break from customary assumptions about women's

---

[117] Hippolytus, *Trad. ap.* 10. 1, ed. and trans. G. Dix, *The Treatise on the Apostolic Tradition* (London: SPCK, 1937), 18. Hippolytus distinguishes between confessors (ὁμολογητής) who have been 'in chains in prison for the Name' (and who thereby earn the office of presbyter) and confessors who were 'not brought before a public authority nor punished with chains nor condemned to any penalty but [were] only by chance derided for the Name' (and who therefore require a laying on of hands to be ordained).

[118] The *Acts of Paul and Thecla* gives evidence of a social milieu strikingly similar to that of the contemporaneous New Prophecy movement of Asia Minor; it shares common emphases on asceticism, women's leadership roles, and the power attributed to martyr-confessors who have gained their freedom. In this context, it is interesting that, like the New Prophetic prophetesses Maximilla and Priscilla, Thecla communicates her teachings in the form of 'oracles' (λόγια; *ATh* 42).

[119] Persuasively argued by Wayne Meeks, 'The Image of the Androgyne', 180 ff. Meeks suggests that Galatians 3: 28 represents a 'baptismal reunification formula' which envisions the 'eschatological restoration of man's original divine, androgynous image' in Genesis 1: 27 (Meeks, op. cit., 197). Elisabeth Schüssler-Fiorenza, noting that the creation of humankind 'male and female' in Genesis 1: 27 introduces procreation, interprets Galatians 3: 28 not in terms of eschatological dissolution of gender distinctions, but as a redefining (or 'depatriarchalizing') of gender relationships (*In Memory of Her: A Feminist Theological Reconstruction of Christian Origins* (New York: Crossroad, 1983), 211).

identity in society. While it may have indeed been perceived as a way of enacting the 'no longer male and female' of the Galatian baptismal formula, it also was 'a symbol of the ambiguities, tensions, and hostility' in early Christian attitudes toward women.[120]

However, Thecla's transvestitism also needs to be understood in the social-historical context of concerns related to women's travel in antiquity. When Thecla tells Paul she will cut her hair short as proof of her resistance to temptation, it is in the context of asking Paul to let her follow him wherever he goes.[121] Later, when she dresses herself like a man, it is again for the purpose of travel.

> Taking with her young men and female servants, she girded herself, sewed her mantle into a cloak in the fashion of men, and went off to Myra . . .[122]

In the apocryphal *Acts of Andrew* (second century CE), transvestitism seems to fulfill the similar social function of enabling women to travel freely (i.e. incognito) in public.[123] In *AA* 19, a woman named Maximilla 'changes her clothes as was her custom' (συνήθως μεταμφιασθεῖσα τὴν ἐσθῆτα) in order to go out from her home and enter the vestibule of the praetorium without being seen (ἵνα μὴ ὀφθῇ).[124] Only after members of her own

---

[120] Nicholas Constas, Introduction to the 'Life of St. Mary/Marinos', in A.-M. Talbot (ed.), *Holy Women of Byzantium* (Washington: Dumbarton Oaks, 1996), 3.

[121] *ATh* 25.   [122] *ATh* 40.

[123] An anthropologist has made a similar observation concerning the role of transvestitism in the folklore of a Muslim community in Afghanistan: 'Concealed identity, whether in male or female guise, implies freedom of movement and freedom from very pervasive community control' (Mills, 'Sex Role Reversals, Sex Changes, and Transvestite Disguise in the Oral Tradition of a Conservative Muslim Community in Afghanistan', 192).

[124] For another occasion where the verb μεταμφιάζομαι describes a woman's change into male clothing, see the *Life of St. Matrona* (*Vita prima*; *Acta Sanctorum* (3 Nov.), 794E). Jeffrey Featherstone and Cyril Mango translate and comment upon the *Life of St. Matrona* in Talbot (ed.), *Holy Women of Byzantium*, 13–64; cf. E. C. Topping, 'St. Matrona and Her Friends: Sisterhood in Byzantium', in J. Chrysostomides (ed.), *ΚΑΘΗΓΗΤΡΙΑ: Essays presented to Joan Hussey* (Camberley Porphyrogenitus, 1988), 211–24. At least thirteen hagiographies of transvestite female saints were produced during the Byzantine period (Talbot, op. cit., 2, n. 6; E. Patlagean, 'L'Histoire de la femme déguisée en moine et l'évolution de la sainteté féminine à Byzance', *Studi Medievalis*, 3/17 (1976), 597–623).

household 'unmask' her is her true identity revealed. A short time later, when Maximilla sends her friend Iphidama to find the prison where the apostle Andrew is staying, Iphidama also 'exchanges her usual clothing'[125] in order to travel without hindrance through the streets of the city (*AA* 28). Finally, in *AA* 46, Maximilla actually disguises herself as Andrew in order to accompany Iphidama to the prison.[126]

In each case, the transvestitism of Maximilla and Iphidama has the purpose of enabling the women to travel safely in public. In late antiquity, Christian women were often discouraged from travelling because of the likelihood of social or sexual contact. One of the Egyptian monastic fathers challenged a female pilgrim from Rome who had come to visit the holy man, 'How dare you make such a journey? Do you not know that you are a woman and cannot go just anywhere?'[127] Jerome even tries to scare the young woman Eustochium into remaining indoors by recalling the violence suffered by Dinah when she left the safety of her home (Genesis 34).[128]

In fact, women who travelled, especially those who travelled alone, faced the ever-present danger of physical or sexual violence against their persons. In the *ATh*, when Thecla ventures out in public on the road to Antioch, even in the presence of Paul, she must fend off the very real threat of rape. Thus, Thecla's change of dress would also have had the very practical function of protection against further assault (sexual or otherwise) during her journeys as a charismatic teacher and missionary.[129] A story told by Eusebius of Emesa confirms this function of cross-dressing in antiquity: a virgin named Theodora escapes from the threat of rape by trading clothes with a Christian brother, Didymus.[130] In

---

[125] The phrase used here to describe this change of dress varies only slightly from the description cited above from the *Acts of Andrew* 19: μεταμφιασθεῖσα τὴν συνήθη ἐσθῆτα.

[126] Maximilla is led out in the 'guise of Andrew' (ἰδέα τοῦ Ἀνδρέα).

[127] *Apophth. Patr. Arsenius* 28 (PG 65. 97A).

[128] Jerome, *Ep.* 22. 25 (PL 22. 411).

[129] In a similar vein, Basil of Ancyra urges virgins to defend themselves against unwanted advances by men by taking on male mannerisms in speech and walk (*De virginitate*, 18–19 (PG 30. 708D); Brown, *Body and Society*, 268).

[130] Eusebius of Emesa, *Homilia* 6. 25–8, Latin text ed. É. M. Buytaert, OFM, *Eusèbe d'Émèse* (Louvain: Spicilegium Sacrum Lovaniense Administration,

early Christianity, transvestitism may indeed have been seen by itinerant women as a very practical means to safeguard themselves against such sexual threats, while still allowing themselves the freedom to travel as charismatic teachers.[131]

The depiction of Thecla as a charismatic figure in the *ATh* may shed light on the social make-up of the second-century communities who preserved her legend. The value placed on Thecla's charisma—as an ascetic, as a confessor, as a cross-dressing itinerant teacher—suggests something about the social roles endorsed by such groups. What might such communities have looked like? They certainly would not have been comprised solely of ascetic vagrants—such charismatic figures do not typically subsist on their own. Instead, they tend to exist in symbiosis with settled communities that offer subsistence and material support.[132]

In the *ATh*, the relationship between Thecla and Tryphaena's household conforms to this sociological model. Following Thecla's release from the arena, Tryphaena invites her into her home: 'Come inside and I will assign to you all that is mine.' There, Thecla rests for a period of eight days, and instructs Tryphaena and her female servants in 'the word of God'.[133] The length of Thecla's stay is significant. The writer of an early church manual entitled the *Didache* (c.100 CE) counsels communities to welcome apostles and those who come 'in the name of the Lord' for a maximum of only two or three days, in order to prevent abuses by visitors of false reputation.[134] That Thecla stays for eight days bespeaks both her favour and Tryphaena's exceptional generosity. Even after Thecla leaves and begins her life as an itinerant teacher, Tryphaena continues to offer financial support ('much clothing and gold') to both Thecla and her former mentor Paul.

The relationship between Tryphaena and Thecla might finally serve as an imaginative model for reconstructing the

---

1953), i. 168–71; Elizabeth Castelli, 'Virginity and Its Meaning for Women's Sexuality in Early Christianity', *Journal of Feminist Studies in Religion*, 2 (1986), 87.

[131] Concern about the threat of sexual violence remains a prominent motif in contemporary women's folklore (Jordan, 'The Vaginal Serpent', 26–44).

[132] Thiessen, *Sociology of Early Palestinian Christianity*, 7.

[133] *ATh* 39.   [134] *Did.* 11–12.

social organization of the communities behind the story. If the legend of Thecla traces its oral roots to settled communities in second-century Asia Minor—perhaps domestic circles of widows who shared a common commitment to the life of chastity—such communities may have served as sources of support for charismatic members who travelled and taught, communicating the story of Thecla and its distinctively ascetic message to settled communities in other locales. Perhaps some of these charismatic women claimed the status of 'confessor' and performed an intercessory function for local communities. Perhaps some even practised transvestitism as a sign of their break from society and as means of facilitating their travel.[135]

In the end, the identity of the earliest female devotees to Thecla remains virtually lost to the contemporary historian. However, I have tried to show that the *ATh* offers a rich set of social data with which to trace the faint contours (i.e. the values and practices) of women's culture in second-century Christianity. The set of practices I have outlined—asceticism, itinerancy, and charismatic function—later prove to be determinative for the development of Thecla's cult in Asia Minor and in Egypt.

---

[135] The anathema proclaimed against women who exchange their garments for a man's garments at the Synod of Gangra (340 CE) would suggest that female transvestitism was practised enough to merit such a sanction (*Canon* 13, ed. C. J. Hefele, *Histoire des Conciles*, i. pt. 2 (Paris: Letouzey et Ané, 1907), 1038). Jerome also inveighs against the practice of female transvestitism in his letter to Eustochium (*Ep.* 22. 27).

The Cult of Thecla at Seleucia in Asia Minor

At the end of the *ATh*, Thecla's final resting place is identified as Seleucia (modern day Silifke, Turkey),[1] a town near the southern coast of Asia Minor, about 100 km south-east of Iconium and 50 km south-west of Tarsus (see map of Asia Minor, Fig. 1). The story concludes with a brief note about her final journey to Seleucia where 'after bearing witness (διαμαρτύρεσθαι) to these things . . . and after enlightening many with the word of God, she slept with a noble sleep'.[2] The author does not elaborate on what Thecla accomplished in that region or how long she lived there. And yet, despite the fact that it receives so little mention in the *ATh*, Seleucia and its environs quickly became a hub for Thecla devotion. A shrine dedicated to Thecla (Hagia Thekla) was established on a hill just to the south of the city (see Fig. 2) and by the fourth century the holy site began attracting pilgrims from Asia Minor and from all over the Mediterranean world. The growth and prosperity of Hagia Thekla as a pilgrimage site from the fourth to the sixth century are indicated especially by two factors: (i) the architectural adaptation and expansion of the site itself, and (ii) new literary activity promoting Thecla's cult (i.e. adaptations and expansions of her legend).

---

[1] The town of Seleucia is often referred to as Seleucia-on-the-Calycadnus. As its name suggests, the town was founded under the Seleucids (between the years 296 and 280 BCE). By the first century BCE Seleucia came under Roman control. For a time in the third century CE (following the year 269), the Sassanids invaded and occupied Seleucia and the surrounding region. However, under Diocletian (284–305 CE), the town was established as the capital of a newly demarcated province, Isauria (Celâl Taskiran, *Silifke* [Seleucia-on-Calycadnus] *and Environs: Lost Cities of a Distant Past in Cilicia* (Ankara: SIM Matbaacılık, 1993), 22–3).

[2] *ATh* 43.

HAGIA THEKLA, THE PHYSICAL SETTING

In the spring of the year 384, a female pilgrim named Egeria took a three-day detour from her itinerary of holy sites to visit Thecla's shrine: 'Only three nights from Tarsus, in Isauria, is the martyr shrine of Saint Thecla; [and] since it was so close we were pleased to travel there.'[3] Having arrived in the town of Seleucia during the day, she decided to climb the hill to Hagia Thekla in the early evening in order to spend the night there. In her travel diary, she records her impression of the sights that greeted her as she reached her destination: 'There in the vicinity of the holy church . . . are innumerable monastic cells for men and women. . . . (Indeed) there are a great many monastic cells all over that hill, and in the middle there is a huge wall that surrounds the church, in which the martyr shrine is located. This martyr shrine is rather beautiful.'[4]

Egeria's report suggests that at the time of her visit there was one church at the site, and that the actual shrine (martyrium) of Saint Thecla was connected with that structure. This remained the case through the first half of the fifth century—a literary work dated *c*.444/8 CE (the *Life and Miracles of Saint Thecla*) also presumes a single, central church, and identifies its liturgical table as the locus of Thecla's shrine[5] (I will discuss this work in detail later in this chapter). Unfortunately, the exact location of the original shrine has not yet been determined. But in any case, sometime in the second half of the fifth century, Thecla's shrine was relocated to a nearby cave at the southern end of the same hill; there, a small, three-aisled basilica was built into the natural grotto of limestone.[6]

---

[3] Egeria, *Itin.* 23. 2 (66 Francheschini).

[4] *Itin.* 23. 2–4 (66 Francheschini).   [5] *Life* 28 (Dag., 280).

[6] The archaeologists who discovered and published the remains of this 'cave church' earlier this century originally believed this structure had to be the fourth-century shrine attested by Egeria (E. Herzfeld and S. Guyer, *Meriamlik und Korykos* (Manchester: Manchester University Press, 1930), 38–46, esp. 43–6; cf. J. Wilkinson, *Egeria's Travels*, rev. edn. (Warminster: Aris & Phillips, 1981), 288–92). However, there is no archaeological evidence *in situ* that can definitively be traced back earlier than the fifth century. Indeed, around 444/8 CE the same *Life and Miracles* (mentioned above) remarks on this grotto as a place of solitude for pilgrims, but does not indicate that it yet housed a church or shrine (*Miracle* 36; Dag., 388). According to this account, the grotto was situated to the west and just opposite the main shrine (νεώς) itself.

Over this cave church another much larger basilica was built later in the fifth century (Fig. 3). This expansive, three-nave structure exceeded 80 m in length (today only the southern half of the main nave remains standing), and was probably built by the Emperor Zeno sometime shortly after the year 476 CE.[7] The story of Zeno's patronage of Hagia Thekla is known from the historian Evagrius (*c*.593 CE). Temporarily exiled from office by a usurper named Basiliskos, Zeno spent time in the region of Isauria, and while there reportedly received a promise from Saint Thecla that his reign would be re-established. According to Evagrius, after Zeno's successful return to Constantinople and the arrest of Basiliskos in 476 CE, the emperor dedicated a large church to the 'protomartyr Thecla' in gratitude for the saint's intercession on his behalf.[8] The layout and dimensions of the church, as well as the style of its sculpture fragments (i.e. capitals), are consistent with a late fifth-century dating.[9]

Indeed, toward the end of the fifth century and into the sixth, there was a flurry of architectural activity at the site. At least two other churches were built in this period, as well as a public bath and a number of large cisterns (Fig. 4). Of these, the so-called North Church (not yet excavated) would have greeted visitors first as they arrived on the path from Seleucia.[10] Further to the south, a so-called 'Domed Church' (so named because the four pillars in the central nave were thought by early excavators to support a roof of this type[11]) exceeded 70 m in length and was characterized by a semi-circular atrium through which visitors entered from the west. Immediately to the west of the Domed Church

---

[7] Dag., 61–3.

[8] Evagrius Scholasticus, *H.E.* 3. 8, ed. J. Bidez and L. Parmentier, 107–8.

[9] Dag., 61.

[10] Even though the North Church has not yet been excavated, O. Feld was able to identify remains of capitals that allow for a late fifth-century dating ('Bericht über eine Reise durch Kilikien', *Istanbuler Mitteilungen*, 13–14 (1963–4), 93–4).

[11] Herzfeld and Guyer, *Meriamlik und Korykos*, 59. More recently, it has been argued that the pillars would not have borne the weight of a domed structure, and instead probably supported a pyramidal roof made of wood, like that found at the monastic church at Alahan in Cilicia (G. H. Forsyth, 'Architectural Notes on a Trip through Cilicia', *Dumbarton Oaks Papers*, 11 (1957), 223–5; cf. M. Gough, 'The Emperor Zenon and Some Cilician Churches', *Anatolian Studies*, 22 (1972), 202–3).

archaeologists have discovered traces of a number of other building projects from this period: the ruins of what may have been
another small basilica, a public bath, and four cisterns.[12] Three
more cisterns have been found 100–200 m further to the south
in the vicinity of the great basilica over the cave.

This flurry of building projects at Hagia Thekla undoubtedly
reflects the changing needs of a rapidly growing pilgrim clientele.
As more and more pilgrims visited the shrine of Thecla outside
Seleucia, more cisterns and baths were needed to provide water
for drinking and bathing, more churches were needed to accommodate increasing numbers of worshippers. Today, these buildings lie in ruins, but their remains testify to the crowds of
pilgrims that once visited Thecla's hilltop shrine.

LITERARY PATRONAGE OF THE THECLA CULT AT
SELEUCIA: THE EXPANSION OF HER LEGEND

The imperial patronage of Zeno (*c*.476 CE) supplied the hard cash
for the architectural adaptation and expansion of Hagia Thekla.
At the same time, other forms of patronage promoted Thecla's
cult in subtler ways. One of these forms of patronage was the production of literary works about the saint. While builders were
busy working with stone, writers took up their pens to write new
and improved versions of Thecla's life and to document the
saint's ongoing miraculous works of healing at her shrine. This
literature provides important social data for understanding the
development of the cult of Saint Thecla at Seleucia and the practices that constituted that cult.

As mentioned in Chapter 1, the story of Thecla originally had
its roots in oral folklore. Toward the end of the second century,
the author of the non-canonical *Acts of Paul* finally published
Thecla's story as part of that larger narrative. However, with the
autonomous development of Thecla's cult at Seleucia, the *ATh*
became detached from the manuscript tradition of the *Acts of Paul*
and enjoyed a separate history of transmission in connection with
her Asia Minor shrine. Egeria (384 CE) relates how, after arriving at Hagia Thekla and having a communal prayer, 'We read

---

[12] Herzfeld and Guyer, *Meriamlik und Korykos*, 77–87.

the Acts of Saint Thecla.'[13] By the late fourth century CE the *ATh* was being read as a work in its own right at Seleucia.

By the fifth and sixth centuries, writers connected with Thecla's pilgrimage centre in Seleucia began producing modified, extended versions of her life. Two examples are especially valuable for the light they shed on cultic practice at Hagia Thekla during this period: (i) the *Life and Miracles of Saint Thecla*,[14] and (ii) a later, expanded version of the *Acts of Paul and Thecla*, which I will refer to as *ATh*[Sel].[15] These works are each largely based on the earlier *ATh*; however, they augment the original legend with additional biographical details about what Thecla did in her final days at Seleucia, and especially her final act as a 'martyr'. These new endings represent writers' attempts in the fifth and sixth centuries to justify the establishment of Thecla's martyr shrine at Seleucia, and to show pilgrim readers how their experience there enjoyed a tangible connection with the 'actual' experience of the saint. At the same time, these expanded accounts offer clues as to social changes in the life of the cult during this period.

The *Life and Miracles of Saint Thecla* is a work in two parts. The first half (the *Life*) consists of a periphrastic biography of the saint based on the events in the *ATh*, but with an extra section at the end that introduces new material about the end of Thecla's life at Seleucia. The second half (the *Miracles*) is a collection of forty-six stories about the many miracles that Saint Thecla performed posthumously on behalf of pilgrims and other devotees at Seleucia.

In all extant manuscripts the *Life and Miracles* is attributed to the theologian Basil of Seleucia (d. *c*.468 CE); however, this attribution proves to be false. Internal evidence shows that it was in fact penned by an anonymous fifth-century rival of Basil, probably a local rhetorician from Seleucia.[16] From details provided in the text, one can estimate fairly precisely its date of composition.

---

[13] *Itin.* 23. 5 (66 Francheschini).

[14] For a critical edition of the *Life and Miracles*, see Dagron (ed.), *Vie et miracles*.

[15] The manuscript tradition of this expanded version of the *Acts of Paul and Thecla* is detailed in *Acta Apostolorum Apocrypha*, ed. R. A. Lipsius and M. Bonnet (Leipzig: Hermann Mendelssohn, 1891), 269–72.

[16] Dagron provides the definitive treatment of the work's authorship and date (Dag., 13–30).

The *Life and Miracles* had to have been written between the years 444 and 448 CE—after the execution of a priest named Severus in 444 (mentioned as having recently occurred under the general Satornilos in *Miracle* 13) and before the end of John's reign as bishop of Seleucia in 448 CE (the author reports that John is still alive in *Miracle* 44).[17] It should be noted that, however, while the *Life and Miracles* dates to 444/8 as a composite *written* work, the miracle stories themselves have *oral* roots that trace back to the middle of the fourth century CE. The very earliest stories seem to date to around the year 353.[18] In the case of the *Miracles*, then, the author's task was an editorial one—that of assembling stories told by pilgrims for several generations (between 353 and 444/8 CE). Thus, he speaks of 'running around here and there, gathering, and collecting miracles, as if gathering them up from the recesses of the distant past and forgotten memory'.[19]

The expanded content of Thecla's biography (*Life* 27–8) reflects a similar cognizance of pilgrims' experience on the part of the author. The narrative continues after Thecla arrives at Seleucia. Finding it raining, she climbs a hill to the south of the city where she takes shelter. There, she spends the remaining part of her life resisting the local 'demons' of paganism,

---

[17] Ibid. 17–19. The date 448 actually provides a *terminus ante quem* for the completion of an *original version* of the *Life and Miracles*—this first edition included almost the entire work we know now (the entire *Life* and the *Miracles* up through *Miracle* 44). There is evidence that the same author made several later additions to this original version. Sometime during the reign of Basil as bishop of Seleucia (*c*.448–68 CE), the author expanded *Miracle* 12 with new autobiographical material—material meant specifically to defend himself against his rival Basil and to show how Saint Thecla's favour rested with him in their ecclesiastical controversy. Perhaps a decade later, this author also added two more miracles (45–6) and a final dedication to the end of the work. This final emendation took place after 468 (the end of Basil's reign as bishop) but certainly before Zeno's great building project around 476, since there is no evidence for Zeno's constructions in the *Life and Miracles*. Furthermore, when the grotto is mentioned, it is described in terms that suggest a natural setting prior to any architectural development. Thus, at the time the *Life and Miracles* was written, the grotto was not yet the location of Thecla's church—instead, it is clear that the sites were still distinct because the author comments that the grotto was located then to the west of the shrine locale (*Miracle* 36).

[18] *Miracles* 5 and 6. The bulk of the *Miracles* seem to range in date from around 370 to 420 CE (Dag., 26–7).

[19] *Miracle* 44. 9–11 (Dag., 404).

teaching (κατηχεῖν) and baptizing (σφραγίζειν) others in Christ. The end of Thecla's life is unconventional—the author reports that she did not actually die. Instead, 'still living, she sank and entered secretly into the earth' (ἔδυ δὲ ζῶσα καὶ ὑπεισῆλθε τὴν γῆν).[20]

Throughout the *Life and Miracles* the author celebrates Thecla's status as a martyr, the first (female) martyr after Stephen.[21] It is curious then that he sees no contradiction in supporting a tradition asserting that Thecla never actually died. Apparently, this tradition was already well known at Seleucia at the time of the author's writing—he cites it as a 'widespread and genuine report' (πολὺς καὶ ἀληθέστερος λόγος).[22] Seemingly, in the *Life and Miracles*, the rhetorical function of this tradition is to emphasize the *living presence* of the martyr-saint, a presence manifested in the healing properties of her shrine.[23] Thus, the author notes that the very spot where Thecla sank into the earth became the site of 'the divine and holy liturgical table' and the source for a spring which produced healing water. By identifying these visible accoutrements of the shrine as the location of Thecla's 'interment', the *Life and Miracles* shows how Thecla's presence was made tangible—physically accessible—to pilgrims visiting Hagia Thekla.

Such descriptions of Thecla's shrine in the *Life and Miracles* reflect the physical setting of Hagia Thekla prior to Zeno's building project (c.476 CE). By contrast, the *ATh*[Sel] (part of the later manuscript tradition of the *ATh* itself) seems to have been produced in the aftermath of Zeno's constructions, or at least after Thecla's shrine had been relocated to the famous grotto. In the *ATh*[Sel], the cave itself becomes the privileged location of Thecla's final acts. This tradition has an aetiological function—to provide biographical support for the relocation of Thecla's shrine to the cave in the latter half of the fifth century. The specific date of this tradition is difficult to determine, although it certainly is

---

[20] *Life* 28. 7–8 (Dag., 280).

[21] The Prologues to both the *Life* and the *Miracles* introduce her as 'the greatest female martyr' (ἡ μεγίστη μάρτυρα) (Dag., 168, 284); cf. *Life* 12; 13; 15; 16; 20; 22; 23; 24; 25; 26; *Miracles* 1; 4; 5; *passim*.

[22] *Life* 28. 7 (Dag., 280).

[23] Indeed, the collection of *Miracles* presume Thecla's power as a 'living martyr', present and active in the life of her devotees.

earlier than the eighth or ninth century (the date of the earliest extant manuscript).[24]

In the *ATh*[Sel], before going to Seleucia Thecla first travels back to Daphne, to the tomb where Paul and Onesiphorus had prayed for her during her trial by fire in Iconium.[25] After this brief stop, she travels to Seleucia and establishes herself in a 'cave' (σπήλαιον) on a nearby mountain (named Kalamos or Rodeon).[26] Thecla's route of travel in the *ATh*[Sel]—with her intermittent stop at Daphne and her path up to the cave—corresponds to the itinerary many late-fifth century pilgrims took on their way to Hagia Thekla. In this context, it is interesting that Thecla is led up to the cave by a 'luminous cloud' (νεφέλη φωτεινή). This symbol of divine protection and guidance recalls the νεφέλη πυρός at Thecla's baptism (*ATh* 34), but it also may be a verbal allusion to the fiery cloud that led Moses and the Israelites in their flight from Egypt (Exodus 13: 21).[27] This expansion of Thecla's life presents her journey, then, as the prototypical pilgrimage to Seleucia, one that was to be emulated by later devotees.

In the cave outside Seleucia, Thecla pursues the life of an ascetic, enduring demonic temptation and eventually attracting a small group of female disciples. These women become established in 'the (ascetic) life' (ὁ βίος) and live together with Thecla.[28] The picture given is one of a semi-eremitical community of monastic women similar to that observed by Egeria. (Later in this chapter, I will discuss in more detail the social roles of monastic women living at Hagia Thekla in the fifth century.)

In the *ATh*[Sel], Thecla's ascetic disciplines and her related ability to perform miraculous works of healing win her widespread fame. Yet, the healings and exorcisms she performs for her many visitors quickly bring her into conflict with local physicians from Seleucia. The doctors, whose livelihood is threatened by her

---

[24] The *ATh*[Sel] tradition is preserved in two manuscripts (G and M). G has been dated paleographically to the ninth or tenth century, and M to the eighth or ninth century (*Acta Apostolorum Apocrypha*, ed. Lipsius and Bonnet, lxxvi–lxxvii).

[25] Ibid. 269–71 (MSS GM*cd*). It is interesting that in preparation for this journey Thecla 'sealed up (κατασφραγίζεσθαι) all of her body'. Just as earlier Thecla changed her dress before her journey to Myra, here too she takes precautions in order to preserve (and perhaps cloak) her body from the threat of public recognition and sexual assault.

[26] Ibid. 271 (MS G).   [27] Dag., 48.

[28] *Acta Apostolorum Apocrypha*, ed. Lipsius and Bonnet, 271.

presence, see Thecla as usurping the favour of Artemis, the goddess of healing whose cult was active in the region. This scenario
parallels Paul's conflict with adherents of Artemis at Ephesus
(Acts 19: 23–41) and again presents a picture of Thecla as the
female equivalent of Paul. Again, it is Thecla's virginity that
is understood as the source of her autonomy and power—the
doctors fear that Artemis heeds Thecla's intercessions specifically
because of the latter's status as a virgin.[29] Out of their jealousy
and anger against Thecla, the physicians plot to have Thecla's
virginity defiled in order to nullify her power of healing. They
reason that if they were able to defile Thecla's sexual purity, the
source of her spiritual potency, then 'neither the gods nor
Artemis would hear her concerning the sick'.[30] With this goal in
mind, they find some 'unruly men', get them drunk, and offer
them bribes to rape Thecla.

Just as in the case of Alexander's earlier assault recounted in
the *ATh*, male sexual aggression presents a threat to Thecla's virginity and to the special powers manifest in the virgin's life. Just
as Alexander's attempted rape led to Thecla's trials amidst the
beasts in the arena, here the threat of sexual violence results in
another (metaphorical) encounter with beasts. The drunk men,
coming to rape Thecla, are described as establishing themselves
'like lions' before the door to Thecla's cave. This simile alludes
back to her encounter with the lions in Antioch, and indicates that
her encounter with these 'evil men' should be read as a final martyr trial. The prayer Thecla utters as the men attempt to take hold
of her further sets this scene in the context of her deliverance from
earlier persecution.

O God . . . you who have saved me from fire, who did not hand me over
to Thamyris, who did not hand me over to Alexander, who saved me
from beasts, who delivered me from the deep, who always has worked
together with me and has glorified your name in me, now rescue me from
these lawless men, and do not appear to mock my virginity, which on
account of your name I have guarded up till now . . .[31]

In the final scene of the expanded legend, Thecla preserves her
virginity and evades her accosters by disappearing into a large

---

[29] The doctors warn each other that Artemis 'hears her because she is a virgin' (*Acta Apostolorum Apocrypha*, ed. Lipsius and Bonnet, 271).
[30] Ibid.   [31] Ibid. 271–2.

rock. The rock opens up and Thecla sinks into it, leaving behind only a piece of her garment.[32]

Here, the ending of the *ATh*[Sel] performs an aetiological function, narrating events in the life of the saint that are meant to give validity to later cultic developments. This part of the narrative has three aims. First, it attempts to validate the veneration of Thecla as a true martyr by showing how her life was brought to an end by hostile forces. The editor concludes the *ATh*[Sel] by acclaiming Thecla as 'the first female martyr and apostle and virgin of God' (ἡ τοῦ θεοῦ πρωτομάρτυς καὶ ἀπόστολος καὶ παρθένος).[33] Lauded as the 'first female martyr', Thecla is compared to the first male martyr Stephen. Her disappearance into the stone may have reinforced this association—Stephen was of course stoned to death (i.e. buried under stones). As in the *Life and Miracles*, the title of martyr is now added to her early associations as virgin saint and itinerant teacher—indeed, in the *ATh*[Sel] her martyrdom is seen as the 'consummation' (τελείωσις) of her 'wandering and travels and ascetic discipline' (ὁδοιπορία καὶ περιόδος καὶ ἀσκήσις).[34]

Second, by highlighting *where* Thecla's martyrdom took place, this expanded ending justifies the late-fifth century relocation of Thecla's shrine to the cave under Zeno's grand basilica. In his conclusion, the author makes this aetiological aim explicit: '[These events] took place by the consent of God for the faith of those who see the revered spot, and as a blessing for later generations . . .'[35]

Third, this ending provides an explanation for the accoutrements of the shrine itself. The large rock into which Thecla sank became the centre of her shrine, the site of the liturgical table and a spring of running water for the sick.[36] The enigmatic disappearance of Thecla in the legend also constitutes an implicit apology for the shrine's lack of any bodily relics.[37] The absence of a body, or any of its parts, would have been problematic in

---

[32] Lipsius and Bonnet, 272.   [33] Ibid.   [34] Ibid.   [35] Ibid.

[36] *Life* 28 (Dag., 280); cf. *Acta Apostolorum Apocrypha*, ed. Lipsius and Bonnet, 272 (MS G).

[37] Bernhard Kötting (*Peregrinatio Religiosa: Wallfahrten in der Antike und das Pilgerwesen in der alten Kirche*, 2nd edn. (Münster: Antiquariat Th. Stenderhoff, 1980), 294–5) identifies the graves of Jesus and Thecla as prime examples of pilgrimage sites not tied to bodily relics.

the context of the late antique association of such relics with the locus of the martyr's power. The story's detail about the piece of Thecla's garment left behind in the rock perhaps reflects the establishment of a derivative relic associated with the martyr. In one manuscript, the garment is in fact described as a relic offered to pilgrims; in another, part of the rock formation is said to be the petrified veil.[38] In any case, the rock and the piece of her garment would have been offered as visual confirmation of Thecla's disappearance to pilgrims upon their visit to the shrine and its altar.[39]

The dilemma over the nature of Thecla's presence was an ongoing concern for the early cult of Thecla. This may be the reason that even in the fifth century, the *Life and Miracles of Saint Thecla* claims that Thecla, in fact, remained alive (ζῶσα) after sinking into the rock.[40] Thecla's living presence at the shrine is vividly portrayed in the miracle accounts that accompany the expanded version of her *Life*. In those accounts, the tradition of Thecla's survival in the stone again functions apologetically to justify her ongoing power and presence even in the absence of any bodily remains at the shrine.

Shrines dedicated to Thecla in other geographical regions would face an even more difficult dilemma; the problem of the absence of Thecla's remains was compounded by the problem of radical geographical dislocation. How could shrines in places far removed from Asia Minor—in Rome or Egypt, for example—claim an immediate connection to the martyr if they did not possess a relic? It was, in part, by renarrating the saint's life that devotees in other locales managed to 'translate' Thecla to their own cultural context.

In the case of Roman devotion to Saint Thecla, a third manuscript tradition of the *Acts of Paul and Thecla*, which I will refer to as *ATh*[Rom], demonstrates how the legend of Thecla was expanded even further to connect Thecla's life to the cult of

---

[38] *Acta Apostolorum Apocrypha*, ed. Lipsius and Bonnet, 272 (MSS G and M).

[39] The natural (and original?) function of the rock within the activity of pilgrimage must have been its issuance of a spring of holy water, meaningful for the pious visitor either in conjunction with her desire for healing at the shrine or as a tertiary relic taken back home in pilgrim flasks.

[40] *Life* 28. 8 (Dag., 280).

the martyrs in that city.[41] *ATh*^{Rom} describes Thecla's subterranean transportation to Rome after disappearing in the rock at Seleucia. Still alive after having sunk into the earth, Thecla 'came to Rome to behold Paul, and she found him fallen asleep. She remained there only a short time, and then she slept with a noble sleep.'[42] While this account implicitly recognizes the significance of traditions connected to Seleucia,[43] it is more interested in justifying the existence of the cult dedicated to Thecla in Rome. It is difficult to date this literary tradition, but texts from the seventh century attest to a 'Church of Saint Thecla'—where she was reputed to have been buried—near a basilica dedicated to Paul in Rome.[44] Thus, this third version of the ending of Thecla's life renarrated the legend of Thecla as a means of 'translating' her to another geographical context of veneration.

For the cult of Thecla in Egypt we lack evidence of any such attempt to expand or recast the *ATh* in terms of a new geographical milieu. There is no literary tradition that tries to transport Thecla from Seleucia to Egypt through a sub-Mediterranean channel. Furthermore, there is a conspicuous absence of any reference to Thecla's physical remains in Egypt. A major question in Part II will be how the 'translation' of Thecla to Egypt may have been negotiated in the absence of these crucial cultic markers.

---

[41] *Acta Apostolorum Apocrypha*, ed. Lipsius and Bonnet, 270 (MSS A, B, C).

[42] Ibid.

[43] In addition to preserving the tradition of Thecla's disappearance into the rock, the tradition's reference to Thecla's 'noble sleep' (καλὸς ὕπνος) in Rome establishes verbal continuity with the original ending to her legend in *ATh* 43, which describes her καλός ὕπνος at Seleucia (*Acta Apostolorum Apocrypha*, ed. Lipsius and Bonnet, 270).

[44] References to this Thecla church appear in the *Notitia ecclesiarum urbis Romae* (an *Itinerary* composed under Honorius I, 625–38 CE) and in the *De locis SS. martyrum que sunt foris civitatis Romae* (*DACL* XV. 2. 2235). Festugiére notes that the first text's reference to the location of Thecla's body *in spelunca* establishes an interesting analogy with the cultic configuration at Seleucia (*Collections grecques de miracles: Sainte Thècle, Saints Côme et Damien, Saints Cyr et Jean [extraits], Saint Georges* (Paris: Picard, 1971), 24). One of the Roman catacombs located on the Via Ostiense is named after Thecla; a second cemetery dedicated to Thecla exists on the Via Aurelia (Holzhey, *Die Thekla-Akten: Ihre Verbreitung und Beurteilung in der Kirche* (Munich: J. J. Lentner, 1905), 66).

WOMEN'S PIETY IN CULTURAL CONFLICT AT
HAGIA THEKLA: ASCETICISM, ITINERANCY,
AND MARTYR CULT

Concern about the absence of bodily relics at Seleucia was not
the only social tension that characterized the life of Thecla's cult
at Seleucia. The description of cultic practice in the *Miracles* hints
at other tensions as well. In the experience of Thecla's female
clientele, one observes the kinds of religious freedom granted to
women as well as the kinds of patriarchal constraints placed upon
them. At the same time, as the cult of Thecla at Hagia Thekla
took on more complex institutional forms and became international in scope, other areas of conflict emerged in connection
with: (i) monasticism and the domestication of the ascetic impulse;
(ii) itinerancy and the routinization of pilgrimage; and (iii) the
cult of the martyr and its competition with religious rivals. This
diverse array of tensions, and the dynamic resolution of those tensions in the person of Thecla the saint, shaped to a large extent
the experience of female devotees to Thecla in fourth- and fifth-
century Asia Minor.

Women's Culture in the Seleucian Cult

The fifth-century *Life and Miracles of Saint Thecla* appends a
collection of forty-six miracles associated with Hagia Thekla to
an expanded narration of Thecla's life. The work portrays a cult
that is strongly patronized by women, and yet at the same time
gripped by elements of patriarchal bias.

That the intercessory activity of Saint Thecla was understood
as being particularly (although not exclusively) directed to the
needs of women is evident at various points within the *Miracles*.
Miracle 12 provides an especially striking illustration of Thecla's
special protection of women. Saint Thecla appears in a vision to
the author himself and tells him that she is about to hurry off to
Macedonia to help 'a woman in danger' (γυνὴ κινδυνεύουσα).[45]
This story consciously seems to play off Acts 16: 9 where the
apostle Paul dreams about a Macedonian man who asks Paul to
come to Macedonia and help him.[46] If the author's vision in the

---

[45] *Miracle* 12. 100–1 (Dag., 322).   [46] Dag., 323, n. 17.

Miracles alludes to Paul's dream in Acts the differences between the accounts are as telling as the similarities. Most striking, the gender of the Macedonian supplicant in the *Miracles* has been altered to mirror that of the saint. In this vignette, Thecla not only assumes the mantle of Paul's ministry, but also distinguishes herself from Paul as a patron saint of women.

The *Miracles* of Saint Thecla presents a picture of a pilgrimage practice and martyr cult suffused with the presence and activity of women.[47] Thecla comes to the aid of a fascinating coterie of female clients: a grandmother and devotee of the divinized Greek hero Sarpedon[48] whose grandson suffered from a tumour (*Mir.* 11); the woman in danger in Macedonia (*Mir.* 12); an aristocratic woman who was saddened by the unbelief of her husband (*Mir.* 14); two women (Aba and Tigriane) who suffered broken legs (*Mir.* 18); a pregnant woman named Bassiane and her female servant (*Mir.* 19); a woman whose husband (the General Vitianos) was cheating on her (*Mir.* 20); a bride whose marriage belt was stolen (*Mir.* 21); a wet-nurse of a child who had lost an eye (*Mir.* 24); virgins who sleep inside the shrine (*Mir.* 32); a female suppliant threatened by the sexual advances of a man (*Mir.* 33); a virgin wandering outside the shrine precinct also exposed to the lustful aggression of men (*Mir.* 34); a noble woman named Kalliste who left her husband to become an actress in the theatre (*Mir.* 42); a common woman named Bassiane who became an apotactite at the shrine and the wayward virgin who stole some of her possessions (*Mir.* 43); two women (Dosithea and

---

[47] While women figure prominently in the miracle cycles of other late antique saints, the editor of the *Miracles* of Saint Thecla seems to have had a special interest in making women (and women's society) a 'sujet central' of his work (Dag., 131).

[48] In Homeric myth, Sarpedon commanded the Lycian contingent allied with King Priam in the Trojan War (Homer, *Il.* 2. 876). After he was killed by Patroclus (*Il.* 16. 426 ff.), he was mourned by his father Zeus (16. 459 ff.) and removed to Lycia for burial by Sleep and Death (16. 666 ff.). In post-Homeric Greek mythology, Sarpedon is said to be the son of Zeus and Europa, and brother of Minos, king of Crete. Having been exiled from Crete after a squabble with his brother, he fled to Cilicia and ruled there (Herodotus, 1. 173; Apollodorus, *Bibliotheca* 3. 1. 2). In this region of southern Asia Minor, a local hero-cult dedicated to Sarpedon developed in antiquity. On the veneration of heroes in the Greek world, see H. J. Rose's article, 'Hero-Cult', in *The Oxford Classical Dictionary*, 505–6.

Theodoule) whose miracle stories are not related in detail (*Mir.* 44); a married woman named Xenarchis who learned to read (*Mir.* 45); and finally, a woman named Dionysia who abandons her family to dwell at Hagia Thekla and a virgin at the shrine named Sosanna who originally recounted Dionysia's miracle story (*Mir.* 46).[49] At one point, in the midst of a series of stories about women who received aid from Thecla, the author begins to tell the story of a woman named Dosithea, but then suddenly breaks off his account, seemingly overwhelmed by the number of stories that could be told about female devotees: 'But enough of this! What's the use of adding a drop of water to the boundless seas?'[50] Later, when the author again begins to list women whose devotion to Thecla was especially praiseworthy, he alludes to 'all the other women [αἱ ἄλλαι πᾶσαι] whom I do not have time to cite'.[51]

Women appear in leadership and administrative roles, as notable members of the cult's clientele, and even as the oral conveyors of the miracle stories themselves. These women are said to have taken up 'the same zeal' for Thecla as men 'who have attained the summit of virtue'.[52] At the same time, however, statements in the *Life and Miracles* concerning the moral weakness of women undercut the work's dynamic portrayals of female devotees.[53]

Despite the prominent roles that women played in the life of the cult, their lives would not have been free of the patriarchal biases that pervaded late antique society. One detects an undercurrent of misogyny in the *Life and Miracles*. In the *Life*, the jewellery that Thecla sloughs off is understood as the 'inventions of female vulgarity'.[54] Later, Paul refuses to baptize Thecla specifically because of the susceptibility of 'this female nature and weakness' to temptation.[55] The category of the feminine was, of

---

[49] The visits to Hagia Thecla made by Marana and Cyra, and by Egeria, add to the profusion of women seeking and receiving aid from Thecla at her shrine at Seleucia.

[50] *Miracle* 44. 6–7 (Dag., 402–4).   [51] *Miracle* 44. 44–5 (Dag., 406).

[52] *Miracle* 44. 22–3 (Dag., 404).

[53] S. Brock and S. Ashbrook Harvey (*Holy Women of the Syrian Orient* (updated edn. (Berkeley: University of California Press, 1987/8), 20) note a similar tension 'between what the author says about women and what he tells us women are actually doing' in Syriac lives of female saints and martyrs.

[54] *Life* 8. 19–20 (Dag., 200).   [55] *Life* 14. 23 (Dag., 226).

course, considered morally problematic in ancient philosophical discourse and early Christian theological writing. In the writings of authors from Philo to Porphyry, women were intimately associated with undesired passions.[56] The Alexandrian theologian Origen believed that 'the flesh, and the weakness of the flesh are represented in woman'.[57] Early Christian exegetes, along with the Hellenistic Jewish counterparts, pointed specifically to Eve's sin in Genesis as evidence for women's fall from rationality into a life of the passions.[58] Much of early Christian literature, written by men, attempted to address (and correct) the problem of women's sexuality. Women were perceived as agents of sexual temptation; they were held morally culpable for leading men astray. Women's

[56] While Philo could describe the masculine as asexual—aligning it with the philosophical concepts of activity, incorporeality, and νοῦς—he associated the feminine with the sensual aspects of passivity, corporeality, and sensory perception/feeling (αἴσθησις). As a result, he saw 'the giving up of the female gender [γένος] by changing into the male' as a philosophical advance (Philo, *Quaestiones et solutiones in Exodum* 1. 8; Marvin Meyer, 'Making Mary Male: The Categories of "Male" and "Female" in the Gospel of Thomas', *New Testament Studies*, 31 (1985), 564). In Porphyry's letter to his wife, he urges her to 'flee everything that is effeminate in your soul as if you had put on the body of a male' (*Ad Marcellam* 33, ed. W. Pötscher (Leiden: E. J. Brill, 1969), 36).

[57] Origen, *In Exod.* (PG 12. 305). Some men thought physical desire was connected with women's menstruation. For instance, Gregory the Great believed women were somehow contaminated by the emotional turmoil accompanying menstruation (*Ep.* 11. 64; PL 77. 1196). Gillian Clark attributes this belief to several possible causes: '. . . perhaps by assimilation to oestrus in other mammals, perhaps by observation of sexual feeling or of the effects of fasting. . . . Voluntary fasting was the standard technique for ascetic women who wished to fight desire' (Gillian Clark, *Women in Late Antiquity: Pagan and Christian Lifestyles* (Oxford: Clarendon Press, 1993), 78).

[58] The North African Christian Tertullian warns women at the end of the second century that they directly share Eve's guilt: 'Are you ignorant of the fact that you are an Eve? The sentence of God on that sex of yours lives in this age; it stands to reason that the guilt must live as well. You are the devil's gateway [*diaboli janua*]. You are the unsealer of that tree. You are the first deserter of the divine law . . .' (*Cult. fem.* 1; CSEL 70. 59–60). In the fourth century, the heresiologist Epiphanius decries the 'disease' (νόσημα) that women were thought to inherit from Eve (*Pan.* 79. 2). For a collection of other early Christian writings that offer similar interpretations of Eve's influence over women, see Elizabeth Clark, *Women in the Early Church* (Collegeville, Minn.: Liturgical Press, 1983), 27–86.

dress and ornamentation,[59] and even simply their physical presence, might arouse sexual passions in an unsuspecting male at any time. As a result, the male authors put the onus on women to keep their dress modest, and to avoid public appearances that provoked lust or undue attention.[60]

The brief mention of eunuchs in the *Miracles* also reflects similar misogynist assumptions. Here, eunuchs are characterized as having a proclivity toward greed, mischief, and cupidity because they are 'half-man, half-woman' (γυνάνδρες), and therefore 'half-barbarous' (ἡμιβαρβάροι).[61] The derogation of men who slipped into forms of effeminacy, a common *topos* in ancient philosophical and early Christian writings, was also a backhanded slap against the weakness of women.[62] The ambivalent attitude

---

[59] Gillian Clark argues that, for male writers of late antiquity, it was the expression of status in women's clothing that attracted male (lustful) attention (Gillian Clark, *Women in Late Antiquity*, 111). On Jerome and Chrysostom's respective attitudes on women's dress, see Elizabeth Clark, *Jerome, Chrysostom and Friends* (New York: Edwin Mellon, 1979), 58–9.

[60] Isolation or physical withdrawal was often advocated as a means for women to avoid being a source of temptation to men (G. Cloke, *'This Female Man of God': Women and Spiritual Power in the Patristic Age* (London and New York: Routledge, 1995), 28–31). Around the turn of the third century, Tertullian writes that women should not appear in public except for . . . visiting the sick and attending worship (Tertullian, *Cult. fem.* 2. 11). Gregory of Nazianzus extols the example of his sister Gorgonia, who 'kept herself inaccessible to the eyes of men' (Gregory of Nazianzus, *Or.* 8. 9; PG 35. 800A). The Egyptian monastic tradition witnesses to this ideal of women's isolation. The anchoress Alexandra tells Melania the Elder: 'A man was disabled in mind because of me, and, so that I not seem to distress or mislead him, I chose to lead myself into this tomb while still alive, rather than cause a soul made in the image of God to stumble.' Her self-imposed isolation in the tomb lasted ten years (Palladius, *H. Laus.* 5; PG 34. 1017D).

[61] *Miracle* 9. 24–5 (Dag., 304).

[62] Peter Brown (*The Body and Society: Men, Women, and Sexual Renunciation in Early Christianity* (New York: Columbia University Press, 1988), 10–11) writes, 'In the Roman world, the physical appearance and the reputed character of eunuchs acted as constant reminders that the male body was a fearsomely plastic thing. . . . No normal man might actually become a woman; but each man trembled forever on the brink of becoming "womanish".' On the status of eunuchs in Byzantium and late antiquity, see the following: K. Ringrose, 'Living in the Shadows: Eunuchs and Gender in Byzantium', in G. Herdt (ed.), *Third Sex, Third Gender* (New York: Zone, 1994), 85–109; Shaun Tougher, 'Byzantine Eunuchs: An Overview with Special Reference to Their Creation and Origin', in Liz James (ed.), *Women, Men, and Eunuchs: Gender in Byzantium* (London

toward women in the *Life and Miracles*—the assumption of women's inferiority mixed with a recognition of their (anomalous) potential for heroic spirituality—reflects the continuation of a late antique conflict between ideals of female autonomy and forms of patriarchal constraint upon those ideals.

As a model for women's piety, Saint Thecla herself is understood to embody this conflict in the *Life*. The *Life* notes at various points how Thecla's spiritual prowess contrasts with, and even exceeds, the conventional role and place of women.[63] By the fourth century CE, the philosophy of early Christian asceticism viewed virginity as a means by which women might discard the feminine passions, and thereby subvert the way of nature. In fourth- and fifth-century literature, one encounters privileged women who are extolled as having attained a manliness of spirit through ascetic discipline.[64] A woman who demonstrated spiritual virility was said to be 'forgetful of her sex and the fragility of her body' (*oblita sexus et fragilitatis corporeae*).[65] In this context, the author of the *Life* may have understood Thecla's change to male dress and appearance, in the received tradition, as an ascetic attempt to hide or obscure her female body.

The accentuation of Thecla's flight from marriage and the household, and of her entry into the public sphere in the *Life*, underscores her movement from womanhood to 'maleness'. Thecla's silent prayer at her baptism notably celebrates the fact that God had liberated her from the female tasks of her private bridal chamber and 'led [her] out in public'.[66] Thecla becomes

and New York: Routledge, 1997), 168–84; Matthew S. Kuefler, 'Eunuchs and Other Men: The Crisis and Transformation of Masculinity in the Later Roman West', (Ph.D. diss., Yale University, 1995); Gary R. Brower, 'Ambivalent Bodies: Making Christians Eunuchs', (Ph.D. diss., Duke University, 1996).

[63] See Dag., 41, n. 3.

[64] Gillian Cloke helpfully collects a number of examples in her book '*This Female Man of God*', 213–15.

[65] Jerome, *Ep.* 108. 14; PL 22. 890. In a similar vein, Augustine comments on the manly philosophy of his mother Monica: 'Having forgotten completely her sex, we believed that some great man was contemplating with us' (Augustine, *Beat. vit.* 2. 10; CCSL 29. 71).

[66] *Life* 20. 9 (Dag., 248). In some manuscripts, these female tasks are identified specifically as weaving (ἱστός) and spinning (ἠλακάτη) (Dag., 248, n. 10). This private, domestic context contrasts with the public venue of the arena where Thecla undergoes her martyr trials (ibid.).

more-than-woman not only in virtue, but also in social location. Thus, the narrator of the *Life* remarks that Thecla's bold plan to leave her home and visit Paul in prison was 'more manly' (ἀνδρικώτερος) than what was expected of a woman.[67] Similarly, Thecla's rejection and humiliation of Alexander on a public street exceeded the courage of a woman.[68] Finally, after Thecla's braving of the beasts in the public arena, the governor marvels at 'the forceful and manly [ἀνδρικός] qualities of the young girl'.[69] In the *Miracles*, Thecla's transcendence of female limitations becomes paradigmatic for the piety of female devotees like Dionysia, whose level of virtue and asceticism was, in the same way, considered 'superior to the female condition'.[70]

In the *Life and Miracles*, Thecla is portrayed as the patron saint of women, and women pervade the life of her cult at Seleucia. However, it is important to recognize that women's devotion to Saint Thecla did not develop in isolation from men. Not only did Thecla's cult attract male adherents (men are also recipients of Thecla's benefactions in the *Miracles*) the cult also remained a forum for patriarchal evaluations of women's piety. Therefore, while women attained a special status and prominence in the cult of Saint Thecla at Seleucia, even their most heroic expressions of piety were constrained in part by the patriarchal ideologies of the day.

Asceticism, Itinerancy, and Martyr Cult in Cultural Tension

The miracle accounts paint a variegated picture of Thecla's female clientele: virgins and wives, pilgrims and resident nuns, ardent devotees of the Christian martyr and followers of rival pagan gods. The heterogeneity of this clientele produced further cultural tensions in the practices related to Thecla's cult at Seleucia: (i) between monasticism and the domestication of the ascetic impulse; (ii) between unregulated itinerancy and the routinization of pilgrimage; and (iii) between the cult of the martyr and its cultic rivals (both pagan and Christian). The piety and autonomy of female devotees to Thecla were in large part defined—both promoted and constrained—by these cultural tensions as the cult at Hagia Thekla was formalized and as the shrine attracted a more varied clientele.

---

[67] *Life* 8. 16 (Dag., 200).   [68] *Life* 15. 59–60 (Dag., 230).
[69] *Life* 23. 1–2 (Dag., 260).   [70] *Miracle* 46. 18–19 (Dag., 408).

Women's Monasticism at Hagia Thekla

Amidst this diversity of women's experience portrayed in the *Miracles*, there is evidence for the formation of a female monastic society connected to Thecla's shrine. Just as in the *ATh*, women's ascetic community serves as a tacit backdrop for the martyr cult of Thecla at Seleucia. At the same time, however, the cult at Seleucia began to attract lay pilgrims whose more ordinary lives reflected the domestication of that ascetic spirit.

In Egeria's account of her pilgrimage to Hagia Thekla, she describes a monastic foundation for both men and women at the site: 'Innumerable monastic cells for men and women' were located around the church dedicated to Saint Thecla.[71] Egeria stayed for two days visiting the monks living in the area, 'the men as well as the women' (*tam viri quam feminae*).[72]

Her account seems to describe a loose, semi-eremitical configuration of individual cells situated around the central shrine (i.e. a lavra):

There are a great many cells all over that hill, and in the middle there is a huge great wall that surrounds the church, in which the martyrium is located.[73]

However, just how this layout would have worked for the separation and/or distribution of male and female monks remains unclear.

Male monastics apparently lived in proximity to the shrine,[74] and male clergy functioned in a public role as assessors (παρέδροι) and guardians (φύλακες) of the shrine. The relationship between the clergy and the monks was quite close: Egeria reports meeting the bishop of Seleucia, 'a holy man who was formerly a monk'.[75] The monastic priests who served as assessors for the shrine seem to have formed an influential caste of clergy (γερουσία τῶν ἱερέων)[76] from which bishops were recruited: one of the assessors mentioned by name in the *Miracles*, Dexianos,

---

[71] *Itin.* 23. 2–3 (66 Francheschini). Dual monasteries were a common arrangement in the fourth and fifth centuries.

[72] *Itin.* 23. 6 (66 Francheschini).   [73] *Itin.* 23. 4 (66 Francheschini).

[74] In addition to the Egeria's testimony to the presence of male monks living at and around the shrine, the *Miracles of Saint Thecla* mentions three monks, Karterios, John, and Philip, 'who each dwelled in that monastic community [φροντιστήριον]' (*Miracle* 44. 37–8; Dag., 404).

[75] *Itin.* 23. 1.   [76] *Miracle* 7. 4 (Dag., 300).

would himself become Bishop of Seleucia (430 CE); another assessor, Menodoros, eventually became Bishop of Aigai.[77] Dexianos was considered the paragon among the group in the balance he struck between Seleucia and Hagia Thekla, between his episcopal and monastic vocations.[78]

Yet, alongside the leadership of male monks and priests, Egeria and the author of the *Miracles of Saint Thecla* both place considerable emphasis on the leadership and presence of women at the shrine. From Egeria, we know that women were active in leadership roles at the martyrium at least by the late fourth century. Egeria speaks of a 'holy deaconess named Marthana' who had befriended Egeria originally during Egeria's visit to Jerusalem and seems to have been in the position to host the pilgrim during her stay at Hagia Thekla.[79] Marthana's reputation at Hagia Thekla is further confirmed in the *Miracles* by her being first in a list of celebrated ascetic women who had severed family ties and installed themselves at the shrine.[80]

Egeria notes that Marthana 'directed some cells of hermits or virgins' (*haec autem monasteria aputactitum seu virginum regebat*).[81] Is it possible that Marthana was overseeing a dual (i.e. male *and* female) semi-eremitical monastic community similar to that established by Gregory of Nyssa's sister Macrina at Annesi in Asia Minor?[82] Despite the precedent of Macrina's leadership of a mixed community, it remains unclear whether Marthana exerted authority over the life of male monastics in the vicinity of Hagia Thekla.[83]

---

[77] Dexianos: *Miracles* 7 and 32 (Dag., 300–2, 374–6); Menodorus: *Miracle* 9 (Dag., 304–8).

[78] Dag., 74–5.   [79] *Itin.* 23. 3.

[80] *Miracle* 44 (Dag., 406); cf. Dag., 58.   [81] *Itin.* 23. 3.

[82] Susanna Elm ('*Virgins of God': The Making of Asceticism in Late Antiquity* (Oxford: Clarendon Press, 1994), 78–105, esp. 104) suggests that Macrina, rather than her brother Basil, may have been the dominant figure in the formation of the community at Annesi. On Macrina's life, see P. Maraval (ed.), *Vie de Sainte Macrine*, SC 178, 35–67; R. Albrecht, *Das Leben der heiligen Makrina auf dem Hintergrund der Thekla-Traditionen: Studien zu den Ursprüngen des weiblichen Mönchtums im 4. Jahrhundert in Kleinasien* (Göttingen: Vandenhoeck & Ruprecht, 1986).

[83] Cloke believes that in Marthana we have the 'unusual case of a [female] person of authority not only over other women, but over a mixed community with no sign of a parallel male head superior' (Cloke, '*This Female Man of God*', 188). Cloke's judgement does not take into account the role of male guardians of the shrine as portrayed in the *Life and Miracles*.

'Hermits' and 'virgins' may refer only to the female monks under Marthana's charge. It is clear, however, that whether or not she oversaw male monks as well, Marthana did serve as the superior of a community of ascetic women. What else do we know about women's monasticism at Hagia Thekla? It is striking that, in the *Miracles*, women rarely appear alone at the shrine.[84] In *Miracle* 24, a grandmother brings her grandson to the shrine for healing of his eye ailment; when the child cries out in pain, 'the women who were there' all cry out with him. In *Miracle* 45, a married devotee named Xenarchis is surrounded by a crowd of women who are never identified. Who are these women?

There are suggestions that the original shrine/church (before its relocation to the grotto toward the end of the fifth century) included living quarters for a community of female monks. An interior door to the shrine apparently led to 'the inner shrine and the holy places and the residence of the virgins' (ὁ νεὼς καὶ τὰ σεμνὰ καὶ ὁ παρθενών).[85] Thus, the group of anonymous women who appear in several *Miracle* accounts may have been identifiable with a small community of 'virgins' who actually lived within the shrine enclosure.

Three miracles give us glimpses of this community of virgins who lived and slept at Hagia Thekla. In *Miracle* 32, when the guardian Dexianos displeases Saint Thecla by removing her treasure to the town of Seleucia in hopes of preserving it from pillaging bandits, 'some of the virgins who were sleeping inside the temple' are awakened by the angry voice of the saint. Because of their fright, they come out of the temple in the middle of the night and tell Dexianos the story of what happened.

---

[84] Dag., 134.

[85] *Miracle* 10. 5–6 (Dag., 308); cf. Dag., 58. Gregory of Nazianzus also refers to Hagia Thekla as 'the *parthenôn* of the sacred virgin Thecla' (ὁ παρθενὼν τῆς ἀοιδίμου κόρης Θέκλας; *De vita sua* 548–9 [PG 37. 1067]). In the fourth century CE, the term *parthenôn* could be used to denote a community of ascetic women (Gregory of Nazianzus, *Or.* 43. 62; Epiphanius, *Pan.* 58. 3, 5, ed. K. Holl, GCS 31 (1922), 361). Athanasius' apparent use of the term in *V. Ant.* 3 (PG 26. 844A) has been identified as a textual corruption by G. Garritte ('Un couvent de femmes au IIIe siècle? Note sur un passage de la Vie grecque de saint Antoine', in E. van Cauwenbergh (ed.), *Scrinium Lovaniense: Mélanges historiques E. van Cauwenbergh* (Louvain: Éditions J. Duculot, S. A. Gembloux, 1961), 157 ff.; Elm, '*Virgins of God*', 97, n. 70; 187; 227, n. 2).

In another story (*Miracle* 42), a poor woman named Bassiane came to Hagia Thekla and 'began to live there, because she had anger against her family'.[86] The description of Bassiane's experience suggests that the ascetic motif of flight from family and society continued to be formative for the composition of this community of resident virgins. This story is also interesting in that it tells how Bassiane was victimized by a theft perpetrated by another virgin living at the shrine. This virgin steals a few of Bassiane's possessions when Bassiane is 'asleep or absent'.[87] After Bassiane appeals to the martyr for help, Thecla reveals the culprit to her and 'to all those around the martyrium'.[88]

Finally, a third story (*Miracle* 46) provides more insight not only into the sleeping arrangements of this ascetic community of women, but also into how the intimacy of that sisterhood was reinforced by the belief that Thecla was present among them. In this account, the saint herself comes to visit a female monk named Dionysia, who shares a room with her 'sleeping companion' (ἡ σύγκοιτος) Sosanna.[89] Thecla enters their room and spends the whole night with the sleeping Dionysia, 'holding her close in her arms'. However, Thecla's presence awakens Sosanna, who, when she props herself up on her elbow to get a better look, is surprised to see a third person sleeping among them. When Sosanna finally recognizes the third figure as the martyr Thecla (the author emphasizes that she took good notice of her) Thecla arises, slips away into a corner of the room, and disappears.

Through her communication and presence with them, Thecla is depicted in intimate solidarity with the community of virgins resident at her shrine. In the story from *Miracle* 32, the virgins sleeping in the sanctuary are able 'to hear the saint's voice in reality' and to communicate her pronouncement to Dexianos. In this way, the virgins at Hagia Thekla essentially function as privileged, oracular mouthpieces for Thecla. In antiquity, oracles were often associated with female seers whose auguries were facilitated by sleep-like trances within a holy sanctuary. The vocabulary of the *Miracles* conforms to the language of such incubation cults in the ancient world (especially the verbs describing Saint Thecla's nocturnal epiphanies—ἐφιστάναι, παριστάναι,

---

[86] *Miracle* 42. 5–6 (Dag., 400).   [87] *Miracle* 42. 9 (Dag., 400).
[88] *Miracle* 42. 16 (Dag., 400).   [89] *Miracle* 46. 5 (Dag., 408).

ἐπιφοιτᾶν).[90] In *Miracle* 46, Thecla's presence with this community of women—even to the extent of sharing their bed—
reflects her role in the *Miracles* not simply as patron saint, but
as an imagined member of the sisterhood. Thecla's appearance
conforms to that of her monastic female followers; the author
describes the saint as a 'young maid' dressed in the conventional
monastic garb of a virgin—'a black, threadbare cloak'.[91] Thus, the
Miracles provide a valuable glimpse into the daily life, the religious experience, and even the clothing of a community of virgins resident at Hagia Thekla.

What social function would this community of 'virgins' have
served in relation to the cult of Thecla? The story of the virgins'
response to the removal of Thecla's treasure (*Miracle* 32) suggests
that these women served, in part, as guardians of the shrine, as
a resident security detail and alarm system.[92] In service to the
shrine, they also may have provided accommodations for ascetic
pilgrims like Egeria, and Marana and Cyra.[93] Egeria's account

---

[90] Dag., 103. On incubation cults in antiquity, see L. Deubner, *De
Incubatione Capita Quattuor* (Leipzig: B. G. Teubner, 1900); *Asclepius:
Collection and Interpretation of the Testimonies*, ed. E. J. Edelstein and L.
Edelstein, 2 vols. (Baltimore: Johns Hopkins University Press, 1945/98), esp. i.
209–54 and ii. 145–58. For a critical study of Christian incubation practices, see
N. Fernandez Marcos, *Los thaumata de Sofronio: Contribución al estudio de la
incubatio cristiana* (Madrid: Instituto Antonio de Nebrija, 1975).

[91] *Miracle* 14. 34 (Dag., 326); *Miracle* 12. 96 (Dag., 320); cf. Dag., 98.

[92] The story of Bassiane and the virgin thief (*Miracle* 42) also portrays the virgins as having a collective sense of accountability in their role as guardians of
the shrine: the thief is reformed after a revelation from Thecla exposes her deed
and shames her before the larger group.

[93] H. Sivan ('Who Was Egeria? Piety and Pilgrimage in the Age of Gratian',
Harvard Theological Review, 81 (1988), 59–72) has questioned whether the
pilgrim Egeria had an ascetic piety. Over against this view, I would argue
that Egeria's written journal (the *Itinerarium*) does betray an interest in ascetic
matters, especially in her descriptions of other monastic pilgrims (see 24. 1
and 49. 1; 67, 90 Francheschini). In this context, it is also noteworthy that
Egeria addresses her journal to a community of women: 'From this place
[Constantinople], ladies, light of my heart, I am writing to you with affection.
. . . So, ladies, light of my heart, remember that you are loved by me whether I
am in the body or out of the body' (*Itin.* 23. 10; 67 Francheschini). This female
readership may very well have been a monastic community of which Egeria was
a member—either a formally organized monastery for women or a loose ascetic
society of wealthy women on the order of Paula, Melania, and company.

of her experience in Jerusalem lends credence to the notion that monks and nuns were a large constituency among late antique pilgrims.[94] Most intriguing, however, are the hints that the community of virgins who lived and slept at Hagia Thekla was the source and repository of some of the miracle stories themselves. The *Miracles* represent a collection of oral accounts that were edited and redacted by a male writer, but there is compelling evidence within the *Miracles* that women played a significant role in the oral transmission of these stories. In *Miracle* 32, as mentioned above, the virgins communicate a privileged message from Thecla to the wayward Dexianos; the Greek terms used to describe this communication convey the meaning of telling a story (ἀπαγγέλλειν and διηγεῖσθαι).[95] The oral background to the miracle legends becomes even more explicit in the account of Thecla's visit with Dionysia (*Miracle* 46). There, Dionysia's room-mate Sosanna is credited as the oral source for the story; she 'recounted' (διηγεῖσθαι) the events accurately to the author.[96] It is striking that the radical vision of an ascetic woman's becoming 'superior to the feminine condition' is communicated in a story whose origin is unequivocally traced to a female source.

The virgins at Hagia Thekla seem to have been, then, a community of storytellers. However, while this monastic community served as the hub of oral tradition at Hagia Thekla, the stories of Thecla's miracles spread abroad and gained currency in a variety of other settings as well. The pervasive character of these oral legends is witnessed by the author of the *Miracles*. He interrupts a story of another female devotee (Dosithea) to state that it would be impossible to reassemble all of the stories that could be recovered 'from each city, land, village, or house'.[97] The author undoubtedly exaggerates the universality of Thecla's influence,

[94] Egeria comments on the *plurimi monazontes* from Mesopotamia, Syria, Egypt, and the Thebaid who crowded the sites in Jerusalem (*Itin.* 49. 1 90 Francheschini; E. D. Hunt, *Holy Land Pilgrimage in the Later Roman Empire, AD 312–460* (Oxford: Clarendon Press, 1982), 152). Pierre Maraval also believes that monastic persons 'comprised perhaps the largest portion of the pilgrimage crowd' (Pierre Maraval, *Lieux saints et pèlerinages d'Orient: Histoire et géographie des origines à la conquête arabe* (Paris: Le Cerf, 1985), 116).

[95] *Miracle* 32. 28 (Dag., 376).   [96] *Miracle* 46. 7 (Dag., 408).
[97] *Miracle* 44. 15–16 (Dag., 404).

but his comments probably accurately reflect the fact that stories of Thecla's miracles were told not only in monastic and clerical communities, but also in the domestic context of late antique households. Occasionally, the *Miracles* shed some light on *married* women and their devotion to Thecla. Despite their emphasis upon ascetic values (e.g. women's flight from family)[98] the *Miracles* do not portray a clientele restricted to an elite, semi-eremitical caste of virgins or a privileged stream of visiting nuns. The miracle accounts also purport to represent the experiences of other women whose commitment to marriage and family is actually reaffirmed by Thecla's intercessions on their behalf.

For instance, in *Miracle* 42 an aristocratic woman named Kalliste leaves her husband and becomes 'one of the women of the theatre'.[99] By corrupting herself in debauchery, she loses her beauty and her husband, who quickly replaces her with an assortment of mistresses. Separated from him, she seeks refuge with the martyr.[100] However, in this case, Kalliste's petition for assistance does not result in a flight from family, but in her reconciliation with her husband. At the temple, Thecla appears to Kalliste, and restores to her both beauty[101] and husband.

In *Miracle* 14, an unnamed woman's concern for her husband's faith frames the events of the story. In this tale, the woman, a faithful Christian, travels the eighty kilometres between her home and the sanctuary at Seleucia, petitioning the martyr for the conversion of her husband, Hypsistios, a man who is described as an 'enemy of Christ, a friend of demons' (i.e. an adherent of a pagan cult).[102] Thecla responds to the woman's appeals by first striking Hypsistios with a malady to soften him up, and then appearing to him as a chambermaid at his bedside[103] and inducing him to confess to a Trinitarian formula of belief.

---

[98] The ascetic motif of flight from family appears in stories like that of Dionysia, who 'began to renounce her husband, child, and home' by lodging with the virgins at the shrine (*Miracle* 46. 1–2; Dag., 408).

[99] *Miracle* 42. 6 (Dag., 400).   [100] *Miracle* 42. 10, 12 (Dag., 400).

[101] The author engages in a play on words here with Kalliste's name; Καλλίστη is once again καλλίστη—'very beautiful' (*Miracle* 42. 26; Dag., 402).

[102] *Miracle* 14. 2–3 (Dag., 324–6).

[103] Because of Thecla's appearance (she is dressed as a virgin), Hypsistios takes her for one of the women of the house (*Miracle* 14. 41, 48; Dag., 328).

In these two miracle accounts, women's devotion to Thecla is literally 'domesticated'—her miraculous activity on their behalf finds its context *within* the household and marriage. However, Thecla's patronage of married women in the *Miracles* also has the effect of bringing ascetic virtues to bear on marriage and family relations. In this context, the wife of Hypsistios demonstrates the ascetic virtues of chastity and temperance of lifestyle along with her faith in Christ. The editor of the *Miracles* likens her endurance in prayer and her childless state to the piety of Anna (the Jewish prophetess who was present at the dedication of the infant Jesus in the Jerusalem Temple (Luke 2: 36–8)).[104] Marriage and procreation remain problematic worldly commitments that can only be redeemed by ascetic virtue. Another female devotee, Xenarchis, 'married and lived with a man, but she attained so great a height of virtue and in this way, although she was married, she was well pleasing to the virgin'.[105] Even in the case of Dionysia, who renounced her marriage in order to devote herself full-time to the sanctuary at Hagia Thekla, one observes how women's families (especially their children) were considered a fertile ground for promoting ascetic virtues. Dionysia's namesake daughter matched her mother in her life, thought, and conduct, and even exceeded her in virtue by maintaining a 'virginity pure and intact'.[106]

Gregory of Nyssa's *Life of Macrina* (written in Asia Minor *c.*380 CE) gives us another glimpse of how ascetic virtues (and Thecla devotion) were promoted in the context of family relationships. Writing in praise of his sister Macrina, Gregory describes how her choice of the ascetic life was sealed even before she was born. According to Gregory, in the days leading up to Macrina's birth, her mother experienced a divine vision. In that vision a heavenly figure appeared to her and declared that her daughter Macrina would bear the secret name, 'Thecla', a

---

[104] *Miracle* 14. 11–14 (Dag., 326).   [105] *Miracle* 45. 2–4 (Dag., 406).

[106] *Miracle* 46. 20–2 (Dag., 408). In the late fourth-century church, marriage itself could be tolerated 'for the purpose of incubating piety' (Cloke, '*This Female Man of God*', 43). Ambrose writes, 'The virgin is an offering for her mother . . . virginity itself cannot exist, unless it have some mode of coming into existence' (Ambrose, *De virginibus* 1. 32, 35; PL 16. 198–9). Jerome states, 'I praise wedlock, I praise marriage, but it is because they give me virgins' (Jerome, *Ep.* 22. 20; PL 22. 406). Finally, Augustine praises the mothers Proba and Juliana for raising their daughters to become consecrated virgins (Augustine, *Ep.* 150; PL 33. 645).

name that would 'foretell the life of the young girl and show the
similarity of her choice of life by her possession of the same
name'.[107] However, in the case of Macrina, the identification of
Thecla as a role model was not meant to augur a break from her
family. To the contrary, Macrina's ascetic discipline was situated
early on within her mother's household. Having resolved 'never
to be separated from her own mother', she lived at home and
helped administer her mother's daily affairs, everything from bak-
ing bread to paying property taxes.[108] Macrina's lifestyle eventually attracted other like-minded virgins, and their household at
Annesi (in Pontus) was transformed into a monastery of which
she became the head. Later, after her father's death, Macrina even
'persuaded her mother to leave behind her customary way of life
. . . and to mingle in the same way of life as the virgins [αἱ παρθένοι]
whom she had made into sisters and equals with her . . .'[109]

Gregory presents the story about the prenatal vision and
Macrina's secret name in order to portray his sister as an exemplary ascetic, a worthy successor to Thecla. At the same time,
could the account suggest something particular about the bond
between this mother and her daughter? Could the two have actually shared a common devotion to Saint Thecla that helped
inculcate ascetic virtues within their household? The historicity
of the vision itself is uncertain,[110] but something in Gregory's
account suggests that Thecla devotion may have been formative
for the monastic community that emerged under Macrina's
direction. In explaining Macrina's secret name Gregory makes a
point of noting that the story of Thecla 'was considered of great
importance among the virgins [αἱ παρθένοι]'.[111] Gregory would
certainly have been generally aware of Thecla's popularity
among ascetic women in Asia Minor, but one wonders if he also
may have had in mind here a local devotion to Saint Thecla
among the virgins at Macrina's monastery.[112]

---

[107] Gregory of Nyssa, *V. Macr.* 2. 33–4.

[108] Ibid. 5.   [109] Ibid. 7. 2–8; cf. 11. 1–13.

[110] Albrecht, *Das Leben der heiligen Makrina auf dem Hintergrund der Thekla-Traditionen*, 239.

[111] Gregory of Nyssa, *V. Macr.* 2. 26.

[112] Gregory of Nyssa frequently makes reference to this group, or 'chorus' (χορός) of virgins that developed around Macrina's leadership (*V. Macr.* 11. 9; 16. 5; 26. 1–2; 32. 4; 33. 15; 34. 24; *Ep.* 19. 7, ed. G. Pasquali, *Gregorii Nysseni Opera* 8. 2, 64; Elm, '*Virgins of God*', 92).

In any case, as in the story of Dionysia's daughter in *Miracle* 46, Gregory's account of Macrina's life emphasizes the lingering tension in late antiquity between the domestication of ascetic virtues and the always-privileged status of the true virgin. Gregory, in praising his mother's virtues, must console himself with the fact that she herself 'did not voluntarily choose marriage'.[113] The life of perpetual chastity as exemplified by Thecla (and Macrina) remained the preeminent model and goal;[114] mothers who came belatedly to the virtue of sexual continence could only hope to see that goal truly fulfilled in the lives of their daughters.

Thus, while the life and miracles of Saint Thecla would have been told in the households of virtuous married women like Macrina's mother, it was primarily *ascetic women*—virgins and women who renounced marriage, pilgrims and resident nuns— who remained the social force behind Thecla's cult in Asia Minor and who were celebrated in stories that bespoke the saint's power. Indeed, as Thecla devotion spread to other locales like Egypt, communities of ascetic women would continue to be the lifeblood of her cult.

The Routinization of Pilgrimage at Hagia Thekla

The *Miracle* accounts and Egeria's travel diary also hint at social tensions associated with the organization of travel at Hagia Thekla. A tradition of unregulated ascetic itinerancy continued in the person of independent virgins who wandered around outside the shrine in imitation of Thecla's example.[115] However, more

---

[113] Gregory of Nyssa, *V. Macr.* 2.   [114] Dag., 131.

[115] As in the *ATh*, the Thecla of the *Life and Miracles* is cast as a wandering disciple of Paul, an ambulant 'stranger' (ξένη; *Life* 15. 42, 45 (Dag., 230); *ATh* 26). See also *Life* 22. 57 (Dag., 260) where Thecla intones 'I am, as you see, a woman, a girl in age, and a stranger [ξένη], and alone' (no parallel in *ATh*). Thecla's life as a wanderer is modelled after Paul himself: while he is a 'stranger and vagabond', she is regarded as a participant in his travels (*Life* 4. 25; 12. 21, 14. 35; Dag., 184, 216, 226). Characteristic of Thecla's wanderings is her lack of any set itinerary—she simply 'strayed about' (περινοστεῖν) in search of Paul. In a later cycle of miracles connected to her shrine (and derivative from the *Life and Miracles*), Thecla is depicted in a manner similar to Syrian wandering ascetics: having come to Seleucia from Iconium, she grew accustomed to 'moving throughout' (διακινεῖν) the area in order to gather up grasses to eat (*Virtuous Acts of the Holy Apostle and Protomartyr Thecla in the Grove of Myrtles* (Κατορθώματα τῆς ἁγίας ἀποστόλου καὶ πρωτομάρτυρος Θέκλας τὰ ἐν τῷ Μυρσεῶνι), lines 24–7; Dag., 416).

regularized forms of travel emerged as the cult of Thecla grew to international dimensions and as the numbers of pilgrims increased.[116] These models of women's itinerancy—unregulated and regularized—coexisted in the life of the Thecla cult. At the same time that the ecclesiastical leadership worked to control and shape the contours of women's pilgrimage travel, wandering ascetics continued to move outside the purview of these social structures.[117]

Pilgrims' experience of the cult of the saints, and the church leadership's ability to shape that experience, were mediated in part by the *ritualization* of pilgrimage travel itself—the process through which it became more routinized, and privileged, as it was organized in special patterns that made it distinct from conventional travel.[118] The specific form of ritualization differed depending on the motives of particular pilgrims. The experience of pilgrims who came to a shrine for healing had a different cadence than that of pilgrims who visited only for purposes of religious piety. For pilgrims seeking healing at early Byzantine shrines, the ritualization of their experience could take various forms: the preparation of a votive lamp, participation in an all-night vigil, the act of receiving holy water or a healing salve connected with the shrine.[119] The experience of pietistic pilgrims like

[116] Victor Turner (*Image and Pilgrimage in Christian Culture: Anthropological Perspectives* (New York: Columbia University Press, 1978), 25 ff.) has identified the process of 'routinization' as a final stage in the development of individual pilgrimage sites.

[117] For an observation of the tension between 'spontaneous modes of peregrination' and ecclesiastical attempts to domesticate those forms of travel, see Turner, *Image and Pilgrimage*, 32. This tension should be seen as part of a larger set of 'competing religious and secular discourses' within pilgrimage practice (J. Eade and M. J. Sallnow, 'Introduction', in *Contesting the Sacred: The Anthropology of Christian Pilgrimage* (London: Routledge, 1991), 2).

[118] Along with Catherine Bell (*Ritual Theory, Ritual Practice* (New York: Oxford University Press, 1992), 90) I define 'ritualization' as the way that certain social practices become privileged by being differentiated from a larger set of analogous practices.

[119] On night vigils and the use of oil, water, and other healing substances at Hagia Thekla, see Dag., 77, 79, 103–7; for a vivid reconstruction of pilgrims' experience at a healing shrine in seventh-century Constantinople, see *The Miracles of St. Artemios: A Collection of Miracle Stories by an Anonymous Author of Seventh-Century Byzantium*, ed. V. S. Crisafulli and J. W. Nesbitt (Leiden: E. J. Brill, 1997), 22–5.

Egeria also became ritualized insofar as their visits to holy places like Hagia Thekla took on a distinct liturgical shape.[120]

The pattern of Egeria's visit to Hagia Thekla conforms significantly to the pilgrimage liturgy that she attended at other holy places. This liturgy seems to have been composed of four basic movements:[121]

1. Prayer, upon arrival at the holy place
2. Reading
3. Prayer (and/or Eucharist)
4. Departure from the holy place

Egeria's description of her visit to Araboth Moab, a plain near the Jordan River, reflects this basic pilgrimage liturgy:

When we entered the same plain, we proceeded to the very spot, and we said a prayer there, and read a certain passage from Deuteronomy in that place—not only the song, but also the blessings he (Moses) uttered over the children of Israel. After the reading, we said another prayer, and giving thanks to God, we set off from there.[122]

Recounting her visit to Mount Sinai, Egeria narrates this liturgical sequence twice in a row—once with regard to her ascent up the mountain to visit the cave of Moses, and a second time with regard to her descent down the mountain to visit the cave of Elijah.[123] Egeria's report of her visit to Hagia Thekla displays a

---

[120] Here I disagree with Turner (*Image and Pilgrimage*, 31) who views pilgrimage practice as inherently extraneous to liturgical forms. On the liturgical context of pilgrimage, see Hunt, *Holy Land Pilgrimage*, 67.

[121] My four-part analysis is a modification and abridgement of Wilkinson's (*Egeria's Travels*, 63–6).

[122] *Itin.* 10. 7 (51 Francheschini).

[123] Egeria's visit to Mt. Sinai has the following ritual structure:

A. *Ascent up Mt. Sinai*: visit to cave where Moses was when he went up the mountain a second time and received the second set of tablets (*Itin.* 2. 4–3. 6; 38–41 Francheschini).

1. Prayer: 'Coming in from Paran, we said the prayer . . .' (2. 4); overnight at the base of Sinai; ascent up the mountain with the monks; met by a presbyter at the top

2. Reading from the Book of Moses: 'The entire passage from the Book of Moses was read at that spot' (3. 6)

3. Eucharist: 'The Offering was made in its regular order and we received Communion' (3. 6)

similar liturgical order. After her arrival at the martyr shrine (23.1–2), (i) a prayer was offered (*facta oratione ad martyrium*) (23.5). Following this prayer, she and the other pilgrims (ii) read the Acts of Saint Thecla (*et lectione actus sanctae Teclae*) (23.5–6).[124] After staying at the sanctuary for two days, 'visiting the holy monks and hermits, the men as well as the women', she (iii) prayed and received Communion (*et facta oratione et communione*),[125] and then (iv) departed for Tarsus (*reuersa sum Tharso ad iter meum*) (23.6).

Egeria's consistent witness to this basic liturgy observed at holy places sheds light on how pilgrimage to Hagia Thekla itself became ritualized—that is, set apart from 'ordinary' forms of travel. From Egeria's account of her visit to Hagia Thekla, one can also see how the pilgrimage liturgy associated with holy sites adapted to the varying time constraints of pilgrim experience. In particular, the pilgrimage liturgy could maintain its integrity over an extended period of time. At Hagia Thekla, Egeria's celebration of this pilgrimage liturgy extends over the entirety of her two-day stay at the shrine, during which she visited the monastic inhabitants of the place.[126] Egeria's narration of her ascent up Mount Sinai indicates a similar protracted liturgy. While the first prayer takes place about 6 km from the base of the mountain, the

---

4. Dismissal from the church: 'When we were exiting the church the priests of the place gave us "blessings"—fruits that grow on the mountain itself' (3. 6)
B. *Descent down the mountain*: visit to cave where Elijah hid from King Ahab (*Itin.* 4. 2–4)
　1. Prayer: '. . . and there too we prayed most earnestly . . .' (4. 3)
　2. Reading: '. . . and we read from the Book of Kings. Indeed, I always asked particularly that there might be a reading from the Bible in such a place' (4. 3)
　3. Eucharist: 'When the Offering was made there . . .' (4. 4)
　4. Departure: '. . . we set off once more . . .' (4. 4)
Each of the two sequences follows the outline of the pilgrimage office, with the celebration of the Eucharist, instead of a second prayer, taking place after the Scriptural reading.

[124] Egeria's response to the reading of the Acts indicates with how much reverence that text was held. After recalling the reading, she notes that 'I gave infinite thanks to Christ our God who deemed me worthy to fulfil my desires in all respects' (*Itin.* 23. 5–6; 66 Francheschini).

[125] Here, the second prayer and Communion are observed together.

[126] *Itin.* 23. 6 (66 Francheschini).

next element of the liturgy, the reading of an appropriate text from Deuteronomy, occurs only after she spends the night at a church at the base of the mountain and then journeys all the way to the top of the mountain late the next morning.[127] In each of these episodes (at Sinai and Hagia Thekla), the duration of Egeria's pilgrimage visit is ritualized; that is, she conceives all of her activity within the parameters of this liturgical structure. The liturgical forms that structured (and routinized) pilgrimage practice also determinatively structured pilgrims' *perception and narration* of their actions.

The reading of sacred texts played an especially important role in the 'cognitive mapping' of pilgrim experience.[128] A text or story could function as a 'marker' that made topography meaningful for pilgrims even in the absence of monumental markers.[129] For instance, an intimate knowledge of biblical history informed Egeria's vision of the Holy Land: her narrative account populates the empty expanse of Palestinian landscape with the events and people of Bible story.[130] Egeria's visual perception of holy places was most often marked by 'on-site' readings of stories connected with those places. The effect of these readings was to bring the events alive, to make them present to the pilgrim viewer. Egeria's reading of the 'Acts of Saint Thecla' upon her visit to Seleucia may have had a similar function for her viewing of the saint's martyr shrine and its environs. Her memory of events in the story would have marked her viewing of the landscape around Seleucia, brought it into specific relation to the final events

---

[127] *Itin.* 2. 4–3. 6 (38–41 Francheschini). Egeria's guides informed her group that it was usual for pilgrims to say a prayer when they caught their first glimpse of Mt. Sinai (*Itin.* 1. 2; 37 Francheschini). Egeria is quite clear regarding the chronology of her ascent up Sinai. After an initial prayer about four miles from the mountain, the group arrived at the foot of Sinai late on Saturday, and then set off up the mountain early the next morning, arriving at the summit around ten o'clock.

[128] Blake Leyerle ('Landscape as Cartography in Early Christian Pilgrimage Narratives', *Journal of the American Academy of Religion*, 64/1 (Spring 1996), 119–43) applies theories of cognitive mapping and the sociology of tourism to the study of early Christian pilgrim experience of the Holy Land.

[129] On the function of books, pictures, and souvenirs as topographical 'markers' in modern tourism, see Dean MacCannell, *The Tourist: A New Theory of the Leisure Class* (New York: Schocken Books, 1976), 109–10, 121–3.

[130] Leyerle, 'Landscape as Cartography', 126–9.

of Thecla's life.[131] The effect would have been heightened for later pilgrims who read expanded versions of Thecla's life (e.g. *ATh*^{Sel}) during their visits to Hagia Thekla. Such pilgrims may have experienced the cluster of monastic cells that dotted the landscape surrounding the shrine as 'on-site markers' of the semi-eremitical community of women that Thecla had reportedly established at Seleucia toward the end of her life.[132]

In addition to the role of liturgy and the reading of holy texts, other social factors also contributed to the routinization of pilgrimage travel in relation to Hagia Thekla. First, pilgrimage was regulated by the social codes of Christian hospitality.[133] One function of the community of virgins at the shrine was the reception of travellers: Marthana's welcome of Egeria and the renewal of their friendship made a great impression upon Egeria at Hagia Thekla. Egeria communicates to her readers the personal connection established by Marthana's hospitality before she narrates the details of her activities at the site.

Second, pilgrimage at Hagia Thekla was also regularized through local military protection—regiments were stationed in Seleucia, offering pilgrims protection from the potential threats of robbery or assault.[134] The military protection available to pilgrims at Hagia Thekla is understood in the *Miracles* to be an extension of Saint Thecla's own power as overseer and protector of her pilgrim clientele. For example, in *Miracle* 16 Thecla offers

---

[131] I take exception with Leyerle (op. cit.) only in her suggestion that Egeria's 'high involvement with the Bible' would have made her experience of the Holy Land of a different order than her visit to Hagia Thekla. Leyerle argues that Egeria's knowledge of biblical history often made detailed geographical description of Holy Land sites unnecessary. Because the events in Scripture could be readily called to memory, the sites themselves 'do not need to be described'. In contrast, Hagia Thekla is described by Egeria in some detail. Leyerle makes the unwarranted assumption that it was the extra-scriptural character of the site that made such a detailed description necessary. In fact, it is probably due more to the fact that, in contrast to the sometimes undeveloped sites of rural Palestine, the monastic community and martyrium at Seleucia actually gave her something tangible to describe—human and monumental markers of the saint's life and death.

[132] *Acta Apostolorum Apocrypha*, ed. Lipsius and Bonnet, 271 (MS G).

[133] See Hunt, *Holy Land Pilgrimage*, 65 and 180, on Christian hospitality toward pilgrims, including the reception of visitors at monasteries.

[134] See, for example, *Miracles* 13 and 28 (Dag., 322–4, 362–6).

protection to a soldier named Ambrosius who, while fulfilling his duties travelling for the emperor, was ambushed by robbers. In response to the soldier's prayers to her on his journey, Thecla preserves him from attack by creating the illusion of a military escort, a battalion of soldiers and cavalry. In this account, Thecla is portrayed as a protector of travellers, in that her intercession was designed to preserved the soldier's 'freedom of movement'.[135]

Finally, the pilgrim routes to the *martyrium* themselves became increasingly fixed. The path to Hagia Thekla from Seleucia, a road that cuts through bare rock as it ascends the hillside to the south, was busy enough to be described as a 'thoroughfare' (λεωφόρος) for pilgrims (Fig. 4).[136] The labours of ancient highway workmen remain evident today—e.g. notches in rocks, drainage works.[137] Other established routes provided access to and from the sea, as pilgrims approached Hagia Thekla from the south-west and north-east (Fig. 2).[138] *Miracle* 15 describes how seafaring pilgrims would disembark when they reached the coast at Isauria and would journey over land to the martyr shrine.[139] At the shrine itself, the architectural adaptations of Hagia Thekla during the fifth and sixth centuries also would have had the effect of redirecting and channelling the movements of the large number of pilgrims approaching and entering Thecla's *martyrium*.[140]

Thus a variety of factors contributed to the routinization of pilgrim experience at Hagia Thekla: the liturgical ritualization of pilgrimage, the social roles of hospitality networks, military escorts, and established pilgrim routes. These patterns were in many ways synonymous with larger trends of pilgrimage

---

[135] *Miracle* 16. 24 (Dag., 334).

[136] *Miracle* 25. 23–4 (Dag., 354).   [137] Dag., 63.

[138] Dagron describes Hagia Thecla as being located on a 'convergence de routes' (Dag., 63–4). One of the *Miracles* speaks of a spot to the west of the sanctuary as the place where one could see the juncture of 'every path and every road from high and low regions' (*Miracle* 36. 29–30; Dag., 388).

[139] *Miracle* 15 (Dag., 330).

[140] On the 'orchestration of space at pilgrimage sites', see Simon Coleman and John Elsner, *Pilgrimage: Past and Present in the World Religions* (London: British Museum Press, 1995), 209 ff.

practice in late antiquity. As was the case with other prominent early Christian martyr shrines, the routinization of travel would have helped facilitate visits by international pilgrims like Egeria, but its primary beneficiaries would have been local devotees from Seleucia and its environs who made up the majority of the shrine's daily clientele.[141]

In this context, it is interesting that the *Miracles* give us a glimpse of another type of movement associated with devotion to Thecla—independent wandering—a form of women's itinerancy that may have resisted the routinization of pilgrimage travel. In *Miracle* 34, two men from Eirenopolis, who came to the shrine not to pray but to carouse, find 'a virgin wandering about [περιπλανωμένη] outside the sacred enclosure'.[142] When the men attempt to seduce her, Thecla intervenes before they can defile her. In the end, the men are unable to escape the severe judgement of the saint; they both drown after falling off a ferryboat that conveyed pilgrims travelling to and from the sanctuary.

Who was this wandering virgin? Was she connected in some way to the community of virgins living at the shrine? When Thecla appears to the men, she asks them why they had driven her disciple away from 'my houses' (οἱ ἐμοὶ οἶκοι) in order to seduce her.[143] Was the woman one of the resident virgins, accustomed to wandering around outside her domicile at the shrine? The woman's movement recounted in *Miracle* 34 seems to diverge from the typical pattern of formal pilgrimage travel (i.e. a set itinerary and a defined destination). Indeed, her movement simulates the homelessness of Thecla herself. Both engage in an

---

[141] The majority of the *Miracles* involve visitors from the surrounding region or members of the local populace (Dag., 24). Other collections of miracles from late antiquity—e.g. those of Saints Cosmas and Damian (Constantinople), Cyrus and John (Alexandria), Demetrios (Thessaloniki), and Artemios (Constantinople) —have a similar 'highly-localised focus' (John Haldon, 'Supplementary Essay —The Miracles of Artemios and Contemporary Attitudes: Context and Significance', in *The Miracles of St. Artemios*, ed. Crisafulli and Nesbitt 39). While the local character of these collections undoubtedly reflects the demographics of late antique pilgrimage practice, it also may be credited to the fact that devotees living nearby would have been most available to tell their stories to the compilers of the collections.

[142] *Miracle* 34. 19–20 (Dag., 380–2).   [143] *Miracle* 34. 31–2 (Dag., 382).

irregular, even aimless, form of itinerancy,[144] and both are preserved from the threat of rape.[145]

As I have mentioned before, the independent wanderings of women and the threat of sexual assault are interrelated; together they shed crucial light on social and ideological conflicts in the promotion of pilgrimage among women. On the one hand, independent female travellers may have kept themselves separate from the social ills often associated with pilgrimage and martyr festivals.[146] On the other hand, by appearing alone in public, such women were thought by men in antiquity to pose the danger of sexual temptation, and often faced the threat of sexual assault themselves.[147] As a result, stories like *Miracle* 34 reflect a male cultural ambivalence toward the status of independent virgins. Such stories attest to the presence of independent, wandering virgins on the periphery of institutionalized pilgrimage. Yet, these stories refrain from endorsing the independence of such women, and even shy away from drawing attention to them, because of the destabilizing effect they had upon organized pilgrimage practice and the piety of men. Independent virgins continued to play a surreptitious role in development of the Thecla's cult in Egypt—a role preserved in the witness of oral traditions about women, but subtly cloaked beneath the reticent rhetoric of male

---

[144] The Syriac hagiography of Mary the Pilgrim vividly portrays the lifestyle of this kind of 'wandering' virgin: for three years at the site of Golgotha Mary 'went about praying, without entering anyone's house or speaking with anyone', and spent her nights among the poor 'in the church or wherever else it might be' (John of Ephesus, *Lives of the Eastern Saints*, in *Holy Women of the Syrian Orient*, ed. and trans. Brock and Harvey, 124).

[145] *Life* 28. 7 (Dag., 280); cf. *ATh* 26.

[146] *Miracle* 34 decries the unjust appropriation of money, the drinking parties and orgies that accompanied such festivals (*Miracle* 34. 10 ff.; Dag., 380). Various Christian writers condemned men who only attended church in order to lay eyes on women—see, e.g. John Chrysostom, *Homily* 73, *in Mt.* (PG 58. 676–7) and Anastasius the Sinaïte, *De Sacra Synaxi* (PG 89. 832).

[147] The immediately preceding story, *Miracle* 33, seems connected in subject matter. It also presents a story of two men from Eirenopolis who come to Hagia Thecla for the pageantry of the festival, one of whom gazes with lust upon a virgin who is among those making obeisance before Thecla's temple (*Miracle* 33. 29–30; Dag., 378). The virgin's public appearance is considered the source of the man's ill fortune, as he is skinned alive by a demon because of his lust.

authors (see Chapter 4). As we shall see, in Egypt as in Asia Minor, the piety of itinerant, ascetic women proved a catalyst for social tensions in the patronage of pilgrimage travel.

Political Conflict and Patronage in the Cult of Thecla

The *Miracles* ultimately reveal how the *charisma* of Thecla the martyr was thought to remain present and active at her shrine near Seleucia. And yet, as these stories bear witness to the perceived spiritual power of the martyr, they likewise bear witness to the political force of her cult. As such, the stories actually narrate thinly veiled conflicts in the life of the cult—the assertion of Thecla's power as a martyr also implied the subversion of competing claims to power.

Ancient pilgrims perceived Thecla's power as a martyr in different forms—the power to protect, the power to heal, and the power to instill belief. First, the *Miracles* portray her not only protecting pilgrims against the hazards of travel but also preserving her temple and treasures, and the town of Seleucia, against the threat of marauders and brigands.[148] In the minds of ardent devotees, Thecla's custodial intercession was thought to extend even beyond Seleucia to villages spread throughout Asia Minor and to scattered locales in the Mediterranean.[149] Thus, *Miracle* 10 celebrates the fact that 'nothing hinders her grace and power in any place'.[150] Second, the *Miracles* celebrate Thecla's power in healing various sicknesses and injuries. She corrects displaced vertebrae,[151] repairs four broken legs,[152] cures a tumor,[153] remedies

---

[148] See, for instance, *Miracle* 28, which celebrates the martyr's victory over local invaders. The author makes a point of emphasizing the fact that Thecla never supported the impious audacity (τόλμα) of the intruders' cause (*Miracle* 28. 39–40; Dag., 364).

[149] Thecla's patronage included her hometown of Iconium (*Miracle* 6; also *Miracle* 27, where she offers protection to the village of Selinonte). Earlier I mentioned an instance where Thecla interceded for a woman as far away as Macedonia (*Miracle* 12. 100–1; Dag., 322).

[150] *Miracle* 10. 40–1 (Dag., 310).

[151] *Miracle* 7 (Dexianos); Dag., 300–2.

[152] *Miracle* 8 (Dexianos); *Miracle* 17 (Leontios); *Miracle* 18 (Tigriane and Aba); Dag., 302, 334–40.

[153] *Miracle* 11 (Aurelios); Dag., 312–14.

a bout of anthrax,[154] restores sight,[155] relieves a kidney malady,[156] and heals an infection of the ear.[157] The saint even becomes renowned for her ability to make sick animals well.[158] Finally, Thecla's power for healing reported in the *Miracles* extends beyond the physical to the spiritual: in particular, she is credited with the power to confer faith in Christ and his resurrection. *Miracle* 14 presents the story of the faithful wife of Hypsistios and her petitions to Saint Thecla that her impious husband might become a Christian. In response, Thecla besets the man with a 'tenacious illness' in order to soften him up before 'she furnished the cure'.[159] After intensifying and prolonging Hypsistios' sufferings, Thecla finally visits him 'in reality, not in a dream', and urges him to embrace the Christian (Trinitarian) faith along with the happiness of health. Most important, Hypsistios' conversion was especially marked, 'after a very long life lived in the faith', by his dying in 'the hope of the resurrection'.[160] In this story, Thecla's 'cure' crucially bridges the gap between her power to relieve physical maladies and her power to heal spiritual ills.

Such depictions of Thecla's comprehensive power as a saint do not completely disguise the conflicts that accompanied such claims to power. The *Miracles* set Saint Thecla in competition with groups who rival her power for protection, healing, and belief: she vanquishes pagan gods, confounds local physicians, and even vies with other saints for the devotion of pilgrims. Thecla's competition with these figures in the stories reflects the struggle

---

[154] *Miracle* 12 (the author); Dag., 312–14.

[155] *Miracle* 24 (a child); *Miracle* 25 (eye epidemic in Seleucia); *Miracle* 37 (a blind Cypriot) (Dag., 350–4, 390). With regard to *Miracle* 37, Dagron notes the popularity of Thecla in Cyprus for the healing of eye ailments (Dag., 391, n. 1). Epiphanius of Salamis, metropolitan of Cyprus from 367 until his death in 403, praises Thecla as a female saint second in status only to the Virgin Mary (*Pan.* 79. 5).

[156] *Miracle* 40 (Aretarchos); Dag., 396–8.

[157] *Miracle* 41 (the author); Dag., 398–400.

[158] *Miracle* 36 (Dag., 386–90) tells of an unknown illness that struck a great variety of the local domestic animals, and how Thecla cured the illness by leading the animals to a source of water close to her sanctuary. A miraculous healing of a horse with a spinal malady is appended at the end of the account.

[159] *Miracle* 14. 19–21 (Dag., 326).

[160] *Miracle* 14. 74–6 (Dag., 328–30).

of the cult itself (i.e. its leaders and institutions) to assert its own primacy in relation to competing social and religious claims. The *Miracles* are framed by Thecla's opposition to pagan deities and their local cultic representatives. In the Prologue to the *Miracles*, the author contrasts his own literary task with that of the 'spokespersons and servants of demonic [pagan] oracles' and the 'interpreters of Pythian tales of wonder' who write about the oracles' promises to appease suffering.[161] The author seeks to show how the deceitful ambiguities of the oracles pale in comparison with the 'clear, true, simple, holy, perfect' remedies and predictions of the saints.[162] The first four miracle accounts are devoted to showing how Saint Thecla deposes a series of pagan deities whose local shrines would have implicitly represented threats to the hegemony of her cultic centre at Seleucia: she silences the oracle and tomb of Sarpedon located on the coast,[163] subjugates the sanctuary of Athena on nearby Mount Kôkysion,[164] chases Aphrodite from the town of Seleucia,[165] and bans Zeus from that same city.[166]

Of these pagan cults, those of Sarpedon and Athena seem to have been the most firmly rooted in the local scene and the most difficult to supplant. Near the end of the *Life*, the editor uses military language to describe Thecla's struggle against their cults. Against Sarpedon, 'who had taken possession of a promontory

---

[161] *Miracles*, Prologue, 23–8 (Dag., 284–6). The author mentions here a stock list of oracles: Zeus of Dodona, the Pythian Apollo at Delphi, the Castalian Spring, Asclepius of Pergamum, as well as the oracles at Epidaurus and the nearby Aigae.

[162] *Miracles*, Prologue, 73–7 (Dag., 288).

[163] In *Miracle* 1 (Dag., 290–2), Thecla renders the 'talkative' (πολυφωνότατος) Sarpedon mute (ἀφωνότατος) with the words of Jesus from Mark 4: 39—'Peace, be still!' On the hero cult and legends of Sarpedon, see the article by O. Immisch in W. H. Roscher (ed.), *Ausführliches Lexikon der griechischen und römischen Mythologie*, 4: 389–413; Dag., 85–7.

[164] *Miracle* 2 (Dag., 292).   [165] *Miracle* 3 (Dag., 292).

[166] *Miracle* 4 (Dag., 294–6). Another account of Thecla's life connected to her shrine describes how Thecla, shortly after arriving in Seleucia, resists the advances of a priest of Zeus who lived in the Capitoline temple in the city. When the priest approaches her on horseback, 'thinking mischievously that she was one of the vulgar young women [τις τῶν τυχουσῶν κορῶν],' Thecla sends 'a power out from herself' that knocks the priest off his horse and renders him mute for three days and three nights (*Virtuous Acts of the Holy Apostle and Protomartyr Thecla in the Grove of Myrtles*, ll. 24–35; Dag., 416).

on the edge of the sea', and against Athena 'who continued to occupy the fortress that bore her name', Thecla 'fortifies herself' (ἐπιτειχίζειν . . . ἑαυτήν) for battle.[167] This imagery is meant to evoke and counteract the martial associations of the two gods— the hero Sarpedon was a deified Lycian general, and Athena was the Greek goddess of war. However, this language also hints at the conflict that developed between the martyr cult of Saint Thecla and pagan cults indigenous to the region. Thus, Thecla's victories over these pagan gods in the *Miracles* reflect the social concerns of local, cultic competition.[168]

Thecla's competition with Sarpedon conspicuously surfaces in three other miracles, each of which pits Thecla's power of healing against local physicians who act as Sarpedon's bungling representatives.[169] Sarpedon's designation as 'the great physician' underscores his association with this caste of physicians and their repeated failures to provide a cure.[170] In *Miracle* 11, we get perhaps the most vivid glimpse of these competing claims for healing power. After the doctors fail to provide the cure for a tumour for the granddaughter of a woman devoted to Sarpedon, Thecla appears to the woman in a vision and prescribes the proper remedy. However, because the remedy is applied sparingly, the tumour persists in some areas. Finally, one of the doctors strikes upon the idea of applying more of the remedy, and the tumour is cured. The partial success of the original treatment apparently provided Thecla's opponents with an occasion for questioning her power to heal, because the editor of the *Miracles* feels the need to mention that the doctor's fortuitous idea was 'inspired, I think, by the martyr' and not by Thecla's rival Sarpedon.[171]

It is interesting how the rhetoric of the *Miracles* defines the terms of this cultic competition. Saint Thecla assimilates the attributes of the pagan rivals she deposes as her means of

---

[167] *Life* 27. 53 ff. (Dag., 278).

[168] *Miracle* 2 provides a prime example of how the writer of the *Miracles* emphasizes the decisiveness of Thecla's victories. The writer avers that Athena could not endure 'the assault of the unarmed stranger [ξένη], the naked young woman [Thecla]' (*Miracle* 2. 9–10; Dag., 292).

[169] *Miracle* 11. 12 (Dag., 312); 18. 30 (Dag., 338); 40. 15, 30 (Dag., 396). The scenario that pits a saint's cure over against a doctor's cure is a trope of miracle collections (Haldon, 'Supplementary Essay', 44 ff.).

[170] *Miracle* 11. 12 (Dag., 312).   [171] *Miracle* 11. 46–7 (Dag., 314).

overturning their claims to priority. She becomes militant in order to contend against the warlike hero Sarpedon and the goddess Athena. She becomes a physician in order to subvert the healing claims of Sarpedon's medical devotees. In *Miracle* 3, where Thecla chases Aphrodite from Seleucia, a subtle allusion to the *Iliad* puts Thecla again in the position of a Christian Athena. The editor of the *Miracles* calls Dexianos (the guardian of Thecla's shrine) 'her Diomedes'—in the *Iliad*, it was Diomedes, counselled and empowered by Athena, who chased the son of Aphrodite from the battlefield.[172] The implication here is that Thecla has become a new Athena, supplanting the outdated pagan goddess. Gregory of Nazianzus' description of Hagia Thekla as a *parthenôn* may also intimate Thecla's role as the supplanter of Athena.[173] Gregory was educated in Athens, and would have been well familiar with Athena's famous temple in that city, the Parthenon. By calling the shrine at Seleucia the *parthenon* of Saint Thecla, he may be indicating that he considered Hagia Thekla a Christian replacement for the pagan site in Athens.

Finally, the *Miracles'* attempts to disparage Sarpedon by emphasizing his non-local character ironically elicit yet another example of how Thecla assimilates and rehabilitates her rivals' attributes. Like Thecla, Sarpedon is a 'stranger' (ξένος), one whose wanderings first brought him to the environs of Seleucia.[174] However, instead of being a badge of autonomy and legitimacy as in the case of Thecla, Sarpedon's identity as a 'stranger' and a 'foreigner' only serves to undercut his claims to local prerogative. The editor of the *Life and Miracles* does not make an attempt to portray Thecla as 'more local' in comparison. Instead, he turns the language of 'strangerhood' on its head: while he discredits Sarpedon, he privileges Thecla as the legitimate, local 'stranger' (ξένη).

Thecla's replacement of her pagan rivals also involves the appropriation of local holy space: Thecla's defeat of Sarpedon, Athena, and Zeus culminates in the Christian takeover of pagan holy sites. The tomb of Sarpedon becomes a 'dwelling place of

---

[172] Homer, *Il.* 5. 115 ff.

[173] Gregory of Nazianzus, *De vita sua* 548–9 (PG 37. 1067).

[174] *Miracle* 1. 4 (Dag., 290). The editor of the *Miracles* is probably referring to the later version of the Sarpedon myth, in which he comes to Cilicia in Asia Minor after having been exiled from Crete.

God'.[175] Athena's mountain sanctuary is now in the possession of 'the martyrs' and inhabited by Christian 'holy men'.[176] Thecla has converted Zeus' temple in Seleucia into 'the dwelling place of her teacher Paul'.[177]

As we see in this case of Thecla's support of a church dedicated to Saint Paul in Seleucia, the control of holy space also had implications for the relationships between different saints and their spheres of patronage. Most notably, the struggle of Thecla's cult to establish its jurisdiction at Seleucia also entailed a subtle competition with the cult of Paul in Asia Minor (based in Tarsus). In the *Life and Miracles*, one observes a delicate arbitration between the two saints' claims to local power and prestige. In *Miracle* 4, the report of a church dedicated to Saint Paul in Seleucia is balanced by a similar report of a church dedicated to Saint Thecla in Paul's native city of Tarsus. The editor of the *Miracles* emphasizes the mutual hospitality of the two saints during each other's festivals: 'Paul is the host of the people of Seleucia, and the virgin of those from Tarsus'.[178] Yet, at the same time, this mutual hospitality engendered a vigorous 'contest for superiority' (ἄμιλλα) and 'rivalry' (ἔρις) between the saints.[179] In the *Life*, the writer tries to mollify the 'jealous competition' (ἀντιφιλοτίμησις) that developed between Seleucia and Tarsus by politely yielding a slight priority of place to the city of Paul.[180] However, in *Miracle* 29, when the controversy between the cities turns overtly hostile, he demonstrates a markedly partisan support for Thecla's centre at Seleucia. In that story, the author reports a dispute between Marianos, the bishop of Tarsus, and the aforementioned Dexianos, the bishop of Seleucia. In a political manœuvre against Dexianos, Marianos issues an interdiction against Seleucia and Hagia Thekla right in the midst of the festival of the virgin, the time of year when the pilgrimage routes were most crowded with travellers.[181] When Marianos dies only

---

[175] *Miracle* 1. 22–3 (Dag., 292).   [176] *Miracle* 2. 6 ff. (Dag., 292).
[177] *Miracle* 4. 4–5 (Dag., 294).   [178] *Miracle* 4. 9–10 (Dag., 294).
[179] *Miracle* 4. 9, 12 (Dag., 294); cf. *Life* 27.
[180] *Life* 27. 46 (Dag., 278).
[181] Eade and Sallnow ('Introduction', in *Contesting the Sacred: The Anthropology of Christian Pilgrimage*, 2) properly recognize (over against Victor Turner's archetypal theory of pilgrim *communitas*) how pilgrimage can be an arena 'for conflict between orthodoxies, sects, and confessional groups'.

five or six days later, the author interprets his fate as the swift judgement of Saint Thecla.[182] Throughout the account, the writer is careful not to impugn the dignity of the apostle Paul; yet the message of Thecla's power over Paul's own privileged representatives rings clear.

Thus, the *Life and Miracles* sheds light on important social conflicts in the cult of the martyrs by asserting Thecla's power over other religious claims and authorities. Such miraculous claims of power were, by nature, transient. The very writing of the work seems an attempt on the part of the writer to combat an internal source of tension in the life of the cult—namely, whisperings that the saint's power had diminished. When the writer himself petitions Thecla to continue to intervene in the lives of the faithful, his appeal reflects the pragmatic concern that a saint is only as powerful as her latest miracle. As an answer to such doubts, at the beginning of the *Miracles*, the writer feels the need to deny that Thecla's healing power ceased with the end of her life.[183] Later, at the end of the work, he even petitions the saint to renew her interventions by performing the special miracle of looking favourably upon his writing: 'If you accept [the writing of this work], then reduplicate [μιμοῦ] your actions again on my behalf.'[184]

In this way, while the miracle stories endorse the validity of Thecla's power and subvert her rivals' claims, they also implicitly privilege the one making the claims. Here, the rhetoric of hagiography and the politics of patronage intersect. The act of reporting Thecla's power in the *Miracles* reflects the editor's own negotiation of status as a literary patron of the cult. How does the author claim the favour of the martyr? He demonstrates how he himself had benefited twice from Thecla's miraculous interventions (*Miracle* 12). First, the saint relieves him from the distress caused by his contraction of the disease anthrax. Later in the same account, Thecla saves the author from excommunication by siding with him in a controversy with an ecclesiastical

---

[182] *Miracle* 29. 29 ff. (Dag., 368). This account details how, on one night of the festival, a visibly angry Thecla reputedly appeared to a resident of Seleucia in a dream and denounced the bishop of Tarsus. The writer is eager to note that Marianos died immediately after this vision (*Miracle* 29. 32 ff.).

[183] *Miracles*, Prologue, ll. 101–2 (Dag., 290).

[184] *Miracles*, Conclusion, ll. 15 ff. (Dag., 410).

rival, Basil of Seleucia.[185] By reporting Thecla's past interventions on his behalf, the author subtly signals that he enjoys her special favour in his present endeavour. By compiling the *Miracles* and aligning himself with the beneficence of the martyr, the author tries to enhance his own standing within the cult in relation to Thecla, as well as in relation to her other patrons and devotees.

The stories about Saint Thecla's wonder-working had, then, a political function: by telling such stories, the author of the *Life and Miracles* attempted to ground the institutional power of Hagia Thekla in the charismatic reputation of the martyr. Reports about the ongoing *charisma* of Saint Thecla belied underlying political concerns of patronage and cultic competition. These concerns, as well as the social tensions concomitant with itinerancy, asceticism, and women's piety, continued to play out in the cult of the saint in Egypt. Their recurrence in the Egyptian evidence suggests important lines of continuity with Thecla traditions in Asia Minor. However, in Egypt, one also finds these enduring cultic markers reworked in ways that conformed to the distinctive culture of Egyptian Christianity.

---

[185] *Miracle* 12 (Dag., 318). Dag., 17–18 argues that the second half of the account (the conflict with Basil) was added later by the author.

PART II

The Cult of Saint Thecla in Egypt

3

Thecla Devotion Among Ascetic Women in Alexandria

INTRODUCTION

Seleucia in Asia Minor was the hub of the Thecla cult in late antiquity. But, at the same time, interest in the saint also spread quickly throughout the Mediterranean world.[1] By the end of the fifth century CE, Thecla was extolled as an exemplary virgin and martyr not only in Asia Minor, but also in Italy,[2] Gaul,[3] Germany,[4] North Africa,[5] Armenia,[6] Cyprus,[7]

[1] Carl Holzhey (*Die Thekla-Akten: Ihre Verbreitung und Beurteilung in der Kirche* (Munich: J. J. Lentner, 1905), 50 ff.) surveys the spread of Thecla devotion in both the East and the West.

[2] Zeno of Verona, *Lib. I, tract. 8, De timore* (PL 11. 322–5); Ambrose of Milan: *De virg., lib. II*, 3. 19 (PL 16. 211); *De virg. lib. I*, 7. 40 (PL 16. 276); *Ep.* 63 ad Vercellens (PL 16. 1198); Ps.-Maximus of Turin, *Sermo* 56 (PL 57. 646) (= Ps.-Ambrose, *Sermo* 48; PL 17. 701); Nicetas of Remesiana, *De lapsu virg.* 3–4 (PL 16. 385–6). The author of the *Caena Cypriani*, probably from Northern Italy, is also familiar with Thecla and the *Acts of Paul*. In addition, a fourth-century sarcophagus fragment from Rome has an inscription of Thecla's name on a relief of the apostle Paul (identified by another inscription) (C. Nauerth and R. Warns, *Thekla* (Wiesbaden: Otto Harrassowitz, 1981), 82–4, fig. 30).

[3] Sulpicius Severus, *Dial.* 2. 13. 5 (PL 20. 159).

[4] A fourth-century gold glass medallion discovered in the cemetery of St. Severin in Cologne bears an image of Thecla in the flames (O. M. Dalton, *Catalogue of Early Christian Antiquities and Objects from the Christian East in the Department of British and Medieval Antiquities and Ethnography of the British Museum* (London: British Museum, 1901) no. 629, pl. 30; Nauerth and Warns, *Thekla*, 22–4, fig. 8).

[5] Augustine of Hippo, *Contra Faustum* 30. 4, ed. J. Zycha, CSEL 25, 751. 8–752. 5.

[6] A church in Etschmiadzin has a relief of Thecla and Paul, dated probably to the fifth century CE (DACL 2. 26. 68–71, fig. 2221; Nauerth and Warns, *Thekla*, 11, fig. 4).

[7] Epiphanius of Salamis, *Pan.* 79. 5 (PG 42. 748).

Palestine-Syria,[8] and Egypt. Among these regions, Egypt seems to have been an especially fertile ground for the cult of Saint Thecla. At least as early as the fourth century CE, the traditions surrounding Thecla's life became known to Egyptian writers and artists. Thecla's name and image appear on a wide variety of media: Greek and Coptic papyri and parchment manuscripts, limestone grave stelae, wall paintings, textile fragments, wooden combs, terra cotta oil lamps, and pilgrim flasks. This material evidence for Thecla devotion spans in date from the fourth to the seventh centuries, and comes from locales all over Egypt: cosmopolitan Alexandria and its environs along the Mediterranean coast, towns and cities along the Nile in Middle and Upper Egypt, and the remote oases of the Western Desert (see map of Egypt, Fig. 5).

The scattered nature of this Egyptian evidence raises important questions for the social historian: What would it mean to reconstruct a picture of Thecla's cult in Egypt from this evidence? What can we learn about the social settings of Thecla devotion? What (if anything) might we learn about how religious practices of women were shaped by that devotion, about how Thecla was adopted as a model for women's piety? Finally, how might a historian of early Christianity integrate both artistic and literary evidence in writing a social history of Thecla's cult in Egypt? Because the surviving evidence for Egyptian devotion to Thecla is more scattered and fragmentary than in Asia Minor, the results of piecing together the social world of that devotion will, of course, be more tenuous.

The manuscript tradition of the *Acts of Paul and Thecla* in Egypt attests to the popularity of Saint Thecla in that country. The spread of Thecla's cult paralleled the geographic spread of the text.[9] In total, five Greek manuscripts of the *Acts of Paul* have

---

[8] Jerome, *Ep.* 22 *ad Eustochium* (PL 22. 424). At the beginning of the sixth century CE, a church at Bethphage on the Mount of Olives apparently claimed to have relics of Saint Thecla. The writer Theodosius (*De situ terrae sanctae* 21, ed. J. Wilkinson, *Jerusalem Pilgrims Before the Crusades* (Warminster: Aris & Phillips, 1977), 191) reports it as 'the church where Saint Thecla is' (*ecclesia ubi sancta Tecla est*). Today there is a monastery dedicated to St. Thecla in Ma'alûlah by Damascus (Syria) but the date of origin for the site is uncertain.

[9] Holzhey, *Die Thekla-Akten*, 53.

been recovered from Egypt; among this collection survive two fragments specifically from the *ATh*—a fourth-century parchment from Antinoopolis (Antinoou) and a fifth-century vellum leaf from Oxyrhynchus.[10] In addition to this Greek tradition in Egypt, the *ATh* was also translated into Coptic.[11]

These Greek and Coptic papyri attest to the dispersion of the text to various parts of Egypt. However, the city of Alexandria, an international centre of commerce and scholarship in late antiquity, would have been the place where the *ATh* first gained currency. The theologian Origen of Alexandria, in the first half of the third century, refers on two occasions to the *Acts of Paul*,[12] and therefore was probably well acquainted with the story of Thecla. On both occasions he quotes from the text as a means of instructing his readers on points of theology—he treats the work approvingly,[13] setting it alongside the teachings of John's Gospel and Paul's Letter to the Galatians. The fact that Origen knows and approves of the *Acts of Paul* is significant. As the head of the Alexandrian catechetical school from 203 to 231,[14] he would have had considerable influence over what books were being taught and read in the academy. Thecla's

---

[10] *P. Ant.* I. 13; *P. Oxy.* I. 6. For other texts of the *Acts of Paul* found in Egypt, see H. A. Sanders, 'A Fragment of the Acta Pauli in the Michigan Collection', *Harvard Theological Review*, 31 (1938), 70–90; G. D. Kilpatrick and C. H. Roberts, 'The Acta Pauli: A New Fragment', *Journal of Theological Studies*, 37 (1946), 196–9; and W. D. McHardy's untitled article in the *Expository Times*, 58 (1947), 279.

[11] A Coptic papyrus (*PHeid*) containing extensive fragments from the *Acts of Paul* was published by C. Schmidt, *Acta Pauli*, 2nd edn. (Leipzig, 1905). This manuscript, a translation from the Greek probably written in the sixth or seventh century, helps confirm that the *ATh* circulated as part of the *Acts of Paul* in Egypt.

[12] Origen, *De principiis* 1. 2. 3; *Comm. in Jo.* 20. 12.

[13] In *De principiis* 1. 2. 3, Origen comments that the theological language (*sermo*) of the *Acts of Paul* seems to have been 'correctly formulated' (*recte . . . dictus*). In his commentary on John, Origen uses a quotation from the *Acts of Paul* ('I am about to be crucified again . . .') to support his argument that there is a second repentance for those who have fallen away (20. 12).

[14] Origen wrote all of *De principiis* and the majority of his commentary on the Gospel of John while head of the catechetical school in Alexandria (J. Quasten, *Patrology* (Westminster, Md.: Christian Classics, 1992), ii. 49, 57).

legend (*ATh*) was transmitted as part of the *Acts of Paul* in
Egypt,[15] and thus in this form it may have been well known to
theological students at Alexandria in the early third century.

From Alexandria the story of Thecla was eventually disseminated to the rest of Egypt, but Alexandria itself early
became an active centre for Thecla devotion. By the mid-fourth
century, the bishop of Alexandria himself, Athanasius, displayed a public interest in Saint Thecla and her story: he made
a visit to Thecla's pilgrimage shrine at Seleucia,[16] and may even
have written a version of Thecla's life.[17] In his treatise *On
Virginity*,[18] Athanasius chose to draw images liberally from the
Acts of Paul and Thecla and presents Thecla as the ultimate model
for women's piety.

Athanasius' interest in the female saint was not an isolated phenomenon. Instead, his interest sprang from a specific social and
political context—namely, his relationship to Alexandrian virgins
whom he sought to direct as bishop.

[15] See n. 11 above.

[16] Gregory of Nazianzus, *Or.* 21. 22 (*In laudem Athanasii*); PG 35. 1105.

[17] A *Life* of Saint Thecla attributed to Saint Athanasius is recorded in an index
of the Library of San Lorenzo de El Escorial in Spain (PG 25. xxvii, no. 17).
According to P. Delehaye (*Cat. Cod. Hag. graec. reg. monast. S. Laurentii
Scorialensis*, in *Analecta Bollandiana*, 28 (1909), 370, no. 19; 375, no. 16; 377,
no. 19) references to this *vita* are found at the Escorial in the following codices:
cod. y II. 5 (M. 310), n. 19; cod. y II. 8 (M. 313), n. 16; cod. y II. 9 (M. 314),
n. 19. On this lost work by Athanasius, see also T. M. Aubineau, 'Les Écrits de
Saint Athanase sur la Virginité', *Revue d'ascétique et de mystique* (1959), 155;
DACL XIII. 2. 2670 above with Anm. 6; M. L. Thérel, 'La Composition et le
symbolisme de l'iconographie du Mausolée de l'Exode à El-Bagawat', *Rivista
di archeologia cristiana* (Miscellanea in onore di Enrico Josi IV), 45 (1969), 266;
Nauerth and Warns, *Thekla*, 'Einleitung', xi.

[18] For a recent judgement on the authenticity of Athanasius' *De virginitate*,
see David Brakke, 'The Authenticity of the Ascetic Athanasiana', *Orientalia*, 63/2
(1994), 27–30. The treatise was composed in Greek but is preserved only in Syriac
and Armenian. An incomplete Syriac text has been edited by J. Lebon,
'Athanasiana Syriaca I: Un Λόγος περὶ παρθενίας attribué à saint Athanase
d'Alexandrie', *Muséon*, 40 (1927), 205–48. A complete Armenian text has been
edited by Robert P. Casey, 'Der dem Athanasius zugeschriebene Traktat περι
παρθενιασ', *SPAW* 33 (1935), 1022–45; see also R. P. Casey, 'Armenian
Manuscripts of St. Athanasius of Alexandria', *Harvard Theological Review*, 24
(1931), 43–59. I will use Casey's system of line reference. My translations are
based on the complete Armenian version.

FEMALE MONASTICISM IN ALEXANDRIA:
A SOCIAL CONTEXT FOR THECLA DEVOTION IN
THE FOURTH CENTURY

Athanasius' treatise *On Virginity* provides a valuable glimpse into the lives of Alexandrian women who seem to have adopted Thecla as their patron saint. As in some of his ascetic correspondence, Athanasius writes for the benefit of local nuns.[19] The treatise is less occasional than his two *Letters* to Alexandrian virgins,[20] but its readership would have been the same community of virgins with whom he was in regular correspondence.[21] We know little about the life of this community—its origins are obscure. A writing attributed to Bishop Peter of Alexandria (d. 311 CE) gives an account of a virgin who was dedicated to the service of the church by her parents.[22] Later, under Bishop Alexander (d. 328), a group of virgins came and sought Alexander's counsel on the ascetic life.[23] At the time of Athanasius' writing, Alexandrian virgins seem to have lived primarily within their own homes, or perhaps occasionally in small, private communities. This domestic form of asceticism was typical of fourth-century Egypt; larger cenobitic foundations for women did not become common until the fifth century.

[19] David Brakke, *Athanasius and the Politics of Asceticism* (Oxford: Clarendon Press, 1995), 27.

[20] Athanasius' first *Letter to Virgins* (*Ep. virg.* 1; written in Greek but preserved only in Coptic) has been edited by L. Th. Lefort, *S. Athanase: Lettres festales et pastorales en copte*, CSCO 150 (Louvain: L. Durbecq, 1955), 73–99. His second *Letter to Virgins* (*Ep. virg.* 2; written in Greek but preserved only in Syriac) has been edited by J. Lebon, 'Athanasiana Syriaca II: Une lettre attribuée à saint Athanase d'Alexandrie', *Museon*, 41 (1928), 169–216. An English translation of both letters is given by Brakke, *Athanasius*, 274–302. When citing passages from these texts, I will use the paragraph numbering of Brakke, as well as the standard page and line references in Lefort and Lebon.

[21] In *On Virginity*, Athanasius' frequent use of the second person singular only seems to have had the purpose of personalizing his admonitions to the community as a whole. This is evident because at other points in his treatise he slips back into the second person plural (e.g. *De virg.* 168 ff., 201 ff.; 1032–3 Casey).

[22] This fragmentary text has been edited and published by H. Koch, *Quellen zur Geschichte der Askese und des Mönchtums in der alten Kirche* (Tübingen: Mohr, 1933), 38–9.

[23] Athanasius, *Ep. virg.* 1. 36 (91. 7–11 Lefort).

In fact, during this period, a virgin living in the home came to be viewed as integral to the well-being of the entire household: one of the pseudo-Athanasian *Canons* (written perhaps a generation after Athanasius) opines that in every Christian house there ought to be a virgin, because her presence would guarantee salvation and protection for the family living there.[24] In the absence of a daughter, a female servant could also assume the role of domestic virgin. Such a role sometimes could carry the advantage of elevated status within the household: a servant dedicated to the virgin life was not expected 'to go out into the streets like the rest of the maids'; instead, she was to be treated as a daughter and placed in charge of administering the house.[25] This was, of course, an ideal that was not always put into practice: the writer of the *Canons* complains about certain rich women who still send their virgin servants on menial errands.[26]

Athanasius and other ecclesiastical leaders in Egypt often urged monastic women to avoid appearing in public.[27] However, a virgin who lived at home with her family would not have been completely isolated from her peers. There is evidence that she would have interacted on a regular basis with other domestic virgins and local communities of monastic women: in his letters, Athanasius raises up older women who have persevered in chastity as examples for younger virgins, and counsels them how to behave when together at church.[28] The writer of the *Canons* envisages another way that a domestic virgin could participate in the life of a local community of virgins: she might be taken to a

---

[24] Ps-Athanasius, *Canon* 98, *The Canons of Athanasius, Patriarch of Alexandria*, ed. and trans. W. Riedel and W. E. Crum (London: Williams and Norgate, 1904; repr. Text and Translation Society, 9, Amsterdam: Philo Press, 1973), 53. 14–15 (Arabic text); 62 (translation).

[25] Ps-Athanasius, *Canon* 104; Riedel and Crum, *Canons*, 57. 8–12 (Arabic text); 66–7 (translation).

[26] Ps-Athanasius, *Canon* 103; Riedel and Crum, *Canons*, 57. 4–6 (Arabic text); 66 (translation).

[27] e.g. Athanasius, *Ep. virg.* 1. 13 (78. 13–19 Lefort); Ps-Athanasius, *V. Syncl.* 94 (PG 28. 1545); Evagrius Ponticus, *Ep.* 7 (ed. W. Frankenberg (Berlin: Weidmannsche, 1912), 572–3 (164^{aa})).

[28] *Ep. virg.* 1. 35 (90. 28–35 Lefort); *Ep. virg.* 2. 8–10 (ed. Lebon, 'Athanasiana Syriaca II', 175–6).

local nunnery where she could spend the night observing the liturgical offices before returning home the next day.[29]

It was to such a loose-knit society of ascetic women that Athanasius presented Thecla as the model virgin in his treatise *On Virginity*. Athanasius twice quotes from the *ATh*, and then concludes the treatise with an exhortation based on the life of Thecla. Why does Athanasius draw special attention to the *ATh* here? What importance does this text hold for the community he addresses? Finally, why does Athanasius select Thecla in particular as the epitome of the virginal life?

In order to answer these questions, it is important to examine how Athanasius' use of the *ATh* fits within his larger rhetorical aims. I will argue that Athanasius is not introducing Thecla as a *new* model for women's piety; instead, he is presenting her as a model *already actively embraced by his audience*.

Athanasius quotes the *ATh* in a section of the treatise in which he recalls the parable of the wise and foolish virgins from Matthew 25. He urges the monastic women of Alexandria not to be like the foolish virgins, who had neglected to fill their lamps with oil and consequently found themselves unprepared for the bridegroom's wedding banquet. Athanasius connects this example with his larger moral agenda in the treatise—that of promoting internal as well as external virtues. Thus, he impresses upon his readers that purity of body without purity of heart is of no avail—'For what profit to [the foolish virgins] was virginity and abstinence?'[30]

In order to give more emotional force to his warning to the Alexandrian ascetics, Athanasius expands upon the Gospel's details by dramatizing the foolish virgins' anguished response to their exclusion from the wedding banquet. He has the foolish virgins appeal to the bridegroom by quoting from the *ATh*: 'Are we not your temple? Have we not fasted on your account and practised abstinence all our life? Why do you not listen to us? Why do you not give us the promise that we heard: "*Blessed are they who have kept their own bodies pure, for they will become a temple*

---

[29] Ps-Athanasius, *Canon* 98; Riedel and Crum, *Canons*, 55. 3–6 (Arabic text); 64 (translation). On virgins living in community, see also *Canons*, 48, 92, 99, 101; on virgins in private homes, see also *Canons*, 97, 104.

[30] *De virg.* 106 (1030 Casey).

of God?" And you would banish us!'[31] Here, Athanasius places
in the mouths of these Matthean virgins a quotation from Paul's
ascetic beatitudes in the *ATh*.[32]

When he associates the *ATh* with the experience of the foolish virgins, Athanasius does not intend to discredit the work. In
fact, Athanasius has the bridegroom respond by quoting the beatitude from the *ATh* again as if it were an accepted teaching:

This you have heard, 'Blessed are they who have preserved their own
bodies by means of purity (for they have become the temple of God)',
but truly you have not heard what follows: 'Blessed are the meek, blessed
are the peacemakers, blessed are the merciful, blessed are the poor,
blessed are the pure in heart', and so forth.

Nine blessings. Have you heard only that one?[33]

Athanasius questions here neither the logic nor the validity of the
apocryphal beatitude; instead, he criticizes the foolish virgins for
using the text to focus exclusively on external, or bodily, expressions of purity. The virgins have not heard 'what follows'.
Unexpectedly, 'what follows' are not the other ascetic beatitudes
from the *ATh*, but an assorted listing of the nine beatitudes in
the Gospel of Matthew (5: 3–11).[34] In this way, Athanasius
establishes the Matthean beatitudes as the necessary correlate and

---

[31] *De virg.* III (1030 Casey).

[32] Indeed, the virgins' response follows the logic of that beatitude. They assume
that they have earned the right to be called 'God's temple' because they have
already purified their bodies through fasting and abstinence: 'Are we not your
temple? Have we not fasted on your account and practised abstinence all our
life?' (*De virg.* III; 1030 Casey).

[33] *De virg.* 117–21 (1030 Casey). The section of text in parentheses above is
included in the Syriac text edited by Lebon ('Athanasiana Syriaca I', 215, trans.
Brakke, *Athanasius* 307).

[34] Not just the content, but also the method of Athanasius' argumentation
seems to reinforce the intertextual connection with the Gospel of Matthew. By
juxtaposing two different sets of teachings, Athanasius seems to be consciously
emulating Jesus' method of qualifying the law in the Sermon on the Mount:

Matt. 5: 21–2, 27–8   You have heard that it was said . . . (teaching of the law)
                      But I say to you . . . (teaching of Jesus in Matthew)
Athanasius, *De virg.* This you have heard . . . (beatitude from the *ATh*)
                      But truly you have not heard what follows . . . (beatitude
                      from Matthew)

In each case, the purpose is not to abolish the former teaching, but to intensify
and internalize the level of its observance.

fulfillment of the *ATh* beatitude. If the foolish virgins—and by extension the Alexandrian virgins—have not heeded these nine beatitudes concerning the inner virtues, they have not truly understood the ascetic beatitude from the *ATh* that they espouse. Athanasius dramatizes the Matthean parable as a dialogue in order to draw his audience, the Alexandrian virgins, into the conversation. By portraying the foolish virgins' appeal in the first person plural ('Why do you not listen to us? Why do you not give us the promise that we heard: "Blessed are they ones who have preserved their own bodies by means of purity . . ."'), Athanasius subtly encourages his female readers to identify with the plight of the foolish virgins. He employs a strikingly similar method earlier in the treatise when he places the Alexandrian virgins in the role of Adam and Eve.

When one [of you] sees herself naked and thinks on the disgrace and considers the expulsion, then she sighs, then she weeps, then she laments, then she shakes her head . . . and curses the day in which she was born, and hears from the Lord [about] what . . . Adam and Eve did as an offence. Adam heard, 'Where are you?' You also hear, 'Virgin, where are you? Where were you then, where are you now . . .' And you will reply with great desolation, 'I heard your voice and was afraid because I was naked, and I concealed myself.' And then God will say, 'Who has told you that you are naked if you have not failed in your vow . . . and loved the mortal more than the immortal?' Oh that fear! Oh that pain! Oh that bitter hour![35]

Athanasius portrays his virgin readers performing the same actions, hearing the same query, and voicing the same answer as their forebears Adam and Eve. Appealing to his readers' senses of sight and hearing,[36] he seeks to create an emotional bond between the Alexandrian virgins and their prototypes in Genesis in order to warn them about the danger of getting 'encompassed by such destruction!'[37]

Similarly, in his interpretation of the Matthean parable, Athanasius subtly lures his readers into the dramatic dialogue. In this context, I do not think Athanasius' use of the *ATh* is

---

[35] *De virg.* 39–50 (1027–8 Casey).
[36] Athanasius wants the virgins to see in their mind's eye their own nakedness, and to hear the Lord's admonition of them.
[37] Athanasius, *De virg.* 51 (1028 Casey).

simply a whim of intertextual fancy. Instead, I believe he is responding to the *actual exegetical interests of female monks living in Alexandria.* The effectiveness of Athanasius' exhortation on the Matthean parable would clearly have depended heavily on his readers' prior acquaintance with the beatitude from the *ATh.* 'Blessed are they who have kept their own bodies pure, for they will become a temple of God'—Athanasius here may even be placing a favourite slogan of the Alexandrian virgins on the lips of their Matthean counterparts. If this is the case, Athanasius' treatise grants us extraordinary insight into the character of this ascetic society of women in Alexandria: the bishop seems to have been addressing women for whom the *ATh* served as a formative text.

Indeed, Thecla's appeal within the Alexandrian community is confirmed by the way Athanasius concludes the work with a resounding exhortation on the life of the female saint. The energy of Athanasius' rhetoric rises near the end of the work as he begins a series of commands that call the virgins to action.[38] He presents his readers with a list of biblical exempla to be gazed upon, remembered, and emulated for their reputed love of chastity—Elijah, Elishah, Daniel, Ananias and his companions, Jeremiah, Miriam, Sapphora, John the Baptist, John the Evangelist, and Paul. At the very end, Athanasius highlights the virgin Thecla. Athanasius orders this list chronologically and follows the patriarchal custom of cataloguing women after men. However, the fact that he treats Thecla last has more significance than mere formula; it also speaks directly to her elevated status as a saint among Alexandrian Christians. Indeed, given the amount of attention she receives over and above the other biblical figures, Athanasius and the community to whom he was writing seem to have considered Thecla as the crowning expression of the virginal life.[39]

While Athanasius devotes only a sentence or two to each of the biblical prophets and apostles, he devotes the entire final paragraph of his treatise to the life of Thecla.

---

[38] *De virg.* 191 ff. (1033–4 Casey); see especially 192 ('Look . . .'); 202 ('Remember . . .'), 206 ('Be zealous . . .'; 'Look at . . .'), 213 ('Remain with . . .').

[39] The status of Thecla as the paragon of virginity in this treatise parallels the place of the Virgin Mary in Athanasius' other ascetic writings (e.g. Athanasius, *Ep. virg.* 1. 9–21, 45; 76–83, 94–5 Lefort).

Now remain with the blessed Thecla. Stop being disturbed by Theocleia. Despise the judge. Take courage when you scatter the enemy. Let the force of the fire not frighten you . . . Take courage, O virgin. Let the force of Alexander not subdue you. Tear his clothes to pieces. Put him to shame and be in good spirits. Despise his lions; view askance the bulls. Trample Satan and his instruments. Show forth the power of Christ in this visible world. Go to Tryphaena and the queen Tryphosa where all saints are truly in delight with all angels. There you will be enrolled with the assemblies forever and ever world without end. Amen.[40]

Here, Athanasius recapitulates Thecla's story in the form of moral exhortation, or *paraenesis*.[41] He recalls the life history of Thecla and urges his readers to re-enact Thecla's heroic actions in their own daily asceticism. Beneath Athanasius' command that the Alexandrian virgins 'remain with the blessed Thecla' lies the ethic of imitation—or *mimesis*[42]—so common to popular moral philosophy of late antiquity. In this case, to remain with a saint is to assimilate oneself to that saint's life. Athanasius' emphasis on the role of imitation in moral formation shows how he sought to shape the piety of his readers with reference to the life of Saint Thecla.

The language and biographical detail of this final section on Thecla reinforces the impression that his readers already had a special interest in Thecla as a saint. First, Athanasius urges the virgins to 'remain' (Armenian *mnal*)[43] with Thecla, a choice of words that implies they were already linked with her. Second, the exhortation presumes of the Alexandrian virgins a precise knowledge of characters (Theocleia, Alexander, Tryphaena[44]) and events (fire, bulls, lions) from the *ATh*.

---

[40] *De virg.* 211–20 (1034 Casey).

[41] In antiquity, *paraenesis* was synonymous with general moral exhortation that presented traditional wisdom and widely applicable examples in order to recall the listener to a life of virtue. On the rhetorical features of *paraenesis*, see David Aune, *The New Testament in its Literary Environment* (Philadelphia: Westminster Press, 1987), 191; Abraham Malherbe, *Moral Exhortation: A Greco-Roman Sourcebook* (Philadelphia: Westminster Press, 1986), 124–5.

[42] On mimetic rhetoric in antiquity, see Hans Koller, *Die Mimesis in der Antike: Nachahmung, Darstellung, Ausdruck*, Dissertationes Bernenses, 1.5 (Berne: A. Francke, 1954). On its application in early Christian writing, see Elizabeth A. Castelli, *Imitating Paul: A Discourse of Power* (Louisville, Ky.: Westminster, 1991).

[43] *De virg.* 211 (1034 Casey).

[44] Who is the queen Tryphosa whom we find paired with Tryphaena? The name Tryphosa does not appear at all in the *ATh*. Instead, one finds the names

The paraenetic character of Athanasius' rhetoric also supports the thesis that his readers would have had prior acquaintance with Thecla's life. In presenting models of virginity to be imitated, Athanasius appeals specifically to the *memory* of his readers.[45] Having recalled for them a series of biblical exemplars from the Old Testament, he continues, 'We have remembered the prophets. Remember [pl.] also what was gained by the coming of the Lord Christ and John the Baptist.'[46] It is also clear from his manner of posing questions to his readers that Athanasius expects them already to be well-acquainted with the events connected to the figures he mentions: e.g. 'Do you [pl.] not know that [John the Baptist] baptized Jesus Christ?'[47] Athanasius' exhortation to the Alexandrian virgins to 'remain' with Thecla is contextualized by such appeals to memory.[48] Consistent with the conventions of paraenetic discourse, he presents the prophets, Christ, John the Baptist, and finally, Thecla, as examples that are already familiar to his readers; with these examples, he aims to remind them about things they already know.

Thus, in his treatise *On Virginity*, Athanasius quotes from the *ATh* and urges his readers (at some length) to imitate Thecla as the consummate model of virginity. His rhetoric presupposes that these readers were already familiar with Thecla's example. What we have here, then, is evidence suggesting that Thecla devotion was practised by fourth-century monastic women in Alexandria.

Tryphaena and Tryphosa together in Paul's epistle to the Romans, chapter 16, verse 12: 'Greet those workers in the Lord, Tryphaena and Tryphosa.' Here, Athanasius probably assumed that the Tryphaena of the *ATh* was historically the person referred to in Romans, and therefore mentioned Tryphosa as Tryphaena's associate.

[45] A. Malherbe notes how the use of examples in paraenetic discourse is often tied to memory: 'The moralist therefore reminds (ὑπομιμνῄσκειν) his hearers of outstanding figures, taking care to describe the qualities of the virtuous men. This call to remembrance is in fact a call to conduct oneself as a μιμητής of the model' (A. Malherbe, 'Hellenistic Moralists and the New Testament', *ANRW* II, 26. 1, 282–3).

[46] *De virg.* 201–2 (1033 Casey).

[47] *De virg.* 202–3 (1033 Casey). Shortly thereafter, Athanasius begins to ask another question that is posed in a similar way, only to be interrupted by a gap in the manuscript: 'Look at John the Evangelist, the Theologian, the Son of Thunder. Are you [pl.] not acquainted, you . . . ?' (*De virg.* 204–5; 1033 Casey).

[48] *De virg.* 211 (1034 Casey).

WOMEN'S DEVOTION TO THECLA IN POLITICAL
CONTEXT: THEOLOGICAL AND ASCETIC FACTIONALISM
IN FOURTH-CENTURY ALEXANDRIA

Athanasius' correspondence with local female monks and his presentation of Thecla as a model for their piety cannot be understood in isolation from the political climate of the day. Fourth-century Alexandria was wracked by ecclesiastical factionalism as competing theological parties and ascetic movements contended for influence both within the city and throughout Egypt.

By the mid-fourth century, three organized theological parties had gained supporters in Alexandria. Local churches supporting Athanasius as bishop comprised one of these groups. A second party, which rejected Athanasius' leadership, consisted of the followers of Arius, who had been a priest in Alexandria early in the fourth century. Arius had gained the reputation early in the century as an eloquent speaker and subtle philosophical thinker. His theology originally sparked a controversy with Athanasius' predecessor, Bishop Alexander (d. 328), which eventually led to the condemnation of Arius at the Council of Nicaea in 325 CE. However, the ruling of this council did nothing to quell the controversy; instead, it inaugurated a period of strife between Alexander's successor Athanasius and Arius. After Arius' death in 336, Athanasius and Arius' followers vied for imperial support, and Athanasius' tenure as bishop was marred by five separate periods of enforced exile during which the Arian church enjoyed the emperor's favour (335–7, 339–46, 356–62, 362–3, 365–6 CE).

A third party, called the 'Melitians' by their opponents because they followed the teachings of Bishop Melitius of Lycopolis, also laid claim to being the true church in Egypt. After the persecutions under Diocletian (303–11 CE), followers of Melitius broke with the Bishop of Alexandria (Peter) over two issues: (i) the extent of Melitius' authority to install bishops during the persecution,[49]

---

[49] In the midst of the persecution, Peter and many of his supporting bishops had gone into hiding. During his absence, Meletius tried to maintain the work of the church in Alexandria by ordaining new bishops and priests there. When Peter came out of hiding he condemned Meletius for usurping his authority, and controversy ensued. Athanasius gives an account of this controversy in his *Apologia contra Arianos* and in his *Historia Arianorum ad monachos* (78–80).

and (ii) the proper way to treat Christians who had lapsed during persecution (Melitius and his followers took a rigourist
stance). While the dispute was temporarily resolved at Nicaea,
under Athanasius it was renewed with the Melitian churches at
Alexandria often allying themselves with Athanasius' Arian
opponents.[50]

In addition to these three main theological parties, other religious movements also established footholds in the environs of
Alexandria, dividing up the political landscape further. In the late
third century CE, Hieracas of Leontopolis established a large
ascetic centre in the southern part of the Nile Delta. Hieracas
and his followers espoused a radical ascetic lifestyle: they considered celibacy a prerequisite for salvation, rejected marriage
altogether, and abstained from eating meat and wine.[51] Athanasius
himself perceived Hieracas as a threat and remarked on his
influence among ascetics in Alexandria: the Alexandrian bishop
devotes a large section of his first *Epistle to Virgins* to condemning Hieracas' outright rejection of marriage.[52]

Finally, there is ample evidence that the Manichaean religion
also had communities in Alexandria. Its adherents, like Hieracas'
followers,[53] were rigorously ascetic—along with sex, they eschewed
meat and all forms of work (they depended on catechumens for
material support). Founded by the Persian prophet Mani in
240 CE, Manichaeism originated in southern Mesopotamia, but
the new religion spread rapidly both to the east (into central Asia)
and to the west (into the Roman Empire). It was introduced in
Egypt quite early—Mani's close friend and disciple Pappos
is reported to have been the first Manichaean missionary on
Egyptian soil.[54] A community of Manichaeans was probably
established in Alexandria sometime during the middle of the third
century (between 244 and 270) when another of Mani's disciples,

---

[50] According to Martin Tetz ('Athanasius von Alexandrien', *TRE* 4. 335), the
Melitians may even have elected their own bishop in Alexandria.

[51] Epiphanius, *Pan.* 67 (PG 42. 172–84).

[52] *Ep. virg.* 1. 22–30 (83. 13–88. 14 Lefort).

[53] In some Byzantine sources, Hieracas himself is associated with the
Manichaean faith (Samuel Lieu, *Manichaeism in the Later Roman Empire and
Medieval China*, 2nd edn. (Tübingen: J. C. B. Mohr, 1992), 183, n. 145).

[54] Alexander of Lycopolis (*c*.300), *Contra Manichaei opiniones disputatio* 2, ed.
A. Brinkmann (Stuttgart: Teubner, 1989), 4. 17–19.

Adda, made a visit to the city.[55] A papyrus dated paleographically to the late third or early fourth century CE may confirm this Manichaean presence in Alexandria: it contains a circular letter probably published by the Alexandrian episcopacy in which Christians are warned to beware of Manichaean teachers.[56]

While the religion went on to spread to various places in Upper Egypt during the fourth and fifth centuries,[57] this Manichaean community remained active in Alexandria. In his *Life of Antony* (*c.*356–62), Bishop Athanasius deems it necessary to distinguish Antony's ascetic piety from that of the Manichaeans.[58] Didymus the Blind (313–98 CE), who was head of the Alexandrian catechetical school, engages in a debate with a Manichaean over the propriety of marriage for Christians: over against his opponent's absolute prohibition of marriage, Didymus argues that it is not wrong for Christians to marry, but that marriage was only wrong for a Christian who had already taken ascetic vows.[59] The visibility of Manichaeans in Alexandria also brought resistance from Arians: the rhetorical skills of a local Manichaean teacher named Aphthonius brought a challenge from the Arian theologian Aetius, who travelled all the way to Alexandria from Antioch in order to engage him in

---

[55] Middle Iranian Manichaean sources report Adda's missionary activities; for a discussion of the chronological problems related to Adda's travels in the Roman empire, see Lieu, *Manichaeism*, 102–3.

[56] *P. Ryl.* III. 469.

[57] Caches of fourth- and fifth-century Manichaean texts have been discovered in Coptic at Medinet Medi and in Greek at Lycopolis (C. Schmidt and H. Polotsky, *Ein Mani-Fund in Ägypten* (Berlin: Akademie der Wissenschaften, 1933), 8–17). Syriac fragments found at Oxyrhynchus likewise attest to the Manichaean presence in Upper Egypt (F. Burkitt, *The Religion of the Manichees* (Cambridge: Cambridge University Press, 1925), 111–19). Recently, archaeologists have uncovered a large find of Coptic Manichaean documents at Kellis in the Dakhla Oasis. For a recent report on this find, see Iain Gardner, 'The Manichaean Community at Kellis: A Progress Report', in P. Mirecki and J. BeDuhn (eds.), *Emerging from Darkness: Studies in the Recovery of Manichaean Sources* (Leiden: Brill, 1997), 161–76. A bibliography of previous work at Kellis is provided in the same volume by Paul Mirecki, Iain Gardner, and Anthony Alcock, 'Manichaean Spell, Manichaean Letter', 1, n. 1.

[58] *V. Ant.* 68. 1, ed. G. J. M. Bartelink, *Vie d'Antoine*, 314.

[59] Didymus, *Comm. in Eccles.* 9. 9a, 274. 18–275. 2, ed. M. Gronewald, *Kommentar zum Ecclesiastes (Tura-Papyrus)*, pt. 5, Papyrologische Texte und Abhandlungen, 24 (Bonn: Rudolf Hubelt, 1979), 8–10.

a debate.[60] Finally, during the reign of Timothy I as Patriarch of Alexandria (380–5 CE), the number of Manichaeans who had surreptitiously entered the ranks of the clergy supposedly became so great that Timothy decided to introduce meat into the clergy's diet in order to weed out the vegetarian Manichaeans in their midst.[61]

The five groups that I have outlined—the churches under Athanasius, the Arians, the Melitians, the followers of Hieracas, and the Manichaeans—divided the political landscape of fourth-century Alexandria. As these groups manœuvred for civic influence, communities of monastic women in Alexandria emerged as a valuable source of grass-roots support.

According to ancient sources, the churches under Arius had considerable success in attracting adherents among ascetic women. Athanasius' predecessor, Alexander of Alexandria, criticizes female followers of Arius who disrupt public lawcourts with their pleas, and especially the 'younger women with them' (αἱ παρ' αὐτοῖς νεώτεραι) who 'walk around every public street in an indecent manner' (περιτροχάζειν πᾶσαν ἀγυιὰν ἀσέμνως).[62] Epiphanius reports that over 700 virgins (ἑπτακόσιαι παρθενεύουσαι) ended up being excommunicated along with Arius.[63]

Alexandrian women were also certainly counted among the followers of Hieracas. The movement comes under criticism for allowing ascetic women and men to live under the same roof.[64] Such virgins who lived together with men are referred to by some ancient writers as *virgines subintroductae*—that is, 'virgins introduced secretly' into households.[65]

---

[60] Philostorgius, *HE* 3. 5, ed. J. Bidez, GCS 21 (1972), 46. 23–47. 8. According to the Arian historian Philostorgius, Aetius so humiliated his Manichaean opponent that he immediately became ill and died within a week.

[61] Eutychius (Said ibn Batriq), *Annales*, ed. L. Cheikho, CSCO 50, 146. 20 ff.; Lieu, *Manichaeism*, 181–2.

[62] Theodoret, *HE* 1. 4, ed. L. Parmentier, GCS 19 (1911) 9; also edited by H. G. Opitz, *Athanasius' Werke* 3. 1, 20 (Urkunde 14).

[63] Epiphanius, *Pan.* 69. 3. 2 (PG 42. 208A).

[64] Epiphanius, *Pan.* 67. 8. 3 (PG 42. 184A–B).

[65] Athanasius opposes this practice in his second *Letter to Virgins* (*Ep.* 2. 20–9; ed. Lebon, 'Athanasiana Syriaca II', 181–7 Lebon). John Chrysostom also wrote two treatises on the *subintroductae*; for an analysis of these works, see Elizabeth Clark, 'John Chrysostom and the *Subintroductae*', *Church History*, 46 (1977), 171–85.

Finally, it is not unlikely that ascetic women played a prominent role in the Melitian and Manichaean churches as well. There is not much information about the participation of women in the Melitian church; yet, we know that the Melitians claimed to represent the true 'Church of the Martyrs' (Ἐκκλησία μαρτύρων),[66] and that women were active participants in the Christian martyr cult in late antiquity.[67] The evidence is more direct in the case of Manichaeism: a third-century papyrus from Egypt warns against women called the 'elect' (ἐκλεκταί) who received special honour (τιμή) among the Manichaeans.[68] In the fourth century (c.370), the Roman writer called Ambrosiaster comments on the special attraction this religion 'above all others' (*prae ceteris*) had for women.[69] From these sources, one can easily imagine that the Manichaean community in Alexandria would have counted numerous ascetic women among its adherents.

In this setting of competition for local monastic support, Bishop Athanasius of course actively attracted his own corps of female monastic supporters in Alexandria. His letters to virgins and his treatise *On Virginity* represent his attempts to consolidate his support among such groups over against his ecclesiastical rivals, and to reassert his own episcopal authority over those

---

[66] Epiphanius, *Pan.* 68. 3 (PG 42. 189A). According to Athanasius, the Melitians would preserve their martyrs' bodies in full view, instead of burying them in the ground (*Ep.* 41 (369 CE); 62. 23–63. 5 Lefort).

[67] Peter Brown (*The Cult of the Saints* (Chicago: Chicago University Press, 1981), 44) argues that martyr shrines and cemeteries were places that afforded women a freedom of movement and association that they could not find anywhere else in late-antique Roman society. As a result male writers often viewed women's participation in the martyr cult with suspicion (e.g. Synod of Elvira (306 CE), *Canon* 35) and took any opportunity to blame superstitious excesses of the cult on them (Jerome, *C. Vigilant.* 7. 361A and 9. 363B; Brown, op. cit., 27).

[68] *P. Ryl.* III. 469. 32–3.

[69] Ambrosiaster, *In ep. ad Tim.* ii. 3. 6–7 (ed. H. Vogels, CSEL 81. 3, 311. 27–312. 8). In claiming that Manichaeism was more popular among women than any of the other so-called heresies, Ambrosiaster certainly shares the late-antique, androcentric assumption among 'orthodox' male writers that women were especially susceptible to 'heretical' teachings (on this subject, see Virginia Burrus, 'The Heretical Woman as Symbol in Alexander, Athanasius, Epiphanius, and Jerome', *Harvard Theological Review*, 84/3 (1991), 229–48). However, his general observation that Manichaeism was popular among women may still bear some relation to social reality.

communities. How then did Athanasius' promotion of Saint Thecla contribute to his political agenda? How does the political situation at Alexandria, and specifically the inter-ecclesial competition for the allegiance of virgins, help elucidate Athanasius' appeal to the example of Thecla in the treatise *On Virginity?*

I believe the answer to this question in part has to do with the fact that Thecla was popular not just within Athanasius' circle, but among ascetic women in other religious factions as well. The Manichaeans' interest in so-called 'apocryphal' literature is the best documented: they are known to have used the apocryphal Acts of Peter, John, Andrew, Thomas, and Paul (including the *ATh*),[70] perhaps even in a common collection.[71] The Coptic version of the Manichaean *Psalm-book* explicitly mentions Thecla; she is admired as 'a despiser of the body' (ΟΥΡΕϥΚΑΤΑΦΡΟΝΗ ΜΠϹⲰΜⲀ) and 'the lover of God' (ΤΜⲀΪⲚΟΥΤⲈ).[72] The Coptic text is dated to the fourth or fifth century;[73] however, it is a translation from the Greek and may

---

[70] Around the year 390 CE, Philaster of Brescia notes that 'the Manichaeans and others have such Acts of the blessed Andrew and the blessed evangelist John and likewise [the Acts] of the apostle Peter as well as the blessed apostle Paul' (*Haer.* 60. 6, ed. F. Marx, CSEL 38, 48. 18–20). Around the same time, the Manichaean Faustus of Milevis lists the witnesses of Peter, Andrew, Thomas, and John together with the *Acts of Paul and Thecla* as authoritative sources in his debate with Augustine (Augustine, *Contra Faustum* 30. 4, ed. J. Zycha, CSEL 25. 751–2).

[71] Knut Schäferdiek ('The Manichean Collection of Apocryphal Acts Ascribed to Leucius Charinus', in Hennecke-Schneemelcher, ii, 87–100) argues that by the fourth century Manichaeans had assembled a collection of works that may be identified with the 'so-called "Journeys [περίοδοι] of the Apostles"' . . . the Acts of Peter, John, Andrew, Thomas, and Paul' later described by Photius (*Bibl.* 114, ed. R. Henry, 2. 84). Faustus may allude to this corpus in his debate with Augustine (Augustine, *Contra Faustum* 30. 4; see previous note). In his *Festal Letter* 39 (367 CE) Athanasius attests to the fact that the Melitians also 'pride themselves over the books that they call "apocryphal"' (21. 13–14 Lefort). Could they have utilized a literary corpus similar to that of the Manichaeans?

[72] *A Manichaean Psalm-book*, pt. 2, ed. and trans. C. R. C. Allberry (Manichaean Manuscripts in the Chester Beatty Collection, Stuttgart: W. Kohlhammer, 1938), ii. 192. 25.

[73] Ibid., ii, p. xix; H. J. Polotsky, *Manichäische Homilien* (Manichäische Handschriften der Sammlung A. Chester Beatty, Stuttgart: W. Kohlhammer, 1934), i, p. x, n. 1.

represent an even earlier tradition in Egypt.[74] The *Psalm-book* mentions Thecla first in a series of female exemplars from the apocryphal Acts including Maximilla and Iphidama from the *Acts of Andrew*, Aristobula and Drusiana from the *Acts of John*, Eubula from the *Acts of Peter*, and finally, Mygdonia from the *Acts of Thomas*.

Elsewhere in the same work, the psalmist presents Thecla as a model of purity and endurance in the face of suffering, recounting events from her life at greater length.

Thecla, the lover of God was offered up onto the fire.
She received the sign of the Cross, and walked toward the fire rejoicing.
Surely, she was not ashamed when she was naked in the midst of the crowd.
She was thrown to the bears, and the lions were loosed against her.
She was tied to the bulls, and the seals were loosed against her.
And all these things she suffered; she was not defeated, nor did she
[. . .]
It was a crown that she desired; it was purity that she fought for.[75]

Thecla is again compared to Drusiana, Maximilla, and Aristobula;[76] however, it is clear given the length of the discourse on Thecla's life that the Manichaeans considered her the paradigmatic virgin exemplar for women. In this context, it is not coincidental that the Manichaean Faustus, in his debate with Augustine, appeals to Thecla's conversion to chastity as direct justification for the Manichaean attitude toward marriage.[77]

In so far as the *Psalm-book* would have been read regularly in Manichaean worship, we may recognize it as evidence that Thecla devotion in fourth-century Alexandria would not have been exclusive to Athanasius' followers. The Manichaeans (and, one would imagine, other groups as well) esteemed the female saint as a privileged model for women's piety.

This evidence lends further credence to my argument that when Athanasius wrote his treatise *On Virginity*, ascetic women

---

[74] From quite early on, Manichaean literature seems to have played a central role in the spread of the cult. On his missionary journey, Mani's disciple Adda was supplied with copies of Mani's writings and accompanied by professional scribes (Lieu, *Manichaeism*, 90–1, 102).

[75] Allberry, *Manichaean Psalm-book*, ii. 143. 4–10.   [76] Ibid., 11–14.

[77] *Contra Faustum* 30. 4, ed. J. Zycha (CSEL 25, 751. 8–752. 5).

in Alexandria were *already* embracing Thecla as their exemplar.
Thus, Athanasius was not so much *introducing* Thecla as a
new model for women's piety, but rather *endorsing* a model that
a number of Alexandrian women already held as their own. By
appealing to the hagiographical interests of his virgin readers,
Athanasius was presenting himself as sensitive to and supportive of those interests. In this way, he hoped to consolidate old
support, and perhaps cultivate new support as well among local
monastic women.

One scholar has argued rightly that, for Athanasius, 'imitation
was a political act'.[78] By presenting women and men with ascetic
models like Thecla to imitate, the Bishop of Alexandria sought
to foster unity and allegiance among his followers over against the
competing claims of his opponents. Thus, on the one hand, in
endorsing Thecla as an exemplary martyr who endured trials
by fire and by beasts, Athanasius was implicitly counteracting
the Melitians' exclusive claims to being the true 'Church of the
Martyrs'.[79] On the other hand, in endorsing Thecla as a supreme
model of virginity, he was trying to redirect the women in his
churches away from the more radical asceticisms of Hieracas and
the Manichaeans.

However, in choosing to cite events from Thecla's life,
Athanasius treads a fine political line. In order to meet the needs
of his audience (the Alexandrian virgins in his own camp),
Athanasius endorses a saint whom he shared in common with his
opponents. At the same time he tries to differentiate himself from
his opponents in the specific lessons he draws from that saint's
life—thus, Thecla's life is not so much an illustration of radical,
external ascetic acts (like those of the Hieracians), but of internal virtues. I would finally contend that Athanasius, in his
choice of an 'apocryphal' exemplar, is consciously adopting the
methods of his so-called 'heretical' rivals[80] in order to draw a wider

---

[78] Brakke, *Athanasius*, 165.

[79] Ibid., 165, 267 sees a similar impulse behind Athanasius' appeal to his followers to endure persecution in imitation of Old Testament exemplars.

[80] We know that Athanasius considered the *ATh* 'apocryphal'—he omits it
from his list of canonical books in his famous *Festal Letter* 39—and that 'apocryphal books' (ⲀⲠⲞⲄⲢⲀⲪⲞⲚ) were, by his own definition, tainted by their association with communities of 'heretics' (ϨⲀⲓⲢⲉⲦⲓⲔⲞⲓ). It seems, however, that
Athanasius appears to have experienced some lingering ambivalence over the

base of support from ascetic women in Alexandria—women who, across party lines, held Thecla as their patron saint.

THE FATE OF THE VIRGINS: A HISTORY OF ALEXANDRIAN DEVOTEES TO SAINT THECLA

Thus, sometime during the middle of the fourth century CE, Athanasius wrote his treatise *On Virginity* to a community of virgins who reverenced Saint Thecla as an exemplar of the ascetic life. I have discussed the social and political position of such women in Alexandria, but what more can be said about their *history*? In his conflict with the Arians, their leader Athanasius was exiled from office five times in the space of thirty years (from 335 to 365 CE). Within the turmoil and upheaval of this period, what was the fate of these virgins who remained loyal to Athanasius, and who seem to have considered Thecla their patron saint?

From the writings of Athanasius, we know that these virgins were frequently embroiled in the persecutions that accompanied the Athanasian–Arian conflict in Alexandria.[81] In 339, during Athanasius' second exile from office, monastic women allied with him were victims of persecution at the hands of the Arian Bishop of Alexandria, Gregory of Cappadocia, and the pro-Arian prefect Philagrius. In his *Epistula ad episcopos encyclica*, Athanasius describes how virgins were stripped naked and dragged through the streets by their hands, and how finally they were 'carried off to the tribunal of the governor, and then thrown into the

---

character of these so-called apocryphal books: 'a useful word' (21. 1–2 Lefort; ⲨⲰⲀⲬⲈ Ⲛ̄ⲬⲢⲨⳠⲓⲘⲞⲚ) can be found in them, but they remain 'sources of dissension' (20. 29 Lefort; ⳘⲈⲚⲀⲢⲬ̄Ⲏ Ⲛ̄ⲦⲀⲤⲓⲤ) for his community.

[81] Carlton M. Badger, Jr., 'The New Man Created in God: Christology, Congregation, and Asceticism in Athanasius of Alexandria', (Ph.D. diss., Duke University, 1990), 225–31. It should be noted that virgins on both sides were vocal participants in the conflict. On the one hand, Athanasius complained that his Arian opponents 'gave permission to the women on their side to harass whomever they wished' (*Hist. Ar.* 59. 2–3; 216. 14–20 Opitz). On the other hand, the public complaints of Athanasius' female followers had provoked a response from the emperor Constantine himself—in a letter, he had told them in no uncertain terms to keep quiet (Sozomen, *HE* 2. 31. 2, ed. Bidez and Hansen, GCS 50, 96. 10–12).

prison'.[82] Unfortunately, this episode would not mark the last time that virgins under Athanasius became political targets.

In 355, with the Arians having gained the favour of the emperor Constantius, Athanasius was condemned at the pro-Arian Council of Milan. In February of 356, a hostile military guard stormed the Church of St Theonas in Alexandria where Athanasius was keeping vigil. A number of virgins were trampled and killed in this raid; they would later be celebrated as martyrs in Athanasius' churches.[83] After only narrowly escaping himself, Athanasius was forced into exile, fleeing to the monasteries of Upper Egypt. In his absence, an imperial appointee, George of Cappadocia, replaced him as bishop and began using violence to quell pro-Athanasian resistance.

The communities of virgins who remained loyal to Athanasius predictably became prime targets for George's campaigns of violence. Athanasius, in his *Defence of His Flight* describes the atrocities committed by the Arian leaders against his followers in Alexandria, among them the community of virgins who supported him there. He writes that, at Easter in the year 357 CE,

Virgins were thrown into prison; bishops were led away in chains by soldiers; houses of orphans and widows were seized along with their loaves of bread; attacks were made upon houses, and Christians were driven out in the night.[84]

At Pentecost of that same year, the Roman military commander in Alexandria, Sebastian, a Manichaean who sided with the Arian cause, intensified the persecution against the virgins.

Having lighted a pyre, and having placed certain virgins near the fire, he tried to force them to say that they were of the Arian faith. And when he saw that they (the virgins) were prevailing, and did not give heed to the fire, he immediately stripped them naked, and beat them in the face in such a way that for some time they could hardly be recognized.[85]

Athanasius' language of exhortation in *On Virginity* makes one wonders if Athanasius may have addressed this treatise to the

[82] Athanasius, *Epistula ad episcopos encyclica* 3–4 (2. 172–3 Opitz); cf. *Hist. Ar.* 11 (2. 188–9 Opitz).

[83] Athanasius, *Hist. Ar.* 81 (2. 228–30 Opitz); cf. *Apol. Const.* 25; *Fug.* 24.

[84] Athanasius, *Fug.* 6. 3 (2. 72 Opitz).

[85] Athanasius, *Fug.* 6. 6–7 (2. 72 Opitz).

Alexandrian virgins in the midst of these persecutions, perhaps with the threat of the pyre imminent: 'Despise the judge. Take courage when you scatter the enemy. Let the force of the fire not frighten you . . .'[86] In such a case, Athanasius would have been appealing directly to the virgins' identification with Saint Thecla as a source of strength in time of crisis. Thecla had withstood the heat of the pyre in Iconium; by imitating Thecla, these women too could be courageous before the fire.

In any event, according to Athanasius, the virgins survived the threat of the fire. As a result, the Arians instigated a final rash of arrests and beatings, and then banished 'all those who had been seized, *even the virgin* (ἡ παρθένος) . . . to the Great Oasis' of the Western Desert.[87] Thus, some of the Alexandrian virgins experienced a fate similar to Athanasius and were exiled from the city. In Chapter 5, I will argue that the virgins banished to the Western Desert were among those who held Thecla as their ascetic exemplar.

However, not all of Athanasius' ascetic supporters were sent into exile. While some of the virgins were banished from the city; others apparently survived the persecutions and remained in Alexandria. The pseudo-Athanasian *Canons* themselves attest to the ongoing regulation of female monastic communities in Alexandria perhaps a generation after Athanasius. Furthermore, a letter written in the early fifth century by the monk Isidore of Pelusium to Alexandrian female monks (μοναστρίαι Ἀλεξανδρίναι) would seem to indicate the continued presence of ascetic communities who embraced Thecla as a primary model for female piety.[88] Isidore commends to his female readers 'the all-praiseworthy Thecla' (ἡ πανεύφημος Θέκλα) above all other women as a teacher of 'the female sex' (τό θῆλυ). For such Alexandrian virgins, Thecla continued to stand as 'an eternal monument of purity' (στήλη αἰώνιος ἁγνείας) and 'the chief of female victories and trophies' (τὸ κεφάλαιον τῶν γυναικείων νικῶν καὶ τροπαίων).

---

[86] Athanasius, *De virg.* 212–13 (1034 Casey).

[87] Athanasius, *Fug.* 7. 2 (2. 73 Opitz). Athanasius uses the singular form, παρθένος, to indicate the collective group (some manuscripts offer an alternative reading of αἱ παρθένοι).

[88] Isidore of Pelusium, *Ep.* 87 (PG 78. 241D–244A). For a recent analysis of Isidore's life and letters, see Pierre Évieux, *Isidore de Péluse*, Théologie Historique, 99 (Paris: Beauchesne, 1995).

Finally, while female monks remained an active presence in Alexandria during the fourth and fifth centuries, ascetic women also began venturing out from the city and into the monastic regions to the west. On the edge of the desert, the cemeteries to the west of the city became a haven for hermits who were trying to escape the bustle and distractions of urban life.[89] Further out, larger monastic foundations grew up at various milepost markers along the desert road that paralleled the Mediterranean coast.[90] These communities, often loosely-knit (semi-eremitic) configurations of monastic cells that eventually grew into more centralized (cenobitic) monasteries, also became centres for pilgrimage. Pious visitors came from Alexandria and from all over the Roman Empire seeking healing and spiritual insight from the holy men and women who resided there.

As one might expect, this monastic region to the west of the city was also fertile ground for Thecla devotion. As female ascetics relocated from Alexandria to these outlying desert communities, they brought with them the forms of piety that had sustained them in the city. Indeed, the biography of one such ascetic, a woman named Syncletica, shows how the social practices of some female monks in this region may have been shaped by their emulation of Thecla.

The *Life and Activity of the Holy and Blessed Teacher Syncletica* (= *Life of Syncletica*) was written around the middle of the fifth century,[91] by a writer who probably lived in the vicinity of

---

[89] In late antiquity, cemeteries were located outside the walls of cities. In places like Rome, the suburban location of cemeteries had a determinative effect on the shape of pilgrimage related to the cult of the martyrs, and on the politics of ecclesiastical patronage (Brown, *Cult of the Saints*, 7–8).

[90] The names of these monasteries express their distance from Alexandria—the Pempton (fifth mile), the Enaton (ninth mile), the Oktokaidekaton (eighteenth mile), and the Eikoston (twentieth mile).

[91] PG 28. 1487–1558. The traditional attribution of the work to Athanasius is certainly spurious (D. Brakke, 'The Authenticity of the Ascetic Athanasiana', *Orientalia*, 63/2 (1994), 39). A comparison of the *Life of Syncletica* with later apophthegmata traditions, and with the earlier writings of Evagrius Ponticus and John Cassian, provides a range *ad quem* and *a quo* for dating the work to the middle of the fifth century. On the influence of Evagrius Ponticus and John Cassian on the work, see Dom Lucien Regnault, 'Introduction' to the *Vie de Sainte Syncletique*, trans. Odile Bénédicte Bernard, Spiritualité Orientale, 9 (Abbaye Notre Dame de Bellefontaine, 1972), pp. x–xiv. Certain sayings of

Alexandria.[92] Syncletica herself probably lived during the latter half of the fourth century and the early part of the fifth: the basic descriptions of Syncletica's experience in the *Life* correspond to the social contours of Alexandrian women's ascetic practice in this period.[93] Syncletica's earliest asceticism took place in the home of her parents. 'But this woman, happening to be still in the care of her father, trained (ἀσκεῖν) her soul in piety for the first time.'[94] This domestic context matches the social setting of the Alexandrian virgins under Athanasius.[95] However, as soon as her parents died, Syncletica left her paternal home and resettled in a tomb of a relative which was 'situated some distance [ἀποικίζεσθαι] from the city'.[96] There, she cut off her hair and

Syncletica in the sixth-century Latin collections of the *Apophthegmata Patrum* seem to have been extracted directly from Syncletica's teachings in the *Life*. These sayings do not appear in an earlier Syriac recension of the apophthegmata (Wilhelm Bousset, *Apophthegmata* (Tübingen: J. C. B. Mohr, 1923), 35–48; cf. Irénée Hausherr, SJ, *Études de spiritualité orientale*, Orientalia Christiana Analecta, 183 (Rome: Pontificum Institutum Studiorum Orientalium, 1969), 21).

[92] When the writer extols the 'singular faith . . . with absolute love' found in Alexandria (*V. Syncl.* 4; PG 28. 1489A) he is probably engaging in propaganda for the city (Regnault, 'Introduction' to the *Vie de Sainte Syncletique*, p. iv).

[93] Various scholars have questioned the historicity of Syncletica's *Life*. Because her name denoted senatorial or aristocratic status, some scholars have questioned whether she was a literary invention of the author. In fact, the author of the *Life of Syncletica* makes a pun on her name when he calls her 'the one who was named for the heavenly council [σύγκλητος]' (*V. Syncl.* 4; PG 28. 1488C; noted by Elizabeth A. Castelli, 'Pseudo-Athanasius', in V. L. Wimbush (ed.), *Ascetic Behavior in Greco-Roman Antiquity* (Minneapolis: Fortress Press, 1990), 267, n. 7). However, playful word play on names was common in ancient biography and Christian hagiography, and does not necessarily obviate the historicity of the biographical subject. Regnault, while acknowledging that much of the work represents literary accretion (he describes Syncletica's discourse as 'fictif'), still recognizes signs of the work's relative veracity: e.g. the author's lack of pretension, and the work's relative disinterest in the miraculous compared to later eastern hagiographies. Finally, he points out that the descriptions of Syncletica's illness are so detailed that they are unlikely to have been created out of whole cloth (Regnault, 'Introduction', pp. iv–vi).

[94] *V. Syncl.* 6 (PG 28. 1489B).

[95] Syncletica's ascetic piety seems to have found support in 'a like-minded sister, along with two brothers who had also been led to the most holy [i.e. monastic] life' (*V. Syncl.* 5; PG 28. 1489A).

[96] *V. Syncl.* 11 (PG 28. 1492D). Although the *Life* does not specify the tomb's location, it was probably in one of the necropolises on the western outskirts of Alexandria. C. Haas ('The Arians of Alexandria', *Vigiliae Christianae*, 47

lived for a number of years as a recluse,[97] until reports of her ascetic prowess attracted a small following of women who took up residence in the tombs around hers.

Early in the *Life*, the biographer of Syncletica calls her a 'genuine disciple of the blessed Thecla' (τῆς μακαρίας Θέκλης γνησία μαθήτρια).[98] In pursuing her ascetic vocation, Syncletica is said to be 'following the same teachings' as her spiritual forebear.[99] This identification of Syncletica as a disciple of Thecla might be interpreted merely as a rhetorical gesture on the part of the hagiographer. However, given the evidence for Thecla devotion among Alexandrian virgins in the fourth and fifth centuries, it is quite possible that this identification had historical roots in the life of Syncletica herself. If we are to judge by the

(1993), 235) has argued that in the fourth century the city of Alexandria was topographically divided: followers of Arius congregated in the eastern suburbs of the city (near the parish church of Boukalis) and followers of Athanasius congregated at the western end of the Via Canopus. Syncletica would have been in the latter camp.

[97] The author uses verbs like ἡσυχάζειν and ἀναχωρεῖν as technical, monastic terms in order to describe Syncletica's solitary way of life as a hermit (*V. Syncl.* 12 and 21 (PG 28. 1493B, 1497C); Castelli, 'Pseudo-Athanasius', 271, n. 28; 275, n. 49).

[98] *V. Syncl.* 8 (PG 28. 1489C).

[99] Ibid., the author of the *Life* goes on to enumerate the common characteristics of Syncletica and Thecla: specifically, they share a common 'suitor' (μνηστήρ) in Christ, and a common 'bridal guide' (νυμφαγωγός) in Paul; they inhabit the same 'bridal chamber' (θάλαμος), wear the same 'garment' (ἱμάτιον), listen to the same scriptural hymns (the Psalms and the songs of Miriam the prophetess), have the same love for the Lord, are worthy of the same 'gifts' (δωρεά), and compete in the same 'contests' (ἀγών) against a common opponent. However, the writer suggests that Syncletica's sufferings (including a debilitating bout with terminal cancer of the throat) even eclipsed those of Thecla: 'And I understand the gentler pains to belong to Thecla, for the evil of the enemy used to attack her through external means while he was conversing with her. But with Syncletica he exhibits his more bitter evil, causing a disturbance from the inside through his own contrary and destructive arguments' (*V. Syncl.* 8 (PG 28. 1492A); cf. *V. Syncl.* 106). Early Christian monastic literature often described the attenuated pain of monastic self-deprivation in more austere terms than the relatively transient distress of martyrdom. The monk was thought to have transformed the suffering of the martyrs into a daily struggle with temptation and physical affliction (M. Villier, 'Le martyre et l'ascèse', *Revue d'ascetique et de mystique*, 6 (1925), 105–42; Castelli, 'Pseudo-Athanasius', 270, n. 19).

sparse biographical details provided in the *Life*, the 'teachings' of Thecla seem to have shaped Syncletica's social practices in specific ways—most notably, in her break with domestic patterns of ascetic life.

Syncletica's abandonment of her parents' home touches particularly on the tensions that would have existed for Alexandrian virgins still living in the homes of their parents. While Syncletica's early ascetic life in the household afforded her paternal protection and the freedom not to have to worry about 'the cares of the body' (αἱ τοῦ σώματος ἐπιμελείαι)[100] it also confronted her with her parents' persistent expectation that she marry in order to continue the family line. One of Syncletica's own teachings perhaps alludes to such tensions in Egyptian society: 'But even when we confine ourselves in our houses, we are not liable to be free from anxiety there . . .'[101] The pressure on Syncletica to wed one of her many suitors was all the greater because her sister and her two brothers had already committed themselves to the monastic life.[102] Whereas Syncletica might have under normal circumstances been free to serve as a household virgin, her freedom to do so was threatened by her parents' anxiety about the future of their lineage. Yet, over against her parents' insistent entreaties, Syncletica steadfastly refused to marry.

It is not coincidental that this rebuff of her parents immediately precedes Syncletica's identification as a 'disciple of the blessed Thecla' in chapter 8 of the *Life*. Thecla's commitment to Paul's gospel of chastity led to a similar rejection of her fiancé Thamyris and her mother Theocleia. Thus, Syncletica, even while still in the home, seems to have made a conscious break with the familial and marital expectations that delimited her social options as a woman—a break that anticipated her physical departure from her home after her parents' death. Her ultimate relocation to the tomb of a dead relative subtly underscored the fact that, for her, her family had effectively ceased to exist—her parents had died, and there was no hope that the family line would continue.

---

[100] *V. Syncl.* 6 (PG 28. 1489B).   [101] *V. Syncl.* 26 (PG 28. 1501C).
[102] *V. Syncl.* 5 (PG 28. 1489A). One brother ended up dying at an early age; the other, after having been persuaded to marry by his parents, severed his marriage contract on the eve of the wedding and ran off to join a monastery.

Syncletica's delay in moving out of her parents' home reflects a type of social conflict that would have accompanied readings of Thecla's life by Alexandrian domestic virgins in the fifth century. For a time, Syncletica physically remains in her home, perhaps out of a lingering and halting sense of obligation to her parents. Yet, in all other respects, she has already divorced herself from her parents' authority: in disregarding their counsel, she acts as the disciple of Thecla, 'following in the same teachings'.[103] In the *Life of Syncletica*, we catch a glimpse of how the 'teachings' of Thecla may have provided an impetus for the disruption of family structures in the lives of Alexandrian virgins.

Syncletica's departure from her parents' household was also marked by an act of self-abnegation that may have been inspired by Thecla's example. After she had renounced all her possessions and settled in the tomb, Syncletica, 'having summoned to herself one of the elders, cut off [ἀποτέμνειν] her own hair'.[104] For Syncletica, this act would have been a visual sign of her break from the world (i.e. cosmopolitan Alexandria),[105] but more specifically, it may also have been a sign of her devotion to Thecla—in the *ATh*, Thecla offers to shave her head as a sign of her unwavering commitment to chastity. Syncletica's biographer makes a point of noting that, because she cut off her hair, she was 'for the first time deemed worthy of the name "virgin"' (ἡ παρθενικὴ προσηγορία).[106] The title of 'virgin' here seems to suggest more than its general meaning of sexual chastity. Given the local context of Thecla devotion among Alexandrian virgins, it may also have indicated a more formal, honorific status that Syncletica was inheriting from Thecla, the prototype of all true virgins.

Syncletica's move out from her home marked a radical break with the earlier domestic model of women's asceticism in Alexandria. Significantly, in the *Life of Syncletica*, this move is closely associated with her identity as a 'disciple of the blessed Thecla.' Like Thecla, Syncletica left her family, changed her

---

[103] *V. Syncl.* 8 (PG 28. 1489C).   [104] *V. Syncl.* 11 (PG 28. 1492D).

[105] The biographer interprets Syncletica's action as a renunciation of both 'cosmetics' and 'cosmos' playing on the common Greek root of these words (*V. Syncl.* 11; PG 28. 1493A).

[106] *V. Syncl.* 11 (PG 28. 1493A).

appearance, and assumed a public role as an ascetic teacher of women.[107] This evidence suggests finally that devotion to Saint Thecla—the practice of emulating her life—may in fact have functioned as a subversive, social stimulus in the lives of fifth-century Alexandrian virgins, prompting women like Syncletica to eschew their roles within urban households and to venture into the desert.[108]

Ultimately, the *Life of Syncletica* reflects the persistence of Thecla devotion among Alexandrian virgins amidst changing social circumstances in the fifth century CE. The work, addressed to ascetic women from a variety of monastic backgrounds (including both eremitical hermits and cenobitic nuns)[109]

---

[107] Indeed, when the author portrays Syncletica's teaching as 'a divine symposium (θεῖον συμπόσιον)' for her female hearers, he draws an analogy to the *Symposium* of Methodius (*c.*300 CE), in which Dame Virtue convenes a colloquium of ten virgins (*V. Syncl.* 30; PG 28. 1505B). In Methodius, Thecla's discourse on virginity wins her first place among the virgins, and earns her the honour of leading the choir of virgins in a final hymn of thanksgiving to Christ, their Bridegroom (*Symposium* 11. 2–3, ed. N. Bonwetsch, GCS 27, 131 ff.). Syncletica's biographer, by describing her teachings as 'divine symposium', effectively inserts Syncletica into Methodius' convocation. He casts her as the eleventh participant in the dialogue. Thus, in the context of her own assembly of virgins, Syncletica comes to share Thecla's pride of place.

[108] Societal tension over the proper place of Alexandrian virgins was ongoing, and is reflected in the teachings of the *Life* itself: 'But it is not possible to avoid these things [sins of the senses] if we continually appear in public . . . out of necessity, therefore, it is proper [for women] to avoid the processions into the marketplace' (*V. Syncl.* 25; PG 28. 1501B–C). Women like Syncletica who abandoned their domestic roles and entered public spaces would have faced considerable resistance from some quarters. Thus, the author of her *Life* refrains from portraying her move from home to tomb as a move from the private to the public sphere; instead, she is thought to have exchanged one private context for another. The tomb enclosure becomes, for this author, Syncletica's second home: 'Then she was again in her paternal chambers, having been trained sufficiently by means of sufferings' (*Life of Syncletica* 13; PG 28. 1493B).

[109] While within the narrative Syncletica instructs a small coterie of monastic disciples, the nature of her teachings reflects the biographer's concern for a wider female readership. The warnings about temptations posed by one's 'sisterly relationship' (σχέσις ἀδελφική) with other virgins, the concerns voiced about going out in public, and the comparisons made in Syncletica's discourse to the ways of married women are all traditional motifs in treatises directed to ascetic women (*V. Syncl.* 25, 27, 42; PG 28. 1501B–C, 1504B, 1512C–D). The diverse character of the work's audience is indicated by the shifting concerns of the teachings attributed to Syncletica. In ch. 94, Syncletica addresses those who 'happen

presumes that its audience was well familiar with the cardinal events in Thecla's life: 'For the martyrdoms of the blessed Thecla are unknown to no one, as she contended bravely in the midst of fire and wild beasts.'[110] In the end, we would like to know more about the institutional forms that Thecla devotion took amidst the growth of monasteries in the region west of Alexandria. Certainly, monastic reverence for Saint Thecla continued to find a literary outlet in newly produced *vitae* of Egyptian saints like Syncletica, but it also would have come to be formally recognized in monastic liturgies,[111] and perhaps even in the dedication of monastic chapels.[112] In addition, as I will show in the next chapter, women's devotion to Saint Thecla played just as an important role in the development of monastic pilgrimage and the cult of the martyrs around Alexandria.

to be in a cenobitic monastery' (PG 28. 1545B) and proceeds to affirm the ceno-bitic vocation alongside the anchoritic life. Elsewhere, however, she privileges the anchoritic life ('our profession'—τὸ ἡμέτερον ἐπάγγελμα) favouring it over two other ascetic options, encratism and chastity within marriage (*V. Syncl.* 23; PG 28. 1500D).

[110] *V. Syncl.* 8 (PG 28. 1489D–1492A).

[111] Two medieval Coptic liturgical manuscripts from the Monastery of Saint Macarius of Scetis celebrate the festal day of Saint Thecla (H. G. Evelyn White, *The Monasteries of the Wadi 'n Natrûn* (New York: Metropolitan Museum of Art, 1926), i. 218, 221). The first of these texts, a *Book of Hymns*, refers to her as 'Saint Thecla the Apostle' (ⲧⲁⲅⲓⲁ ⲑⲉⲕⲗⲁ ⲧⲁⲡⲟⲥⲧⲟⲗⲟⲥ).

[112] There is literary evidence from the twelfth century CE for a church dedic-ated to Saint Thecla in the northern delta. It was closely associated with two monasteries in the vicinity—one for men, the other for women (René-Georges Coquin and Maurice Martin, SJ, 'Monasteries in the Gharbiyyah Province', in *The Coptic Encyclopedia*, v. 1651–2).

4

Pilgrimage and the Cult of Saint Thecla in the Mareotis[1]

The Christian practice of pilgrimage flourished especially in the fourth, fifth, and sixth centuries CE. While the Holy Land remained the primary destination for pious travellers,[2] Egypt, as the cradle of monasticism, also attracted visitors in droves. As I mentioned in the previous chapter, the monastic establishments west and south-west of Alexandria—Pempton, Enaton, Oktokaidekaton, Nitria, Scetis (Wadi Natrun)—became fixtures on the itineraries of pilgrims hoping to get a first-hand glimpse of holy men and women. Collections of monastic stories such as the *Apophthegmata Patrum*, the *Conferences* of John Cassian, and the legends about Daniel of Scetis record many such encounters.[3]

However, holy men and women were not the only targets of pilgrimage. With the rise of the Egyptian cult of the martyrs, martyr shrines (*martyria*) also became major centres for pilgrim activity. The bodies of Christian martyrs were thought to be repositories of healing power, a power made portable in the form of souvenir artefacts sold to pilgrims at or near the shrines. Such shrines were rarely isolated structures. More often, they were surrounded by a complex of other buildings and institutions serving the needs of pilgrims: churches, shops, hostels, public baths, and even the *martyria* of other local saints.

---

[1] An earlier version of this chapter appeared as an article entitled, 'Pilgrimage and the Cult of Saint Thecla in Late Antique Egypt', in David Frankfurter (ed.), *Pilgrimage and Holy Space in Late Antique Egypt* (Leiden: Brill: 1998), 303–39.

[2] For a study of late antique pilgrimage to the Holy Land, see E. D. Hunt, *Holy Land Pilgrimage in the Later Roman Empire, AD 312–460* (Oxford: Clarendon Press, 1982).

[3] PG 65. 71–440; CSEL 13 (1886); *Vie (et Récits) de l'Abbé Daniel le scétiote*, ed. L. Clugnet (Paris: Librairie A. Picard et fils, 1901).

The material artefacts and architecture of such shrines, along with the hagiographical literature produced on their behalf, provide important evidence for the social practices related to pilgrimage and the cult of the martyrs in late antique Egypt. In this chapter, I use such material and literary evidence to argue for the existence of a Thecla shrine closely associated with women's pilgrimage in the region south-west of Alexandria.

EGYPTIAN PILGRIM FLASKS WITH THE IMAGE OF SAINT THECLA

About 46 km south-west of Alexandria in the Mareotis district, the ancient pilgrimage centre of the Egyptian martyr Saint Menas lies in ruins. Rediscovered in 1905, its remains are over-shadowed now by the walls of a vast Coptic monastery built in 1959 to commemorate the same saint. The modern Arabic name for this site is Abu Mina (see Fig. 6).[4]

In antiquity, Mareotis was the Greek name for (i) an ancient city south-west of Alexandria (also known as Marea), (ii) the administrative district of that city,[5] and (iii) the large freshwater lake in that district. In Graeco-Roman times, Lake Mareotis and its Alexandrian port served as a crucial trade link for the transportation of goods and foodstuffs from the interior of Egypt. Under the Romans, the Mareotis district became an important grain supplier for the capital city, as well as an area known for its wine and pottery production.[6] In late antiquity, the shores of

---

[4] In Egyptian Arabic names of Coptic saints, *Abu* renders the Coptic title of respect ⲀⲠⲀ.

[5] The Mareotis region formed a petty kingdom of the Twenty-seventh Dynasty. At different points in Egyptian history, the region functioned as a nome (administrative district) of Lower Egypt. The nome was bounded on four sides: by the Mediterranean to the north, by the town of Saïs to the east (on the Bolbitine branch of the Nile), the Nitriote nome (the Wadi Natrun) to the south, and the Western Desert frontier (around longitude 29°) to the west.

[6] Anthony de Cosson, *Mareotis* (London: Country Life, 1935), 40; C. Haas, *Alexandria in Late Antiquity* (Baltimore and London: Johns Hopkins University Press, 1997), 38. A. J. Butler describes the Mareotis at the beginning of the seventh century, on the eve of the Arab conquest: '[T]here is abundant evidence to show that in the seventh century of our era there were many flourishing towns, palm groves, and fertile tracts of country, where now little is known or imagined to be but a waste of rocks and burning sands' (A. J. Butler, *The Arab Conquest of Egypt and the Last Thirty Years of the Roman Dominion*, 2nd edn. (Oxford: Clarendon Press, 1978), 9).

Lake Mareotis began to recede, and the desiccation of the region gradually increased after the Arab Conquest; by the twelfth century, the lake had dried up completely. In modern times, part of the Nile was redirected to fill the lake basin again, and recent efforts by the Egyptian government have raised the water-table in the area. As a result, pockets of greenery have begun to spring up in the sandy terrain out toward Abu Mina.

Fifteen hundred years ago, the dry Mareotis district was dotted by small towns and cultivated plots, and Menas' shrine was a bustling way-station for Christian pilgrims from Alexandria and from all over the Mediterranean world.[7] Around the shrine, a small city grew up in support of the pilgrimage industry. Pilgrims enjoyed the benefits of heated baths, a shopping district, a wide array of hostels (from budget to luxury), large paved court-yards, and at least five places of worship, including the Martyr Church itself (built over the presumed site of Menas' tomb),[8] a baptistery, and three other large basilicas.[9] The 'Great Basilica,' annexed to the Martyr Church in the sixth century, was the largest in Egypt, measuring over 65 m in length, and 50 m in width across its transept.[10] Its size bore witness to the volume of pilgrims who frequented Abu Mina.

Outside the doors of the Martyr Church, in the streets of the town, the plaintive cries of the sick who came to the shrine for healing would have commingled with the sharp barks of artisans in their shops hawking their special wares. Popular among these wares were small clay flasks (*ampullae*) holding holy water or oil, souvenir 'blessings' (εὐλογίαι) stamped with the image of the saint. Thousands of pilgrims who streamed through the doors of Saint Menas' church carried these 'blessings' with them as they re-embarked on their journeys home. The humble clay flasks held the treasure of the saint's healing power, a power to which the

---

[7] Pierre du Bourguet compares the site's fame to that of the present day Lourdes (P. du Bourguet, *Coptic Art* (London: Methuen, 1971), 82).

[8] On the architectural development of the Martyr Church and the subterranean shrine, see P. Grossmann, *Abu Mina I: Die Gruftkirche und die Gruft* (Mainz am Rhein: P. von Zabern, 1989).

[9] For an archaeological description of the entire pilgrimage centre, see P. Grossmann, *Abu Mina: A Guide to the Ancient Pilgrimage Center* (Cairo: Fotiadis, 1986); id., 'The Pilgrimage Center of Abû Mînâ', in D. Frankfurter (ed.), *Pilgrimage and Holy Space in Late Antique Egypt*, 281–302.

[10] Richard Krautheimer, *Early Christian and Byzantine Architecture*, 4th edn. (New Haven and London: Yale University Press, 1986), 111.

pilgrims now could claim personal access. Today, hundreds of these *ampullae* survive in museum collections throughout the Mediterranean world; the geographical range of their discovery also testifies to the scope of the pilgrimage practice related to Menas' sanctuary. Ultimately, the spread of the saint's fame from Egypt 'to every distant land' (ϢⲀ ⲚⲈⲬⲰⲢⲀ ⲦⲎⲢⲞⲨ ⲈⲦⲞⲨⲎⲨ)[11] would have been coextensive with the physical dispersion of these small clay vessels and of the pilgrims who carried them.

The form of these *ampullae* varies but little.[12] The bodies of the flasks are circular (or occasionally slightly oval) and flat, originally moulded in two halves and then joined together. The neck of the flask and its two handles were added later by hand.[13] However, on a number of the *ampullae* that survive today, the more fragile handles, and often the necks as well, have broken off entirely. The numerous depictions of Saint Menas in low relief on the face of these flasks also follow a formulaic pattern (Figs. 7 and 9).[14]

---

[11] 'Prologue' to the Coptic *Miracles of St. Menas*, in *Apa Mêna: A Selection of Coptic Texts Relating to St. Menas*, ed. J. Drescher (Cairo: Publications de la Société d'archéologie copte, 1946), 8. 1. 7–8. For the Coptic texts in *Apa Mêna* I provide page, column, and line references. Claiming that a martyr shrine had international fame was a trope of miracle cycles: see, e.g. the *Miracles of St. Thecla* (Dag., 288, 310) and Sophronius, *Miracles of SS. Cyrus and John* (PG 87. 3. 3612).

[12] The formulaic character of the *ampullae* stems largely from the circumstances of their production: the flasks essentially had to be produced *en masse* for a considerable, and constant, pilgrim clientele. Indeed, according to Haas (*Alexandria in Late Antiquity*, 38), the Mareotis region 'boasted a number of pottery kilns [factories?]' including one near Taposiris Magna that registers as one of the largest discovered in the ancient Mediterranean world (at least 7.5 metres in diameter).

[13] See Kurt Weitzmann (ed.), *Age of Spirituality: Late Antique and Early Christian Art, Third to Seventh Century* (New York: Metropolitan Museum of Art/Princeton University Press, 1979), 576, no. 515.

[14] On Menas iconography, see Carl Maria Kaufmann, *Zur Ikonographie der Menasampullen mit besonderer Berücksichtigung der Funde in der Menasstadt nebst einem einführenden Kapitel über die neuentdeckten nubischen und äthiopischen Menastexte* (Cairo: F. Diemer, Finck & Baylaender, 1910). For some examples, see Drescher (ed.), *Apa Mêna*, pl. 5 and 6; E. D. J. Dutilh, 'Early Symbolism', *Bulletin de la Société archéologique d'Alexandrie*, 6 (1904), 61–8; Zsolt Kiss, *Les Ampoules de Saint Ménas découvertes à Kôm el-Dikka (1961–1981)* (Warsaw: PWN-Éditions scientifiques de Pologne, 1989); Oskar Wulff, *Altchristliche und mittelalterliche byzantinische und italienische Bildwerke*, iii. pt. 1, Altchristliche Bildwerke (Berlin: Georg Reimer, 1909), esp. pl. 18 and 19.

Within a circular border of raised dots or a laurel wreath, a curly-haired Menas (sometimes haloed) stands in a full frontal posture with both of his arms outstretched in the common pose of the *orans*.[15] Dressed in a short tunic, the saint is typically flanked by two camels who bend their heads reverently toward his feet.[16] Two small crosses frequently fill the space on either side of the saint's head, although on larger flasks this space often accommodates a Greek superscription identifying the figure as 'Saint Menas' (*O ΑΓΙΟΣ ΜΗΝΑΣ*).

The reverse side of these Menas *ampullae* displays a fair diversity of subject matter. On the majority of the flasks, a similar image of Menas mirrors the front relief.[17] Other decorative motifs are occasionally represented—palm branches, garlands of leaves, medallions with crosses,[18] stars,[19] a ship,[20] and benedictory texts of the saint.[21] Yet, most notably, on a number of surviving Menas flasks, the figure of a woman appears on the reverse—the image of the holy martyr Thecla 'among the beasts' (*ad bestias*).[22]

The scene of Thecla's second martyr trial among the beasts appears on sixteen different, published examples of Menas

---

[15] In the context of early Christian burial and the cult of the martyrs, the *orans* comes to symbolize the prayer and intercession of the deceased (or more specifically, the martyr) on behalf of the faithful viewer.

[16] The motif of the camels is connected to the legends concerning Menas' death—I will discuss these legends later. The consistency of this iconography of Menas with the camels, which also appears in a fifth-century marble relief of St. Menas found among the ruins at Dekhela (a town several miles west of Alexandria), may suggest that these images are reproductions of an original relief from Menas' tomb chamber at Abu Mina (K. Weitzmann (ed.), *Age of Spirituality* (New York: Metropolitan Museum of Art/Princeton University Press, 1979), 573–4, no. 512).

[17] See, e.g. Weitzmann (ed.), *Age of Spirituality*, 576, no. 515; Dutilh, 'Early Symbolism', nos. 3–6, 11–12, 23, 28, 29; Wulff, *Altchristliche*, nos. 1363–4, 1372, 1374–5, 1377–86, 1389, 1391.

[18] Dutilh, 'Early Symbolism', nos. 9, 22; Wulff, *Altchristliche*, nos. 1371, 1376.

[19] Dutilh, 'Early Symbolism', nos. 26–7.

[20] Ibid., no. 222; Wulff, *Altchristliche*, no. 1387.

[21] 'A blessing of Saint Menas.' Because of the limited surface space, these blessings are often abbreviated: see, e.g. Wulff, *Altchristliche*, no. 1365—*TOY ΑΓΙΟΥ ΜΗΝΑ ΕΥΛΟΓ(ια)*; and no. 1390—*ΑΓΙΟΥ ΜΗΝΑ ΕΥ(λογια)*.

[22] On depictions of saints and martyrs among the beasts in ancient Christianity, see H. Leclercq's article, 'Ad bestias', in DACL I. 449–62.

ampullae (or *ampulla* fragments) that date to the fifth or sixth century (480–560 CE)[23] (these are described and catalogued in Appendix A, 'A Catalogue of Published Ampullae with Saint Thecla'). Fifteen of these sixteen examples (nos. 1–15) derive from an identical iconographic prototype (Figs. 8 and 10). (Yet another similar, unpublished piece is still stored among the inventory of flasks discovered at Abu Mina.)[24] On these *ampullae* Thecla stands with her body slightly turned; her curving torso leans slightly to the viewer's right. She is stripped naked to the waist, revealing the curves of her breasts. On the lower half of her body, an apron or long skirt drapes down to the ground; the material is tied in a T-knot at her waist and clings closely, as if wet, to the contours of her legs. Her face is bordered by hair that falls down around her shoulders and by a halo whose outline resembles a capital omega (Ω).[25] The features of her face remain indecipherable, worn by pilgrim hands and the passage of time.

The scene seems to represent a conflation of martyr scenes from the life of Thecla, incorporating images most notably from Thecla's time in the arena at Antioch. Thecla's arms seem to be tied behind her—their lower halves are not visible.[26] She is bound between two bulls, whose torsos emerge from behind

---

[23] Recently, the excavation of pottery remains at Kôm el-Dikka in Alexandria has allowed Zsolt Kiss to establish a definitive chronology and typology of Menas flasks. By using stratigraphic methods, he has been able to date ampulla fragments with Thecla's image to the period between 480 and 560 CE. Kiss labels this period Phase I, because it is the earliest phase of ampulla production evidenced at Kôm el-Dikka (Kiss, *Les Ampoules de Saint Ménas*, 14–18). Gabrielle Kaminski-Menssen has also argued on stylistic grounds that the Thecla flasks correspond with the earliest ampullae of Phase I that have come to light in Alexandria (*Bildwerke aus Ton, Bein und Metall*, ed. G. Kaminski-Menssen, Liebieghaus-Museum alter Plastik, Bildwerke der Sammlung Kaufmann (Kassel: Verlag Gutenberg, 1996), iii. 41 ff.).

[24] Josef Engemann, *per verbis*, 9 April 1997. Prof. Engemann is currently cataloguing the pottery discovered at Abu Mina.

[25] Wulff, *Altchristliche*, 266, no. 1361. C. Nauerth and R. Warns (*Thekla* (Wiesbaden: Otto Harrassowitz, 1981), 36–7) conjecture that Thecla may be adorned with a head of 'sumptuous hair' (üppiges Haar) that mixes with her halo.

[26] A seventh-century icon from the Monastery of St. Catherine on Mt. Sinai depicts Thecla in a similar posture (*The Monastery of Saint Catherine at Mount Sinai: The Icons*, i. *From the Sixth to the Tenth Century*, ed. K. Weitzmann (Princeton: Princeton University Press, 1976), 44–5, pl. 67, B 19–20; Nauerth and Warns, *Thekla*, 43–7, fig. 17).

Thecla's body to the right and to the left.[27] While the bulls' bodies lurch away from Thecla in opposite directions, their heads turn inwards and they stare back towards the saint. Below the bulls, at Thecla's feet, crouch another pair of animals. To the right, a bear leans back slightly on its haunches with its head upraised.[28] To the left, a lion(ess) bows its head to lick Thecla's feet.[29] A sixteenth *ampulla* (Cat. no. 16), taller than the others and dating to the seventh century,[30] manifests several minor variations on this scene of Thecla *ad bestias* (Fig. 11). Within a circular medallion, a more crudely limned figure of Thecla again stands with her hands (tied?) behind her back, but now her upper torso is modestly draped in a robe that reaches to her feet. In this scene, she is flanked by only two beasts—on the right an animal (probably a poor representation of the bear) turns to her with head upraised and mouth open, while on the left a lion with a large mane rears up at her. The bulls are absent; instead, an inscription arches above the scene, definitively naming the figure, 'Saint Thecla'—*H ΑΓΙΑ ΘΕΚΛ[Α]*.[31] In a circular band around

---

[27] *ATh* 35.   [28] *ATh* 33.

[29] *ATh* 28. The depiction of the lion may also allude to the lioness's defence of Thecla in the arena (*ATh* 33).

[30] This red terracotta flask, with a slightly longer neck and a short base, stands 27 cm tall with a diameter of 17.5 cm (Weitzmann, *Age of Spirituality*, 576–7, no. 516). Weitzmann dates the piece iconographically, comparing the 'schematic figures' on the flask to a relief portrait of Apa Schenute in Berlin (J. Beckwith, *Coptic Sculpture 300–1300* (London: Alec Tiranti, 1963), fig. 115).

[31] A sixth-century Egyptian oil lamp (Fig. 30) provides a close iconographic parallel to this representation of Thecla (C. M. Kaufmann, 'Archäologische Miscellen aus Ägypten', *Oriens Christianus*, 2/3 (1913), 108, fig. 3; *Bildwerke der Sammlung Kaufmann*, ii. *Lampen aus Ton und Bronze*, ed. Wolfgang Selesnow, Liebieghaus-Museum alter Plastik, Frankfurt am Main (Melsungen: Verlag Gutenberg, 1988), 168, cat. no. 302, pl. 41). Thecla stands flanked by two beasts—a lion on the left, a bear on the right. Thecla is the only figure depicted (she is not paired with Menas as on the pilgrim flasks from Abu Mina). Instead of having her arms bound behind her, she raises them in the posture of an *orans*. In addition, the orientation of the beasts' heads is inverted: instead of rearing their heads back up toward Thecla, they now bow down at her feet (perhaps reflecting the iconographic influence of Menas' camels). However, despite these minor variations, the schematic representation of Thecla (e.g. her triangular torso) and the placement of the two animals is reminiscent of the ampulla in the Louvre. Two other oil lamps with similar depictions of Thecla are preserved in museum collections in Florence and Trier (*La collezione di lucerne del Museo Egizio di Firenze*, ed. M. Michelucci Academie Toscana di scienze a lettere 'La Colombaria', 39 (Florence: Leo S. Olschki, 1975), 113–14, no. 398 (pl. 23); C. Nauerth,

the border of the medallion reads another Greek inscription, which confers the 'Blessing of St Menas, Amen' (*ΕΥΛΟΓΙΑ ΤΟΥ ΑΓΙΟΥ ΜΗΝΑ ΑΜΗ[Ν]*). On the other side of the flask, a similar blessing circumscribes an *orans*—most likely Saint Menas himself (Fig. 12).[32]

THE PAIRING OF SAINTS THECLA AND MENAS: GEOGRAPHY AND GENDER IN THE ALEXANDRIAN CULT OF THE MARTYRS

These *ampullae* with Thecla's image raise important questions about how pilgrimage travel may have served as a social context

'Nachlese von Thekla-Darstellungen', in G. Koch (ed.), *Studien zur frühchrist-lichen Kunst und Kultur des Orients*, Göttinger Orientforschungen II. series, Studien zur spätantiken und frühchristlichen kunst (Wiesbaden: Otto Harras-sowitz, 1982), vi. 17 and pl. 6, fig. 6).

[32] Kaufmann sees this *orans* as another representation of Thecla (Kaufmann, *Zur Ikonographie der Menasampullen*, 141). However, the male lineaments of the figure—accentuated by toga, pantaloons, and staff—favour an identification of the figure with Menas. (Despite the literary legend about Thecla's cross-dressing, early Christian iconography does not portray her in male guise.) This Menas *orans* is flanked by liturgical accoutrement. On the left, a hanging lamp or cen-sor is suspended from a shell-shaped structure, perhaps a baldachin. On the right stands what appears to be an ornate metal bowl with a domed cover and cross. Just as *ampullae* discovered in Palestine have provided scholars with images of the contemporaneous architecture and topography of the Holy Land, so too the miniature images on this Menas flask may hint at the decoration of Menas' sanc-tuary. On the *ampullae* of the Holy Land, see André Grabar, *Ampoules de Terre Sainte* (Paris: C. Klincksieck, 1958); and Gary Vikan, *Byzantine Pilgrimage Art* (Washington: Dumbarton Oaks, 1982). While Weitzmann (*Age of Spirituality*, 577) cannot find any iconographic parallel of such sanctuary images accompany-ing an *orans* of Menas or Thecla, the *Encomium* of Saint Menas relates that from the beginning an oil lamp hung in the sanctuary directly over his tomb (*Apa Mêna*, 65. 2. 5). This tradition is also preserved in the Ethiopic *Martyrdom* (*Texts Relating to Saint Mêna of Egypt and Canons of Nicaea in a Nubian Dialect*, ed. E. A. Wallis Budge (London: British Museum, 1909), 57, 72). According to the *Encomium*, an oil lamp also played a role in Menas' conception. At the feast of the Holy Virgin, his barren mother had dipped her finger in the oil of a burning lamp in hope of having a child, and the Christ child in Mary's arms had uttered the word, 'Amen'. When the child was born, his mother remembered hearing this word and—by moving the letter 'A' from the beginning to the end—arrived at a name for her son—'Mena' (*Apa Mêna*, 43–4). This word play between 'Amen' and 'Mena' is preserved in the blessing on the *ampulla*: 'Blessing of St. Mena, Amen.'

for Thecla devotion in fifth-, sixth-, and seventh-century Egypt. At the same time, however, these *ampullae* prompt a more immediate question. Why does Saint Thecla appear on this pottery connected with Saint Menas' sanctuary in the Mareotis? That is, what factors led to the pairing of these two saints in the iconography of late antique pilgrimage paraphernalia?

One factor may have been that Menas shared with Thecla a curious geographical connection with Asia Minor. Actually, little is known for certain about Menas as an historical figure—the early accounts of Menas' life are quite legendary (and sometimes contradictory) in character.[33] The two main sources, the *Martyrdom* and the *Encomium*, both portray Menas as a native Egyptian who is conscripted as a soldier under Diocletian and stationed in Phrygia.[34] There, when the emperor decrees that all citizens have to make offerings to the gods, the Christian Menas deserts the army and flees to the wilderness. Returning later, he confesses his faith publicly and refuses to take part in the sacrifices. As a result, the governor has him tortured and finally beheaded.

The tradition about the transfer of Menas' relics back to Egypt appears in both the Greek and Coptic legends, although the details vary considerably. In the *Martyrdom*, it is Menas' family which transports his body back to Egypt.[35] Only the Coptic version mentions the location of Menas' shrine—the martyr's

---

[33] On historiographical problems with the sources for Menas' life, see Drescher (ed.), *Apa Mêna*, pp. i–x; H. Delehaye, 'L'Invention des reliques de Saint Ménas à Constantinople', *Analecta Bollandiana*, 29 (1910), 117 ff.).

[34] There are three prose versions of the Greek Martyrdom catalogued in *Bibliotheca Hagiographica Graeca Sociorum Bollandianorum*, editio altera (Brussels: Société des Bollandistes, 1909), 175 (nos. 1250, 1253, 1254). I use the version found in *Analecta Bollandiana*, 3 (1884), 258–70. The Coptic Martyrdom and Coptic Encomium, both based on the Greek Martyrdom, have been edited by James Drescher (*Apa Mêna*, 1–6, 35–72). For a concise summary of these accounts of Menas' life, see Martin Krause, 'Menas the Miracle Maker, Saint', in *The Coptic Encyclopedia*, v. 1589–90.

[35] In the Coptic *Martyrdom*, Menas' sister takes up his remains and brings them by ship to Egypt. Interestingly, in one tradition this sister is called Thecla (*The Difnar of the Coptic Church*, ed. De Lacy Evans O'Leary (London: Luzac, 1930), iii. 18b–19a). However, this appellation is quite late and is probably derivative of the iconographic pairing of Thecla and Menas (*Apa Mêna*, 99, n. 2).

body is placed on the back of a camel, which miraculously carries it from Alexandria to its final resting place. The eighth-century Coptic *Encomium* is far more expansive. In that account, Menas' former regiment is reassigned to Egypt to defend the Mareotis against barbarian invasions, and the soldiers take his 'holy remains' with them as protection. On the voyage to Egypt, the presence of Menas' bones wards off the attack of sea monsters with 'faces like camels'.[36] Later, the theme of camels surfaces yet again—after the soldiers have arrived in Egypt and thwarted the barbarian invasion in the Mareotis, they place Menas' body on the back of a camel in order to convey the martyr home with them. However, when the camel persistently refuses to budge, the soldiers conclude that God intended them to bury the saint's body there. After a crippled boy from a nearby village stumbles upon the concealed tomb and is healed, the site becomes publicly recognized as Menas' *martyrium*, a place invested with miraculous properties of healing.

The variations in these literary accounts resist contemporary attempts to identify a 'historical Menas'. These legends none the less articulate common assumptions about Menas during the rise of his cult in late antiquity. Devotees would have identified him as a native Egyptian, martyred in Asia Minor and then imported as a saint back to Egypt.[37] In this context, Menas' migrant reputation may have evoked compelling parallels with the status of Thecla in Egypt. Like Menas, Thecla suffers a 'martyrdom' in southern Asia Minor—the region of Phrygia, the location of Menas' martyrdom, actually neighbours the district of Cilicia,

---

[36] This event serves as a not-so-subtle literary allusion to the iconographic tradition of Menas flanked by two dromedaries. The sea creatures in the story even mirror the posture of the camels on the *ampullae*: 'Sometimes too they would take on a gentle nature and lower their long necks and do homage to the saint's remains' (*Encomium; Apa Mêna*, 61. 1. 12–20). Later, the allusion to the iconography becomes explicit—when the leader of the regiment depicts the image of Menas on a wooden tablet, he also includes 'the likeness of the animals which he had seen at sea, being in the likeness of the camels beneath his feet, reverencing him' (*Encomium; Apa Mêna*, 7–10).

[37] This predominant viewpoint contrasts with a much later Coptic tradition—reflected only in the Prologue to Menas' collection of *Miracles*—that has the saint remain in Egypt during his entire life and martyrdom (*Apa Mêna*, 7–10; Grossmann, *Abu Mina: A Guide*, 9).

home to Thecla's shrine at Seleucia.[38] At the same time, the importation of Thecla's cult to Egypt follows the same path as the geographical relocation of Menas' *martyrium*.

Yet, such thematic and geographic connections between the saints do not, in and of themselves, fully explain the frequent pairing of Thecla with Menas on the *ampullae*. After all, the images or names of other saints with diverse regional associations are also paired with Menas (albeit less frequently). The monk Isidore of Pelusium (eastern Nile Delta) appears on a few clay fragments.[39] A single Menas *ampulla* has on its reverse the haloed figure of a young Abbakon, martyred in Rome in 270 CE.[40] Another flask carries the monogram of Peter (*ΠΕΤΡΟΥ*)—perhaps the well-known archbishop and martyr Peter of Alexandria, or even the name of a local superintendent of Abu Mina.[41] Finally, a few other flasks pair Menas with a certain Saint Athenogenes.[42]

[38] In this context, the Coptic authors who write about Menas seem to have felt the need to defend the Egyptian character of his cult. In the Greek *Martyrdom*, Menas' body is taken back to Egypt, but there is no mention of Menas' shrine in the Mareotis. The writer may have been more interested in the Phrygian connections of the saint. By contrast, the Coptic *Martyrdom* includes an interpolated episode that has the saint's Egyptian shrine as its primary referent. In this new episode, after Menas is thrown into the hold of a ship and taken to prison (a journey perhaps intended to evoke a Nile voyage), he has a vision of Christ in which the Saviour offers him explicit assurances and promises concerning the foundation of the martyr's shrine in Egypt (*Apa Mêna*, 97–100).

[39] Isidore was a close relative of the Alexandrian patriarchs Theophilus and Cyril, two important patrons of Menas' sanctuary (Kaufmann, *Zur Ikonographie der Menasampullen*, 137–9, fig. 84; *Recueil des inscriptions grecques-chrétiennes d'Égypte*, ed. M. Gustave Lefebvre (Service des antiquités de l'Égypte, Cairo: Imprimerie de l'Institut français d'archeologie orientale, 1907), no. 727 (from Elephantine) and no. 732 (from Alexandria).

[40] Wulff, *Altchristliche*, pl. 17 and 19, no. 1359. Abbakon, buried on the Via Cornelia, was apparently Persian by background. In trying to find the slightest connection between Abbakon and Menas, Kaufmann suggests that the depiction of this Persian martyr may relate to the fact that Abu Mina remained unharmed during the Persian occupation of Egypt. A more likely explanation may be that the *ampulla* was made to order for a patron who had close connections with Abbakon's cult, or perhaps someone who was simply named after him.

[41] In raising the latter possibility, Kaufmann points to the absence of the title *Ο ΑΓΙΟΣ* and alludes to a known example of someone being assigned by the Alexandrian bishop to manage the shrine (Kaufmann, *Zur Ikonographie der Menasampullen*, 141–2).

[42] Ibid. 143–5; id., 'Archäologische Miscellen aus Ägypten I', *Oriens Christianus*, 2/3 (1913), 105–6 and fig. 1.

Thecla stands out conspicuously among this group as the only female saint to appear on pilgrim flasks from Abu Mina. What is it about her identity as a *female* saint that may have also motivated, and contextualized, her pairing with Menas? In the previous chapter, I discussed at some length how female saints like Thecla were privileged as gendered models for women's piety. For instance, in his first *Letter to Virgins*, Athanasius urges his virgin readers to emulate the Virgin Mary and a series of other biblical women, while in the *Life of Antony* he gives priority to the prophet Elijah as the appropriate exemplar for male monks.[43] Could the patrons of Menas' cult have chosen to pair Menas and Thecla in order to provide distinct, gendered models for male and female pilgrims?

Such a motivation is not unlikely. Artistic and architectural evidence related to the Menas cult also reflects a concern for distinctions between the sexes among the pilgrim clientele. A small ivory box (pyxis), perhaps designed to hold incense or relics, bears the familiar image of Menas as an *orans* between two kneeling camels (Fig. 13).[44] What is especially noteworthy are the other details. Menas stands within an architectural setting (perhaps a schematic representation of his shrine), and welcomes the arrival of pilgrim supplicants approaching from either side. On the left, two women advance with hands extended toward the saint, while on the right two men mirror their posture. The groups are

---

[43] Athanasius, *Ep. virg.* 1. 12, 21 (77. 35–78. 7; 82. 19–83. 12 Lefort); *V. Ant.* 7 (ed. Bartelink, 154–7). In *Ep. virg.* 1. 21, alongside Mary Athanasius highlights Sarah, Rebecca, Rachel, Leah, Susannah, Elizabeth, and Miriam as models of faith for the Alexandrian virgins. On the presentation of men and women as gendered models for imitation, see S. A. Harvey, 'Women in Early Byzantine Hagiography: Reversing the Story', in Lynda L. Coon, Katherine J. Haldane, Elisabeth W. Sommer (eds.), *That Gentle Strength: Historical Perspectives on Women in Christianity* (Charlottesville, Va.: University of Virginia Press, 1990), 39.

[44] Weitzmann, *Age of Spirituality*, 575–6, no. 514. The provenance of this sixth-century piece has been debated. Beckwith argues that the ivory was carved in Constantinople, but it may have been a higher quality product of Menas' Egyptian shrine (Beckwith, *Coptic Sculpture*, figs. 35, 36). While Weitzmann admits that it could conceivably have been produced at a Menas sanctuary outside Egypt, he also notes that the style of the relief resembles that of a Wiesbaden pyxis with Nilotic themes (Weitzmann, no. 170), as well as that of a Maximinianus cathedra whose Egyptian provenance is disputed (Weitzmann, figs. 60, 65).

spatially separated from one another by the two pillars of the central arch.

Actual divisions of space in the architecture of Abu Mina confirm an emphasis on the social differentiation of male and female pilgrim clientele. Excavations of the baptistery at Abu Mina (located immediately to the west of the Martyr Church) have shown that at least as early as the late fifth century the building was divided into two rooms, each equipped with a font (*piscina*) and a sunken basin. The provision of two rooms may have allowed male and female catechumens to be baptized separately, one group in the main enclosure (which was octagonal and covered with a dome) and the other in the smaller chamber to the south.[45] The physical separation of men and women in the baptistery finds a secular parallel in the construction of the town's Double Bath, which was completed in the sixth century. The plan of the bath includes 'two similar, but strictly separated parts' designed to accommodate the respective needs of male and female pilgrims worn out from their long journey.[46]

The urge in early Christian pilgrimage to segregate the experience of women, by means of physical barriers as well as social mores, would have reinforced the presentation of individual, gendered models for female pilgrims. This privileging of female saints for female devotees is further confirmed in the case of another late antique pilgrimage cult where a male and female saint were paired—that of Saints Artemios and Febronia in the Church of Saint John the Baptist in Constantinople.[47] The association of

[45] Grossmann, *Abu Mina: A Guide*, 17–18. More recently, Grossmann ('The Pilgrimage Center', 284) has suggested that the second, smaller font may have had a seasonal usage—in particular, for times when there were smaller numbers of neophytes seeking baptism.

[46] Grossmann, *Abu Mina: A Guide*, 20.

[47] The cult of Saint Febronia arose in Syria during the sixth century CE; by the seventh century her cult had spread to Constantinople where she became linked with Artemios. In the Church of Saint John the Baptist, where Artemios' relics were preserved, an oratory was dedicated to Saint Febronia during this period. For a brief analysis and translation of her Syriac *Life* (late sixth or early seventh century CE), see *Holy Women of the Syrian Orient*, ed. and trans. S. P. Brock and S. A. Harvey (Berkeley: University of California Press, 1987/8), 150–76. On Febronia's place in the cult of Saint Artemios, see *The Miracles of St. Artemios* ed. V. Crisafulli and J. W. Nesbitt (Leiden; New York; Cologne: E. J. Brill, 1997), esp. 13–14.

Febronia with Artemios is elucidated in one of the *Miracles of St. Artemios*, a story of a woman whose daughter is suffering from a hernia.[48] In this story, Artemios does not perform the healing; instead, in a dream he tells the mother to take her daughter to 'sister Febronia'.[49] After rushing to the church, the mother has a second dream, in which she sees the female saint applying a wax salve to the girl's genitals; she then awakens and discovers her daughter healed. Why did Febronia intercede instead of Artemios? According to the hagiographer, it was precisely because the patient was a woman: '[B]ecause of the female patient's sense of modesty, Febronia undertook henceforth to treat ailments of this sort.'[50] Thecla may have been adopted as Menas' hagiographical partner for a similar reason—to address the needs of female pilgrims.[51] And yet, neither Thecla's identity as a female saint nor her status as a martyr from Asia Minor would have provided her with an exclusive claim to be Menas' partner. The question remains—why was Thecla *in particular* selected for this role?

EVIDENCE OF A THECLA SHRINE IN THE MAREOTIS

Why was Saint Thecla privileged as the partner of Menas? An episode from the *Miracles of Saint Menas* supplies another

---

[48] *Miracle* 24 (ibid. 140–4).

[49] Ibid. 140. 23.

[50] Ibid. 142. 28–144. 1. The cult of Saint Febronia had an early association with women's piety. The *Life of Febronia* (late sixth or early seventh century CE) records the establishment of her martyr shrine in a women's convent in Nisibis, Syria, and claims to have been written by one of the nuns from that convent. This claim has sparked a debate over female authorship of the work (*Holy Women of the Syrian Orient* ed. and trans. Brock and Harvey, pp. xiv–xv, 19–20, 150).

[51] It is interesting that both Thecla and Febronia undergo a process of defeminization in their martyr trials; in the case of Febronia, her breasts are cut off by her persecutors (*Life of Febronia*, 600–1; *Holy Women of the Syrian Orient*, ed. and trans. Brock and Harvey, 168). In fact, the *Life of Febronia* explicitly invokes Thecla as an example for Febronia immediately before her persecution (*Life of Febronia*, 591; *Holy Women*, ed. and trans. Brock and Harvey, 163). One wonders whether their defeminized image made Thecla and Febronia ideal candidates for pairing with a male saint. John Nesbitt ('Introduction', *The Miracles of Artemios*, 13–14) argues that the pairing of Febronia and Artemios may have been suggested in part by their common suffering of sexual mutilation during martyrdom (Artemios' lower abdomen was crushed between two rocks, and as a result he gained his reputation as a healer of hernias).

answer.[52] One of the stories in that collection tells of a rich woman who decides to travel to Abu Mina in order to dedicate her possessions to the saint.[53] (In the Coptic, the woman remains anonymous; in the Greek, she is named Sophia.) Departing from her hometown of Philoxenité, the port town on Lake Mareotis that accommodated pilgrims in transit to Abu Mina,[54]

[52] The Greek text, from an eleventh century manuscript has been published by Ivan Pomialovskii (*Zhitie prepodobnago Paisiia Velikago i Timofeia patriarkha aleksandriiskago poviestvovanie o chudesakh Sv. velikomuchenika Miny*, Zapiski Istoriko-filologicheskago fakulteta Imperatorskago S.- Peterburgskago Universiteta (St. Petersburg: Tip. Imperatorskoi Akademii Nauk, 1900), 62–89). The fragmentary Coptic text, from a ninth century manuscript in the Pierpont Morgan Library in New York, has been edited and translated by James Drescher (*Apa Mêna*, 7–34). In addition, he also published 'Further Miracles' of Saint Menas from another manuscript in that same collection (ibid. 73–96). Drescher (ibid. 105) argues that the Coptic text represents an earlier reading than the Greek text, pointing out several places where the Greek seems to err by mistranslating the Coptic. The dating of the work is difficult. The folkloric stories themselves certainly precede the ninth-century Coptic MS—they likely reflect life at Abu Mina during the cult's heyday from the late fifth to the seventh centuries. In their present form, however, they can be dated no earlier than the reign of Anastasius (491–518 CE) based on a consideration of internal evidence (ibid. 112, n. 1).

[53] This story appears as the fourth miracle in the Coptic collection (22. 1. 15–22. 2. 32 Drescher). The Greek text presents the story as the third miracle in the collection (Pomialovskii, *Zhitie*, 68. 28–70. 26).

[54] According to the *Encomium*, the prefect of the Emperor Anastasius (491–518 CE) had the village of Philoxenité constructed in order to provide for the needs of pilgrims after their lake crossing. The new town included hospices, rest-houses, and porticoes for rest, depositories for storage, and a market-place for provisions. Such a building project would have been consistent with the reign of Anastasius, who, because of his prudent financial policies, was able to spend 'liberally on public works, and especially on the fortification of the frontiers' (A. H. M. Jones, *The Later Roman Empire 284–602* (Baltimore: Johns Hopkins University Press, 1964), i. 236). The ruins of a port facility discovered about thirty kilometres south-west of Alexandria are now thought to be the Byzantine site of Philoxenité (Haas, *Alexandria in Late Antiquity*, 38–9, fig. 5; 372, n. 58; M. Rodziewicz, 'Alexandria and District of Mareotis', *Graeco-Arabica*, 2 (1983), 201–3; figs. 6, 10). While the *Miracles of St. Menas* claim that Anastasius' prefect named the village after himself, there is no record of a prefect named Philoxenus under that emperor. Drescher notes that a Philoxenus served as legate under Zeno (479 CE), and another of the same name served as consul under Justinian (525 CE) (*Apa Mêna*, 148, n. 1). Zeno did actively promote the cult of Menas during his reign—he has been credited with the construction of the Great Basilica at Abu Mina, and the sanctuary city may originally have been named after him as Zenonopolis (Grossmann, *Abu Mina: A Guide*, 13; *Apa Mêna*, 147,

she travels alone on foot through the desert 'until she approaches the martyr shrine of Saint Thecla' (ϢⲀⲚⲦⲈⲤⲠⲰ̱ ⲈⲠⲘⲀⲢⲦⲨⲢⲒⲞⲚ Ⲛ[ⲐⲀⲄⲒⲀ] ⲐⲈⲔⲖⲀ).[55] In the vicinity of this shrine of Thecla, a soldier sexually assaults her;[56] however, she is miraculously saved by Saint Menas, who arrives on horseback and carries her to the safety of his sanctuary.[57]

Could the pairing of Menas and Thecla on the pilgrim flasks be due to the proximity of another shrine dedicated to Saint Thecla in the Mareotis? This Miracle of Saint Menas survives as the only explicit witness to such a shrine in late antiquity, but its testimony is not without merit as evidence for the shrine's existence. While the miraculous content of the *Miracles of St. Menas* has led scholars to dismiss many of them as accounts of

n. 1). The later Arabic text of the *Encomium* attributes the construction of the town to Justinian (*Apa Mêna*, 70–1). However, if the town of Philoxenité was, in fact, constructed under Anastasius, it more likely took its name from Philoxenus of Mabbug (*c.*440–523 CE), a leading contemporary theologian favoured by the emperor because of his pronounced Monophysite beliefs.

[55] *Miracles of St. Menas* (*Apa Mêna*, 22. 2. 27–31). Drescher situates the subsequent events of the story 'a mile from' this martyr shrine, based on his reconstruction of a small lacuna that follows in the Coptic text: [ϢⲀⲦⲚ Ⲟ]ⲨⲘⲒⲀⲒⲞⲚ. The Greek text claims that the woman actually 'arrived at the temple of the holy and triumphant protomartyr Thecla' (ἔφθασε τὸν ναὸν τῆς ἁγίας καὶ καλλινίκου πρωτομάρτυρος Θέκλας; Pomialovskii, *Zhitie*, 69. 11–12).

[56] The language of the story emphasizes the violent, sexual nature of the assault. Having espied the woman walking alone, the soldier 'wanted to commit a mad act of debauchery against her' (ἠβουλήθη τὸν τῆς ἀκολασίας οἶστρον πρᾶξαι εἰς αὐτὴν) and grabbed hold of her. Later, after demanding sex—'Come here, let's sleep together' (δεῦρο, κοιμηθῶμεν ὁμοῦ)—the soldier utters a barefaced threat, 'If you disobey, I have in my sword the power to kill you' (ἐὰν δὲ παρακούσῃς, ἀποκτεῖναί σε ἔχω ἐν τῇ ῥομφαίᾳ μου). Finally, despite Sophia's protest that he not coerce her (μὴ καταναγκάσῃς με τοῦτο πρᾶξαι), it is emphasized that the soldier 'seized her violently' (ἐκράτει αὐτὴν σφοδρῶς) and 'threw her down to defile her' (ἔρριψεν αὐτὴν . . . φθεῖραι αὐτὴν) (Pomialovskii, *Zhitie*, 69. 16–17, 22–3; 70. 1, 6–7, 11–12).

[57] The Coptic text breaks off after the appearance of the soldier—'Behold, one of the soldiers . . .' The rest of the story is provided by the Greek text. In the end, not only is the woman rescued, but the soldier receives punishment at the hand of Saint Menas. As the soldier prepares to rape the woman, he ties the reins of his horse to his foot to keep the animal from running away. However, when Menas arrives on horseback and rescues the woman, he also grabs the reins of the other horse and drags the soldier all the way to Abu Mina! This ordeal proves redemptive for the soldier—upon recognizing the glory of the saint, he repents and becomes a faithful devotee of Menas.

actual historical events, the stories reveal much about the social and material setting of Menas' pilgrimage centre.[58] In the case of the miracle about the woman (Sophia) rescued from rape by St Menas, the ancient editor of the collection would have had little reason to fabricate 'the martyr shrine of Saint Thecla' as the setting for the story, and indeed would have had a compelling interest in placing the story in an authentic social context. In fact, by employing the definite article—*the* martyr shrine of Saint Thecla, instead of *a* martyr shrine—the editor (or original story-teller) actually seems to have presumed his or her audience's familiarity with the site. Unfortunately, the remains of this shrine have long been cloaked by a veil of desert sand. Given this absence of archaeological evidence, it is only possible to conjecture at the physical character and location of Thecla's *martyrium* in the Mareotis.

What such a Thecla shrine in the Mareotis would have looked like of course remains a mystery. One can only imagine what shapes, colours, and images would have greeted the eye of the visitor upon entering. None the less, it may be helpful to sift through the scattered monumental evidence related to Thecla from Egypt—art forms that would have been fixed within analogous architectural settings—in order to hazard a guess at the types of material culture that may have been found within her late antique shrine near Abu Mina.

The walls of Egyptian martyr shrines in late antiquity were often adorned by textile hangings and relief sculptures of the honoured saint, as well as by graffiti left by pilgrims. A Coptic curtain fragment depicting Thecla as an *orans* (fourth or fifth century CE) is preserved in the Textile Museum of Washington, DC (Fig. 14).[59] To the right of the saint burns a large candle

---

[58] Although he decries the genre of the *Miracles of St. Menas* as tainted by 'paganism' and 'puerility', Delehaye admits that such stories remain 'precious documents for the history of the great sanctuaries,' especially in so far as they grant insight into the place of saints' shrines 'in the life of the Christian population' (H. Delehaye, in *Analecta Bollandiana*, 43 (1925), 65 (my translation from the French)).

[59] Nauerth and Warns, *Thekla*, 60–2, fig. 22; The Textile Museum, Washington, invoice no. 71.46. Height = 33.4 cm; width = 38 cm. On that textile, only the last two letters of her name (Λ Λ) survive in bold lettering above her head. Nauerth and Warns dismiss earlier theories that the figure is male by pointing out the jewellery adorning Thecla's forehead and ears.

mounted on a tall lampstand. It is likely that its counterpart originally stood on the left, but this portion of the textile has since been worn away. These lampstands not only would have provided iconographic symmetry; they also probably reflected the actual physical placement of the curtain within a shrine enclosure. The textile thus may have hung on a wall between standing lanterns or in a niche bordered by columns.[60]

In addition, a relief of Thecla—perhaps an image similar to her representation *ad bestias* on the Menas flasks—may have occupied a central wall of the shrine. In the case of Menas, a fifth-century marble relief resembling his depiction between two camels survives in the Graeco-Roman Museum in Alexandria.[61] Unfortunately, with regard to Thecla, no satisfying parallel to the *ampullae* image survives in sculpture. A Coptic limestone relief depicting a topless, skirted Thecla between two leaping (canine) beasts is in fact housed in the Brooklyn Museum;[62] however, questions about its authenticity remove it from consideration as an analogue for a relief that might have been found in the Mareotis shrine.[63]

Finally, the interiors of many late antique tombs and *martyria* also became marked by graffiti left behind by pilgrims. This

---

[60] Nauerth and Warns, *Thekla*, 62.

[61] Weitzmann, *Age of Spirituality*, 573–4, no. 512. The sculpture itself was not originally from Abu Mina; it was discovered in the excavations of El Dekhela, a town just to the west of Alexandria. However, comparing the sculpture to an ivory of Saint Menas in Milan, Weitzmann suggests that the sculpture, with its lack of architectural background, 'may reproduce the original cult image more faithfully'.

[62] Nauerth and Warns, *Thekla*, 63–9, fig. 23; earlier published in *Pagan and Christian Egypt: Egyptian Art from the First to the Tenth Century A. D.* (Brooklyn: Brooklyn Museum, 1941), no. 59; and in *Late Egyptian and Coptic Art: An Introduction to the Collection in the Brooklyn Museum* (Brooklyn: Brooklyn Museum, 1943), pl. 20.

[63] Coptic art historians during the last fifty years have regularly cited this relief in their discussions of the emergence of a Coptic style in sculpture (K. Wessel, *Koptische Kunst: Die Spätantike in Ägypten* (Recklinghausen: Aurel Bongers, 1963), 168; Beckwith, *Coptic Sculpture 300–1300*, 55, no. 121; P. du Bourguet, *Coptic Art* (London: Methuen, 1971), 176, fig. 12; A. Effenberger, *Koptische Kunst* (Leipzig: Köhler und Amelang, 1975), fig. 54). However, Donald Spanel of the Department of Egyptian and Classical Art at the Brooklyn Museum has determined that the relief is inauthentic (*per verbis*, 6 June 1996). Based on iconographic considerations—especially the shallow, woodcut-like appearance of the relief—he believes that the relief is either a forgery or a later replica of an original.

graffiti often consisted simply of names hastily scratched on plaster or stone,[64] but it also could occasionally take the form of dedicated gifts inscribed with petitions for blessings from the saint.[65] The sixth- or seventh-century bronze cross engraved with a petition to Saint Thecla in the Dumbarton Oaks collection in Washington, DC, would have functioned as such an *ex voto* offering (Fig. 15).[66] While the provenance of the piece is not certain, its characteristic form matches a type of cross found most commonly in Egypt.[67] At the top of the cross's vertical arm, immediately above the inscription, a tiny bust of Thecla depicted as an *orans* has been etched into the metal. Below, an inscription invokes the help of Saint Thecla on behalf of four persons, one of whom is a namesake of the saint. The fact that the cross is embedded in lead indicates that it was originally mounted on another surface, probably on a pillar or wall of a church or shrine.[68]

---

[64] The Piacenza pilgrim (*c.*570 CE), writing of his travels in the Holy Land, describes how he scrawled his parents' names on a couch at the site where the wedding at Cana took place: 'There, although I am unworthy, I wrote the names of my parents' (*Antonini Placentini Itinerarium* 4, ed. P. Geyer, CSEL 39. 161). At the Necropolis of El Bagawat in the Kharga Oasis of Egypt, the graffiti of pilgrim visitors, ancient and modern, still cover the walls of many funerary chapels (A. Fakhry, *The Necropolis of El-Bagawat in Kharga Oasis* (Service des Antiquités de l'Égypte, Cairo: Government Press, 1951)).

[65] For example, in the late sixth century, a Roman pilgrim named John had a votive plaque placed at the entrance to the shrine of Saints Cyrus and John near Alexandria, a plaque which testified that he had been healed of blindness by the saints (Sophronius, *Miracles of SS. Cyrus and John* 69; PG 87. 3. 3423 ff.).

[66] *Catalogue of the Byzantine and Early Medieval Antiquities in the Dumbarton Oaks Collection*, ed. Marrin C. Ross (Washington: Dumbarton Oaks, 1962), i. 58, no. 67; Vikan, *Byzantine Pilgrimage Art*, 44–5, fig. 37.

[67] Josef Strzygowski (*Koptische Kunst*, Catalogue général des antiquités du Musée du Caire (Vienna: Adolf Holzhausen, 1904), pl. 34, nos. 9177 (5th–6th cent.), 9178, 9180) catalogues three similar Coptic crosses with similar flaring arms and rounded projections at the corners. The size of the Thecla cross (h: 7.7 cm; w: 6.2 cm) is fairly equivalent to cross no. 9177 in Strzygowski (h: 8.1 cm; w: 5.8 cm). Another example of this type has been found in Palestine (G. M. Fitzgerald, *Beth-Shan Excavations, III, 1921–1923, The Arab and Byzantine Levels* (Philadelphia, 1931), 42, pl. 38, no. 21).

[68] The depiction of saints on the pillars of shrines is attested elsewhere: for example, in the *Encomium of Saint Menas* (*Apa Mêna*, 42) Menas' mother, visiting a church dedicated to the Virgin Mary, prays before a pillar on which Mary's image was painted.

This meagre monumental evidence—a curtain fragment, a limestone relief of questionable authenticity, a small bronze cross—admittedly does not allow much of a foothold for imaginative 'reconstructions' of Thecla's shrine in the Mareotis. Questions of dating and provenance to the side, even the act of drawing visual analogies rests on the somewhat tenuous assumption that different shrines dedicated to the same saint would have shared certain similar physical traits. In the end, however, these analogies have the vital function of spurring the historian's visual imagination regarding this lost *martyrium* of Saint Thecla in the Mareotis, of helping the historian to better visualize the textures and hues of sacred space in late antiquity.

On the equally vexing question of the site's location, some scholars have hypothesized that Thecla's sanctuary must have been located near the village of Dekhela (the modern settlement lies approximately eight miles from Alexandria on the Mediterranean side of Lake Mareotis).[69] In that locale, archaeologists have discovered fourteen monastic epitaphs, a marble bas-relief of Saint Menas, and Corinthian capitals with Christian insignia—perhaps the meagre remains of a fifth or early sixth-century monastic edifice.[70] However, the location of El Dekhela does not conform to the geography of the miracle account. The pilgrim Sophia encounters the Thecla shrine while travelling on foot to Abu Mina from Philoxenité, a town located on the opposite (southern) shore of Lake Mareotis. Therefore, especially given the absence of the conventional description of a lake crossing, the shrine described in the *Miracles of St Menas* could not have been located on the Mediterranean (northern) side of the lake. Instead, it would have lain somewhere in the Western Desert between Lake Mareotis and the pilgrimage city of Abu Mina. A definitive resolution to this debate over the shrine's location of course must await a serendipitous discovery by some future archaeologist.

[69] Kaufmann, *Zur Ikonographie der Menasampullen*, 96; Klaus Wessel, *Coptic Art* (New York: McGraw-Hill, 1965), 18.

[70] E. Breccia, and W. E. Crum, 'D'un édifice d'époque chrétienne à El-Dekhela et de l'emplacement du Ennaton', *Bulletin de la Société archéologique d'Alexandrie*, 9, NS, 2/1 (1907), 3–12. The oldest of the inscriptions carries the date of 524 CE; therefore, Breccia dates the edifice to the sixth century at the latest (Breccia, op. cit., 11).

Even barring such a discovery, the reference in the *Miracles of St Menas* to a 'martyr shrine of Thecla' provides invaluable insight into the pairing of Saints Menas and Thecla on the *ampullae*. In particular, it reveals this pairing of Menas and Thecla as primarily a local phenomenon of the Mareotis—the iconographic expression of cultic cooperation between neighboring martyr shrines.

CULTIC COMPETITION BETWEEN THE SHRINES OF SAINTS MENAS AND THECLA: A STUDY IN THE APPROPRIATION OF ORAL TRADITION

The *Miracles of St Menas* exhibit significant characteristics of oral folklore—their roots likely trace back to the storytelling of the pilgrims themselves.[71] *Miracle* 5 in the Greek tradition presents an example of folkloric borrowing—it tells of a crippled man who is told by Menas to visit the bed of a mute, female devotee in order that they both might receive healing. (The initial shock of the encounter spurs the woman to shout out and the man to run away!) Interestingly, the story is recorded elsewhere as a miracle of Saints Cyrus and John at Menouthis (Aboukir, Egypt), and as a miracle of Saints Cosmas and Damien.[72] In addition, the account has parallels in the healings of Asclepius.[73]

Indeed, the legend about Sophia's miraculous deliverance from rape conforms to a recurrent *topos* in folkloric literature. The motif of a woman's escape from an undesired lover continues to appear in modern folktales from Iceland to India.[74] Consistent with the hagiographic interests of the *Miracles* as a whole, this

---

[71] Drescher (*Apa Mêna*, 106) describes the *Miracles of St. Menas* as 'quite independent short stories' that 'largely derive from the common stock of folk-lore'.

[72] H. Delehaye, 'L'invention des reliques de S. Ménas', 131–2; Sophronius, *Miracles of SS. Cyrus and John* 30 (PG 87. 3. 3520); L. Deubner, *Kosmas und Damian* (Leipzig and Berlin: B. G. Teubner, 1907), 162–4.

[73] H. Delehaye, *Les légendes hagiographiques* (Brussels: Bureaux de la Societé des Bollandistes, 1905), 174; O. Weinreich, *Antike Heilungswunder: Untersuchungen zum Wunderglauben der Griechen und Romer* (Giessen: Alfred Topelmann, 1909), 179–82. For a collection of literary and epigraphic sources related to Asclepius, see *Asclepius: Collection and Interpretation of the Testimonies*, 2 vols., ed. E. J. Edelstein and L. Edelstein (Baltimore: Johns Hopkins University Press, 1945/8).

[74] Stith Thompson (ed.), *Motif-Index of Folk Literature*, rev. edn. (Bloomington and London: Indiana University Press, 1955), 377–9 (T320–328).

story in its present form celebrates Saint Menas' efficacious intervention on behalf of a woman threatened by sexual assault. However, given the fact that the woman's rescue took place near a shrine dedicated to Saint Thecla, it is curious that this individual Menas legend accords with the oral story-form most closely associated with the cult of Thecla in Asia Minor—the tradition of a wandering woman who escapes the threat of rape.

This story tradition, possibly with oral roots in the social experience of female devotees, stands behind Thecla's initial encounter with Alexander in the *ATh*, when she deflects his lustful advances by tearing his clothes and humiliating him in public. It also infuses the later narratives about Thecla and her female devotees connected with her pilgrimage centre in Seleucia. At the end of the expanded version of the *ATh*, Thecla is again forced to elude the impassioned advances of 'unruly men' who try to rape her. As her final act, she disappears into a large rock, which becomes the centrepiece of her shrine locale. In the *Life and Miracles of Saint Thecla*, two consecutive stories (*Mirs.* 33 and 34) describe how Thecla came to the rescue of female devotees imperiled by sexual assault when they wandered alone outside the temple precincts.

The social dislocation of the pilgrim Sophia, who leaves her home and husband in secret and travels on foot through the desert alone,[75] correlates with the experience of such itinerant women connected to Thecla's shrine at Seleucia. In particular, the description in the Greek text of how Sophia was discovered 'wandering around' (περιπατοῦσα) outside Thecla's shrine in the Mareotis is reminiscent of the account in *Miracle* 34 of the *Life and Miracles of Saint Thecla* of a virgin 'wandering about' (περιπλανωμένη) Thecla's sanctuary at Seleucia.[76] In both legends, the solitary wanderings of the women leave them vulnerable to sexual assault by men inspired by the devil,[77] and both are

---

[75] *Miracles of St. Menas* (*Apa Mêna*, 22. 2. 27–31); Pomialovskii, *Zhitie*, 69. 8–11.

[76] Ibid. 69. 12–13; *Miracle* 34. 19–20 (Dag., 380–2).

[77] In each case, the demonic inspiration for the deed is prompted by the men's/man's initial visual encounter with the women. In *Miracle* 34 of the *Life and Miracles of St. Thecla*, the narrator pauses to note that the demon enabled the men to find the woman (*Miracle* 34. 19–21; Dag., 380–2). In the story of Sophia in the *Miracles of Saint Menas*, as soon as the soldier sees her walking alone the devil enters into his heart (ἰδὼν τὴν γυναῖκα, εἰσῆλθεν ὁ διάβολος εἰς τὴν καρδίαν; Pomialovskii, *Zhitie*, 69. 14–15).

rescued by the miraculous act of a saint. In the *Life and Miracles of Saint Thecla*, Saint Thecla comes to the virgin's aid, while in the story of Sophia, it is Saint Menas who intercedes. The confluence of themes in this Menas legend is remarkable— a story-type involving the attempted rape of an itinerant woman is again coupled with the designation of a Thecla shrine as local setting. The parallels between the Menas-Sophia story and the legends related to Thecla's cult folklore seem too suggestive to explain away as mere coincidence. How might one account for these similarities? Given the folkloric background of Menas' *Miracles* and the proximity of a Thecla shrine, I propose that the Menas cult here may have *appropriated and redacted an oral legend originally connected with the Thecla cult*. In such an original oral setting, Thecla would have been credited with thwarting the soldier's sexual aggression and rescuing her female devotee; the account of Saint Menas' intercession would, in this case, have derived from a later oral stratum, or perhaps even from the literary redaction itself.[78]

Such a hypothesis raises the possibility not only of cultic co-operation, but also of competition between the two devotional sites.[79] This rivalry comes to expression in the basic topography and plot movement of the Menas legend. The woman Sophia is literally carried away from the Thecla shrine (where she had been accosted) to the doorstep of Menas' basilica where she finally takes refuge. Thus, in its redacted structure, the story manages to promote the shrine of Saint Menas as a privileged locus of divine protection, while tacitly branding the area around Thecla's *martyrium* as unsafe, a place where unsuspecting female pilgrims might be ambushed at any moment if it were not for Menas' far-reaching benefaction.

---

[78] The aforementioned *Miracle* 5 in the Greek *Miracles of Saint Menas* provides correlative evidence for the appropriation of legends connected with different cultic figures (Delehaye, 'L'invention des reliques de Saint Ménas', 131–2).

[79] In the last twenty years, social theorists in the fields of political economy and organizational management have given the phenomena of institutional co-operation and competition a great deal of attention. The interdependence of these two factors has even led to the coining of a new word, 'co-opetition' (A. Brandenburger and B. Nalebuff, *Co-opetition* (New York: Doubleday, 1996)). On pilgrimage as an arena for competition and conflicting interpretation, see J. Eade and M. J. Sallnow (eds.), *Contesting the Sacred: The Anthropology of Christian Pilgrimage* (London: Routledge, 1991).

The pairing of Menas and Thecla on the *ampullae* may then also be seen as an outgrowth of this cultic competition, an attempt by the Menas cult to subsume Thecla devotion under its own auspices. By co-opting stories and images connected with the local Thecla cult (thereby assimilating certain recognizable patterns of Thecla devotion), the Menas shrine perhaps sought to capture and redirect the attention of her devotees in the region. In this way, cultic borrowing would have served competitive ends. This social dynamic approximates the 'isomorphism' seen when modern business competitors, such as telephone companies, fast-food restaurants, and twenty-four hour convenience stores, come to resemble one another as they share the same institutional environment.[80] Ancient pilgrimage was a comparable, institutional environment: in pilgrimage, social practices such as religious veneration, travel, and commerce gave rise to concrete organizational forms, such as shrines, road systems, hostels, and artisans' shops, and these forms—even among competitors (such as Menas and Thecla)—tended to be isomorphic.

The theory of isomorphism suggests that pilgrimage shrines competing for the same clientele will develop similar networks of roads, shops, and shrines. Therefore, whether it be in the contemporary business arena or in ancient pilgrimage systems, competition coexists alongside and within forms of institutional exchange and mutuality. Thus, while the pairing of Menas and Thecla on the pilgrim flasks would have publicly conveyed a picture of concord and alliance,[81] such a picture may also have belied a subtle competition for local precedence and power.[82]

---

[80] Paul J. DiMaggio and Walter W. Powell, 'The Iron Cage Revisited: Institutional Isomorphism and Collective Rationality in Organizational Fields', in W. W. Powell and P. J. DiMaggio (eds.), *The New Institutionalism in Organizational Analysis* (Chicago and London: University of Chicago Press, 1991), 63–82, originally published under the same title in *American Sociological Review*, 48 (1983), 147–60.

[81] Peter Brown, observing the frequent pairing of saints in late-Roman Christian communities—e.g. Peter and Paul in Rome, Felix and Fortunatus in Aquileia—explicates these doublets in terms of a public need for symbols of unity in the face of social division: '[T]he feast of a pair of saints was a feast of concord in a potentially deeply divided city' (Peter Brown, *Cult of the Saints* (Chicago: University of Chicago Press, 1981), 97).

[82] William A. Christian, Jr., in his study of pilgrimage practice in sixteenth-century Spain, notes that the designation of two saints as joint patrons of a shrine

WOMEN'S ITINERANCY AND PILGRIMAGE: THE SOCIAL
PRACTICES OF THECLA DEVOTION IN THE MAREOTIS

In addition to disclosing faint traces of this cultic rivalry between Menas and Thecla, the story of Sophia from the *Miracles
of Saint Menas* potentially provides other important clues about
the social practices related to this Thecla shrine—especially,
women's itinerancy and pilgrimage in the Mareotis. The story
presumes that this Thecla shrine shared a common pilgrimage
network with Abu Mina. Sophia travels the road from
Philoxenité to Abu Mina, and she encounters one of the soldiers
stationed in the area to protect pilgrims from banditry—
'Behold, a man, a certain soldier from among the ones guarding
the road on account of robbers . . .'[83] According to the Coptic
Encomium, the Emperor Zeno 'assigned 1200 soldiers' to guard
the pilgrim road, and arranged it so that the revenues of the
Mareotis would fund the maintenance of this regiment.[84] The
larger pilgrimage centres in late antiquity often benefited from
similar forms of military protection.[85]

Notably, however, in the story of Sophia this system of protection breaks down. Walking the desert alone without the
added safety of a large group of pilgrims,[86] Sophia ends up being

most often resulted from social tensions in the life of the cult: 'If on the most
critical occasions, over a certain period, the general advocate consistently failed,
then a community might associate with it a co-patron (often of the opposite
sex) . . .' (*Local Religion in Sixteenth-Century Spain* (Princeton: Princeton
University Press, 1981), 92–3). In such cases, the relationship between co-patrons
was determined by both the extent and limitations of the saints' power.

[83] Pomialovskii, *Zhitie*, 69. 13–14. Brigandage was not uncommon in the lake
district (Haas, *Alexandria in Late Antiquity*, 37).

[84] *Encomium* (*Apa Mêna*, 69. 2. 24–31; 70. 1. 6–10).

[85] A military regiment also helped secure the pilgrimage route to Thecla's
centre at Seleucia (*Miracles* 13 and 28; Dag., 128). On the Sinai peninsula, 800
trained soldiers were assigned to protect monasteries and hermits, according to
the *Antonini Placentini Itinerarium* (ed. P. Geyer, CSEL 39. 186).

[86] Susanna Elm notes that female pilgrims often travelled in groups, and in
high style. Monks, priests, and occasionally bishops joined Egeria in her travels,
and the entourage of Jerome accompanied Paula and her daughter Eustochium.
In perhaps the most extreme example, Poimenia's supplies were carried with her
on a ship with eunuchs, slaves, and the Bishop Diogenes (S. Elm, '*Virgins of God*'
(Oxford: Clarendon Press, 1994), 274; Hunt, *Holy Land Pilgrimage*, 76–7).

attacked by one of the very people hired to protect her. Just as in the stories related to Saint Thecla's cult in Asia Minor, so too in this story set in the shadow of an Egyptian shrine dedicated to Thecla one finds evidence for the experience of solitary, itinerant women even in the midst of more routinized forms of pilgrimage.[87]

Might the legend of Sophia reflect the fact that Thecla's shrine was associated with wandering women—women who found themselves at the unprotected margins of the late antique pilgrimage clientele? The stories surrounding Thecla's cult in Asia Minor emphasize strongly her association with the women's itinerancy and asceticism.[88] Moreover, the demographics of late antique Egyptian asceticism provide an indigenous, cultural context for such a clientele. The monastic writers of the fourth, fifth, and sixth centuries occasionally refer to the life of ascetic nomads in the Egyptian desert. In the *Apophthegmata*, Abba Bessarion's life is compared to that of 'the birds, or sea creatures, or animals on dry land . . . household concerns did not enter his mind; the desire for particular places [τόπων ἐπιθυμία] never seemed to gain control of his soul. . . . He appeared altogether free of bodily passions . . . always in the open air [αἴθριος], being burnt by the blaze of the sun . . . like a vagabond [ὁ πλανώμενος] on the edge of the desert.'[89] Itinerancy was one of the options for monks who sought detachment [ξενιτεία] from the world.[90] Abba Ammonas endorses it as one of three appropriate pathways

[87] On the one hand, independent female travellers had the virtue of remaining independent of the social ills attached to pilgrimage and the festival days of martyrs. On the other hand, by appearing alone in public, such women faced the threat of sexual assault, as they were seen by males as available sexual prey. Various accounts decry the thievery, drinking parties, and sexual promiscuity that accompanied Christian martyr festivals (see e.g. *Miracle* 34 in the *Life and Miracles of Saint Thecla*). Christian writers also frequently condemned men who only attended church in order to lay eyes on women (John Chrysostom, *Hom. in Mt.* 73 [PG 58. 676–7]; Anastasius the Sinaïte, *De sacra synaxi* [PG 89. 832]; Dag., 379, n. 8).

[88] In addition to the community of resident virgins at Seleucia attested in the *Life and Miracles of Saint Thecla*, one may note other prominent female pilgrims like Egeria, and Marana and Cyra, who made a point of visiting Thecla's Asia Minor shrine (Egeria, *Itin.* 22–3; Theodoret of Cyrrhus, *H. rel.* 29).

[89] *Apoph. Patr. Bessarion* 12 (PG 65. 141D–144A).

[90] On the phenomenon of wandering monks in late antiquity, see B. Kötting, *Peregrinatio Religiosa* (Münster: Antiquariat Th. Stenderhoff, 1980), 304.

to ascetic withdrawal: 'Either to wander [πλάζεσθαι] in the desert places, or to go out to a foreign land where no one recognizes me, or to confine myself to a cell.'[91] The freedom of a life of nomadic asceticism posed an irresistible temptation for some foreign pilgrims visiting the monastic areas outside Alexandria. The fifth-century Gallic bishop Claudianus Mamertus (*c.*425–74 CE) thus exhorts his readers to eschew the external 'pilgrimage of place' and embark instead on an internal pilgrimage of the soul: 'On that account let us no longer stay as strangers [*peregrinemur*] in Alexandria, but turn away from Egypt, having sailed over the sea of errors and crossed the desert of ignorance, so that we may enter the homeland of truth and the country of promise.'[92] The geographical scope of this exhortation suggests that Claudianus is imagining not Holy Land pilgrimage, but rather 'the ascetic peregrinations of a monastic character'.[93] In addition, the nomadic life also posed a temptation to local monks who viewed it as the final step in their renunciation of social attachments. In this context, the Alexandrian desert mother Syncletica (fifth century CE) warns cenobitic monks against the hazards of such a lifestyle: 'If you find yourself in a monastery do not go to another place, for that will harm you a great deal. Just as a bird who has abandoned her eggs causes them to be watery and sterile, so a virgin or monk cools and extinguishes the faith when she or he moves from place to place.'[94]

Judging by Syncletica's instruction, nomadic wandering was an option not only for male monks. Women, too, left home and family for the open spaces of the desert. Evagrius Ponticus, the mystical writer who lived as a monk at Nitria, Egypt, at the end of the fourth century, feels the need to warn virgins to 'flee the

---

[91] *Apoph. Patr. Ammonas* 4 (PG 65. 120B).

[92] Claudianus Mamertus, *De statu animae* 3. 11, ed. A. Engelbrecht, CSEL 11. 175; cf. *De statu animae* 1. 22 (CSEL 11. 80).

[93] H. von Campenhausen, 'The Ascetic Idea of Exile in Ancient and Early Medieval Monasticism', in *Tradition and Life in the Church: Essays and Lectures in Church History*, trans. A. V. Littledale (Philadelphia: Fortress Press, 1968), 239–40. Campenhausen's article originally appeared as a monograph in German under the title *Die asketische Heimatlosigkeit im altkirchlichen und frühmittelalterlichen Mönchtum*, Sammlung Gemeinverständlicher Vorträge und Schriften aus dem Gebiet der Theologie und Religionsgeschichte, 149 (Tübingen: J. C. B. Mohr (Paul Siebeck), 1930).

[94] *V. Syncl.* 94 (PG 28. 1545); cf. *Apoph. Patr. Syncletica* 6 (PG 65. 421D–424A).

stories of wandering old women' (διηγήματα γραῶν φεῦγε κυκλευουσῶν).[95] In one of his many correspondences (*Letter* 7), Evagrius beseeches a bishop 'to prevent those [women] who have renounced the world from needlessly walking around [Syriac *rdâ'*] over such roads'.[96] In another letter (*Letter* 8), Evagrius urges his exhortees to teach virgins and monks 'not to take a long journey or to travel [Syriac *rdâ'*] through deserted lands without examining the matter seriously'.[97] While part of his concern may lie with the dangers and distractions of conventional pilgrimage, Evagrius especially questions the propriety of women who seek to retreat from the world by means of incessant wandering: 'I wonder whether a woman roaming about [Syriac *meṭkarkâ'*] and meeting myriads of people can achieve such a goal [of withdrawal from the world].'[98]

Attempts by monastic and ecclesiastical leaders to curb the movements of women were legion in late antiquity,[99] but the warnings voiced by Evagrius, Syncletica, and Claudianus

[95] Evagrius Ponticus, *Sententiae ad virginem*, 13, ed. Hugo Gressmann, *Nonnenspiegel und Mönchspiegel des Euagrios Pontikos*, Texte und Untersuchungen zur Geschichte der altchristlichen Literatur, 39/4 (Leipzig: J. C. Hinrichs, 1913) 147. In his *Sententiae ad monachos*, Evagrius gives ascetic men a similar warning concerning the false tales of 'wandering monks' (κυκλευταὶ μοναχοί; *Sententiae ad monachos* 81 (Gressmann, 160)).

[96] Evagrius Ponticus, *Ep.* 7, ed. W. Frankenberg (Berlin: Weidmann, 1912), 572–3 (164[aa]), trans. Elm, '*Virgins of God*', 277.

[97] Ibid. Susanna Elm concludes that Evagrius speaks of virgins and monks when he refers to the exhortees' 'sisters' and 'sons' who have 'renounced the world'.

[98] Ibid. The addressees of Evagrius' *Letters* 7 and 8 are never named although internal evidence suggests a connection with ascetic communities in Palestine. In *Letter* 7, Evagrius writes concerning 'the chaste deaconess Severa', who is identified elsewhere (*Letters* 19 and 20) as a member of Melania the Elder's monastic society in Jerusalem (Elm, op. cit.). Evagrius maintained a regular correspondence with Melania while he was in Egypt, and *Letter* 8 may have been addressed to her as well.

[99] e.g. see Athanasius' first *Letter to Virgins*, where he presents the Virgin Mary as a model of settled ascetic existence: 'She neither had an eagerness to come out of her house, nor did she at all know the streets; rather, she remained in her house at rest . . . And she did not wander in and out, but only as it was necessary for her to go to the temple' (*Ep. virg.* 1. 13, 15; 78. 13–16; 79. 17–19 Lefort). Such efforts to keep ascetic women restricted to their dwelling places extended even to the policing of their thoughts: 'When you sing psalms, let your mind agree with your spirit and let your thoughts not wander [Armenian: *yacim*] outside . . . "because the Lord lodges solitaries in a house" . . .' (Athanasius, *De virg.* 92–3, 95–6; 1029 Casey). In *De virg.* 12 (1027 Casey) Athanasius similarly urges, 'Do not wander [*yacim*] outside by means of your imagination.'

Mamertus seem to reflect their acquaintance with a specific class of itinerants within Egyptian monasticism.[100] These 'perpetual pilgrims' posed special problems for church leaders in their attempts to regularize ascetic practice (and pilgrimage) in the Egyptian desert.[101] And yet, at the same time, the monasteries and shrines that dotted the desert landscape west and south-west of Alexandria—the very institutions patronized by such church leaders—would have served as a subsistence network, a critical source of food and temporary shelter, for ascetic pilgrims and wanderers of all descriptions.[102]

In this context, amidst the throngs of pilgrim clientele who flocked toward Saint Menas' sanctuary, the shrine of Thecla in the Mareotis may have held a particular attraction for wandering women who felt themselves called to imitate Thecla's own ascetic homelessness (ξενιτεία). Indeed, the legend of Sophia attests to the physical hazards such women would have faced as solitary itinerants.

A series of Egyptian legends about female monastic transvestites, set in the middle of the fifth to the beginning of the sixth century CE, seems to confirm Thecla's association with itinerant, ascetic women in Egypt.[103] The stories take the life of Thecla as

---

[100] Even in *Letters* 7 and 8, where Evagrius may be writing to Palestinian monastic communities, his concerns about wandering women are conditioned by his experience in the Egyptian monastic centre at Nitria.

[101] Commenting on this literature, Elm (*'Virgins of God'*, 281) writes, '[W]omen who chose perpetual *xeniteia* were clearly condemned. These differentiations in our sources can be seen as attempts to control and steer. Clearly, women (and men) on the road were even less 'controllable' by ecclesiastical authorities than those in the desert.'

[102] William Christian (*Local Religion*, 122–3) observes a similar phenomenon in sixteenth-century Spain: 'The existence of this kind of national network, the chains of hospices for pilgrims, and the hospitality for pilgrims at larger shrines, encouraged the flowering of a kind of pilgrim vagabond.'

[103] John Anson, 'The Female Transvestite in Early Monasticism: The Origin and Development of a Motif', *Viator*, 5 (1974), 1–32, esp. 11 ff. On the phenomenon of the transvestite female saint in late antiquity, see also A.-M. Talbot, *Holy Women*, 1–64; E. Patlagean, 'L'histoire de la femme désguisée', *Studi Medievalis*, 3/17 (1976), 597–623; and M. Delcourt, *Hermaphrodite: Myths and Rites of the Bisexual Figure in Classical Antiquity* (London: Studio Books, 1961), 84–102. The following seven transvestite legends have a specifically Egyptian setting: 1. Anastasia: Latin text in *Acta Sanctorum* (2 Mar.), 40–1; 2. Apollonaria/Apolinaria: in *Acta Sanctorum* (1 Jan.), 257–61; James Drescher (ed.), *Three Coptic Legends: Hilaria. Archellites. The Seven Sleepers*, Supplément

their subtext—in each, a young woman disguises herself in male clothing in order to leave home secretly for the ascetic life. The transvestite disguise allows the woman to travel about freely, and eventually to assimilate herself undetected into a community of male monks where she advances in monastic piety. The geographical setting of these stories is significant—the young women most often follow a path from (or via) Alexandria into the monastic territories west of the city. In two of these legends, the Greek *Life of Apolinaria* and the Coptic *Life of Hilaria*, the protagonists' pilgrimage routes actually take them through the Mareotis to Abu Mina (and from there southward to the monastic centre at Scetis).[104]

aux Annales du service des antiquités de l'Égypte, cahier no. 4 (Cairo: Institut français d'archéologie orientale, 1947), 152–61; 3. Athanasia: Latin and Greek texts in *Acta Sanctorum* (4 Oct.), 997–1000; 4. Euphrosyne: Latin text in *Acta Sanctorum* (2 Feb.), 533–44; Syriac text and English translation in *Select Narratives of Holy Women from the Syro-Antiochene or Sinai Palimpsest*, ed. A. S. Lewis, Studia Sinaitica 9–10 (London: C. J. Clay and Sons, 1900); 5. Hilaria: in PO 11 (Paris, 1916), 624–38; Coptic version and English translation in Drescher (ed.), *Three Coptic Legends*, 1–13, 69–82; 6. Theodora: Latin text in *Acta Sanctorum* (3 Sept.), 788–91; 7. Eugenia: Latin text in PL 73. 605–24; Greek metaphrastic version in PG 116. 609–52; Syriac text and English translation in *Select Narratives*, ed. Lewis; English trans. of the Armenian text in *The Apology and Acts of Apollonius and Other Monuments of Early Christianity*, ed. F. C. Conybeare (London: Swan Sonnenschein; New York: Macmillan, 1894), 134–89.

[104] While Hilaria's stop at Abu Mina is only mentioned in passing, Apolinaria's visit is described in detail. The story tells how Apolinaria, along with a eunuch and an old man, take a boat across Lake Mareotis, disembark at Philoxenité, and traverse the desert road to Abu Mina. Six of the seven transvestite legends (Anastasia, Apolinaria, Athanasia, Euphrosyne, Hilaria, and Theodora) have their female protagonists pursue the monastic life in the desert of Scetis and the Wadi Natrun near Alexandria. This fact has prompted John Anson to argue that these legends 'may have been mass-produced by a school of Egyptian scribes at a time when the desert of Scetis had become the acknowledged center of the monastic movement'. In this context, he describes these works as a 'literary cycle' that eventually became widely disseminated in the Latin West by the sixth century (Anson, 'The Female Transvestite', 12–13). On the monastic background of these legends, see also E. Amélineau, 'Histoire des deux filles de l'empéreur Zenon', *Proceedings of the Society of Biblical Archaeology*, 4/10 (Feb. 1888), 181–206. On their character as a literary cycle, see René Aigrain, *L'Hagiographie: Ses sources, ses méthodes, son histoire* (Poitiers: Bloud & Gay, 1953), 229–230. A folkloric study of these legends may also elucidate some of their shared scenarios and plot motifs, although more detailed work needs to be done in this area before specific conclusions can be drawn.

That the life of Thecla serves as the prototype for this group of legends is made explicit in the *Life of Eugenia*.[105] The (fictional) events of the story are set much earlier (during the reign of the emperor Commodus, 180–92 CE), and Eugenia is portrayed as the wealthy daughter of Philip, the Roman eparch assigned to Alexandria.[106] Into Eugenia's hands falls a copy of the *Acts of Paul and Thecla* ('the book of the story of the discipleship of Thecla the holy virgin, and of Paul the Apostle').[107] While travelling in her litter from Alexandria to a nearby village along with her eunuchs and servants, she studies passages from this 'book of Thecla'.[108] Eugenia's reading has an immediate effect on her: imitating Thecla's example, she cuts her hair and dresses herself like a man, a sign of her rejection of family ties and commitment to the virginal life. (This physical transformation is central to each of the transvestite legends.) The connection to Thecla is reinforced later; when the author describes the reaction of Eugenia's

---

[105] Drescher (*Three Coptic Legends*, 123–4) notes a number of legendary features that the *Life of Eugenia* shares with the *Life of Hilaria*.

[106] The early setting of the story induces Conybeare (*Apology and Acts*, 147–56) to date the legend as early as the second century (he also posits a late third-century recension). However, Conybeare's arguments prove untenable. The legend more likely derives from a time period much closer to that of the other transvestite legends from Egypt, perhaps the fifth century. Such a date is confirmed by external witnesses. The late sixth-century poet and Bishop of Poitiers, Venantius Fortunatus, juxtaposes the names of Eugenia and Thecla in one of his poems (*Carmina*, ed. Frid. Leo, in *Monumenta Germaniae Historica*, iv., pars prior (Berlin: Weidmann, 1881), 192): 'we are encouraged that you seek after those things | that Christ granted Eugenia and gentle Thecla.' Almost a century earlier, Avitus, Bishop of Vienne (450–518), outlines the story of Eugenia in his poem *De laude castitatis* (PL 59. 378B).

[107] *Life of Eugenia* 2, in *Select Narratives of Holy Women*, ed. Lewis, 2 (fol. 22a); cf. *Apology and Acts*, ed. Conybeare, 158. The mention of *Acts of Paul and Thecla* appears only in the Syriac and Armenian versions; the Latin substitutes 'the teaching of that most blessed Apostle Paul' (*eius beatissimi Pauli apostoli doctrina*; PL 59. 607B). In fact, the Latin omits any and all references to the female saint. In this context, the textual tradition seems to support the hypothesis that the Syriac and Armenian versions offer an earlier reading. Given the apocryphal reputation of the *ATh* in the Latin church, it is more likely that Thecla would have been deleted from the original text, rather than added to it at a later time.

[108] *Life of Eugenia* 3, *Select Narratives of Holy Women*, ed. Lewis, 3 (fol. 22b); cf. *Apology and Acts*, ed. Conybeare, 158. In the Latin version, Eugenia travels out to the suburbs of Alexandria for the express purpose of mingling with the Christians (PL 73. 607C).

household upon discovering her absence, he borrows a phrasing reminiscent of the *Acts of Paul and Thecla* (10): 'For her parents were mourning for their daughter; and her brothers for their sister; and her servants for their mistress.'[109] In the *ATh*, it is Thecla's family (her mother, fiancé, and maidservants) who mourn a similar loss.[110]

Eugenia's change of appearance, besides facilitating her break from family, also allows her the freedom to travel on her own. Abandoning the rest of her retinue, Eugenia and two of her eunuchs walk along the road where they soon mingle with a large crowd of Christian pilgrims singing songs led by the Bishop Helenus.[111] Under the guidance of Helenus, Eugenia eventually establishes herself *incognito* at a local male monastery (under the name of Eugenius). There, as a result of her exemplary piety, she is promoted to head abbot and exercises the gift of healing. This gift of healing results in a major twist in the plot when Eugenia/Eugenius is falsely accused of making sexual advances to a woman who had been healed by her. In defence of herself and her fellow monks, she is finally forced to reveal her sex at the court of the Alexandrian governor.[112]

Although the *Life of Eugenia* is thoroughly legendary, certain details reflect implicit social assumptions about pilgrimage and Thecla devotion in late antique Egypt. Consider, for instance, the picture of Eugenia reading a copy of the *ATh* as she travelled on

---

[109] *Life of Eugenia* 8; *Select Narratives of Holy Women*, ed. Lewis, 12 (fol. 31b); cf. Conybeare, 168. The Latin and Greek editors retain this reading: *lugebant universi confusi: parentes filiam, sororem fratres, servi dominam* (PL 73. 610D–611A); ἐπεβοῶντο πικρῶς, οἱ πατέρες τὴν θυγατέρα, οἱ ἀδελφοὶ τὴν γνησίαν, οἱ δοῦλοι τὴν δέσποιναν (PG 116. 624B); cf. *ATh* 10.

[110] *ATh* 10: 'And they wept bitterly, Thamyris missing his betrothed, Theocleia her child, the maidservants their mistress' (καὶ οἱ μὲν ἔκλαιον δεινῶς, Θάμυρις μὲν γυναικὸς ἀστοχῶν, Θεοκλεία δὲ τέκνου, αἱ δὲ παιδίσκαι κυρίας).

[111] *Life of Eugenia* 4, *Select Narratives of Holy Women*, ed. Lewis, 5 (fol. 25a); cf. Conybeare, 161 (PL 59. 608B).

[112] After Eugenia's revelation, her family is converted and 'all Alexandria was like one church' (*Life of Eugenia* 16; *Select Narratives of Holy Women*, ed. Lewis, 22 (fol. 41a); cf. Conybeare, 178; PL 59. 615C). The rest of the story narrates her father's martyrdom and burial in Egypt (chs. 17–20), and Eugenia's own martyrdom (along with a virgin named Basilia) in Rome (chs. 20–30). The events in Rome may actually represent a later addition to the original legend, an attempt to yoke the reputation of the Alexandrian virgin more closely to the Roman cult of the martyrs. Conybeare himself notes a disjuncture in the text at chapter 20.

the road out from Alexandria. Early Christian pilgrimage accounts regularly highlight the reading of sacred texts as a constituent part of the pilgrim experience. The late fourth-century pilgrim Egeria reports that during her visit to Thecla's *martyrium* at Seleucia (Asia Minor) she and the other pilgrims 'read the Acts of Saint Thecla' (. . . *et lectione actus sanctae Teclae*).[113] Sometimes pilgrims even carried private texts with them to read en route to a holy place. The fourth-century bishop John Chrysostom refers to the practice of wealthy women in his time carrying miniature Gospels on chains around their necks.[114] In the fifth century, the Egyptian monk Isidore of Pelusium makes a similar connection in one of his letters when he alludes to 'the women now [who wear] the miniature Gospels' (τὰ εὐαγγέλια μικρά).[115] Such miniature codices, especially popular in Christian circles in antiquity,[116] fulfilled an apotropaic as well as a devotional function for those carrying them.[117]

---

[113] Egeria, *Itin.* 23. 5–6. Egeria's response to the reading of the Acts indicates with how much reverence that text was held. After recalling the reading, she notes that 'I gave infinite thanks to Christ our God who deemed me worthy to fulfil my desires in all respects.' Indeed, her reading of the *ATh* at Seleucia parallels her reading of Scripture during her stops at pilgrim sites in the Holy Land.

[114] John Chrysostom, *Hom. in Mt.* 72 (PG 58. 669)—ὡς πολλαὶ νῦν τῶν γυναικῶν εὐαγγέλια τῶν τραχήλων ἐξαρτῶσαι ἔχουσι; E. Nestle, 'Evangelien als Amulet am Hals und am Sofa', *Zeitschrift für die neutestamentliche Wissenschaft*, 7 (1906), 96; *Voluminum Codicumque Fragmenta Graeca cum Amuleto Christiano*, ed. E. Schaeffer, Papyri Iandanae, fasc. 1 (Lipsius: B. G. Teubner, 1912), 31; Leiv Amundsen (ed.), 'Christian Papyri from the Oslo Collection', *Symbolae Osloenses*, 24 (1945), 140, n. 3.

[115] Isidore of Pelusium, *Ep.* 150. 2. See also Gregory of Tours' epitome of the *Acts of Andrew*, where a woman named Trophima has the Gospel 'on her bosom' (*Liber de Miraculis Beati Andreae Apostoli* 23, ed. M. Bonnet in *Monumenta Germaniae Historica*, i. *Scriptores Rerum Merovingicarum. Gregorii Turonensis Opera*, ed. W. Arndt and B. Kruesch, 1/2 (Hanover, 1885), 821–46).

[116] Forty-seven out of the fifty-five known miniature codices contain Christian texts, including a number of apocryphal works: the *Shepherd of Hermas* (P. Oxy. xv. 1783, 1828), the *Acts of John* (P. Oxy. vi. 850), the *Acts of Peter* (P. Oxy. vi. 849), the *Didache* (P. Oxy. xv. 1782), an unidentified Gospel (P. Oxy. v. 840), the *Protevangelium of James* (P. Grenf. i. 8), and the *Acts of Paul and Thecla* (P. Ant. i. 13); Harry Y. Gamble, *Books and Readers in the Early Church: A History of Early Christian Texts* (New Haven and London: Yale University Press, 1995), 235–6; cf. C. H. Roberts, *Manuscript, Society and Belief in Early Christian Egypt* (London: Oxford University Press, 1979), 12.

[117] Chrysostom's mention of miniature Gospels worn by women in *Homily* 72 (cited above) comes in the context of his commentary on Matthew 23: 5, which

Might the account of Eugenia perusing the *Acts of Paul and Thecla* as she travelled give us a glimpse of a similar, social practice related to women's pilgrimage and Thecla devotion in Egypt? The textual tradition of the *ATh* in Egypt bears out this supposition: two of the Greek manuscripts of the *ATh* discovered in Egypt are from miniature codices. The smaller of the two (7.3 by 6.7 cm), a vellum leaf found at Oxyrhynchus, Egypt, dates to around the fifth century.[118] The second example, a parchment sheet found at Antinoopolis, Egypt, from the fourth century, was originally part of a deluxe codex probably owned by a well-to-do Christian—the skin is 'thin and translucent to an unusual degree' and the script is delicately written.[119] Such pocket codices of the *ATh* would have been eminently portable; they would have lent themselves well to the needs of pilgrim travel.[120] Remarkably, the picture of Eugenia reading the *ATh* in transit not only matches with other ancient views on books and their portable use, it also conforms to specific manuscript evidence related to Thecla in Egypt.[121]

disparages the use of amulets (φυλακτήρια). Indeed, elsewhere, Chrysostom asserts that these women who suspend Gospels from their necks carry them around everywhere 'as a form of powerful protection' (ἀντὶ φυλακῆς μεγάλης; *Hom. ad. pop. ant.* 19. 14 (PG 49. 196); cf. *Hom. in Cor.* 43). On 'The Magical Use of Christian Books', see Gamble, *Books and Readers*, 237–41; cf. Roberts, *Manuscript, Society and Belief*, 10–11.

[118] *P. Oxy.* I. 6. The manuscript contains text from *ATh* 8 and 9. Grenfell and Hunt date the leaf according to paleographic criteria, noting its 'somewhat irregular uncial' script.

[119] *P. Ant.* I. 13 (7.2 by 8.7 cm). On the basis of paleography, Roberts dates the text slightly earlier than a similar pocket codex containing the text of Jonah, which has been dated to the fourth or fifth century (H. C. Youtie, 'A Codex of Jonah', *Harvard Theological Review*, 38 (1945), 195 f.).

[120] Roberts (*Manuscript, Society and Belief*, 11) writes, 'Some of the parchment codices may have been imports into Egypt, brought by travellers or pilgrims at a time when Egypt was open to the outside world (and particularly the Christian world) as it had not been two centuries earlier.'

[121] The connection between Thecla devotion and literacy also has precursors in the legends connected to the saint's cult in Asia Minor. In the *Life and Miracles of Saint Thecla*, Thecla is described often as a lover of letters (*Miracles* 37, 38, 41; Dag., 129). In *Miracle* 45 (Dag., 406–8), a woman named Xenarchis receives a book as a gift. She accepts it with pleasure but laments the fact that she does not know how to read. After expressing her hope in the martyr's intercession, she unties the codex, opens it, and bends over it reverently 'as if to contemplate or perhaps to kiss it'. As soon as her eyes light upon the letters, she begins to

The scene in which Eugenia publicly reveals her identity, may also allude to a familiar artefact connected with Egyptian pilgrimage and the cult of Thecla. After Eugenia heals the wife of an Alexandrian senator, the latter tries to seduce her, thinking she is a man. When she refuses, the spurned woman lodges an accusation against Eugenia, claiming that Eugenia made sexual advances to her. Brought before the court in fetters, Eugenia decides she must confess her biological gender in order to protect the reputation of the Egyptian monks. First, she explains, 'I became a man for a short time, being emulous and imitating my teacher Thecla: she who despised and rejected the desires of this world, and became worthy of the good things of heaven by means of her chastity and her life.'[122] Then, as visible proof of her sex, Eugenia rips open her garment to reveal her breasts to the crowd.

In the story, this audacious act has the effect of exonerating Eugenia from Melania's false accusation. However, given her explicit identification with Thecla, Eugenia's act would also have had other associations for Egyptian readers in late antiquity. According to the text, she 'rent the garment which she wore *from the top as far as her girdle* . . . and the chaste breasts which were upon the bosom of a pure virgin were seen'[123] (my italics). Here, the *Life of Eugenia* presents a visual tableau that conforms remarkably to the iconography of the pilgrim flasks. It is as if the image of Thecla stamped in clay has actually imprinted itself on the bodily posture of Eugenia. The story thus reinterprets the life of Thecla through the prism of pilgrimage iconography. In this context, the *Life of Eugenia* may be read as more than simply a collection of motifs borrowed from legendary stock. Rather, the story reflects the writer's intimate acquaintance with local pilgrimage related to Saint Thecla around the sixth century.

read 'fluently and without hesitation, so well that the women around her were stupefied'. These women respond by paraphrasing John 7: 15 where the Jews are amazed at Jesus' knowledge of Scripture: 'How does this woman know letters without having been taught?' Here, the woman Xenarchis is put in the place of Christ.

[122] *Life of Eugenia* 15, *Select Narratives of Holy Women*, ed. Lewis, 20 (fol. 39a); cf. Conybeare, 176–7.

[123] *Life of Eugenia* 15, *Select Narratives of Holy Women*, ed. Lewis, 21 (fol. 39b); cf. Conybeare, 177; PL 59. 614D.

The pieces of evidence that I have treated—the Thecla *ampullae*, the story of Sophia, transvestite legends like that of Eugenia— show how religious travel provided a social context for the importation of Thecla devotion into late antique Egypt. In the stories of female monastic pilgrims who 'became male,' Thecla's legend was recast with new characters in a new geographical milieu. In the story of Sophia, one recognizes Thecla's endur- ing association with itinerant, ascetic women. In the form of portable clay flasks bearing her image, and in the form of a local shrine, the power of Saint Thecla was made visually and tan- gibly accessible to her pilgrim clientele. The *ampullae*, in particu- lar, remind us that pilgrims' devotion to Thecla would have been an acutely sensory experience.[124] It was in the textured lines of these earthen vessels that Egyptian pilgrims finally came to see and touch the presence of this foreign, female saint.

---

[124] On the sensory experience of pilgrims in late antiquity, see Vikan, *Byzantine Pilgrimage Art*, 5 ff.; also Georgia A. Frank, 'The Memory of the Eyes: Pilgrimage to Desert Ascetics in the Christian East During the Fourth and Fifth Centuries', Ph.D. diss., Harvard University, 1994, 70 ff.

5

The Spread of Thecla Devotion
Outside Alexandria and Its Environs

Egypt consists of several regions each with distinct geographical and cultural characteristics: Alexandria and the Mediterranean coast, the Nile Delta, the Nile Valley, the Fayûm (a large, cultivated oasis close to the Nile south-west of the Delta), the more remote oases of the Western Desert, and so forth. As I have shown in Chapters 3 and 4, Alexandria and its environs along the Mediterranean coast were a centre for Thecla devotion in late antique Egypt. In this region, reverence for the female saint thrived in the religious practices of women's monasticism and pilgrimage. A letter written by Isidore of Pelusium to Alexandrian female monks shows that the Thecla cult was also active elsewhere in the Nile Delta. However, Egyptian devotion to Saint Thecla was by no means limited to Alexandria and the Delta.

Indeed, extant material and literary sources confirm that even as early as the fourth century CE the cult of Saint Thecla had begun to spread southward into the Fayûm, the Nile Valley, and the Western Desert. Fourth- and fifth-century codices from towns in the Nile Valley preserve fragments from the *Acts of Paul and Thecla*. A textile fragment, a wooden comb, and a limestone relief from this same period preserve images from Thecla's life. In the Fayûm as well as in towns along the Nile, sixth-century papyri record churches and shrines dedicated to Thecla, and grave inscriptions give evidence of Egyptian women named after the female saint. In the Kharga Oasis of the Western Desert, wall paintings of Saint Thecla also survive from the fourth and fifth centuries.

What can be said about the cult of Saint Thecla in these regions? The first half of this chapter will focus on evidence for Thecla devotion in the Kharga Oasis of the Western Desert; the second half on the development of her cult in the Fayûm and the Nile Valley. As I reconstruct the practices and institutions related to Thecla devotion in these areas, I will be raising important questions about the ways that her cult spread and adapted to new, local settings. What social factors—people, world-views, conflicts—helped shape the cult of Saint Thecla in different locales? What geographical variations are evident? How were Thecla traditions transformed (for instance, in literature and art) as her cult incorporated elements of local culture? Finally, what do we know about women's devotion to Thecla in these regions? In seeking answers to such questions, I will show how Thecla devotion in Egypt was informed not only by the transcultural practices of monasticism and pilgrimage, but also by indigenous customs related to Egyptian burial and the cult of the martyrs.

DEVOTION TO SAINT THECLA IN THE KHARGA OASIS: EVIDENCE IN ART

Wall Paintings of Saint Thecla at El Bagawat

Given its isolation, the Kharga Oasis is an unexpected place to find early Christian evidence for Thecla devotion. Over 600 km south of Cairo and 240 km south-west of the Nile Valley from Asyut, the oasis is a swath of green in the vast, barren sea of sand known as the Western Desert (see map of Egypt, Fig. 5). In antiquity as well as in more recent epochs, the oasis and its main town of Hibis served as a remote desert way station for caravan routes connecting the Nile Valley with Nubia and parts south.[1] Even today, the isolation of the Kharga Oasis still impresses itself on the modern traveller. A bus ride from Cairo takes at least ten hours, the last four of which wind through uninhabitable waste-land—a lunar landscape devoid of human settlement. Kharga's physical isolation from the Nile Valley is accentuated by the surrounding geology. The oasis forms a depression in the desert

---

[1] The famous Darb el-Arbain (the 'Road of the Forty') links the Kharga Oasis with Fasher in the Sudan and Asyut in the Nile Valley. Today, the camel caravans of the Rashida Bedouin still frequent this route (C. Vivian, *Islands of the Blest: A Guide to the Oases and Western Desert of Egypt* (Maadi, Egypt: Trade Routes Enterprises/International Publications, 1990), 39–40).

floor bordered on three sides by steep escarpments, a mountain (Gebel et Taref), and a belt of high sand dunes.[2] From pharaonic times, the Kharga Oasis and its neighbour Dakhla to the west (together known as the Great Oasis) gained notoriety as places of exile.[3] This reputation continued in late antiquity when the oases became a punitive destination for Christians banished during the Christological controversies of the fourth and fifth centuries.[4] I have already noted in Chapter 3 that a group of Athanasius' supporters were exiled to the Great Oasis in 357 CE by their Arian opponents.[5] I will return to them in this chapter. It should be observed, however, that these followers of Athanasius were not alone in their fate. A decade later when the Arians themselves fell into disfavour under the pagan emperor Julian (361–3 CE) some of their number were likewise banished to the Great Oasis.[6] In the early fifth century, Palladius reports

---

[2] H. E. Winlock, *The Temple of Hibis in el Khargeh Oasis*, pt. 1. *The Excavations*, Metropolitan Museum of Art Egyptian Expedition Publications XIII (New York: Metropolitan Museum of Art, 1941), 1.

[3] Vivian, *Islands of the Blest*, 31, 33. During the Dynastic periods, Dakhla Oasis was dubbed the 'Oasis to Which We Deport'.

[4] Recent archaeological finds indicate that the Dakhla Oasis also became home to a sizeable Manichaean community in late antiquity (see Chapter 3, n. 57).

[5] Athanasius, *Fug.* 7 (PG 25. 652C). Athanasius himself may also have passed one of his self-imposed exiles at the Kharga Oasis; however this local tradition lacks explicit textual support. In his *Apology to Constantius* (probably written in 357 CE shortly before *De fuga*) Athanasius reports that he embarked on a journey out from his place of hiding and through 'the desert' in order to confer with the Emperor Constantius. He aborted the trip while en route after hearing news that his prominent supporters in Italy, Spain, and Gaul had been banished at the Council of Milan (Athanasius, *Apol. Const.* 27; PG 25. 629A). Athanasius' journey may have taken him through the Western Desert; however, his route, along with his point of origin, remain obscure, as the exiled bishop had a vested interest in keeping his whereabouts secret.

[6] The early Byzantine theologian John of Damascus, in an account of an Arian martyr named Artemius, describes how Artemius' companions were separated from him and sent 'to an Oasis of Arabia' (ἐν Ὀάσει τῆς Ἀραβίας). The writer has in mind the area around the Kharga Oasis because he proceeds to distinguish this 'Oasis Major' (Ὄασις μεγάλη) from another 'Oasis Minor' (Ὄασις μικρά), common designations differentiating the larger Kharga and Dakhla Oases to the south from the smaller Bahariyya Oasis to the north (*Martyrdom of St. Artemius* 39; PG 96. 1288C). In the early fifth century, this same distinction between the Greater and Lesser Oases of the Egyptian desert is maintained by the Egyptian historian Olympiodorus, whose work is summarized by Photius, the Byzantine historian (Photius, *Bibl.* 80. 61a–b, ed. R. Henry, *Bibliotheque* (Paris: Belles Lettres, 1959), 180).

the exile of some of John Chrysostom's supporters. One of them, a popular priest of Antioch named Constantius was 'exiled to (the) oasis by imperial order', but managed to evade capture by fleeing to Cyprus.[7] Another supporter, Demetrius the Bishop of Pessinus (Pisinum), seems to have been deported to the Oasis without incident.[8] Finally, in the aftermath of the Council of Ephesus (431 CE), Nestorius, a successor to Chrysostom in the episcopal seat of Constantinople, was banished to the Kharga for alleged theological heresy.[9] He remained there from 436 until 451 CE, when he was taken hostage in a barbarian raid.[10] Amidst this stream of outcasts and transients, a fairly sizeable Christian community managed to establish a foothold at the oasis by the mid-fourth century.

The existence of this more permanent Christian settlement is evidenced by the remains of an extensive necropolis on the edge of the desert, 5 kilometres north of the modern town and just east of the ancient site of Hibis.[11] Two hundred and sixty-three mud-brick chapels, many identifiably Christian, cluster on a series of barren ridges, their hulls baked dry as dust by the unrelenting heat of the desert sun. This same area had been used as a burial ground in Roman times: a group of pagan tombs are cut into the small

---

[7] Palladius, *Dial.* 16. 93, *Dialogue sur la vie de Jean Chrysostom*, ed. Anne-Marie Malingrey and Philippe Leclercq (SC 341 (Paris: Le Cerf, 1988)), 310.

[8] Palladius, *Dial.* 20. 43–4, ed. Malingrey and Leclercq, 396; also 310–11, n. 4. Palladius specifies that Demetrius was exiled to 'the oasis in the neighbourhood of the Mazici'. The Mazici were a Berber tribe of the Western Desert who made raids in the territory around Kharga in the fifth century.

[9] See Socrates ('Scholasticus'), *Hist. eccl.* 34 (PG 67. 816A): '[Nestorius] was banished to the Oasis, where he still remains.' (Διὸ καὶ ἄκρι νῦν καθῃρημένος, εἰς τὴν Ὄασιν κατοικεῖ). See also George the Monk ('Hamartolos'), *Chronicon* 105. 6 (PG 110. 741C): 'Nestorius was banished to the Oasis.' (Νεστόριος δὲ ἐξωρίσθη εἰς Ὄασιν)

[10] In two letters to the governor of the Thebaid (preserved by the sixth-century historian Evagrius) Nestorius speaks of his time at the 'Oasis of Hibis' (Ὄασις ἡ Ἴβις), and of the horrors he faced during his 'barbarian captivity' (βαρβαρικὴ αἰχμαλωσία). Nestorius' captors were the Blemmyes (Blemmyans), a tribe of Ethiopian nomads who invaded the Thebaid around 450 CE (Evagrius Scholasticus, *HE* I. 7. 258–60, ed. J. Bidez and L. Parmentier, 13–16).

[11] Little of the ancient town has been excavated. However, the Temple of Hibis (dedicated to the god Amun-Re) has been well preserved. Built in the sixth century BCE, the temple was adapted to accommodate a Christian church in the fourth century CE (Winlock, *The Temple of Hibis in el Khargeh Oasis*, 45–8).

cliff face that drops off to the west of the Christian tombs.[12]
Today, the necropolis is called El Bagawat.[13]

The chapels of El Bagawat testify to the active funerary practices of the Christian community resident in the Kharga Oasis
from the fourth to the seventh centuries. The above-ground
chapels were built over the actual graves. The graves themselves
usually took one of two forms: either an oblong recess in the
ground or a well-like shaft with burial alcoves.[14] On the interior
of the chapel walls, triangular niches held braziers for incense
burned in honour of the dead.[15] A number of the chapels were

---

[12] A number of the Christian tombs themselves may also be adaptations of
earlier pagan burial space. The original religious character of many of the above-
ground chapels remains indeterminable because no decoration survives. However, the Metropolitan Museum of Art uncovered remains of pagan burials in
some of the chapels at El Bagawat early in this century (W. Hauser, 'The
Christian Necropolis in Khargeh Oasis', *Bulletin of the Metropolitan Museum of
Art*, 27 (March 1932), 38–50). These finds prompted Hauser to push the beginning of the necropolis back to the middle of the third century CE, and to argue
that 'the chapels were begun by the pagan community, and that as Christianity
spread among the leading families, instead of abandoning the cemetery, they went
on using their burial vaults and building new tombs which they decorated with
the *crux ansata*, the monograms of Christ, the *A Ω*, and biblical and allegorical
scenes' (ibid. 50). Ahmed Fakhry (*The Necropolis of El-Bagawat in Kharga Oasis*
(Cairo: Government Press, 1951), 2) agrees that Christians 'continued to bury
their dead in the same necropolis where their ancestors were buried and where
their pagan neighbours and relatives were also burying their dead'. The discovery
of papyri containing the archives of a society of embalmers and gravediggers
(including both pagans and Christians) confirms the contiguity of pagan and
Christian burial practice at the Kharga in the third century CE (Hauser, 'The
Christian Necropolis in Khargeh Oasis', 50).

[13] According to C. K. Wilkinson ('Early Christian Paintings in the Oasis of
Khargeh', *Bulletin of the Metropolitan Museum of Art*, 23/2 (1928), 29) the name
El Bagawat may be a corruption of the Arabic *kabawat* ('the domes'), which
would allude to the characteristic style of roof employed in the construction of
the chapels.

[14] P. Grossmann, 'Bagawat, Al-, Location and Architecture', in *The Coptic
Encyclopedia*, ii. 326.

[15] W. de Bock, *Matériaux pour servir à l'archéologie de l'Égypte chrétienne*
(St. Petersburg: Eugene Thiele, 1901), 10) originally thought these niches were
for the lighting of lamps. However, Ahmed Fakhry, observing the lack of soot
on the plaster within these niches, raised questions about this theory. The discovery of a decorated limestone brazier for incense (with burnt remains) inside
a niche in Chapel 36 made clear the use of this space (Fakhry, *Necropolis of
El-Bagawat*, 26–7).

equipped with forecourts, antechambers, and apses.[16] These constructions were designed to accommodate the flow of visitors and the celebration of memorial liturgies.[17] Some chapels have remains of semicircular couches and masonry tables where visitors ate meals in honour of the dead.[18]

A visit to the chapels at El Bagawat would have been an intensely visual experience. In various chapels vividly coloured wall paintings greet the eyes of the visitor: simple *ankh*-crosses painted in rich burgundy; geometric designs in yellows, reds, and blues; green vine tendrils ripe with grapes; multi-hued peacocks and phoenixes with plumes or wings outstretched. Two of the chapels—the Chapel of the Exodus (no. 30) and the Chapel of Peace (no. 80)—contain wall paintings of biblical scenes and figures. In both, one finds images of Saint Thecla.

The Chapel of the Exodus, one of the earliest chapels in the necropolis (mid-fourth century CE),[19] is located at the northern end of the cemetery. It derives its name from its noteworthy depiction of Moses and the Israelites fleeing a phalanx of Egyptian soldiers, a scene that encircles the lower perimeter of the chapel dome. Moses' approach to the Promised Land (depicted as a large architectural structure) dominates the northern face of the dome and confronts the visitor as he or she enters from the south (Fig. 16). A host of other biblical scenes— executed throughout in a similar, schematic style[20]—populate the

[16] See Fakhry's classification of chapel types (ibid. 19–22, 31, table 1).

[17] Several of the mausolea—including a multi-room building complex at the northern end of the cemetery (Chapels 23–5) and a three-aisled basilica near its centre (Chapel 180)—actually functioned as small churches.

[18] Grossmann, 'Bagawat, Al-, Location and Architecture'.

[19] The early dating of the Chapel of the Exodus has been based by Fakhry (*Necropolis of El-Bagawat*, 2, 9) on its architectural type, the decoration of its façade, its placement in relation to surrounding structures, and the character of its iconography. On the architectural relationship of the Chapel of the Exodus to the structures later built around it, see de Bock, *Matériaux*, 16 ff.; and C. M. Kaufmann, *Ein altchristliches Pompeji in der libyschen Wuste* (Mainz: Franz Kirchheim, 1902), 13 ff. See also Grossmann's 'Plan of the complex in the northern area of al-Bagawat' (*The Coptic Encyclopedia*, ii. 328) where he also includes the chapel in the earliest stage of building construction.

[20] Henri Stern ('Les peintures du mausolée "de l'Exode" à El-Bagaouat', *Cahiers archéologiques*, 11 (1960), 119) notes in particular the artist's limited repertoire in the portrayal of human portraits and bodily movements, his simplified variations on types of clothing, and his stylized depiction of buildings and trees.

arched wall space below this rendering of the Exodus: to the north (facing the door), Adam and Eve in the Garden and Noah in the Ark; to the west, Daniel in the lions' den, the three men in the furnace, and the torture of Isaiah; to the south (above the entrance), the arrival of Abraham's servants at the home of Rebecca, three scenes from the life of Jonah, and the tribulation of Job; and to the east, a seated Susannah, Jeremiah before the Temple, and Abraham's attempted sacrifice of Isaac.

Amidst all these figures from Hebrew scripture, in the middle of the eastern arch a scene from the life of Thecla catches the eye (Figs. 17–19). Thecla stands in the pose of an *orans*, arms outstretched and head upraised. To the left of her head, an inscription in Greek (recently destroyed)[21] identified her as THEKLA. Her visage now obscured, Thecla is dressed in a tan robe, the skin of her arms and legs a light reddish brown. Around her, dark red flames lick at her legs and torso.

Above, an amorphous, dark grey thundercloud looms. The cloud is flecked with large, white-dotted x's, probably meant to represent hail; below, a sheet of lighter grey vertical dashes descends in a torrent upon Thecla's head and the fire that engulfs her. The scene is a vivid rendering of Thecla's trial by fire in chapter 22 of the *Acts of Paul and Thecla*.

The public executioners spread out the wood and commanded her to mount the pyre. Then, having made the sign of the cross, she climbed up on the wood. They ignited it; and although a great fire burst forth, the fire did not touch her. For God, showing compassion, raised a tumultuous noise beneath the earth; and above, a cloud full of rain and hail cast a shadow and its entire volume poured out, so that . . . the fire was quenched and Thecla was saved.

Similar portraits of Thecla in the fire have been discovered on fourth-century gold glass medallions from Cologne, and on a fifth-century Coptic textile from ancient Panopolis (Akhmim) in Egypt.[22]

---

[21] Within the past century, many of the identifying inscriptions in the chapel were defaced. Fakhry (*Necropolis of El Bagawat*, 44) reports that, in 1926, the chief-guard of the Egyptian Antiquities, who had been instructed to prevent further graffiti to the chapel, unwittingly destroyed the Greek inscriptions, thinking them to be the work of modern vandals.

[22] The two gold-glass fragments, now kept in the British Museum, depict Thecla as a naked *orans* standing between tongues of flame within a circular border. One of these pieces was discovered in the cemetery near St. Severin in

Thecla's perseverance amidst the fire (and amongst the beasts) earned her early acclaim as a 'protomartyr' of the Christian church.[23] Here in the Chapel of the Exodus, the artist portrays Thecla in a similar light. Along with the three men in the furnace on the western arch, she serves as a visual example of faithful endurance in the face of suffering, and of God's deliverance.

The depiction of Thecla in a funerary chapel in the Western Desert is, in itself, intriguing. Even more remarkable, however, is the fact that Thecla is the only non-biblical figure, and indeed (excepting perhaps an unlabelled shepherd scene) *the only Christian figure*, to be depicted in the Chapel of the Exodus. No apostles and no other saints (Egyptian or otherwise) make an appearance. Even if one were to regard a shepherd on the eastern arch as a depiction of Christ the Good Shepherd,[24] Thecla's location in relation to this scene would only reinforce her privileged place as the only Christian saint of the chapel—Thecla and the shepherd occupy equivalent, symmetrically balanced spaces on either side of a large tree that bisects the eastern arch.

Is Thecla's presence in the chapel a meaningless anomaly, or does her presence in fact attest to her elevated status among Christians living at the oasis? A second wall painting of Thecla in the same necropolis would seem to indicate an enduring, vibrant, local interest in the female protomartyr. In the fifth- or

Cologne (*Catalogue of Early Christian Antiquities*, ed. O. M. Dalton (London: British Museum, 1901)), no. 618, 629; C. Nauerth and R. Warns, *Thekla* (Wiesbaden: Otto Harrassowitz, 1981), 22–4). The Coptic textile, which depicts Thecla similarly, also had a funerary provenance. It was discovered during excavations of a cemetery at Achmim (Robert Forrer, *Die frühchristlichen Alterthümer aus dem Gräberfelde von Achmim-Panopolis* (Strasburg: F. Lohbauer, 1893), pl. 16, fig. 10; Nauerth and Warns, op. cit.).

[23] For example, see the Prologue to the fifth-century *Life and Miracles of Saint Thecla* where the author introduces Thecla as 'apostle and martyr,' and later as 'protomartyr' (*Life*, Prologue, 2–3, 26–7, 35 (Dag., 168–70); *Miracles*, Prologue, 1–2, 4–5 (Dag., 284)). In the Prologue of the *Life*, Thecla earns the title 'apostle and martyr'. (*Life*, Prologue, 2–3, 26–7, 35; Dag., 168–71).

[24] C. M. Kaufmann and later Henri Stern question whether the shepherd should be interpreted as a portrayal of Christ given its non-central placement on the eastern arch of the chapel. Other representations of the Good Shepherd in early Christian catacombs and sarcophagi generally occupy a central space in iconographic compositions (Kaufmann, *Ein altchristliches Pompeji*, 43, n. 1; Stern, 'Les peintures du Mausolée "de l'Exode", à El-Bagaouat', 106–7).

sixth-century Chapel of Peace, Thecla appears again, now paired with her mentor, the apostle Paul (Fig. 20).[25] Here, the artistry is more refined, the body lines and gestures more fluid. On the south side of the dome (above the doorway), the two figures sit facing each other on gold-coloured stools, their legs crossed. On the left Thecla wears a loose fitting greenish-grey dress and a veil down to her waist; her eyes are cast down toward her lap where she holds a yellow book or a writing tablet. Thecla writes in the book with a pen, while Paul sits across from her on the right, gesturing toward the book with a pointing stick he holds in his hand. Greek inscriptions above their heads identify them as THEKLA and PAULOS. Thecla's importance is accentuated by the female company she keeps: Eve stands immediately to her left, the Virgin Mary to her (and Paul's) right.[26] The rest of the dome only accommodates a handful of other figures: allegorical personifications of Prayer, Justice, and Peace (from whom the chapel takes its name), as well as select personages from the Septuagint —Adam (next to Eve), Abraham sacrificing Isaac with Sarah looking on, Daniel, Jacob, and Noah. This scene of Thecla being instructed by Paul indeed may not have been the only one of its type in the necropolis; a badly preserved wall painting in the fifth-century Chapel 25 (part of a large building complex in front of the Chapel of the Exodus) retains hints of a similar scene.[27]

---

[25] C. K. Wilkinson mistakenly identifies the two figures as two Egyptian saints named Thecla and Paul, presumably from the Coptic *Martyrdom of Paese and Thecla* (Wilkinson, 'Early Christian Paintings in the Oasis of Khargeh', 29–36; on the *Martyrdom of Paese and Thecla*, see my discussion later in this chapter).

[26] The Holy Spirit is depicted as a dove above Mary's shoulder on the right, an indication that the painting is of the Annunciation.

[27] The painting occupies the western wall of the chapel's inner chamber. Now almost entirely obliterated, it depicts two persons seated in chairs facing one another. Both sit with legs crossed. The figure on the right appears to be female. She is veiled (?) and holds in her hands a rectangular object, perhaps a book, of burnt orange colour. The figure on the left is that of a man: a loose hood or scarf hangs down behind his head, and he holds out an unidentifiable object in his hand. What remains of a large *ankh* cross fills the centre of the arched wall space above the scene. To the right of the woman, a square structure of muted red spans the corner of the west and north walls, perhaps connected to another scene, now obscured. A scene of Abraham and Isaac, only slightly better preserved (and the only other extant painting in the chapel), is also found on the north wall (Fakhry, *Necropolis of El-Bagawat*, 80, 87–8).

The Community Behind the Wall Paintings:
Alexandrian Virgins in Exile

The wall paintings of Thecla in the Chapel of the Exodus and the Chapel of Peace provide artistic evidence for Thecla devotion in the Kharga Oasis as early as the fourth century CE. This artistic evidence for Thecla devotion in the Kharga Oasis would seem to be confirmed by contemporary documentary evidence: two fourth-century ostraca recently unearthed at Kysis in the southern part of the Kharga Oasis attest the presence of local women named after the female saint.[28] How then did the cult of Saint Thecla find its way to this remote locale? What kind of community, what kind of social practices, may have stood behind the art at El Bagawat? For an answer, I turn back to the group of Athanasius' followers who were exiled to the oasis in the middle of the fourth century.

In his *Apologia de fuga sua*, the Bishop of Alexandria reports on the atrocities committed by the Arians against his followers in Alexandria. Ascetic women in Athanasius' camp seem to have been special targets for Arian persecution. He writes that at Easter of 357 CE virgins were imprisoned and the houses of widows were confiscated.[29] At Pentecost of the same year, the Arian commander, 'having lighted a pyre . . . placed certain virgins near the fire and tried to force them to say that they were of the Arian faith. And when he saw that they were prevailing, and did not give heed to the fire, he immediately stripped them naked, and beat them in the face in such a way that for some time they could hardly be recognized.'[30] Following this torture of the virgins, the Arians instigated another rash of arrests and beatings, before banishing 'all those who had been seized, *even the virgin* . . . to the Great Oasis'.[31]

Some these virgins exiled to the oasis probably were among those who revered Thecla as their patron saint (see Chapter 3). Athanasius addressed his treatise *On Virginity* to such a community of Alexandrian virgins, exhorting them to continue

---

[28] *O. Douch* I. 20. 1 (306–430 CE); III. 226. 2 (4th cent. CE).

[29] Athanasius, *Fug.* 6 (PG 25. 652A).   [30] Ibid. (PG 25. 652B).

[31] Athanasius, *Fug.* 7 (PG 25. 652C). The singular use of 'virgin' here seems to be collective.

modelling their lives after that of Saint Thecla. I believe that he wrote this treatise to the virgins while they were still in Alexandria, as they were facing the prospect of torture and exile. Indeed, his exhortation on the life of Thecla may also have alluded to the threat of the Arian persecution: 'Now abide with the blessed Thecla . . . Despise the judge . . . Let the force of the fire not frighten you.'[32]

These virgins would have brought their devotion to Saint Thecla with them in exile to the Kharga Oasis. Indeed, an iconographic detail in the Chapel of the Exodus may in fact suggest a connection with this community of ascetic women.[33] Immediately below the scene of Thecla amidst the flames, seven female figures process in a line to the left, each carrying a lighted torch (Fig. 21). An inscription (now defaced) originally identified the figures as *parthenoi*—'virgins'.[34] Does the art in the Chapel of the Exodus here provide access to the lives of the early Christians who frequented El Bagawat in the fourth century? If so, what else does the art divulge about its ancient patrons? How might the chapel itself be connected with ascetic women exiled from Alexandria?

In order to begin to answer such questions, it is important to view the image of Saint Thecla in its iconographic context. On the eastern arch of the Chapel of the Exodus, three enigmatic scenes have been painted immediately below Thecla's trial by fire. I have already mentioned the procession of seven virgins (παρθένοι). These figures hold torches (or lamps) and walk upon a pathway that leads from a small, square structure (perhaps an arched doorway or domed building) to the façade of a temple with seven steps and four columns.[35] Below the virgins, another scene depicts two figures leading camels packed for a journey in the opposite direction (to the right). Carrying staffs, they walk amidst

---

[32] Athanasius, *De virg.* 211–13 (1034 Casey).

[33] M. L. Thérel ('Le composition et le symbolisme de l'iconographie du mausolée de l'Exode à El-Bagawat', *Rivista di archeologia cristiana*, 45 (1969), 223–70) was the first to argue this connection.

[34] A later pilgrim, mimicking the original inscription, wrote *parthenoi* a second time above the line of virgins (de Bock, *Matériaux*, 23).

[35] The square structure is maroon and crossed by taupe lines. The pillars of the temple are golden brown; edged with darker coffee lines with a maroon inside border.

a sparse grove of bushes or small trees in the direction of the square structure. Finally, to the right of the square structure, there is a third scene: an unidentified figure stands alone in a darkened area beneath a large tree (Fig. 22). The area, mauve with tan highlights and interspersed with maroon vertical dashes, has an irregular, arched border. The figure is an *orans*—with arms outstretched and head in right profile, it gazes upwards toward the apex of the arch.

A procession of virgins, two persons leading camels, and a solitary *orans* in a darkened space—how do these scenes relate to the visual presentation of Thecla as a martyr-saint? What, if anything, do these neighbouring images tell us about the expectations, experiences, and assumptions of the fourth-century community of Christians in the Kharga Oasis?

The identity of the anonymous *orans*, in particular, has sparked considerable debate among art historians.[36] Recently,

---

[36] Some have suggested that the figure is Abraham's wife Sarah (in connection with a painting depicting the Sacrifice of Isaac located to the right of the *orans* (Kaufmann, *Ein altchristliches Pompeji*, 39–40; O. Wulff, *Altchristliche und byzantinische Kunst*, i. *Die altchristliche Kunst* (Berlin: Akademische Verlagsgesellschaft Athenaion m.b.h., 1918), 97; Fakhry, *Necropolis of El Bagawat*, 63). It is unclear why the artist of the Chapel of the Exodus would have depicted Sarah standing in a darkened area under a tree. Sarah appears alongside Abraham and Isaac in the Chapel of Peace, although in that later painting Sarah's position in relation to the sacrifice scene is quite different. Others have argued that the *orans* may represent another scene from the *Acts of Paul and Thecla*: an image of Paul praying for Thecla (*ATh* 23; Nauerth and Warns, *Thekla*, 14 ff.), or an image of Thecla herself disappearing into the rock at Seleucia (*ATh*[Sel] 44; A. Grabar, *Martyrium* (Paris: Collège de France, 1946), ii. 21; Stern, 'Les peintures du Mausolée "de l'Exode", à El-Bagaouat', 104–6; J. Schwartz, 'Nouvelles études sur des fresques d'El-Bagawat', *Cahiers archéologiques*, 13 (1962), 4–5). Two factors militate against the interpretation that the figure is Paul. First, we have no artistic parallel for a scene of Paul praying for Thecla, and the anonymous *orans* does not exhibit any of the conventional features of Pauline iconography. In early Christian art, Paul usually appears as a balding man with a long, pointed beard—on the iconography of Paul, see E. Dassmann, *Paulus in frühchristlicher Frömmigkeit und Kunst* (Opladen: Westdeutscher Verlag, 1982). Second, the lack of an identifying inscription makes it even more unlikely that the figure is Paul. Given the fact that names or labels accompanied the other biblical figures in the chapel, one would certainly expect the same in the case of the apostle. In this context, one would not expect to find Paul anonymously represented in a chapel devoid of other apostolic figures. The interpretation of the *orans* as an image of Thecla's disappearance into the rock

however, a compelling interpretation of the *orans* has been suggested, one that grounds the wall painting in the immediate social context of early Christian funerary practice: *the anonymous* orans *is a representation of the deceased buried in the tomb below the Chapel of the Exodus.*[37] Such an interpretation makes sense of the surrounding images: the darkened space around the deceased represents the tomb or chapel itself; the square structure immediately to the left represents the door to the chapel.[38]

On the walls of early Christian burial chambers, it is not uncommon to find portraits of the dead in the form of *orantes*. The catacombs of Rome abound with examples.[39] Such *orantes* are sometimes accompanied by inscriptions naming the deceased.[40] Often, however, they are not—the deceased simply remain anonymous.[41]

The use of the *orans* type to represent the deceased was not restricted to early Christian burial practice in Rome; it had antecedents in ancient Egyptian art and hieroglyphs. In earlier

runs into problems of dating. The legend about Thecla's disappearance can be dated no earlier than the middle of the fifth century CE, and therefore is probably later than the chapel itself. Indeed, we lack iconographic analogues for such a scene prior to the fourteenth century (R. Warns, 'Weitere Darstellungen der heiligen Thekla', in G. Koch (ed.), *Studien zur frühchristlichen Kunst* (Wiesbaden: Otto Harrassowitz, 1986), ii. 94–101, pl. 25 and 26. 1). A Coptic limestone relief of Thecla in the Brooklyn Museum was once cited as a possible parallel (Nauerth and Warns, *Thekla*, 14, n. 2; 63–9) but Donald Spanel of the Brooklyn Museum (*per verbis* 6 June 1996) has since determined the work to be inauthentic (probably a forgery).

[37] Thérel, 'Le composition et le symbolisme', 269.

[38] Thérel (ibid.) notes that the depiction of the door is inspired by the 'stèle fausse-porte' of Egyptian tombs.

[39] See, e.g. *Roma sotterranea: Le pitture delle catacombe romane*, ed. J. Wilpert (Rome: Desclée, Lefebvre, 1903), ii, pl. 43, 64, 84, 88, 90, 92, 118, 163, 185, 188.

[40] In the Catacomb of St. Callixtus, six *orantes* in one cubiculum are identified by inscriptions as Dionysia, Nemesius, Procopius, Eliodora, Zoe, and Arcadia (Fabrizio Mancinelli, *The Catacombs of Rome and the Origins of Christianity* (Florence: SCALA, 1981), 23, fig. 43; *Roma sotterranea*, ed. Wilpert, ii, pl. 110).

[41] In the case of a late third-century painting in the Catacomb of Priscilla, the *orans* of a deceased woman is not identified by name—she is known to art historians only as the 'Veiled Woman' (*Domna velata*). The same wall depicts other scenes from her life (J. Stevenson, *The Catacombs: Rediscovered Monuments of Early Christianity* (London: Thames and Hudson, 1978), 61, 88 (fig. 63); also *Roma sotterranea*, ed. Wilpert, ii, pl. 79–81).

times, the figure standing with arms stretched upward had been a determinative component in hieroglyphic writing of the verb 'to mourn,' and the ancient letter *ka* (which resembled arms held aloft) had symbolized the magical essence of the dead.[42] During the Graeco-Roman period, the *orans* was regularly used to depict the deceased on Egyptian funerary stelae. Indeed, the anonymous *orans* in the Chapel of the Exodus shares several distinctive features with *orantes* on contemporary stelae from the fourth century CE:[43] the torso of the figure appears in frontal view; the head and lower limbs are in right profile. The depiction of the feet in profile, and the vertical orientation of the forearms, have especially been identified as artistic conventions native to Egypt.[44] Finally, the doorway to the tomb and the darkened space surrounding the figure (the tomb itself) serve a similar 'framing' function to the architectural borders regularly employed on the stelae reliefs. Thus, in portraying the deceased as an *orans*, the artist of the Exodus Chapel borrowed forms from Egyptian iconography as well as from ancient Christian art.[45]

Who was the person buried in the Chapel of the Exodus? Reporting on the banishment of his followers to the oasis,

---

[42] Roger V. McCleary, 'Funerary Stelae with the Orans-Motif: Workshop Traditions of Terenuthis during the Roman Occupation', Ph.D. diss.; University of Toronto, 1985, 447.

[43] McCleary, 'Funerary Stelae', 450 ff.

[44] Hilda Zaloscer, 'Gibt es eine koptische Kunst?', *Jahrbuch der österreichischen byzantinischen Gesellschaft*, 16 (1967), 236, 240–4, fig. 1–2; F. A. Hooper, *Funerary Stelae from Kom Abou Billou*, Kelsey Museum of Archeology Studies, no. 1 (Ann Arbor: University of Michigan, 1961), 20 (see also pl. 1–9 (a,b)). Hooper contrasts the posture of the Graeco-Roman *orantes* to the more horizontal orientation of the arms in late Christian reliefs.

[45] The Christian adaptation of earlier Egyptian funerary conceptions explains other decorative motifs in the chapel as well, especially the prevalence of ankh crosses and Nile boats. The paintings of Nile boats on the dome of the Chapel of the Exodus, like those on the stelae from Kom Abu Billou, would signify the continuity with 'the ancient Egyptian conception of the afterlife as a voyage' (McCleary, 'Funerary Stelae with the Orans-Motif', 499, n. 233; cf. Stern, 'Les peintures', 96, n. 5; C. Bonner, 'The Ship of the Soul on a Group of Grave-Stelae from Therenuthis', in *Proceedings of the American Philosophical Academy*, 85 (1942), 84–91). In this context, McCleary's disassociation of the Christian *orans* from its earlier pagan counterpart is overstated (op. cit., v). He bases his conclusion on a comparison of funerary reliefs, but does not take into account the influence of ancient Egyptian motifs in other media.

Athanasius notes that the Arians 'drove them away so cruelly that some of them died on the way while others died in the place of exile itself'.[46] Could the deceased have been an Alexandrian exile to the Kharga Oasis, one of the virgins in Athanasius' circle who held Thecla as their patron saint?[47]

The iconographic details seem to suggest that the deceased was, in fact, an ascetic devotee of Thecla. First, the fact that the artist painted a procession of virgins next to the *orans* is significant. This scene probably provides a glimpse into the ascetic community of the deceased.[48] Second, the iconographic placement of the *orans* immediately below the image of Thecla seems to confirm that the deceased had a special affinity for the female saint (Fig. 23). The portrayal of the dead in the presence of a favoured saint or martyr was a recurrent motif in early Christian funerary art.[49] On a fourth-century wall painting in the Roman Catacomb of Domitilla, the deceased—a woman named Veneranda—is shown being led into heaven by the martyr Petronilla.[50] Depicted as an *orans*, she is identified by an inscription as the person buried in that grave chamber (the Arcosolium of Veneranda). Other examples of the *orantes* in the company of saints survive in the Catacomb of Saint Thecla and the Catacomb of Marcus and Marcellinus in Rome.[51]

The connection between Thecla and the deceased portrayed in the Chapel of the Exodus does not depend merely on spatial proximity, but also on similarity of bodily posture. The *orans*, with

---

[46] *Fug.* 7 (PG 25. 653A).

[47] With only rare exception (e.g. the theory of Nauerth and Warns (n. 36 above)) art historians have viewed the *orans* as a female figure. Representative of this view is Oskar Wulff, (*Altchristliche und byzantinische Kunst*, 98) who remarks on the *orans'* 'weibliche Gestalt'.

[48] Thérel ('Le composition et le symbolisme', 265) writes that the virgins 'represent dedicated virgins who settled in the Khargeh Oasis and for whom the mausoleum was built' (my translation).

[49] See examples from the Roman catacombs in *Roma sotterranea*, ed. Wilpert, ii, pl. 243 and 245 (Catacomb of St. Thecla), and pl. 249 (Catacomb of SS. Marco and Marcellinus).

[50] U. M. Fasola, *Die Domitilla-Katakombe und die Basilika der Märtyrer Nereus und Achilleus*, 3rd edn., ed. Ph. Pergola, trans. into German by K. Köberl (Città del Vaticano: Pontificia Commissione di Archeologia Sacra, 1989), 40, fig. 9.

[51] *Roma sotterranea*, ed. Wilpert, ii, pl. 243, 245, 249. The Catacomb of Saint Thecla in Rome exhibits no paintings of its namesake.

head upraised and arms outstretched, seems to mimic Thecla's intercessory pose. In this way, the chapel artist was emphasizing a mimetic link between the two figures—in death, the deceased is understood to have attained the image of her model Thecla. One finds a curious parallel in another wall painting of Thecla in Egypt. In a necropolis near ancient Athribis (the modern village of Winnînah, near Sûhâg) there is a rudimentary image of Thecla standing between two poorly conceived lions (Fig. 24).[52] While some have mistaken the *orans* for Daniel,[53] the accentuated female lines of the figure suggest otherwise.[54] Indeed, an important iconographic detail specifically identifies the *orans* as Thecla—the lion on the left licks the woman's foot, an allusion to *ATh* 28 where a lioness befriends Thecla and kisses her feet.[55]

What is even more interesting about this painting is the presence of another (smaller) female figure immediately to the right of Thecla—again, probably a depiction of the person buried in this chapel. Perhaps only one-third the size of Thecla, she wears a similar garment and replicates Thecla's pose with both hands upraised. As at El Bagawat, the similarity of posture may have

[52] de Bock, *Matériaux*, pl. 29, fig. 2; W. de Grüneisen, *Les caractéristiques de l'art copte* (Florence: Instituto di edizioni artistiche fratelli alinari, 1922), pl. 41, fig. 2; noted in K. Wessel, *Reallexikon zur byzantinischen Kunst*, (Stuttgart: Anton Hiersemann, 1966), i. 1115; and Warns, 'Weitere Darstellungen der heiligen Thekla', 84. The necropolis has received little archaeological attention; consequently its structures have not been dated (A. L. Schmitz, 'Das Totenwesen der Kopten: Kritische Übersicht über die literarischen und monumentalen Quellen', *Zeitschrift für Ägyptische Sprache und Altertumskunde*, 65/1 (1930), 19, no. 17). The more thoroughly excavated necropolises across the Nile at ancient Panopolis (Akhmim) spanned a range of centuries, from the fourth to the ninth CE (Schmitz, 'Das Totenwesen der Kopten', 17–19, no. 16; Forrer, *Die frühchristlicher Alterthümer*. The primitive quality of the paintings at Athribis may suggest a dating early in this period, but a systematic study of the necropolis is necessary before any final conclusions are drawn.

[53] de Grüneisen, *Les caractéristiques*, 68; Schmitz, 'Das Totenwesen der Kopten', 19.

[54] Wessel (*Reallexikon zur byzantinischen Kunst*, i. 1115) notes that the figure's dress and hairstyle are 'weiblich'. The figure of Thecla contrasts with another male *orans* found in the same chapel (de Bock, *Matériaux*, pl. 29, fig. 1; de Grüneisen, *Les caractéristiques*, pl. 41, fig. 2).

[55] Wessel (*Reallexikon zur byzantinischen Kunst*) mistakenly states that the lion bites the foot of the *orans*. In fact, the tip of the lion's tongue extends to touch the foot.

been a way that the artist chose to emphasize the mimetic bond between the saint and the person who had died. Thus, this wall painting near Athribis provides an iconographic context for interpreting the *orans* in the Chapel of the Exodus as a female devotee of Thecla, in this case one of the Athanasian virgins exiled to the Kharga Oasis.

The writings of Athanasius provide a firm, historical context for locating a community of virgins at the Kharga Oasis in the fourth century, and the wall paintings in the Chapel of the Exodus would seem to provide tangible evidence that this community of virgins carried their devotion to Thecla with them as they passed into exile. The iconographic details of the eastern arch suggest that these women probably understood their torture in Alexandria as a sharing in the sufferings of Thecla. They, like Thecla before them, faced the fire and prevailed. Seeing the rain descend to quench the flames around Thecla, the virgins at the oasis would have recalled their own deliverance from the Arian pyre. Perhaps herein lies an explanation of the vertical dashes that fall like rain upon the *orans* of the deceased—they are a visual reminder of the blessings God had showered upon the virgins in preserving them from the fire in Alexandria. In this way, the wall painting again gives subtle expression to the community's desire to emulate their model Thecla in the endurance of suffering.

Indeed, the images contiguous to that of Thecla in the Chapel of the Exodus—the figures leading camels, the *orans*, and the procession of virgins—may be viewed in the context of this ascetic community's experience of exile in the Kharga. First, there are hints of a local topography in the images. The darkened space around the *orans* would represent the tomb or chapel itself. The square structure immediately to the left is the door to that chapel. The lower scene where two figures lead camels toward the tomb door may depict an event from the history of the Alexandrian community—specifically, the exiles' initial arrival to the oasis after their long journey from Alexandria. The figures traverse a landscape dotted intermittently with small trees or bushes. Even today, scattered patches of vegetation greet the visitor as he or she approaches the oasis from the north. In this context, the tall tree above the *orans* may not be just a decorative motif; it may also stand for the oasis itself—the fertile spot where the Alexandrian expatriates were forced to resettle, and where some of them would ultimately be buried.[56]

The procession of virgins carrying lamps or torches may have called to mind the actual funerary processions of the community at El Bagawat;[57] but it also would have had eschatological associations for ancient Christian viewers. The path the virgins tread—a thin line painted in a shade of light lavender-taupe—originates at the tomb door and eventually leads up the steps of a temple-like structure (Fig. 21). Elsewhere on the eastern arch, the prophet Jeremiah stands before an almost identical edifice—there, clearly a representation of the Jerusalem Temple (Fig. 25).[58] In this context, the seven virgins approaching the Temple probably are meant to represent the celestial choir of virgins, who lead the deceased up toward the heavenly Jerusalem.[59] Above them,

---

[56] Other depictions of vegetation in the chapel also have topographic references. Two large trees mark the borders of the Promised Land before Moses and the Israelites. Also, Adam and Eve are ushered out of a Garden of Eden that is lush with fruit trees, grape vines, and foliage.

[57] The use of lamps was commonplace in ancient funerary processions. At Dura-Europos, a third-century fresco of the women visiting the tomb of Christ shows them carrying lighted tapers (C. H. Kraeling, *The Christian Building*, Excavations at Dura-Europos, Final Report 8/2 (New Haven: Dura-Europos Publications, 1967), 213, pl. 44–6, Susan B. Matheson, *Dura-Europos: The Ancient City and the Yale Collection* (New Haven: Yale University Art Gallery, 1982), 28–30, fig. 25, 25A). In late antiquity, the tombs themselves were also adorned with lamps and candles. In the early fifth century, Paulinus of Nola (*Carmen* 14. 99–103) describes the tomb of St. Felix as crowded with lanterns that burned day and night. In the late sixth century, Venantius Fortunatus (*Carmen* 3. 7. 41, 46) compares the candles in martyr shrines to the innumerable stars of the night sky.

[58] Both Jeremiah and the Jerusalem Temple were once identified by Greek inscriptions: ΕΡΕΜΙΑΣ and ΙΕ[ΡΟ]ΥΣΑΛΗΜ (de Bock, *Matériaux*, 23; Fakhry, *Necropolis of El Bagawat*, 62).

[59] Seven virgins appear elsewhere in early Christian literature as escorts to the Jerusalem Temple or to the celestial realms (Hildegard Heyne, *Das Gleichnis von den klugen und törichten Jungfrauen* (Leipzig: H. Haessel, 1922), 72–9). In particular, in the *Protevangelium of James* Mary is accompanied to the Temple as a child by seven 'pure virgins of the tribe of David' (trans. Hennecke-Schneemelcher, I. 430). In the work *Pistis Sophia*, a retinue of seven virgins escorts the soul during its ascent to the realm of light (*Koptisch-gnostische Schriften*, i. *Die Pistis Sophia*, ed. C. Schmidt, GCS 13 (1905), 212. 25 ff.). The motif of a female retinue welcoming the deceased also appears in early Christian art. In a fourth-century fresco in the Coemeterium Maius in Rome, a woman

the exemplary virgin Thecla oversees their work; she is the head of this choir of virgins, the patron saint of the deceased.

I want to argue that this procession of virgins is part of a larger iconographic narrative on the eastern arch of the Chapel of the Exodus. Placed beneath the image of Thecla, the narrative consists of three elements, arranged counterclockwise (see Figs. 17 and 18):

(3) procession of virgins
(ENTRY INTO HEAVENLY JERUSALEM)

(2) *orans* of the deceased
(TOMB IN THE OASIS)

(1) two figures leading camels
(EXILE TO THE OASIS)

The first scene depicts the exiles' journey from Alexandria. The second reflects the community's experience of death in the oasis. The third expresses an eschatological hope—namely, that the soul of the deceased would ascend to the heavenly Jerusalem. The procession is a scene of triumph, signifying the fact that even though the virgins might be banished to the oasis, they could not ultimately be defeated. Persecuted and dislodged from their homes, they could still anticipate a final victory paralleling Thecla's own victory over martyrdom.

While the *orans* serves as the visual crux of this iconographic cycle (the narrative literally turns on it), the direction of movement in the final scene reinforces the central theme of the chapel: the exodus of the faithful from a place of exile. It is no coincidence that the virgins proceed in the same direction as the line of Israelites bound for the Promised Land immediately above. The procession of virgins is the culminating scene of the narrative, and as such, it gives visual expression to the exiled community's hope for an exodus from their own captivity in the oasis.

buried there is likewise depicted as an *orans*. On the left, she is welcomed to a heavenly banquet by five female figures; on the right a line of women advance toward her with torches lit (J. Wilpert, *Die gottgeweihten Jungfrauen in den ersten Jahrhunderten der Kirche* (Freiburg am Breisgau; St. Louis, Mo.: Herder, 1892), pl. 2, fig. 5).

The depiction of Jerusalem as the destination of faithful virgins would have especially resonated with the experience of this exiled community. From one of the letters of Athanasius, we know that these same Alexandrian virgins had once made a pilgrimage to Jerusalem and had expressed a longing to return some day to the Holy Land. Significantly, in that letter their mentor Athanasius compares their sight of the Holy Sepulchre in Jerusalem to a vision of Paradise.[60] For the Alexandrian virgins, now in exile, the memory of this pilgrimage experience may have served as a metaphor for a hope that was both earthly and eschatological—a hope for an ultimate return to Jerusalem, if not in life at least in death.

Thus, the contexts of exile and burial help us understand how this complex of images would have functioned for an ancient viewer, for an Alexandrian virgin visiting the grave of a departed sister. By witnessing the deceased's welcome into the heavenly Jerusalem, the chapel visitor would have anticipated her own entry into the communion of saints, her own reunion with her patron saint Thecla. The tomb of the *orans* is depicted as a privileged door of entry into this communion, a place where the distance between earth and heaven is effectively bridged.[61] In this way, the chapel itself was marked as sacred space for the ancient viewer.

Other images in the Chapel of the Exodus reinforce this impression of the tomb(s) as sacred space. Upon entering the chapel, the visitor is immediately struck by the prominent scene of Moses leading the Israelites up to a large structure painted on the northern face of the dome, presumed to represent the Promised Land or the heavenly Jerusalem (Fig. 26).[62] The central section

[60] Writing to the virgins shortly after their return to Alexandria, Athanasius consoles them with the memory of Christ's tomb: 'We grieve with you, maidservants of Christ, because as you were separating from the holy places you shed streams of bitter tears. As you were travelling, you were also weeping because you were leaving far behind the cave of the Lord, which is the image of Paradise or, rather, which surpasses it . . . you too were in great distress as you departed from the holy places because you desire and long for the courts of the Lord' (*Ep. virg.* 2. 1–2 (ed. Lebon, 'Athanasiana Syriaca', 170. 3–7; 171. 39–41); trans. D. Brakke, *Athanasius*, 292–3).

[61] On tombs as sacred space, see Peter Brown, *The Cult of the Saints* (Chicago: Chicago University Press, 1981), 1–4, 86 ff.

[62] Fakhry, *Necropolis of El Bagawat*, 55–6.

of the structure—with its meshlike grillwork, dome, and cross— resembles depictions found in late antique pilgrimage art of the small structure (*aedicula*) built over the remains of Christ's burial place in the fourth-century Church of the Holy Sepulchre in Jerusalem.[63] The colonnaded façade in the painting also resembles ancient depictions of that church's exterior and its adjacent courtyard (the Anastasis Rotunda).[64] Yet, at the same time, this colonnaded façade also bears a striking resemblance to the characteristic tomb architecture at El Bagawat (Fig. 27).[65] Here then, in the iconography of the Chapel of the Exodus, there is a merging of two locales: the necropolis of El Bagawat is visually conflated with the Holy Land itself, with the site of Christ's resurrection.[66] Visitors to the Chapel of the Exodus could imagine their visit to the necropolis in part as a re-enactment of Moses'

[63] A. Grabar, *Ampoules de Terre Sainte (Monza-Bobbio)* (Paris: Librairie C. Klincksieck, 1958), *passim*; J. Engemann, 'Palästinische Pilgerampullen im F. J. Dölger Institut in Bonn', *Jahrbuch für Antike und Christentum*, 16 (1973), 5 ff. A similar ampulla bearing the image of Christ's tomb can be found in the collection at Dumbarton Oaks in Washington (M. C. Ross, *Catalogue of the Byzantine and Early Mediaeval Antiquities in the Dumbarton Oaks Collection*, i. *Metalwork, Ceramics, Glass, Glyptics, Painting* (Washington: Dumbarton Oaks, 1962), no. 87; Gary Vikan, *Byzantine Pilgrimage Art* (Washington: Dumbarton Oaks, 1982), 20–4).

[64] A seventh- or eighth-century bread stamp in the Cleveland Museum of Art depicts the Church of the Holy Sepulchre and the Anastasis Rotunda with a similar portico (Krautheimer, *Early Christian and Byzantine Architecture*, 63, fig. 27C).

[65] The artist probably did not aim to copy one particular local structure, as Kaufmann argues (*Ein altchristliches Pompeji*, 44 ff.). Instead, he or she was incorporating the general architectural features of the necropolis into the painting— especially the style of façade identified as types 6 and 7 by Fakhry (*Necropolis of El Bagawat*, 25–6). Kaufmann's argument that the painting depicted the large complex of chapels (nos. 23–5) immediately in front of the Chapel of the Exodus is problematic not only because of a divergence of architectural details, but also because of problems in dating. The chapel complex in question was constructed *after* the Chapel of the Exodus (de Bock, *Matériaux*, 16–17).

[66] David Frankfurter ('The Cult of the Martyrs in Egypt Before Constantine: The Evidence of the Coptic *Apocalypse of Elijah*', *Vigiliae Christianae*, 48 (1994), 33) speaks of an analogous tendency to merge conceptions of holy space in the late third-century cult of the martyrs. He argues that author of the Coptic *Apocalypse of Elijah*, when speaking of 'holy places', imagines an eschatological synthesis of 'on the one hand, the vast network of native Egyptian shrines and temples, and on the other, the reputation of the Holy Land . . . as a network or concentration of shrines'.

journey to the threshold of the Promised Land, itself an allegory (for Christians) of the soul's journey to the realm of heavenly repose. But, in the dim light of the chapel, an Alexandrian virgin also would have been encouraged imaginatively to re-enter the earthly city of Jerusalem and the Church of the Holy Sepulchre, to draw near in anticipation to the heavenly Jerusalem, to enter into fellowship with Thecla, with the deceased, and with the community of saints.

For the exiled community of virgins, the act of viewing the paintings in the Chapel of the Exodus would have reminded them of their connection with the deceased and Saint Thecla. Even the visitors' physical posture while viewing the paintings—head tilted back,[67] arms upraised in the conventional ancient attitude of prayer[68]—would have reinforced such a connection. Standing in the darkened space of the chapel, gazing up at the biblical congregation of saints on the dome walls above her, a virgin of the oasis would have seen herself not only mirroring the *orans* posture of the deceased, but also physically emulating the image of the virgin martyr Thecla.[69]

---

[67] In the early fifth century CE, Paulinus of Nola (*Carmen* 27. 511–13; CSEL 30. 285) witnesses the typical physical posture of pilgrims viewing the paintings in the church of St. Felix at Nola: 'Now I want you to gaze at the paintings on the portico . . . and to tire your inclined neck [*supinum collum*] a little while you view everything with your face tilted back [*reclinatus vultus*].'

[68] Hooper (*Funerary Stelae*, 20 and 39, n. 65) observes that, in Egyptian funerary art, upraised hands seem to express 'an act of worship' synonymous with 'the Greek posture of prayer with hands raised and palms turned upwards toward heaven'. In addition, he comments on the early and widespread use of the *orans* as a symbol for a person in mourning.

[69] Late antique and early Byzantine writers describe in vivid terms how visual art could evoke deep-felt emotional responses and move viewers toward imitation (William Loerke, '"Real Presence" in Early Christian Art', in T. G. Verdon (ed.), *Monasticism and the Arts* (Syracuse, NY: Syracuse University Press, 1984), 29–51, esp. 30–1; Leslie Brubaker, 'Perception and Conception: Art, Theory, and Culture in Ninth-Century Byzantium', *Word and Image*, 5/1 (Jan.–Mar. 1989), 19–32. At the turn of the fifth century, Asterius of Amasea wrote of his own response to a painting on the martyrdom of St. Euphemia: 'But now I cry and emotion hinders my speech: for the artist has painted the drops of blood so vividly that you might say that they were truly pouring down upon her lips, and that you might depart having wept yourself' (Asterius of Amasea, *Description of a Painting on the Martyrdom of St. Euphemia*, ed. F. Halkin, *Euphémie de Chalcédoine* (Brussels: Société des Bollandistes, 1965), 7). The sight of the drops of blood trickling like tears down the martyr's face brings tears to

The Limits of Iconographic History: The Uncertain Fate of Thecla's Devotees in the Kharga Oasis

Despite what it elucidates about the values and viewing habits of early Christian exiles in the Kharga Oasis during the fourth century, the art at El Bagawat reveals almost nothing about the subsequent history of the Alexandrian virgins and the development of Thecla devotion in the region. While some of the virgins may have eventually returned to Alexandria during the periods when Athanasius came back into favour, others may have remained as part of an expatriate community in the oasis. Archaeological excavations in the vicinity of El Bagawat give evidence of a monastic presence in the Kharga in the fifth and sixth centuries CE,[70] and the painting of Thecla in the Chapel of Peace (Fig. 20) would seem to reflect a continued local interest in the saint during this period. In the Chapel of Peace, Thecla's close visual association with Eve and Mary seems to bear out her enduring role as a model

the writer's own eyes—tears not only of sympathy, but also of mute imitation. In the ninth century, the writer Photius specially supports the notion that viewing the images of the martyrs promotes imitation: 'Martyrs have gone through great struggles . . . and books preserve their memory. Their deeds are also seen being performed in visual images—(indeed) the painting brings the struggles of those blessed martyrs more vividly to mind . . . While both words and images convey these deeds, it is viewers rather than hearers who are led toward imitation' (Photius, *Homily*, 17. 5, ed. B. Laourdas, *Photiou Homiliai (ΦΩΤΙΟΥ OMIΛIAI)*, (Makedonikon Spoudon Parartema 12 (Thessaloniki: Hellenika periodikou syggramma, 1959), 170. 17–21).

[70] Just north of El Bagawat, archaeologists have discovered the remains of several monastic foundations. A kilometre north of the necropolis, the Monastery of Mustapha Kachef seems to have functioned as a hostel for travellers to and from the oasis. On the ceiling of its church have been found Christian inscriptions from the fifth and sixth centuries (Vivian, *Islands of the Blest*, 56–7). In the valley below Mustapha Kachef, Egyptian archaeologists have recently excavated what appears to be an earlier monastic structure, which they have dubbed the Monastery of El Bagawat. The two-storied complex includes two apsidal chapels, a number of monastic cells, and a kitchen with an oven and circular *triclinia* for the preparation and sharing of meals. There have been no published reports yet on this excavation. Little remains in the way of inscriptions, but during a visit to the site in April 1997, I was able to discern the word 'peace' (εἰρήνη) painted on the walls of two rooms (one on the apse of a small chapel). While 'peace' is a common early Christian motif, its appearance in this context is interesting given the existence of the contemporaneous Chapel of Peace nearby at El Bagawat.

of women's piety. However, Thecla's pairing with Paul in that chapel also perhaps bespeaks a subtle domestication of Thecla's status in this later period. In contrast to the Chapel of the Exodus where Thecla appears in solitary, ecstatic triumph over the pyre, in the Chapel of Peace Thecla is veiled, her eyes downcast as she is instructed by the apostle. Did the subordination of Thecla to a figure of male authority in the art mirror similar ecclesiastical attempts to control and direct communities of virgins who settled in the oasis? Unfortunately, in the absence of any other evidence, this question must remain unanswered.

THE SPREAD OF THECLA DEVOTION IN THE FAYÛM AND THE NILE VALLEY

The cult of Saint Thecla in Egypt outside the environs of Alexandria was not restricted to a remote community in the Kharga Oasis. Thecla devotion also spread to other areas—specifically, to towns of the Fayûm and the Nile Valley (see Fig. 5). In these regions, the cult of Saint Thecla thrived, but it also underwent important cultural changes. Once a Mediterranean phenomenon, it eventually became thoroughly assimilated into the native Egyptian cult of the martyrs.

Social Factors: Egyptian Pilgrims and Monastic Communities

The evidence for Thecla devotion in the Fayûm and the Nile Valley is quite diverse. Manuscript fragments of the *Acts of Paul and Thecla* from the fourth and fifth centuries CE have been discovered at Antinoopolis (Sheikh-Ibada) and Oxyrhynchus (al-Bahnasâ).[71] Images of Thecla appear on a fourth-century wooden comb (Fig. 28) and a fifth-century textile from Panopolis (Fig. 14),[72] a fourth- or fifth-century limestone relief probably from Oxyrhynchus (Fig. 29),[73] a sixth-century oil lamp from the

---

[71] *P. Ant.* i. 13; *P. Oxy.* i. 6.

[72] Forrer, *Die frühchristlichen Alterthümer*, 15–16, pl. 12, fig. 2 (comb); pl. 16, fig. 10 (textile); Nauerth and Warns, *Thekla*, 22–4 (textile); 51–3, fig. 19 (comb).

[73] Weitzmann, *Age of Spirituality*, 574–5, no. 513. Weitzmann notes that the style of the relief bears a striking resemblance to fourth- and fifth-century Coptic sculptures from Oxyrhynchus and Ahnas. Thecla's posture is similar to

Fayûm (Fig. 30),[74] and an undated wall painting in a necropolis near Athribis (Fig. 24).[75] During the sixth, seventh, and eighth centuries churches, streets, and shrines were dedicated to her in Arsinoe (Medinet el-Fayûm),[76] Oxyrhynchus,[77] and Aphrodite (Atfih).[78] A late sixth-century church built at the entrance of

her portrait on the pilgrim flasks from Abu Mina. She stands with arms held behind her back, and a halo adorns her head. The curved lines of her body are accentuated. A T-shaped skirt, belted at the waist, hangs down in front. She is flanked on the lower left by a lion, on the lower right by a lioness. However, the two angels that hover at her shoulders are unattested elsewhere. Their presence may reflect the popularity of angel reverence in Middle Egypt (see n. 103).

[74] *Bildwerke der Sammlung Kaufmann*, i. *Lampen aus Ton und Bronze*, ed. Wolfgang Selesnow, Liebieghaus-Museum Alter Plastik (Frankfurt am Main) (Melsungen: Verlag Gutenberg, 1988), cat. no. 302, pl. 41; C. M. Kaufmann, 'Archäologische Miszellen aus Ägypten', *Oriens Christianus*, 2/3 (1913), 108, fig. 3.

[75] de Bock, *Matériaux*, pl. 29, fig. 2; de Grüneisen, *Les caractéristiques de l'art copte*, pl. 41, fig. 2.

[76] Six Greek papyri spanning this period record an 'Avenue of Saint Thecla' (λαύρα τῆς ‘Αγίας Θέκλης) in the city of Arsinoe (*Stud. Pal.* VIII. 717 (8th cent.); VIII. 762 (6th cent.); X. 6 (7–8th cent.); *SB* I. 4890, 4892, 5127. The street was apparently so named because there was a church dedicated to the saint located along it (Aristide Calderini, *Dizionario dei nomi geografici e topografici dell'Egitto greco-romain* (Cairo: Società reale di geografia d'Egitto, 1935–) vol. 2. 4, 250; also Luciana Antonini, 'Le chiese cristiane nell'Egitto dal IV al IX secolo secondo i documenti dei papiri greci', *Aegyptus*, 20 (1940), 170, no. 15). A sixth-century tax record also from the Fayûm witnesses a payment by 'the steward of (the church of) Saint Thecla' ((ὁ οἰκονόμος τῆς ἁγ)ίας Θέκλης) (*Stud. Pal.* VIII. 104).

[77] The discovery of a fragment of the *Acts of Paul and Thecla* at Oxyrhynchus indicates that a local interest in Thecla may be traced from at least the fifth century CE (*P. Oxy.* I. 6). In addition, two sixth-century papyri from Oxyrhynchus document the existence of a church (or perhaps two churches?) of Saint Thecla in that city. One papyrus, dated 587 CE, mentions a man named John who was 'a deacon and steward of Saint Thecla' (διάκονος καὶ οἰκονόμος τῆς ἁγίας Θ[έ]κλας) (*P. Oxy.* XVI. 1993. 18–20 (dated 587 CE); Antonini, 'Le chiese cristiane', 179, no. 30). The other lists three holders of ecclesiastical office in the same or a similar institution dedicated to the female saint: a 'guardian of the church' (ἐκκλησιέκδικος), a 'presbyter of Saint Thecla' (πρεσβύτερος τῆς ἁγίας Θέκλας) and one who is called both 'presbyter and steward of the same holy church' (πρεσβύτερος καὶ οἰκόνομος τῆς αὐτῆς ἁγίας ἐκκλησίας) (*P. Oxy.* XXIV. 2419. 3–5). The limestone relief of Thecla in Kansas City (see n. 73) may have adorned an interior wall of such a church.

[78] *P. Lond.* IV. 1420. 189 (706 CE); IV. 1421. 40, 65, 67 (720 CE); Stefan Timm, *Das christlich-koptische Ägypten in arabischer Zeit* (Wiesbaden: Dr. Ludwig Reichert, 1992), vi. 2732–3.

the Luxor Temple in Thebes may even have been dedicated to Saint Thecla—the original excavators of the site found her name inscribed on one of its walls.[79] Finally, a number of women were named after the female saint during this period: papyri and inscriptions attest namesakes of Thecla in the Fayûm, and in various towns along the Nile, including Hermopolis (al-Ashmûnayn), Oxyrhynchus, Aphrodite, Hermonthis (Armant), Thebes (Luxor), and Syene (Aswan).[80] The diversity of this evidence reflects the different ways the cult of Saint Thecla was made accessible to the inhabitants of these areas: through the production of books, the decoration of household items and burial spaces, the founding of public religious institutions, and the naming of children, Thecla's reputation as a martyr saint was promulgated in a variety of social and geographical settings.

In light of this evidence, some important questions arise for the historian studying the development of the cult of the martyrs in Egypt. How was the cult of Saint Thecla imported into the Nile Valley and the Fayûm? What social practices contributed to the spread of Thecla devotion? The wall painting of Saint Thecla in the Chapel of the Exodus is among our earliest evidence for the cult of Saint Thecla outside Alexandria and the Delta. Could the Alexandrian virgins have planted seeds of Thecla devotion in towns along the Nile as they stopped en route to the oasis (or perhaps even upon their return)? One gets a sense from the writings of Athanasius that local communities supported him in his travels back and forth from his places of exile—such might have been the social setting in which Thecla's story was first communicated to Christians living in the cities of the Nile Valley.

Even if this community of women from Alexandria had a personal role in transporting Thecla's cult, it is clear that additional factors are necessary to account for its spread to so many

---

[79] M. Abdul-Qader Muhammad, 'Preliminary Report on the Excavations Carried Out in the Temple of Luxor, Seasons 1958–1959 and 1959–1960', *Annales du service des antiquités de l'Égypte*, 60 (1968), 252–4, 272, pl. 30. Peter Grossmann and Donald S. Whitcomb ('Excavation in the Sanctuary of the Church in front of the Luqsur-Temple', *Annales du service des antiquités égyptiennes*, 72 (1992–3), 25–34) dated the church to the late sixth century based on its architectural decoration and the deposition of ceramic debris at the site.

[80] See 'Appendix B: Egyptian Namesakes of Saint Thecla'.

different towns in the Fayûm and along the Nile. One of these factors may have been pilgrimage related to the cult of the martyrs. Is it possible that there were pilgrims from the Fayûm or the Nile Valley who travelled to Hagia Thekla near Seleucia (Asia Minor), or to Abu Mina, and who brought back with them a desire to establish shrines to Saint Thecla in their home towns? The *Life and Miracles of Saint Thecla* attests to the fact that Egyptians travelled to Thecla's shrine in Asia Minor: it celebrates the ascetic piety of a devotee who hailed from Egypt, 'Paul the Egyptian.'[81] However, the shrine of Thecla near that of Saint Menas in the Mareotis (discussed in Chapter 4) would have been a more accessible place where Egyptian pilgrims might have encountered Thecla's cult. While many of the visitors to Abu Mina would have come from nearby Alexandria,[82] the site would also have attracted pilgrims from more distant places such as the Fayûm and the Nile Valley.[83] Indeed, the cult of Saint Menas, closely linked with that of Thecla, was active in these areas: from Greek papyri we know that churches were dedicated to Saint Menas in Arsinoe (Fayûm) and Oxyrhynchus by the sixth century.[84] In addition, at Medinet Habu near Thebes, six Coptic frescoes of Menas on horseback have been recovered, probably dating from the eighth century CE.[85] It may not be coincidental that during the sixth century there were churches separately

---

[81] *Miracle* 44. 24–5 (Dag., 404).

[82] Five of the thirteen *Miracles of Saint Menas* published by Pomialovskii involve pilgrims to Abu Mina who live in Alexandria (*Miracles* 2, 4, 7, 10, 12 Pomialovskii (ed.) *Zhitie*, 66–8, 70–3, 79–81, 86–9). Similarly, in the collection of miracles related to Saints Cyrus and John at Menouthis (PG 87. 3. 3423–3676), the majority of miracles involve people from the Delta or the surrounding area. On pilgrimage related to this pair of saints at Menouthis, see D. Montserrat, 'Pilgrimage to the Shrine of SS Cyrus and John at Menouthis in Late Antiquity', in D. Frankfurter (ed.), *Pilgrimage and Holy Space in Late Antique Egypt*, 257–79. On the localized character of late antique shrines, see J. Haldon, 'Supplementary Essay', in *The Miracles of St. Artemios*, ed. Crisafulli and Nesbitt (Leiden; New York; Cologne: E. J. Brill, 1997), 38–9.

[83] B. Kötting (*Peregrinatio Religiosa* (Münster: Antiquariat Th. Stenderhoff, 1980), 99–101) cites inscriptional and literary evidence for pilgrims who visited Abu Mina from places as distant as Smyrna, Piacenza, and Rome.

[84] *Stud. Pal.* VIII. 762 (Arsinoe); *P. Oxy.* XVI. 1993. 18–20 and XXIV. 2419. 3–5 (Oxyrhynchus).

[85] D. N. Wilbur, 'The Coptic Frescoes of Saint Menas at Medinet Habu', *Art Bulletin*, 22 (1940), 36–103.

dedicated to both Thecla and Menas in Arsinoe and Oxyrhynchus. Could it be that the cult of Saint Thecla was imported into these cities together with the cult of Saint Menas, that the cults of these two saints were introduced by pilgrims who had visited both of their shrines in the Mareotis? If this is so, it may explain why the iconography of Thecla found on a sixth-century oil lamp from the Fayûm (Fig. 30) resembles so closely her image on a pilgrim flask from Abu Mina (Fig. 11; Cat. no. 16).[86] The veneration and conveyance of such artefacts would have been primary means by which pilgrims introduced Thecla's cult and image to towns in the Nile Valley.[87] Pilgrim flasks containing holy water would have transported a sense of the saint's miraculous power and could have served as focal points for cultic enthusiasm.

Pilgrimage was probably not the only factor in the spread of Thecla's cult. Monastic communities may also have been instrumental in promoting Thecla devotion. Correspondence between monks was one way that traditions about Thecla were spread: as mentioned in Chapter 3, the monk Isidore of Pelusium wrote a letter to Alexandrian ascetic women in which he celebrates the example of Saint Thecla.[88] Similar letters could have introduced Saint Thecla to monastic communities along the Nile. Monastic communities also may have played an important role in standardization of the liturgical celebration of Thecla as a martyr,[89] and in the copying of manuscripts, such as the miniature codices of the *ATh* from Antinoopolis and Oxyrhynchus.

Papyrological evidence from Aphrodite supports the notion that monastic communities provided a social context for the cult of Saint Thecla in the Nile Valley. Two early eighth-century papyri from that town mention a '*topos* of Amma Thecla'.[90] In late antique Egypt, the term *topos* (Coptic, ΜΑ) could refer

---

[86] *Lampen aus Ton und Bronze*, ed. Selesnow, cat. no. 302, pl. 41 (oil lamp); Weitzmann, *Age of Spirituality*, 576–7, no. 516 (pilgrim flask). I discuss the iconographic parallels in Chapter 4, n. 31.

[87] In Chapter 4, I argued that miniature codices like the one found in Oxyrhynchus (*P. Oxy.* I. 6) may very well have been pilgrimage artefacts.

[88] *Ep.* 87 (PG 78. 241D–244A).

[89] According to eleventh- and thirteenth-century Coptic liturgical manuscripts owned by the Monastery of Saint Macarius in Scetis (Wadi Natrun), Saint Thecla's feast day falls on the 25th of the month Epep (H. G. Evelyn White, *The Monasteries of the Wadi 'n Natrûn* (New York: Metropolitan Museum of Art, 1926), i. 218, 221).

[90] *P. Lond.* IV. 1420. 189 (706 CE); IV. 1421. 40, 65, 67 (720 CE).

both to a monastery and to the shrine of a martyr, the holy 'place' where the saint's relics were deposited. Papyri from the sixth to eighth centuries attest over fifty (other) monasteries at Aphrodite, a number of which are identified as *topoi*.[91] When the formula '*topos* of saint so-and-so' was used to refer to a monastery, it intimated that the saint was considered to be specially present at the site—i.e. that the monastery contained a shrine dedicated to that saint.[92] An eighth-century Theban document gives an account of two parents who bring their sick son to the 'holy *topos*' of the Monastery of Apa Phoibammon.[93] When they pour water from the shrine over the boy's body, he is healed by 'God and the prayers of that martyr'.[94] As a result of this miracle, the couple decide to give their son over to the service of monastery and the administrator in charge of the shrine. The '*topos* of Amma Thecla' at Aphrodite was probably just such a monastic establishment—namely, one that contained a shrine, and perhaps even relics,[95] of the female saint.

The 'Egyptianization' of Saint Thecla: The Creation of a New Coptic Martyr Legend

Monasticism and pilgrimage would have been important social contexts for the spread of Thecla devotion in the Fayûm and the Nile Valley, just as they were for the development of her cult around Alexandria and in Asia Minor. This continuity of practice

[91] Calderini, *Dizionario dei nomi geografici e topografici dell'Egitto greco-romano* vol. 1. 2, 325 ff.; P. Barison, 'Richerche sui monasteri dell'Egitto bizantino ed arabo secondo i documenti dei papiri greci', *Aegyptus* 18, (1938), 98–122; Timm, *Das christlich-koptische Ägypten in arabischer Zeit*, iii. 1443 ff.

[92] H. E. Winlock and W. E. Crum, *The Monastery of Epiphanius at Thebes*, 2 vols. (New York: Metropolitan Museum of Art, 1926), 111–14; Frankfurter, 'The Cult of the Martyrs in Egypt', 44, n. 39.

[93] *Koptische Rechtsurkunden des achten Jahrhunderts aus Djême (Theben)*, ed. W. E. Crum and G. Steindorff (Leipzig: J. C. Hinrichs, 1912), no. 91; L. S. B. MacCoull, 'Child Donations and Child Saints in Coptic Egypt', *East European Quarterly*, 13/4 (1979), 410–11.

[94] *Koptische Rechtsurkunden*, ed. Crum and Steindorff, no. 91, 12–13.

[95] The creation of bodily relics *ex nihilo* was well known in the Egyptian cult of the martyrs: the monk Shenoute, for one, condemns the widespread falsification of relics in the Thebaid (*Discourses* 8 ('Those Who Work Evil'); codex HD 239: ii. 24 ff.; catalogued by Stephen L. Emmel, 'Shenoute's Literary Corpus', (Ph.D. diss.; Yale University, 1993), iv. 979–80). On the ubiquity of martyrs' relics in Egypt, see De Lacy Evans O'Leary, *The Saints of Egypt* (Amsterdam: Philo Press, 1974), 12 ff.

notwithstanding, as the cult of Saint Thecla spread it was also transformed in significant ways. One of these ways was the wholesale rewriting of traditions associated with Thecla's name —the creation of a *new, distinctively Egyptian* martyr saint named Thecla.

How and why would the traditions surrounding Saint Thecla be replaced by that of a namesake martyr? The evidence concerning Thecla devotion in another town, Antinoopolis provides some answers. Antinoopolis thrived during the fourth and fifth centuries as the capital of the Thebaid, and as a cradle of Egyptian monasticism.[96] Writing in the fifth century, Palladius reports that over 1,200 hermits inhabit the city.[97] Moreover, he adds that 'in that city of Antinoopolis, there are twelve monasteries of women, who hold fast to the most excellent way of life'.[98]

Amidst these monastic establishments, devotion to Saint Thecla seems to have taken root quite early. The earliest extant manuscript of the *Acts of Paul and Thecla*—a single parchment sheet of a fourth-century miniature codex—was discovered at Antinoopolis.[99] A Greek epitaph on a gravestone from Antinoopolis also reflects the high esteem in which the female saint was held. The inscription offers a final petition on behalf of the person who has died ('the blessed servant of God, David'):

Lord Jesus Christ and holy [Ap]a Colluthus and holy [Am]a The[cl]a, give rest to his soul. Have mercy on him in [your (?)] kingdom.[100]

---

[96] James E. Goehring ('Monastic Diversity and Ideological Boundaries in Fourth-Century Christian Egypt', *Journal of Early Christian Studies*, 5/1 (1997), 61–84, esp. 65–73) highlights the diversity of monastic expression at Antinoopolis during the fourth through sixth centuries, pointing especially to literary and documentary evidence for 'the peaceful coexistence of Melitian and non-Melitian ascetics'.

[97] Palladius, *H. Laus.* 96 (PG 34. 1203B). The same accounting is given by Heraclides (*Paradise* 45; PL 74. 330B). John Moschus attests to the survival of this monastic community in the late sixth or early seventh centuries CE (*Pratum Spirituale* 143, 161; PL 74. 190–1, 200–1).

[98] Palladius, *H. Laus.* 137 (PG 34. 1235D).   [99] *P. Ant.* 1. 13.

[100] *SB* 1. 1564. 4–6. The date of the stele is uncertain. Preisigke edits this portion of the text as follows:

line . . . 4 Κ(ύρι)ε Ἰ(ησο)ῦ Χρ(ιστο)ῦ καὶ ὁ ἅγιος
line 5 [ἄπ]α Κολλοῦθος καὶ ἡ [ἁ]γία . . . α Θέ[κλ]α ἀνάπαυσον τήν ψυχήν αὐτοῦ
line 6 [ἐ]λέησον αὐτόν ἐν τῇ Βασιλείᾳ [σου(?)].

However, G. Lefebvre (*Annales du Service des Antiquités de l'Egypte*, 9 (1908), 176, no. 812) reads [ἄμ]α before Θέκλα in line 5.

The petitioner privileges Thecla alongside Christ as an inter-
cessor for the dead, and also places her on a level with Saint
Colluthus, a famous local martyr under Diocletian who had a
shrine at Antinoopolis.[101] A Coptic text in the Pierpont Morgan
collection—the *Martyrdom of Saint Colluthus*—reports the details
of Colluthus' interview with the governor of Antinoopolis and his
sentencing to death by burning.[102] The fact that Thecla is mentioned in the same breath as Christ and this home-town martyr
must reflect her high status in the area.

Just how was the cult of Saint Thecla promoted in this local
context? The devotees of Colluthus could point to the site of his
martyrdom in Antinoopolis, and to his reputation as a healer.[103]
But questions concerning Thecla may have nagged at the minds
of Coptic Christians. What claim did this foreign-born saint have
to a holy place or a healing power in this city? The *Acts of Paul
and Thecla* situates Thecla's life and death in Asia Minor—
why should she be viewed as specially present to the residents
of Antinoopolis? Such cultural concerns eventually led to an
attempt to 'Egyptianize' the legend of Saint Thecla. In the process, a new *Martyrdom* was written, and a new, *distinctively* Coptic
Thecla was invented.

---

[101] A Coptic text speaks of 'the body of holy Apa Colluthus in his marty-
rium on the mountain of his city Antinoopolis' (ΠⲤⲰⲘⲀ ⲘⲠⳉⲀⲅⲓⲟⲤ ⲀⲠⲀ
ⲔⲟⲗⲗⲟⲨⲐⲟⲤ ⳉⲘⲠⲉϥⲘⲀⲣⲧⲨⲣⲓⲟⲚ ⲉⲧⳉⲘ ⲠⲦⲟⲟⲨ ⲚⲦⲉϥⲠⲟⲗⲓⲤ
ⲀⲚⲦⲓⲚⲟⲟⲨ); W. Till, *Koptische Heiligen- und Martyrerlegenden*, 1st pt.,
Orientalia Christiana Analecta, 102 (Rome: Pont. Institutum Orientalium
Studiorum, 1935), 173. 4–6). Later, in the same text, his shrine is referred to as
'the place [ⲦⲟⲠⲟⲤ] of the holy Apa Colluthus' (Till, op. cit., 173. 19).

[102] P. M. Codex M 591, T. 28, Ff. 88V–92 (ninth century CE), ed. E. A. E.
Reymond, and J. W. B. Barns, *Four Martyrdoms from the Pierpont Morgan Coptic
Codices* (Oxford: Clarendon Press, 1973), 25–9. Because this martyr account is
remarkably free of the usual hagiographic excess, Reymond and Barns argue for
its authenticity, contrasting it with later, more 'epic' versions of Colluthus' life.
They place Colluthus' *Martyrdom* in the same category as the *Acts of Phileas and
Philoromus*, a (rare) martyrology that has been viewed favourably by critical his-
torians (ibid. 8, 11 ff.; W. H. C. Frend, *Martyrdom and Persecution in the Early
Church* [Grand Rapids, Mich.: Baker Book House, 1965), 495 and 528, n. 134).

[103] According to all accounts, Colluthus was by profession a physician. The
introduction to his *Martyrdom* therefore tries to establish lines of continuity
between Colluthus' work as a physician and his ongoing healing power as a martyr:
'The martyr account of the holy martyr of Christ Colluthus, and the physician
and healer of everyone who receives from the body and blood of Christ purely
. . .' (P. M. Codex M 591, T. 28, Ff. 88 V i. 1–10; Reymond and Barns, 25).

The Coptic *Martyrdom of SS. Paese and Thecla*[104] details the lives (and martyrdoms) of an Egyptian man named Paese and his sister Thecla, a young widow who lives in the city of Antinoopolis.[105] Like the *Martyrdom of S. Colluthus*, the story is set during the persecution of Christians under Diocletian. Unlike that straightforward account of Colluthus' trial, the *Martyrdom of SS. Paese and Thecla* abounds with stereotypical characters, sensational scenes, and inconsistent historical details —characteristics that have earned for most Egyptian martyrologies the reputation of literary fiction.[106]

Paese, a local Christian man who lives across the river from Antinoopolis near Hermopolis Magna, travels to Alexandria to visit a sick friend named Paul. There, Paese is arrested for the faith and tortured horribly:[107] he is placed on the rack with torches lit under him; he is dragged, flogged, doused with vinegar, and then set on fire; finally, he is lathered in pitch, bound in chains, and thrown into a fiery furnace. At each new torture, the angel Raphael intercedes and heals him of his wounds.

Meanwhile Paese's sister Thecla, also an active Christian, is inspired to travel to Alexandria and join her brother. When she goes to the dock at Antinoopolis to find transportation, she hires a boat 'with the angel Raphael standing upon it, and Gabriel sitting [in it], and Saint Mary the Holy Virgin and Elizabeth the mother of John the Baptist sitting in front'. However, Thecla does

---

[104] The earliest reference to the story of Paese and Thecla appears in a Greek papyrus from the fifth or early sixth century CE (*P. Berl. Sarisch.* 3). The Coptic text that I will be using immediately precedes the martyrology of Saint Colluthus in the ninth-century P. M. Codex M 591, T. 28, Ff. 49–88R (Reymond and Barns, 33–79). Four other fragmentary manuscripts of this Coptic work are extant. Two of these manuscripts (Borg. Copt. 109, fasc. 144 and 143) are edited by Walter Till, *Koptische Heiligen- und Martyrerlegenden*, 71–4, 74–84; neither has been dated. Another fragment (Vienna K 9437), dating to the ninth century, appears in *Stud. Pal.* xv. 247. Finally, portions of this text appear in a tenth-century Bohairic manuscript published by Evelyn White, *The Monasteries of the Wadi 'n Natrûn*, i. 113–18 (no. 21).

[105] According to the text, Thecla 'married a husband in the city of Antinoopolis', but this husband 'died while he was young' (*Martyrdom of SS. Paese and Thecla* 50 V i. 27–9; ii. 7–9; Reymond and Barns, 34).

[106] Reymond and Barns (1–6) note that many Egyptian martyrologies share features with Greek epic romance and drama.

[107] *Martyrdom of SS. Paese and Thecla* 57 V ii. 14 ff. (Reymond and Barns, 42 ff.).

not recognize them for who they are—during the first half of her journey she thinks the angels are sailors and the women are members of the ruling elite.[108] It is only later that Mary, after anointing Thecla with oil, reveals the identity of the other passengers and appoints Raphael as Thecla's guardian during her impending persecution.[109]

In Alexandria, Thecla is arrested, and her tortures prove even more heinous than her brother's.[110] On the rack, her skin is scraped away until her ribs are exposed. Her breasts are slashed, and her sides are burned by torches. After her heels are pierced, she is hung upside down by a chain until the blood drips from her mouth and nose. Her head is bored with an awl, and boiling pitch is poured down upon her brain.[111] More tortures follow: a

---

[108] *Martyrdom of SS. Paese and Thecla* 68 R i. 17–ii. 3 (Reymond and Barns, 56).

[109] The characterization of Raphael as Thecla's guardian throughout the *Martyrdom of SS. Paese and Thecla* reflects popular conceptions in the cult of the martyrs concerning the power of angelic intermediaries. Coptic magical texts from this period routinely invoke the assistance of both the archangels and the martyrs. While Gabriel is most commonly cited in these spells, Raphael's name frequently surfaces, both individually and as a member of a choir of seven. For instance, one ritual spell from the eighth or ninth century summons Raphael, the other archangels, the three youths in the furnace from Daniel, and all the 'confessors' (ϨΟΜΟΛΟΓΙΤΗⳞ), for healing and protection (*Berlin* 11347; Walter Beltz (ed.), 'Die koptischen Zauberpapiere und Zauberostraka der Papyrus-Sammlung der Staatlichen Museen zu Berlin', *Archiv für Papyrusforschung und verwandte Gebiete*, 31 (1985), 32–5; Angelicus M. Kropp, *Ausgewählte koptische Zaubertexte*, 3 vols. (Brussels: Fondation égyptologique reine Élisabeth, 1930–1), ii. 113–17). In a 'spell for good fishing' from the British Library (*c*.600 CE), the petitioner bids God to make Raphael his special guardian: 'So you must ordain Raphael the archangel for me . . .' (*London Oriental Manuscript* 6795; Kropp, *Ausgewählte koptische Zaubertexte*, i. 32–4). Raphael's interventions to heal Thecla or rescue her from torture provoke accusations of magic from her persecutors. While such accusations were a common motif in martyr literature (see, e.g. *ATh* 15, 20), they also reflect Coptic social assumptions concerning the practice of magic. On the relation of the cult of the martyrs and the cult of the angels in pilgrimage contexts, see also V. Turner, *Image and Pilgrimage in Christian Culture* (New York: Columbia University Press, 1978), 158.

[110] *Martyrdom of SS. Paese and Thecla* 75 R i. 20 ff. (Reymond and Barns, 64 ff.).

[111] On the fragmenting of the female body in Coptic texts, see Terry Wilfong, 'Reading the Disjointed Body in Coptic: From Physical Modification to Textual Fragmentation', in Dominic Montserrat (ed.), *Changing Bodies, Changing Meanings: Studies on the Human Body in Antiquity* (London and New York: Routledge, 1998), 116–36. Wilfong argues that Coptic sources—medical,

burning pyre, hot tar poured down her throat, an attempt to drown her at sea.[112] Each time the archangel Raphael intercedes and rescues Thecla along with her companions.

Exasperated, the Alexandrian commander hands Thecla and her brother over to his military counterpart in the Thebaid (their home district): 'Take these two magicians, and do this favour for me: take them with you to the south . . .'[113] Thus, it is finally near Hermopolis, outside a village named Tepôt, that Thecla and her brother attain martyrdom (they are beheaded).[114]

One can read this fantastical story for social-historical insight into the early medieval cult of the martyrs and the development of traditions related to the name of Thecla in Egypt. Indeed, its author actively seeks to promote the establishment and maintenance of martyr shrines. Standards are set for those who administer the offerings given to 'the house of a saint' (ΠΗ̅Ι̅ Ν̅ΟΥΠΕΤΟΥⲀⲀⲂ): 'If the presbyter, or the deacon, or the administrator performs well the service of the saint without neglect', he will receive blessing from the saint; but, the one who destroys 'the offering that is given to the shrine (ΤΟΠΟⲤ)' will receive punishment.[115] Moreover, heavenly rewards are promised

---

magical, hagiographical, homiletic, and monastic—generally treat women's bodies as a collection of disjointed parts, while they treat men's bodies more in terms of a unified whole. Based on his reading of the martyrdom of Shenoufe, however, he contends that in Coptic martyr accounts this trend is curiously reversed: it is the body of the male martyr (not the female martyr) that is more fully dismembered (ibid. 130–3). The body-part-specific tortures inflicted upon Thecla in the *Martyrdom of SS. Paese and Thecla* would seem to counter that claim. Perhaps a broader study of Coptic martyrdoms is warranted to determine how the female body is constructed in other sources.

[112] *Martyrdom of SS. Paese and Thecla* 81 V i. 24 ff. (Reymond and Barns, 71 ff.).

[113] *Martyrdom of SS. Paese and Thecla* 86 R ii. 19–24 (Reymond and Barns, 76–7).

[114] A seventh-century Greek document records Tepôt in a list of place names in the Hermopolite nome (*Stud. Pal.* xxv. 27). Another mention of the village in the Bohairic martyrdom of Anoub (with variant spelling ΤΟΥϤⲰΤ instead of ΤΕΠⲰΤ) indicates that it was located on the western (Canopic) branch of the Nile just north of the town of Shetnoufe (*Acta Martyrum* I, ed. I. Balestri and H. Hyvernat, CSCO 3. 1; (Paris: Typographeo Reipublicae, 1907) i. 225 f.; Reymond and Barns, 182–3, n. 109).

[115] *Martyrdom of SS. Paese and Thecla* 80 R i. 26–V i. 19 (Reymond and Barns, 70).

to the person who 'builds a martyr shrine in the name of a saint, or . . . covers the body of one in graveclothes, or . . . gives an offering on the day of a saint, or offers alms to the poor and the strangers in our midst on the day of his commemoration, or gives a gift to the house of a saint, or produces a book for the house of God in his name, or purchases a Gospel and places it in his martyr shrine as a memorial to him'.[116] This litany of charitable deeds ends appropriately with a self-referential nod to the literary patronage of the saints. The *Martyrdom of SS. Paese and Thecla* itself constitutes such a book written in the saints' name; it was likely placed in a church or shrine dedicated to one or both of the martyrs and read on the day of their commemoration. By marking such a literary effort as particularly blessed, the author of the martyrology also implicitly manages to sanction his own role within the life of the cult.

On a literary level, the *Martyrdom of SS. Paese and Thecla* reads as a hagiographical reworking of the original Thecla legend. The Coptic martyrology recycles several familiar scenarios and plot motifs from the *ATh*, and the Egyptian Thecla inherits a number of traits from her onomastic predecessor. In particular, the three interrelated themes of chastity, itinerant 'stranger-hood' (discussed in Chapter 1), and martyrdom[117]—along with the theme of androgyny—play important roles in her characterization.

Widowed at a young age, Paese's sister Thecla first commits herself to a life of continence in the service of the martyrs: 'Many wealthy men of the city exhorted her (to marry), saying "We want to take you as our wife"; but as for her, she was not persuaded by them, but remained faithful to the saints . . .'[118] Her rejection of marriage recalls the original Thecla's spurning of Thamyris (*ATh* 7–10). Indeed, in a vision, Paese learns that his sister Thecla will be rewarded in heaven because of her 'chastity'.[119]

---

[116] *Martyrdom of SS. Paese and Thecla* 79 R i. 23–ii. 15 (Reymond and Barns, 69).

[117] Thecla, along with Paese and Paul, earns three crowns in heaven: one for her 'lot as a stranger', one for her 'blood that will be poured forth over Christ's name', and one because of her 'chastity' (*Martyrdom of SS. Paese and Thecla* 80 V ii. 31–81 R i. 6; Reymond and Barns, 70).

[118] *Martyrdom of SS. Paese and Thecla* 51 V i. 2–9 (Reymond and Barns, 35).

[119] *Martyrdom of SS. Paese and Thecla* 81 R i. 5–6 (Reymond and Barns, 70).

Also as in the *ATh*, the Egyptian Thecla is physically separated from the male protagonist of the story (in this case, her brother Paese), and the plot is motivated by her travels to reunite with him. Her eventual reunion with Paese in the prison is reminiscent of Thecla's initial visitation with Paul in *ATh* 18.

[Thecla] went in to Paul and, having sat down at his feet, she heard about the magnificent acts of God. And Paul feared nothing, but conducted himself with the boldness of God; and her faith increased as she kissed his fetters. (*ATh* 18)

She discovered [Paese] fettered with the saints—there was great favour upon his face, after the manner of an angel of God. She advanced toward him, and kissed him . . . (*Martyrdom of SS. Paese and Thecla* 72 R ii. 15–23)

In this context, Thecla's brother himself becomes a surrogate for the apostle Paul in the story.[120] Imprisoned in Alexandria, Paese goes on to describe himself as a 'stranger in this city' (ⲞⲨⲰⲘⲘⲞ ⲠⲚⲦⲈⲒⲠⲞⲗⲓⲤ), echoing the Iconians' descriptions of the apostle Paul in the *ATh*.[121] Significantly, the Egyptian Thecla identifies with her brother's (and the original Thecla's) 'lot as a stranger' (ⲦⲘⲚⲦⲰⲘⲘⲞ).[122] Called from her home in Antinoopolis to travel the many miles to Alexandria, martyrdom for her both literally and figuratively constitutes a pilgrimage. From prison, she writes a letter to her son, 'I wander (ⲤⲰⲣⲘ) from strange places, and all our fathers lived as strangers (ⲢⲰⲘⲘⲞ); for our father David said, "I am a sojourner (ⲢⲘⲚϭⲞⲓⲗⲉ), abiding just like all my fathers did." '[123] Here, the language of itinerancy has come to signify the martyr's journey.

Besides her dedication to chastity and her self-identification as a wandering 'stranger', the Egyptian Thecla also shares in (and indeed exceeds) her predecessor's martyr trials. Her trial by fire

---

[120] The name of Paese's best friend, Paul, further suggests this connection. While Paese functions as the surrogate for the apostle, Paul's name is attached to a secondary character in the narrative.

[121] *Martyrdom of SS. Paese and Thecla* 54 V i. 28–9 (Reymond and Barns, 38); cf. *ATh* 8 and 13.

[122] *Martyrdom of SS. Paese and Thecla* 80 V ii. 33 (Reymond and Barns, 70). In the Coptic version of the *ATh*, the feminine form of 'stranger' (ⲰⲘⲘⲰ) is twice applied to Thecla (*Acta Pauli*, ed. Schmidt, 21. 3; 22. 11).

[123] *Martyrdom of SS. Paese and Thecla* 82 V ii. 17–25 (Reymond and Barns, 73).

recapitulates the earlier martyr scene from the *ATh*,[124] and both Theclas are ultimately delivered by means of a miraculous act of divine intercession. While a thunderstorm quenches the flames in the *ATh*, in the Egyptian martyrology the Virgin Mary and the archangel Raphael intercede in Alexandria and make the fire seem 'like a dewy wind blowing at dawn'.[125]

In addition, the ideal that a woman should 'become male', so prominent in the *ATh*, finds new expression in this Coptic text. Indeed, for Paese and his sister Thecla, martyrdom itself becomes the supreme, masculine act. Raphael twice appears to Paese in prison and urges him to 'become strong' (ϢⲰⲠⲈ ⲚⲞⲨⲢⲰⲘⲈ Ⲛ̄ⲬⲰⲰⲢⲈ) like a man.[126] It is significant that Raphael also identifies Thecla as a woman 'strong in her soul' (ⲬⲰⲰⲢⲈ Ϩ̄Ⲛ̄ⲦⲈⲤⲯⲨⲬⲎ).[127] Thecla's own move toward 'manliness' is manifested physically during her martyr trials— at one point, the Alexandrian commander has both her breasts slashed.[128] This act of carving off her breasts has the function of 'defeminizing' Thecla.[129] Indeed, the author emphasizes her (masculine) strength by bracketing this event with an inclusio:

Now this blessed woman bore this torture with great strength [Ⲙ̄Ⲛ̄Ⲧ ⲬⲰⲰⲠⲈ]. Afterward [the commander] had both her breasts slashed, and he also had four burning torches brought, and he placed them under her sides. *The blessed Thecla bore these tortures with strength* [Ⲙ̄Ⲛ̄Ⲧ ⲬⲰⲰⲠⲈ].[130]

Of course, later when the angel Raphael arrives and heals her breasts 'as if she had not been tortured at all',[131] the reader recognizes that Thecla's physically 'de-sexed' state is only temporary; it functions as a liminal moment, an event that discloses

---

[124] *Martyrdom of SS. Paese and Thecla* 77 R i. 12–17 (Reymond and Barns, 66); *ATh* 22.

[125] *Martyrdom of SS. Paese and Thecla* 77 R ii. 5–7 (Reymond and Barns, 66).

[126] *Martyrdom of SS. Paese and Thecla* 61 V i. 19–21; 66 R ii. 29–31 (Reymond and Barns, 47, 54).

[127] *Martyrdom of SS. Paese and Thecla* 66 V ii. 6–7 (Reymond and Barns, 54).

[128] *Martyrdom of SS. Paese and Thecla* 75 R i. 31–3 (Reymond and Barns, 64).

[129] On the modification (and fragmentation) of gendered bodies in Coptic texts, see Terry Wilfong, 'Reading the Disjointed Body in Coptic', 116–36.

[130] *Martyrdom of SS. Paese and Thecla* 75 R i. 26–ii. 9; (Reymond and Barns, 64; my italics).

[131] *Martyrdom of SS. Paese and Thecla* 75 V i. 2–6 (Reymond and Barns, 64).

the virility of her spirit and anticipates her final suffering and glorification as a martyr.

In borrowing from the *ATh*, the author of this martyrology has demonstrated considerable independence of composition, undoubtedly drawing from other traditions. And yet, lines of convergence remain in the presentation of narrative scenarios, in the characterization of the female protagonists, and above all in the duplication of the name Thecla. Indeed, the characterization of this Coptic namesake shows how a new Egyptian Thecla could be created out of the stuff of the original Thecla legend.

I want to argue that the *Martyrdom of SS. Paese and Thecla* was produced in order to link Thecla's name and legacy more closely to the towns and countryside of the Nile Valley. Antinoopolis gains repute as Thecla's 'home town'—the place where she dedicated herself to a chaste life and offered aid to imprisoned saints. In fact, later traditions preserved in the *Arabic-Jacobite Synaxarium* and in the *Calendar of Abou'l-Barakât* point to her enduring hagiographical association with that city and its environs.[132]

The conclusion of the *Martyrdom of SS. Paese and Thecla* provides a specific aetiological background for the discovery of Thecla's (and Paese's) relics across the river from Antinoopolis

---

[132] *Le Synaxaire arabe jacobite (rédaction copte)*, iii. *Les mois de Toubeh et d'Amchir*, ed. R. Basset, PO 11. 5 (1915), 811–12; *Le Calendrier d'Abou'l-Barakât*, ed. E. Tisserant, PO 10.3 (1915), 266. The *Synaxarium* summary seems to be yet another rewriting of the traditions surrounding Thecla, Paese, and Paul. Paul is portrayed as the son of Syrian parents who have resettled in Egypt at Hermopolis (al-Ashmûnayn). Seeking martyrdom, he travels to Alexandria where he openly confesses his Christian faith. After being sent back to Antinoopolis for questioning, he is tortured and then executed. Two friends of his from Antinoopolis, Thecla and her brother Abaisi (= Paese?), recover his body and bury it. This Thecla of Antinoopolis is herself celebrated as a separate martyr in the Coptic calendar (O'Leary, *Saints of Egypt*, 260; Antonini, 'Le chiese cristiane nell'Egitto,' 136) although her characterization demonstrates marked correlations with the tradition preserved in the *Martyrdom of Paese and Thecla*. The mention of a martyr named Thecla in the *Calendar of Abou'l-Barakât* is also probably derivative of the tradition related to Paese and Thecla. In the *Calendar*, Thecla is paired on her feast day with a Saint Macrobius, probably identifiable with Macrobius of Hermopolis (al-Ashmûnayn), the city near Thecla's (and Paese's) presumed place of burial (M. de Fenoyl, *Le sanctoral copte* (Beirut: Imprimerie catholique, 1960), 128; P. du Bourguet, SJ, 'Christian Subjects in Coptic Art: Saint Thecla', *The Coptic Encyclopedia*, ii. 541).

in the Hermopolite nome. At the end of the work, Thecla and her brother are not executed in Alexandria; instead, they are conveyed as prisoners on a boat travelling south and beheaded at an unnamed location (**ⲞⲨⲞⲨⲰϨ**) north of the village of Tepôt.[133] The author, claiming the privilege of an eyewitness, vouches for the preservation of the martyrs' remains: 'I saw how the angel Raphael, having stretched out his hands, collected the blood of these saints, and did not allow it to touch the earth.'[134] He then relates the story of how an old man stumbled upon the bodies of Paese and Thecla with the help of another angel: after wrapping them in graveclothes, 'he took them to a high place and buried them until the day when God was ready to reveal them'.[135] In narrating these events, the author seeks to authenticate the active veneration of Thecla's and Paese's relics in this region.

Finally, the *Martyrdom of SS. Paese and Thecla* also hints at the social tensions that underlay the creation of new martyrs in early medieval Egypt—namely, the lines of co-operation and competition that existed between cultic locales. The story repeatedly casts Thecla's persecution in terms of an overt rivalry between Christ and Apollo, who is portrayed as the god of the Alexandrian commander.[136] Yet, while Thecla is made to wage open war again this stock pagan adversary, her hagiographer also would have her engage in a far subtler diplomacy with the local traditions of

---

[133] *Martyrdom of SS. Paese and Thecla* 86 V i. 26 (Reymond and Barns, 77). The editors Reymond and Barns (183) translate **ⲞⲨⲰϨ** as 'hamlet'. Crum (*The Coptic Dictionary*, 508) gives the definition, 'dwelling-place'; however, he notes that its meaning remains in many cases 'obscure' and 'doubtful'.

[134] *Martyrdom of SS. Paese and Thecla* 87 V i. 20–9 (Reymond and Barns, 78). The author also assures the reader that during the night local sheepdogs guarded the bodies of the saints and 'did not allow anyone to touch them' (*Martyrdom of SS. Paese and Thecla* 87 V ii. 16–20; Reymond and Barns, 78).

[135] *Martyrdom of SS. Paese and Thecla* 88 R ii. 14–23 (Reymond and Barns, 78–9).

[136] Early in the narrative, the Alexandrian commander challenges Paese: 'Why has Jesus not come and helped you; why has he not rescued you from my hands? Because there is no god who has power like Apollo.' Later, Thecla responds to him by defying Apollo's power to heal: 'Let Apollo walk, and come to me in this place, and I will worship him . . . I have never seen a god raised up and brought to a person; but rather, it is our Lord Jesus Christ who goes to everyone and saves those who hope in Him . . . If Apollo is a living god, the next time you are sick, let him heal you' (*Martyrdom of SS. Paese and Thecla* 59 R ii. 22–31; 76 R ii. 32–76 V ii. 10; Reymond and Barns, 43–4, 65–6).

other female saints. Specifically, Thecla's river journey to Alexandria allows the author to trace a cultic topography along the
Nile, and to forge links with the cult of the Virgin Mary at
Hermopolis (al-Ashmûnayn)[137] and the cult of a young Egyptian
virgin-martyr named Heraei at Tammah (in the nome of
Memphis).[138] During her travels, Thecla learns of Mary's legendary residence in Hermopolis during the Holy Family's exile
in Egypt, and is miraculously anointed with oil by Mary. Thecla
also visits the home of Heraei in the town of Tammah; there Heraei
too receives Mary's blessing in preparation for martyrdom. Along
with Elizabeth and a maidservant, Mary and Heraei accompany
Thecla on her journey and act as a female community of support
during the time leading up to Thecla's martyr trials.

And yet, the benefaction of Mary and sorority of Heraei in the
story also belies subtle lines of competition within the cult of the
saints. It is noteworthy that during the latter part of the narrative, these other female characters disappear. A central figure
in Thecla's journey and early martyr trials, Mary is notably absent
following Thecla's rescue from the pyre.[139] Thus, just as the
martyrologist seeks to localize Thecla's martyr tradition in the
environs of Hermopolis, he effectively removes all competing local
claims from the picture. Further mentions of Mary and her cult

---

[137] The first night of her journey, Thecla asks Mary (whom she still does not
recognize) what city she is from. Mary responds by telling her that she had been
living 'in the city of Shmoun', Greek Hermopolis Magna (*Martyrdom of SS.
Paese and Thecla* 69 V i. 6–8, 13–18; Reymond and Barns, 57). The legend of
the Holy Family's sojourn in Hermopolis appears as early as the fifth century
in the writings of Palladius and Sozomen (Palladius, *H. Laus.* 52 (PG 34. 1137);
Sozomen, *H.E.* 5. 22 (PG 67. 1281); M. Jullien, 'Traditions et légendes coptes
sur le voyage de la sainte-famille en Égypte', *Les missions catholiques*, 19 (1887),
22–3). This tradition later flowered in the Middle Ages (O. Meinardus, *In the
Steps of the Holy Family from Bethlehem to Upper Egypt* (Cairo: Dar al-Maaref,
1963), 45–8).

[138] The legend of Heraei is celebrated in a martyrology published by F. Rossi
(*I papiri copti del museo egizio di Torino* (Turin, 1887–8), i. 5, 32 ff.). In that
account, she is said to be not yet fourteen years old, while in the *Martyrdom of
SS. Paese and Thecla* her age is twelve (*Martyrdom of SS. Paese and Thecla* 70
V ii. 18 ff.; Reymond and Barns, 59). Heraei also appears in the Egyptian mar-
tyrdom of Apater and Irai (*Les Actes des martyrs de l'Égypte*, ed. H. Hyvernat
(Paris, 1886), 78 ff.; Reymond and Barns, 169, n. 63).

[139] *Martyrdom of SS. Paese and Thecla* 77 R ii (Reymond and Barns, 66).

in Hermopolis perhaps would only have overshadowed the writer's attempts to establish Thecla as the female martyr *par excellence* in that locality. This milieu of cultic competition may finally also explain why the original Saint Thecla is never mentioned in the martyrology of her Coptic namesake. The writer is not interested so much in portraying a life that merely reflects the example of Saint Thecla; instead, he seeks, in some sense, to *elide* the original image of Thecla and *replace* her with an Egyptian surrogate. In the process, the original Thecla gets lost in the Coptic 'translation'.

The creation of new martyr traditions was quite common in late antique and early medieval Christianity, and Egypt was no exception. In the fifth century, for example, the Egyptian monk Shenoute laments the practice, condemning those who try to pass off corpses' bones as martyr relics.[140] A less hostile observer might view the production of new martyr accounts as the creative expression of local pieties. At any rate, the result was often a proliferation of martyr accounts associated with the same name. Later martyr traditions tried to connect the name of Thecla with different cities and regions throughout the Mediterranean, including Sicily,[141] Rome,[142] Salerno (Italy),[143] Aquileia (Italy),[144] Claromontanum (France),[145] Hadrumetum (Tunisia),[146] Gaza (Palestine),[147] Khirbet Mâmâs (Palestine),[148] and even

[140] Shenoute, *Discourses* 8 ('Those Who Work Evil'); codex HD 239: ii. 24 ff.; catalogued by Stephen L. Emmel, 'Shenoute's Literary Corpus', (Ph.D. diss., Yale University, 1993) iv. 979–80.

[141] *Acta Sanctorum* (2 May), 502–50; Giuseppe Morabito, 'Alfio, Filadelfio, et al.', *Bibliotheca Sanctorum*, 1 (1961), 832–4.

[142] Lipsius and Bonnet, 270 (MSS A, B, C). Umberto Fasola, 'Tecla', *Bibliotheca Sanctorum*, 12 (1969), 175, 180–1; see Fasola's bibliography for archaeological publications on the Catacomb of Saint Thecla on the Via Ostiensis.

[143] *Acta Sanctorum* (2 Jan.), 190–4; Antonio Balducci, 'Archelaide, Tecla e Susanna', *Bibliotheca Sanctorum*, 2 (1962), 375–6.

[144] *Acta Sanctorum* (1 Sept.), 605–8; Fasola, 'Tecla'.

[145] *Acta Sanctorum* (6 Sept.), 537; Gérard Nathon, 'Tecla', *Bibliotheca Sanctorum*, 12 (1969), 173–4.

[146] *Acta Sanctorum* (6 Aug.), 551–2; Thomas Špidlík, 'Bonifacio e Tecla', *Bibliotheca Sanctorum*, 3 (1969), 335–6.

[147] Eusebius, *De martyribus Palestinae* 3.1 (PG 20. 1409); Fasola, 'Tecla'.

[148] Joseph-Maria Sauget, 'Mamante, Tecla, Basilisco', *Bibliotheca Sanctorum*, 8 (1966), 612–13.

Alexandria.[149] Hagiographical traditions about an Alexandrian martyr named Thecla are only preserved in summary accounts, but they appear to have been later adaptations of the Paese and Thecla legend. The Arabic and Ethiopic *Synaxaria* record the martyrdoms of an Egyptian woman named Thecla and her close friend (or sister) named Mugi. As in the *Martyrdom of Paese and Thecla*, Thecla travels to Alexandria in a boat guided by Mary and Elizabeth, and endures persecution in that city. In the case of the *Synaxaria*, however, she is said to hail from a place called Qarâqus (Farâqes) in Lower Egypt, and is martyred near Alexandria in a town called Damtouâ (Demutu).[150] A tradition preserved in a Greek martyrology may indicate another variation on this legend: there, Thecla has a sister named Andropelagia, and both are said to be martyred in Alexandria itself.[151] These variant traditions were probably attempts by the medieval Coptic church in Alexandria to adopt this Egyptian Thecla as their own.[152] Thus, the *Martyrdom of SS. Paese and Thecla* is not the only example of this impulse to create new, local martyr traditions; but it is unique for the insight it offers into the cult of Thecla in the Nile Valley, and the social factors that motivated the creation of a namesake saint.

CONCLUSION

Ascetic treatises, miracle stories, and martyr accounts; pilgrim flasks, wall paintings, and grave stelae—these literary and

---

[149] *Le Synaxaire éthiopien*, ii. *Mois de Hamlé*, ed. I. Guidi, PO 7 (1911), 413–14; *Synaxarium Alexandrinum*, ed. I. Forget, CSCO 19 (versio), Scriptores Arabici (Lavanio: Marcellus Istas, 1926), 239–40; *Le Synaxaire arabe jacobite (rédaction copte)*, v. *Les mois de Baounah, Abib, Mesoré et jours complémentaires*, ed. R. Basset, PO 17 (1923), 687; Joseph-Marie Sauget, 'Tecla e Mugi', *Bibliotheca Sanctorum*, 12 (1969), 184–5; *Acta Sanctorum* (2 Sept.), 666–7.

[150] E. Amélineau, *La géographie de l'Égypte à l'époque copte* (Paris: Imprimerie nationale, 1893), 120, 178.

[151] *Acta Sanctorum* (2 Sept.), 666–7.

[152] This proliferation of Thecla legends may have given rise to the later Alexandrian tradition that a martyr named Thecla was the scribe of the *Codex Alexandrinus*. On this tradition, see H. J. M. Milne, *The Codex Sinaiticus and the Codex Alexandrinus* (London: British Museum, 1938), 28–9; also John Gwynn, 'Thecla (11)', in W. Smith and H. Wace (eds.), *A Dictionary of Christian Biography, Sects, and Doctrines* (New York: AMS Press, 1984), 897.

material artefacts give evidence of communities that gave rise to the cult of Saint Thecla in Egypt. Each artefact has the power of bringing us, as historians, into closer contact with the everyday lives of Egyptian Christians who venerated Thecla as a saint. By reading for ourselves Athanasius' urgent appeals to Alexandrian virgins, by handling a clay flask worn smooth by pilgrim hands, by stooping through the doorway of a burial chapel, or by deciphering an ancient gravestone, we are able to enter imaginatively the social world of Egyptian Christians who venerated Saint Thecla. What finally can be said about that world?

Despite the sometimes piecemeal nature of the evidence, I have described common practices associated with Thecla's cult across the geographical boundaries of Asia Minor and Egypt. Just as in Asia Minor, Thecla devotion in Egypt remained firmly grounded in the practices of asceticism and pilgrimage related to the cult of the martyrs. Indeed, even when the cult of Saint Thecla was transformed through the creation of new namesake martyr traditions, asceticism and pilgrimage continued to be promoted as ideals for devotees. Thus, the Coptic martyr Thecla in the *Martyrdom of SS. Paese and Thecla* is said to earn a reward in heaven not simply for the blood that she sheds in martyrdom, but also for her 'chastity' (i.e. her asceticism) and her 'lot as a stranger' (i.e. her itinerancy).[153]

I have also emphasized the fact that women played leading roles in the development and spread of Thecla devotion. The origins of the Thecla cult may be traced to communities of ascetic women who originally transmitted her legend orally. In the fourth and fifth centuries CE, women were active as pilgrims and as resident virgins at Thecla's shrine near Seleucia, Asia Minor. In Egypt during this same period, Alexandrian female monks under Athanasius revered Thecla as their patron saint; these same virgins exported Thecla devotion to the Kharga Oasis when they were exiled there during the Arian Controversy. During the fifth and sixth centuries, itinerant women were an integral part of the clientele at Thecla's shrine in the Mareotis. We might expect, then, that in the Fayûm and the Nile Valley the cult of Saint Thecla continued to be associated with the religious practices of

---

[153] *Martyrdom of SS. Paese and Thecla* 80 v ii. 31–81 R i. 6 (Reymond and Barns, 70).

women.[154] Indeed, the fact that Thecla's image appears on a woman's comb and the evidence for women naming their children after Thecla indicate that her cult was active not just among monastic women but also among women in families and households. The practice of naming female children after Thecla (documented in Appendix B) may even be seen as a popular expression of the urge to imitate the female martyr among married women.[155]

Sedentary virgins living in urban households, suburban tombs, and desert monasteries; solitary ascetic wanderers and wealthy pilgrims travelling in organized groups; women in Christian households who named their children after Thecla, who had Thecla's image etched into their combs, embossed on their oil lamps, and carved onto the face of their gravestones—no matter their background, what bound these female devotees of Saint Thecla together was a common desire to emulate the female saint. An ethic of imitation consistently informed the promotion of Thecla as a saint in Egypt. The Bishop Athanasius exhorts Alexandrian virgins to 'abide with the blessed Thecla,' and to re-enact in their lives her ascetic struggle. The biographer of

---

[154] In most cases, the papyrological and inscriptional evidence is not helpful for the task of reconstructing female devotion to Thecla in these regions. It should be noted, however, that this evidence is equally unhelpful for the task of reconstructing specifically *male* devotion to Thecla. There are a few references to male clergy connected to churches of Saint Thecla, but they hold clerical offices one would expect to be held by men during this time period: *oikonomos, diakonos, ecclesiekdikos, presbyteros* (*Stud. Pal.* VIII. 104; *P. Oxy.* XVI. 1993. 18–20; *P. Oxy.* XXIV. 2419. 3–5).

[155] In a culture that both celebrated and feared the power of names (as evidenced by the use of names in ancient magical incantations) the propagation of namesakes often reflected parents' hopes that their daughters would receive the protection, and one day embody the virtues, of the saints. In his biography of his sister Macrina, Gregory of Nyssa describes how his mother, just as she was about to give birth to Macrina, had a dream in which the child was given the secret name of Thecla. Gregory goes on to explain that this secret name was intended 'to foretell the life of the girl and to mark, by the identity [ὁμωνυμία] of the name, the similitude [ὁμοιότητα] of life purpose' (Gregory of Nyssa, *V. Macr.* 2, ed. Pierre Maraval (SC 178), 148; PG 46. 961B–C; on the association of Macrina with Thecla, see Ruth Albrecht, *Das Leben der heiligen Makrina auf dem Hintergrund der Thekla-Traditionen* (Göttingen: Vandenhoeck & Ruprecht, 1986)). In the *Life and Miracles of Saint Thecla*, a woman named Thecla is even thought by her mother to resemble the saint in form and stature (*Miracle* 11; Dag., 314).

Syncletica presents her as a disciple moulded in Thecla's image, and urges his monastic readers to envision both Thecla and Syncletica as models for their own piety. In her *Life*, Eugenia explicitly emulates Thecla by donning male clothing, a gesture that signifies her break from family and her freedom to travel. In the wall painting in the Chapel of the Exodus (El Bagawat), the artist depicts the deceased in the same posture as her patron Saint Thecla, and evokes in the (implied) viewer a similar visual identification with the saint. The author of the *Martyrdom of SS. Paese and Thecla* creates a new, Coptic namesake martyr in the original Thecla's image—through such literary patronage Thecla is finally 'Egyptianized' as a model for women's piety.

An Egyptian grave stele in the Coptic Museum in Cairo (Fig. 31)[156] provides a rare, personal glimpse into one Egyptian woman's identification with Saint Thecla. The stele displays the roughly carved relief of a female *orans*. A Greek inscription, scrawled like a graffito around and below the figure, identifies the deceased as a namesake of Saint Thecla: 'Lord, give rest to the soul of your servant Thecla. . . .' Standing on a pedestal shaped as a parallelogram, this Thecla wears only a short apron; her torso and breasts are exposed. A cross has been incised over each upraised arm. The artisan seems to have made an ill-fated attempt to etch two animals on either side of the figure. On the right, the head, body, and tail of a crudely drawn animal are faintly visible. On the left, he or she apparently abandoned the project after only a few unsuccessful scratches.

On this grave stone, the deceased is not physically juxtaposed to her patron saint. *Instead, the artist seems to have actually conflated the image of Saint Thecla with that of the deceased.* Here, the portrait of Thecla from the pilgrim flasks—where she appears topless and flanked by beasts—infuses the funerary image of her namesake.[157] The commissioning of one's own gravestone was not uncommon in antiquity: it is likely that this

---

[156] *Coptic Monuments*, ed. W. E. Crum, Catalogue général des antiquités égyptiennes du Musée du Caire (Cairo: Imprimerie de l'Institut français d'archéologie orientale, 1902) 142, and pl. 52, nr. 8693; DACL xii. 2. 2313, 2318, fig. 9098.

[157] Nauerth and Warns (*Thekla*, 48–50) argue that the parallelogram beneath the woman's feet represents Thecla's 'baptismal pool' in the arena, that the crosses above her function as baptismal symbols, and that the stele recalls the common baptism of the two Theclas.

woman was familiar with such representations of the saint and arranged to have herself depicted in the image of Thecla on her own stele.

This stele confirms the fact that Egyptian women understood their devotion to Saint Thecla as a form of imitation. In their own lives, and in their deaths, female devotees saw themselves as conforming to the image of the female saint.[158] Of course, the ethic of *imitatio Theclae*—the imitation of Thecla as a moral exemplar—did not result in a monochromatic piety among Egyptian women; it in fact produced diverse forms of religious practice. The practices of devotees varied in accordance with their social context. Yet, the virgin living in an urban household, the wandering desert ascetic, the wealthy international pilgrim, the married woman living near a shrine each would have shared a common desire to imitate Thecla the saint. For such women in late antiquity, Thecla's example was a source of empowerment. By imitating the female apostle and protomartyr, devoted women laid claim to her *charisma*, a spiritual power made accessible to them in the shrines and sacred artefacts of the Thecla cult.

---

[158] On death as the ultimate assimilation with one's models, see S. Harvey, 'Women in Early Byzantine Hagiography', 51.

APPENDIX A

A Catalogue of Published Ampullae with Saint Thecla[1]

Key: H = Height; Dm = Diameter; W = Width; Th = Thickness

1. Ampulla, fragment.
   a. *Location*: Alexandria, Graeco-Roman Museum.
   b. *Size*: Dm 11.5 cm.
   c. *Dating*: 5th century CE (Wilpert); on the basis of iconographic and inscriptional forms.
   d. *Bibliography*: (1) E. D. J. Dutilh, 'Symbolisme des antiquités chrétienne'/'Early Symbolism', *Bulletin de la archéologique d'Alexandrie*, 6 (1904), 45–6, 63–4; no. 7, Pl. 1 and 2 (misidentified as a relief of Menas). (2) J. Wilpert, 'Menasfläschen mit der Darstellung der hl. Thecla zwischen den wilden Tieren', in *Römische Quartalschrift*, 20 (1906), 90–1 (no image provided).
2. Ampulla, fragment.
   a. *Location*: Alexandria (Kôm el-Dikka), Centre d'archéologie méditerranéenne de l'Académie polonaise des sciences et Centre polonais d'archéologie méditerranéenne de l'Université de Varsovie au Caire, Inv. W 1/3720/81. Discovered at Kôm el-Dikka, Alexandria.
   b. *Size*: H 4 cm; W 4 cm.
   c. *Dating*: 480–560 CE (Kiss); on the basis of stratigraphic location of discovery.
   d. *Bibliography*: Zsolt Kiss, *Les ampoules de Saint Menas découvertes à Kôm el-Dikka (1961–81)* (Varsovie: PWN—Éditions Scientifiques de Pologne, 1989), no. 4, fig. 5.
3. Ampulla, fragment.
   a. *Location*: Alexandria (Kôm el-Dikka), Centre d'archéologie méditerranéenne de l'Académie polonaise des sciences et Centre polonais d'archéologie méditerranéenne de l'Université de Varsovie au Caire, Inv. R/1584/70. Discovered at Kôm el-Dikka, Alexandria.

---

[1] Previously published in 'Pilgrimage and the Cult of Saint Thecla in Late Antique Egypt', in David Frankfurter (ed.), *Pilgrimage and Holy Space in Late Antique Egypt* (Leiden: Brill, 1998), 335–9.

b. *Size*: H 10.5 cm; W 6.5 cm; Th 3.5 cm.

c. *Dating*: 480–560 CE (Kiss); on the basis of stratigraphic location of discovery.

d. *Bibliography*: Zsolt Kiss, *Les ampoules de Saint Menas découvertes à Kôm el-Dikka (1961–81)* (Varsovie: PWN—Éditions Scientifiques de Pologne, 1989), no. 5, fig. 6.

4. Ampulla, fragment.

a. *Location*: Alexandria (Kôm el-Dikka), Centre d'archéologie méditerranéenne de l'Académie polonaise des sciences et Centre polonais d'archéologie méditerranéenne de l'Université de Varsovie au Caire, no inventory number. Discovered at Kôm el-Dikka, Alexandria.

b. *Size*: H 5 cm; W 3 cm.

c. *Dating*: Undetermined.

d. *Bibliography*: Zsolt Kiss, *Les ampoules de Saint Menas découvertes à Kôm el-Dikka (1961–81)* (Varsovie: PWN—Éditions Scientifiques de Pologne, 1989), no. 6, fig. 7.

5. Ampulla, fragment.

a. *Location*: Berlin, Frühchristlich-byzantinische Sammlung, Nr. 1361.

b. *Size*: Dm 6.5 cm.

c. *Dating*: 4th–5th cent. CE (Wulff); no criterion provided.

d. *Bibliography*: O. Wulff, *Altchristliche und mittelalterliche byzantinische Bildwerke* I (Berlin: Georg Reimer, 1909), 266, no. 1361, Taf. 69.

6. Ampulla, two fragments.

a. *Location*: Frankfurt am Main, Liebieghaus Museum alter Plastik, Inv.-Nr. 2775.2.

b. *Size*: H 19 cm; Dm 10 cm.

c. *Dating*: 480–560 CE (Kaminski-Menssen, 41–4); on the basis of Kiss's stratigraphic findings.

d. *Bibliography*: (1) Claudia Nauerth, 'Nachlese von Thekla-Darstellungen', in G. Koch (ed.), *Studien zur spätantiken und frühchristlichen Kunst und Kultur des Orients* (Göttinger Orientforschungen II. Reihe, Band 6; Wiesbaden: Otto Harrassowitz, 1982), 14–15, Taf. 4, Abb. 1, Fc (only one of the two fragments). (2) Gabrielle Kaminski-Menssen, *Bildwerke aus Ton, Bein und Metall*, Liebieghaus-Museum alter Plastik, Bildwerke der Sammlung Kaufmann, Band III (Kassel: Verlag Gutenberg, 1996), 55–6, Kat.-Nr. I 2, Taf. 3.

7. Ampulla, fragment.

a. *Location*: Frankfurt am Main, Liebieghaus Museum alter Plastik, Inv.-Nr. 2775.27.

b. *Size*: H 13 cm; Dm 13 cm; W 0.8 cm; Th 3.7 cm.

c. *Dating*: 480–560 CE (Kaminski-Menssen, 41–4); on the basis of Kiss's stratigraphic findings.

d. *Bibliography*: (1) Claudia Nauerth, 'Nachlese von Thekla-Darstellungen', in G. Koch (ed.), *Studien zur spätantiken und frühchristlichen Kunst und Kultur des Orients* (Göttinger Orientforschungen II. Reihe, Band 6; Wiesbaden: Otto Harrassowitz, 1982), 14–15, Taf. 4, Abb. 1, Fb. (2) Gabrielle Kaminski-Menssen, *Bildwerke aus Ton, Bein und Metall*, Liebieghaus-Museum alter Plastik, Bildwerke der Sammlung Kaufmann, Band III (Kassel: Verlag Gutenberg, 1996), 62, Kat.-Nr. I 27 A–B, Taf. 10.

8. Ampulla, fragment.
   a. *Location*: Frankfurt am Main, Liebieghaus Museum alter Plastik, Inv.-Nr. 2775.29.
   b. *Size*: H 6 cm; Dm 12.5 cm; Th 4.2 cm.
   c. *Dating*: 480–560 CE (Kaminski-Menssen, 41–4); on the basis of Kiss's stratigraphic findings.
   d. *Bibliography*: (1) Claudia Nauerth, 'Nachlese von Thekla-Darstellungen', in G. Koch (ed.), *Studien zur spätantiken und frühchristlichen Kunst und Kultur des Orients* (Göttinger Orientforschungen II. Reihe, Band 6; Wiesbaden: Otto Harrassowitz, 1982), 14–15, Taf. 4, Abb. 1, Fd. (2) Gabrielle Kaminski-Menssen, *Bildwerke aus Ton, Bein und Metall*, Liebieghaus-Museum alter Plastik, Bildwerke der Sammlung Kaufmann, Band III (Kassel: Verlag Gutenberg, 1996), 63, Kat.-Nr. I 29 A–B, Taf. 10.

9. Ampulla, fragment.
   a. *Location*: Frankfurt am Main, Liebieghaus Museum alter Plastik, Inv.-Nr. 2775.30.
   b. *Size*: H 9.5 cm; Dm 11 cm.
   c. *Dating*: 480–560 CE (Kaminski-Menssen, 41–4); on the basis of Kiss's stratigraphic findings.
   d. *Bibliography*: (1) Claudia Nauerth, 'Nachlese von Thekla-Darstellungen', in G. Koch (ed.), *Studien zur spätantiken und frühchristlichen Kunst und Kultur des Orients* (Göttinger Orientforschungen II. Reihe, Band 6; Wiesbaden: Otto Harrassowitz, 1982), 14–15, Taf. 4, Abb. 1, Fe. (2) Gabrielle Kaminski-Menssen, *Bildwerke aus Ton, Bein und Metall*, Liebieghaus-Museum alter Plastik, Bildwerke der Sammlung Kaufmann, Band III (Kassel: Verlag Gutenberg, 1996), 63, Kat.-Nr. I 30, Taf. 10.

10. Ampulla.
    a. *Location*: Frankfurt am Main, Liebieghaus Museum alter Plastik, Inv.-Nr. 2775.31.

b. *Size*: H 13 cm; Dm 13 cm.

c. *Dating*: 480–560 CE (Kaminski-Menssen, 41–4); on the basis of Kiss's stratigraphic findings.

d. *Bibliography*: (1) Claudia Nauerth, 'Nachlese von Thekla-Darstellungen', in G. Koch (ed.), *Studien zur spätantiken und frühchristlichen Kunst und Kultur des Orients* (Göttinger Orientforschungen II. Reihe, Band 6; Wiesbaden: Otto Harrassowitz, 1982), 14–15, Taf. 4, Abb. 1, Fa. (2) Gabrielle Kaminski-Menssen, *Bildwerke aus Ton, Bein und Metall*, Liebieghaus-Museum alter Plastik, Bildwerke der Sammlung Kaufmann, Band III (Kassel: Verlag Gutenberg, 1996), 63, Kat.-Nr. I 29 A–B, Tafel 10.

11. Ampulla (Figs. 7–8).

    a. *Location*: London, British Museum, EA69839.

    b. *Size*: Dm 17.7 cm.

    c. *Dating*: 6th–7th century CE (Friedman); no criterion provided.

    d. *Bibliography*: (1) 'Recent Acquisitions', in *British Museum Society Bulletin*, 54 (March 1987), 27. (2) Florence D. Friedman, *Beyond the Pharaohs: Egypt and the Copts in the 2nd to 7th Centuries A.D.* (Providence: RI: Museum of Art, Rhode Island School of Design, 1989), 227, no. 140.

12. Ampulla (Figs. 9–10).

    a. *Location*: London, British Museum, E.C. 882.

    b. *Size*: H 14 cm.

    c. *Dating*: Not determined.

    d. *Bibliography*: (1) O. M. Dalton, *Catalogue of Early Christian Antiquities and Objects from the Christian East in the Department of British and Mediaeval Antiquities and Ethnographs of the British Museum* (London: British Museum, 1901), no. 882, pl. 32. (2) Claudia Nauerth, and Rüdiger Warns, *Thekla: Ihre Bilder in der frühchristlichen Kunst* (Wiesbaden: Otto Harrassowitz, 1981), 35 ff. and Abb. 16. (3) Claudia Nauerth, 'Nachlese von Thekla-Darstellungen', in G. Koch (ed.), *Studien zur spätantiken und frühchristlichen Kunst und Kultur des Orients* (Göttinger Orientforschungen II. Reihe, Band 6; Wiesbaden: Otto Harrassowitz, 1982), Taf. 5, Abb. 2.

13. Ampulla, fragment.

    a. *Location*: New Haven, Yale University Art Gallery, Whiting Palestinian Collection, 1912. 311.

    b. *Size*: H 8.5 cm; W 11.5 cm.

    c. *Dating*: 4th–5th century CE (Kleiner/Matheson); no criterion provided.

    d. *Bibliography*: (1) Charles Alfred Kennedy, 'The Whiting Collection of Palestinian Pottery at Yale.' (Ph.D. diss., Yale

University, 1961), 134–5, no. 441 (W311). (2) Diana E. E. Kleiner and Susan B. Matheson (eds.), *I Claudia: Women in Ancient Rome* (Austin: University of Texas Press, 1996), 102, fig. 70.

14. Ampulla.
    a. *Location*: Unknown.
    b. *Size*: Not available.
    c. *Dating*: 4th–5th century CE (Kaufmann, 1910); on the basis of the dating of Wulff (see cat. no. 5) and Wilpert (see cat. no. 15).
    d. *Bibliography*: (1) C. M. Kaufmann, *Zur Ikonographie der Menasampullen* (Cairo: F. Diemer, Finck, & Baylaender, 1910), 142 and fig. 85. (2) C. M. Kaufmann, *Die heilige Stadt der Wüste* (Kempten-München: J. Kosel and F. Pustet, 1924), 88 and Abb. 52. (3) H. Buschhausen, 'Frühchristliches Silberreliquiar aus Isaurien', in *Jahrbuch der österreichischen-byzantinischen Gesellschaft*, 11/12 (1962–3), fig. 10. (4) A. Grabar, *Martyrium: Recherches sur le culte des reliques et l'art chrétien antique* (Paris: Collège de France, 1946), II.7 and pl. 63. (5) K. Weitzmann, *The Monastery of Saint Catherine at Mount Sinai: The Icons* (Princeton: Princeton University Press, 1976), fig. 21. (6) Claudia Nauerth and Rüdiger Warns, *Thekla: Ihre Bilder in der frühchristlichen Kunst* (Wiesbaden: Otto Harrassowitz, 1981), 35 ff. and Abb. 15.

15. Ampulla.
    a. *Location*: Unknown.
    b. *Size*: Not available.
    c. *Dating*: 5th century CE (Wilpert); on the basis of iconographic and inscriptional forms.
    d. *Bibliography*: (1) J. Wilpert, 'Menasfläschen mit der Darstellung der hl. Thecla zwischen den wilden Tieren', in *Römische Quartalschrift*, 20 (1906), 87. (2) C. M. Kaufmann, *Die heilige Stadt der Wüste* (Kempten-München, 1924), 100 and Abb. 62. (3) DACL XI.1.386, fig. 7979.

16. Ampulla, with base (Figs. 11–12).
    a. *Location*: Paris, Museé du Louvre, Départment des antiquités grecques et romaines, MNC 1926.
    b. *Size*: H 27 cm; Dm 17.5 cm.
    c. *Dating*: 7th century CE (Weitzmann); based on stylistic considerations.
    d. *Bibliography*: (1) Gustave M. Lefebvre, *Recueil des inscriptions grecques-chrétiennes d'Egypte.* (Service des antiquités de l'Égypte; Cairo: Imprimerie de l'Institut français d'archéologie orientale, 1907), 136, no. 692 (no image provided). (2) C. M. Kaufmann, *Zur Ikonographie der Menasampullen* (Cairo: F. Diemer, Finck, & Baylaender, 1910), 141 (no image provided).

(3) Kurt Weitzmann, ed., *Age of Spirituality: Late Antique and Early Christian Art: Third to Seventh Century* (New York: Metropolitan Museum of Art/Princeton University Press, 1979), 576–8, no. 516. (4) Claudia Nauerth and Rüdiger Warns, *Thekla: Ihre Bilder in der frühchristlichen Kunst* (Wiesbaden: Otto Harrassowitz, 1981), 25–30, and Abb. 10 f.

APPENDIX B

Namesakes of Saint Thecla in Late Antique Egypt[1]

'Lord, give rest to the soul of your servant Thecla. She died in the Lord . . .'[2]

(Epitaph inscribed on a Greek gravestone from Egypt)

Thecla is one of a handful of saints' names, and the only female Christian name besides Mary, widely used by the Christian inhabitants of Egypt in late antiquity.[3] One papyrologist has observed that regional variation in the popularity of saints' names in Egypt would make an interesting study.[4] Here, I will focus my attention on the frequency, distribution, and religious context of the name Thecla in this region.

By studying namesakes of Saint Thecla in Egypt, I hope to gain further (indirect) insight into the popularity of the saint and her cult in late antique Egypt. The evidence for the practice of naming Egyptian children after Thecla comes from papyrological and epigraphic sources. I will proceed by asking four types of questions of this evidence:

---

[1] This appendix appeared originally as an article in the *Bulletin of the American Society of Papyrologists*, 36 (1999) 71–81.

[2] Κ̄Ε̄ ⲀⲚⲀⲠⲀⲨⲤⲞⲚ ⲦⲎⲚ ⲮⲨⲬⲎⲚ ⲦⲎⲤ ⲀⲞⲨⲀ̄ⲎⲤ ⲤⲞⲨ ⲐⲈⲔⲀⲀ̄Ⲥ ⲈⲔⲞⲓⲘⲨⲐⲎ ⲈⲚ Κ̄Ⲱ . . . (*Coptic Monuments*, ed. W. E. Crum, Catalogue général des antiquités égyptiennes du Musée du Caire (Cairo: Imprimerie de l'Institut français d'archéologie orientale, 1902), 89, no. 8385; *Recueil des inscriptions grecques-chrétiennes d'Égypte*, ed. Gustave M. Lefebvre, Service des Antiquités de l'Égypte (Cairo: Imprimerie de l'Institut français d'archéologie orientale, 1907), 22–3, no. 101). The same formula—'Lord, give rest to the soul of your servant Thecla . . .'—also appears on another Greek stele in the Cairo Museum (*Coptic Monuments*, ed. Crum, 126 and pl. 34, no. 8598; *Recueil des inscriptions grecques-chrétiennes d'Égypte*, ed. Lefebvre, 24, no. 107; Lefebvre corrects an error in Crum's transcription).

[3] Roger Bagnall ('Religious Conversion and Onomastic Change in Early Byzantine Egypt', *Bulletin of the American Society of Papyrologists*, 19/3–4 (1982), 110–11) compiles a list of seven such names that can be said to derive exclusively from Christian saints: Phib, Phoibammon, Shenoute, Tatianos, Thekla (Thecla), Theodoros, and Victor.

[4] Ibid.

1. *Chronological*: Is it possible to develop a chronology of this onomastic practice? For instance, how early does Thecla's name appear? When did her name achieve the widest popularity?
2. *Geographical*: How dispersed was the use of her name? In what different places does it appear?
3. *Linguistic*: Does the evidence for naming children after Thecla cross linguistic boundaries? That is, does the name appear in both Greek and Coptic sources? Furthermore, do we observe any onomastic variants derived from the name Thecla? What significance do these variations have?
4. *Religious*: What can we discern about religious assumptions (if any) behind the practice of naming children after the female saint?

First, how early does the name Thecla appear among the inhabitants of Egypt? One would expect the earliest evidence to be from the fourth century, when the cult of Saint Thecla began to attract attention in urban centres like Alexandria. According to the editors of the Oxyrhynchus papyri, however, the name Thecla appears even earlier: in a *libellus* from the period of the Decian persecution (*c*.250 CE), a woman named Thecla is identified as the daughter of a man who made sacrifices to the Emperor.[5] If this reading were correct, it would be quite noteworthy, for it would tell us that her parents were Christians,[6] in all likelihood Christians familiar with the female saint and her story. In addition, it would indicate a remarkably rapid spread of Thecla devotion to the Nile Valley only fifty or seventy-five years after the composition of the *ATh*.

Such early evidence for a namesake of Thecla in Egypt aroused my doubt, and I thought it necessary to have the editors' reading checked. Nikolaos Gonis' recent examination of the papyrus in the British Library confirmed my suspicion: after close study he concluded that it was impossible to read θέκλα from the traces.[7] Thus, the editors' reconstruction of the name Thecla in this third-century *libellus* proves untenable.

The earliest documented evidence for a namesake of Thecla in Egypt comes in fact, as we might expect, from the middle of the fourth century

[5] *P. Oxy.* XII. 1464. r. 10.

[6] John R. Knipfing, 'The Libelli of the Decian Persecution', *Harvard Theological Review*, 16 (1923), 360.

[7] Nikolaos Gonis, *per litt.*, 11 June 1998. The original editors dotted the first, third, and fourth letters of the name (θ, κ, and λ) to indicate their imperfect preservation on the papyrus. According to Gonis, there are in fact 'insignificant remains' of the first letter, the third cannot be kappa in the writer's hand, and the fourth is more likely iota than lambda. I owe thanks to Roger Bagnall, who arranged for Nikolaos Gonis to examine the papyrus for me and who facilitated our communications.

CE. A letter dated to this period from Oxyrhynchus is addressed by a man named Thonius to his 'spouse and sister Thecla'.[8] The verso of the papyrus preserves the original address, 'Deliver to Thecla in the house of Lallochus.'[9] From elsewhere in the Nile Valley, two papyri— one a land register from the mid-fourth century, the other a lease of land dated 394 CE—record namesakes of Thecla in the city of Hermopolis (al-Ashmûnayn).[10] Of particular interest, two fourth-century ostraca recently unearthed at Kysis in the Kharga Oasis attest women named Thecla, a discovery that further confirms the popularity of the female saint among Christians living in that remote region.[11]

While there are likewise only a handful of references to namesakes of Thecla from the fifth century,[12] papyri from the sixth and seventh centuries attest the burgeoning popularity of Thecla's name. Indeed, the increase in the number of women named Thecla during this period can be depicted graphically by comparing the number of namesakes attested century by century in three geographical locations: Oxyrhynchus, Hermopolis/the Hermopolite nome, and Aphrodite.

Table 1

Date	Oxyrhynchus	Hermopolis	Aphrodite	Total
4 CE	1	3	0	4
5 CE	3	4	0	7
6 CE	12	5	10	27
7 CE	5	4	1	10
8 CE	0	0	9	9

[8] *P. Oxy. Descr.* XI. rp. r. 1 (*P. Oxy.* I. 182. r. 1–2), ed. Dominic Montserrat, *et al.*, 'Varia Descripta Oxyrhynchita', *Bulletin of the American Society of Papyrologists*, 31 (1994), 49, pl. 9. The editors date the letter to the fourth century CE based on paleographic comparison with the Papnuthis archive in *P. Oxy.* XLVIII. 3387 (358 CE), 3390 (342 CE).

[9] *P. Oxy. Descr.* XI. rp. v. 1 (*P. Oxy.* I. 182. v. 1), ed. Montserrat, 'Varia Descripta', 49.

[10] *P. Herm.* XXII. v. 6 (394 CE); *P. Herm. Landl.* I. rp. 25. 408 (4th cent. CE).

[11] *O. Douch* I. 20. 1 (306–430 CE); III. 226. 2 (4th cent. CE). For a discussion of wall paintings of Saint Thecla in the Kharga Oasis, and an argument for a community of ascetic female devotees exiled there in the fourth century CE, see Chapter 5.

[12] From Oxyrhynchus: *P. Köln* II. 102. r. 3 (418 CE); *P. Oxy.* L. 3599. r. 7, 23 (460 CE); *P. Wash. Univ.* II. 95. 11 (4th–5th cent. CE); from the Hermopolite nome: *SB* V. 7758. r. 5 (497 CE); *PSI* I. 66. 12, 34, 37 (5th cent. CE?).

These raw totals are simply the number of namesakes documented in each century;[13] in the absence of some constant for comparison, they do not provide a direct basis for determining the popularity of the name Thecla. However, when one considers these numbers in relation to the Heidelberg database records for each century, one can begin to calculate with more precision the frequency of the name's occurrences.[14]

Table 2

Date	Total namesakes from 3 nomes	Heidelberg database records	Frequency of occurrence
4 CE	4	1819	.0022 (0.22%)
5 CE	7	358	.0196 (1.96%)
6 CE	27	1026	.0263 (2.63%)
7 CE	10	436	.0229 (2.29%)
8 CE	9	330	.0273 (2.73%)

Charting the *frequency* of the name Thecla in three regions—Oxyrhynchus, Hermopolis/the Hermopolite nome, and Aphrodite—gives us a more accurate indication of its popularity over time. It is interesting that the greatest proportional rise in the name's popularity occurred from the fourth to the fifth century; during that period its frequency in our sources increased ninefold. The sudden increase in the occurrence of Thecla's name in the fifth century may very well be related to the fact that it was during this period that pilgrimage related to the cult of Saint Thecla first emerged as an active religious practice in Egypt (see Chapter 4). In the three centuries following, as the popularity of the saint increased, so did the popularity of the saint's name, although the increase in its frequency of usage was more incremental.

The popularity of Thecla's name during the sixth and seventh centuries is also evidenced by the 'density' of different namesakes within particular papyri. An early sixth-century document (5–14 July 521 CE) from Aphrodite refers to three distinct women named Thecla:

---

[13] The figures I provide are based on discrete namesakes of Thecla documented in papyri found on the TLG database.

[14] My figures for the total number of papyri recovered for each century comes from the Heidelberger Gesamtverzeichnis der griechischen Papyrusurkunden Ägyptens (available on the web at www.urz.uni-heidelberg.de/institute/fak8/papy/hagedorn/).

a mother of Anouphis, a mother of Mousaios, and a mother of Enoch.[15] Likewise, a seventh-century Greek papyrus recording the purchase of a share of a house testifies to the prevalence of the name Thecla in Oxyrhynchus: the writer (Elizabeth) not only has a mother named Thecla; she also addresses her correspondence to another Thecla with a husband named Philemon.[16] This latter Thecla, the wife of Philemon and the daughter of Dio, is identified often in another papyrus from 647 CE as the owner of a house in Oxyrhynchus.[17] Yet another Thecla, identified as the daughter of a man named Jacob Cana, also surfaces in the same document.[18] The appearance of multiple namesakes in a single papyrus reinforces the impression that Thecla's name would have been encountered frequently in the daily social interactions of Egyptians during this period.

Having discussed namesakes of Thecla from a chronological perspective, I now want to raise questions concerning geography and linguistic culture. How widespread was the practice of naming children after Thecla? In addition to the data for Hermopolis, Oxyrhynchus, and Aphrodite, there is also evidence for namesakes in a number of other locales (almost anywhere that provides documentary evidence in some quantity). I have already mentioned fourth-century ostraca from the Kharga Oasis that refer to women named Thecla in that region. A seventh-century marriage contract from Apollonopolis Magna (Edfu) mentions another Thecla, who in this case was the mother of a man named Philemon.[19] In addition, grave stelae inscribed with the name Thecla have been discovered in the Fayûm,[20] at Hermonthis (Armant),[21]

---

[15] *P. Cair. Masp.* III. 67328. 4. 5; 67328. 7. 4; 67328. 10. 4. Another sixth-century papyrus (dated 27 April 553) from Aphrodite lists another Thecla, mother of a man named Palos (*P. Cair. Masp.* III. 67303. 8).

[16] *SB* VI. 8987. 2, 7, 24 (Oct. 644–Feb. 645 CE).

[17] *SB* VI. 8988. 7, 11, 20, 21, 23, 25, 53, 57, 68, 87, 101. This papyrus, although discovered in Apollinopolis Magna, witnesses persons and events in Oxyrhynchus.

[18] *SB* VI. 8988. 10. Another seventh-century papyrus published in the same volume names two other Theclas—the mother of Atretis, and the mother of Anoutis (*SB* VI. 9595. 3, 8).

[19] *SB* VI. 8986. rp. 8; cf. *SB* VI. 8987. 24 and *P. Edfou* I. 4. r. 4.

[20] *Le monuments coptes du Musée de Boulaq*, ed. Albert Gayet, Mémoires publiés par les membres de la Mission Archéologique Français au Caire III. 3 (Paris: Ernest Leroux, 1889) pl. 28, fig. 33; *Recueil des inscriptions grecques-chrétiennes d'Egypte*, ed. Lefebvre, no. 84. Three other stelae of uncertain provenance may have originated in the Fayûm (ibid., nos. 96, 101, and 107).

[21] Ibid., no. 420.

and in the vicinity of Syene (Aswan).[22] The iconography on the stele from the Fayûm depicts the deceased holding a child—perhaps this Thecla had been a young mother at the time of her death, perhaps she and her child were buried together (Fig. 32).[23]

Namesakes of Thecla were found not only among the Greek papyri or the Greek population. In excavations of the Monastery of Epiphanius (c.580–640 CE) at Thebes (Luxor), the name Thecla appears in both Greek and Coptic materials. A Greek graffito found in Cell B offers the following petition: '[Lord, a]nd power of the great saints, help your servant Menas, Tur . . . , . . . kion, Thecla and Kir. Amen.'[24] A Coptic ostracon discovered in the original monastery conveys a message to a woman named Thecla (and others) from a person in prison.[25] Seven other Coptic papyri and ostraca with namesakes of Thecla have been recovered from Thebes and its environs:[26] among them, three are personal letters written by the namesakes themselves.[27] Outside of Thebes, the

---

[22] *Recueil des inscriptions grecques-chrétiennes d'Egypte*, ed. Lefebvre, no. 574. Three papyri from Syene also refer to women named Thecla (*P. Lond.* v. 1733. 33; *P. Münch.* I. 5r. rp. 1; *P. Münch.* III. 1. 102. r. 9).

[23] This depiction of a woman named Thecla with her child may reflect the influence of Egyptian scenes depicting Isis and Horus and/or the Virgin and Child. On the influence of Isis iconography on early Christian images of Mary, see Michael Carroll, *The Cult of the Virgin Mary: Psychological Origins* (Princeton: Princeton University Press, 1986), 8.

[24] W. E. Crum and H. G. Evelyn White, *The Monastery of Epiphanius at Thebes*, pt. 2, *Coptic Ostraca and Papyri; Greek Ostraca and Papyri* (New York: Metropolitan Museum of Art, 1926), 145, no. 689. (*SB* IV. 7501. 3) Another Greek papyrus also attests a namesake of Thecla in the vicinity of Thebes (*P. Herm.* 31. 5).

[25] Ibid., 51, no. 177. 30.

[26] *Koptische Rechtsurkunden des Achten Jahrhunderts aus Djême (Theben)*, ed. Walter Crum and Georg Steindorff (Leipzig: J. C. Hinrichs, 1912), nos. 23. 23; 48. 12, 14; 100. 73, 75 (all dated to the eighth century CE); *Coptic Ostraca from Medinet Habu*, ed. Elizabeth Stefanski and Miriam Lichtheim, University of Chicago Oriental Institute Publications (Chicago: University of Chicago Press, 1952), lxxi, nos. 165, 166, 209 (seventh or eight century CE); *Coptic and Greek Texts of the Christian Period from Ostraka, Stelae, etc. in the British Museum*, ed. H. R. Hall (London: British Museum, 1905), 98, pl. 68, IV. 1 (seventh or eighth century CE). For a list of Coptic sources in which namesakes of Thecla appear, see W. Till, *Datierung und Prosopographie der Koptischen Urkunden aus Theben*, Österreichische Akademie der Wissenschaften, Philosophisch-historische Klasse, Sitzungsberichte 240 (Vienna: Hermann Böhlaus, 1962), i. 216.

[27] *Coptic Ostraca from Medinet Habu*, ed. Stefanski and Lichtheim, nos. 166, 209; *Coptic and Greek Texts*, ed. Hall, 98, pl. 68, IV. 1; see also *Varia Coptica*, ed. W. E. Crum (Aberdeen: Aberdeen University Press, 1939), no. 94, a letter of unknown provenance in which a woman named Thecla addresses correspondence to a man named Pous on both the recto and the verso.

name Thecla is also found in a Coptic papyrus from Aphrodite dated 709 CE.[28]

Several variants of *Θέκλα* are attested in this documentary evidence. In the Coptic sources, one finds the name rendered ⲐⲎⲔⲖⲀ, ⲐⲎⲔⲖⲈ, ⲐⲈⲔⲖⲈ, and even ⲐⲈⲔⲖⲞⳠ.[29] The Greek sources attest other (mis-)spellings. Two eighth-century papyri from Aphrodite (now in the British Museum) include the form Taekla (*Ταεκλα*) in a list of names.[30] A miscellaneous fragment in the same collection contains the name Tekla (*Τεκλ[α]*).[31] This spelling seems to have been an early variant—two papyri from Hermopolis dated to the fourth and sixth centuries also refer to women named Tekl[a].[32] Finally, a funerary stele in the Cairo Museum bears the inscription, Thekkla (*Θεκκλα*).[33] The appearance of such alternative spellings further indicates how the saint's name was assimilated in different ways by Egyptian onomastic custom.

Before I move on to the question of what religious assumptions lay behind the phenomenon, let me summarize my findings thus far. First, regarding chronology, namesakes of Saint Thecla are attested in Egyptian documentary evidence from the fourth to the eighth century CE. An increase in the popularity of the name Thecla in the fifth century (and in centuries following) may be linked to the emergence of pilgrimage practice related to her cult in Egypt during that period of time. Second, Thecla's name was in use across a wide geographical range—from the Fayûm in the north to Syene (Aswan) in the south, with evidence for namesakes especially numerous in cities like Oxyrhynchus, Hermopolis,

---

[28] *P. Lond.* IV. 1519. In addition, four Coptic ostraca of unknown provenance include references to women named Thecla: *Coptic Ostraca from the Collections of the Egypt Exploration Fund, The Cairo Museum and Others*, ed. W. E. Crum (London: Egypt Exploration Fund/Kegan Paul, Trench, Trübner, 1902), 75, no. 447. 4; *Varia Coptica*, ed. Crum, nos. 52. 2; 94. 1, 14; *Coptic and Greek Texts*, ed. Hall, 123, pl. 85, l. 11.

[29] *Coptic Ostraca*, ed. Crum, 75, no. 447. 4 (ⲐⲎⲔⲖⲀ); *Coptic Ostraca from Medinet Habu*, ed. Stefanski and Lichtheim, no. 166. 1 (ⲐⲎⲔⲖⲀ); *Koptische Rechtsurkunden*, ed. Crum and Steindorff, no. 100. 73 (ⲐⲎⲔⲖⲈ); *Coptic and Greek Texts*, ed. Hall, 123, pl. 85, l. 11 (ⲐⲈⲔⲖⲈ); 98, pl. 68, IV. 1 (ⲐⲈⲔⲖⲞⳠ ⲈⳠⳠⳠⲀⳠ . . .).

[30] *P. Lond.* IV. 1488a; IV. 1555. 13 (date undetermined). The form Taekla may very well have been the result of Coptic confusion over the name Thecla. Someone may have thought the initial *t-* was the Coptic feminine article prefixed to the actual name *(h)ekla*. To this root, the Coptic possessive article (*ta-*) was then added to form *Ta-ekla*, meaning 'the (female) one belonging to *(H)ekla*' (Roger Bagnall, *per litt.*, 10 Aug. 1998).

[31] *P. Lond.* IV. 1491. D, Fr 2 (8th cent. CE).

[32] *P. Stras.* V. 310. 8 (4th cent. CE); *P. Stras.* IV. 194. v. 1 (6th cent. CE).

[33] Crum, *Coptic Monuments*, no. 8586, pl. 32.

and Aphrodite. Third, her name is attested across linguistic boundaries (in both Greek and Coptic sources) and in a number of variant onomastic forms (e.g., Têkla, Têkle, Tekle, Teklos, Taekla, Tekla, and Thekkla). Finally then, what religious assumptions lay behind the appropriation of a saint's name? We have only hints. In a fourth-century papyrus from the Kharga Oasis and a sixth-century papyrus from Aphrodite, we learn of two women named Thecla who named their sons Paul – in each case, perhaps a mother's expression of devotion to the apostolic pair.[34] A sixth-century papyrus from Oxyrhynchus provides an example of how a family's knowledge of the pairing of saints in the Egyptian cult of the martyrs could influence a family's decision to name their daughter after the female saint. It mentions a man named Menas who has a daughter named Thecla:[35] Saints Thecla and Menas were commonly paired on pilgrim flasks from the fifth and sixth centuries.[36] Perhaps most notably, on an Egyptian grave stele in the Coptic Museum (Fig. 31),[37] a deceased woman named Thecla is portrayed in the image of her patron saint. She wears only a short apron, and her torso and breasts are exposed. On either side, the artisan seems to have attempted to etch two animals (with little success – only the head, body, and tail of one animal is visible on the right). Here, the funerary portrait of a namesake is made to resemble the image of Saint Thecla found on the pilgrim flasks, where the saint appears topless and flanked by beasts. In this stele, we see how Egyptian namesakes understood their devotion to Saint Thecla ultimately as a form of imitation:[38] in their lives, and in their deaths, they saw themselves as heirs to both the name and image of the female saint.

---

[34] *O. Douch* I. 20. 1 (4th cent. CE); *P. Mich.* XIII. 668. r. 1 (542/557 CE). There are also two cases of namesakes from Oxyrhynchus who were married to men named Paul (*P. Köln* II. 102. r. 2 (418 CE)).

[35] *P. Oxy.* XXVII. 2478. r. 14 (595/6 CE). A papyri from Antinoe refers to a husband and wife named Menas and Thecla (*P. Coll. Youtie* II. 92 rp. 8; 569 CE).

[36] See 'Appendix A: A Catalogue of Published Ampullae with Saint Thecla'.

[37] *Coptic Monuments*, ed. W. E. Crum, Catalogue général des antiquités égyptiennes du Musée du Caire (Cairo: Imprimerie de l'Institut français d'archéologie orientale, 1902), 142 and pl. 52, no. 8693; DACL XII. 2. 2313, 2318, fig. 9098.

[38] Peter Brown ('The Saint as Exemplar', in *Saints and Virtues*, 13) argues that for men and women in late antiquity, '[the] assignment of name had meant to take at baptism a guide and companion, who could act almost as an ideogram for one's own soul'.

FIGURES

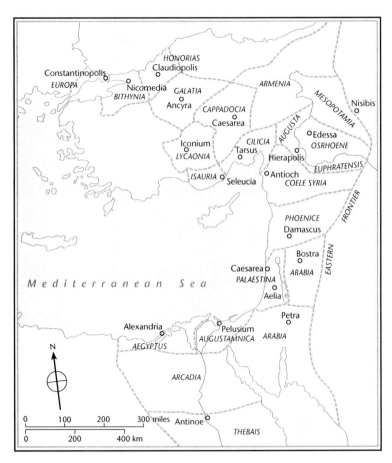

Fɪɢ. ɪ. Eastern Roman provinces in the fourth century, showing Isauria and its capital Seleucia (from Wilkinson, *Egeria's Travels*, ii; courtesy of Aris & Phillips).

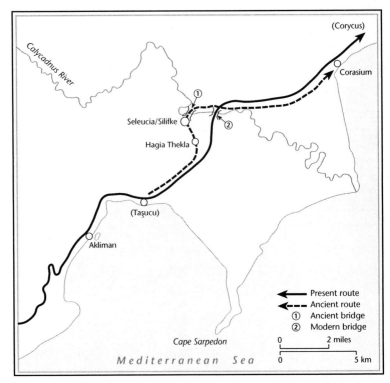

FIG. 2. Seleucia and its environs, showing ancient and modern routes to Hagia Thekla (from Dagron, *Vie et miracles*, 163; courtesy of the Société des Bollandistes).

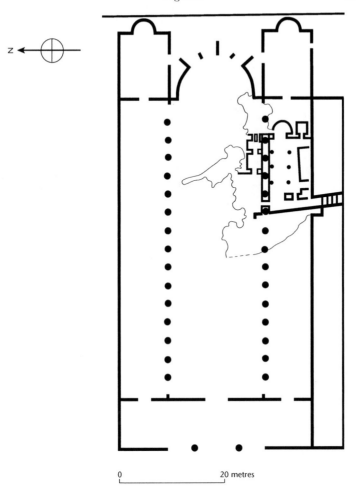

z

0   20 metres

FIG. 3. The Great Basilica and cave chapel at Hagia Thekla (from Dagron, *Vie et miracles*, 165; courtesy of the Société des Bollandistes).

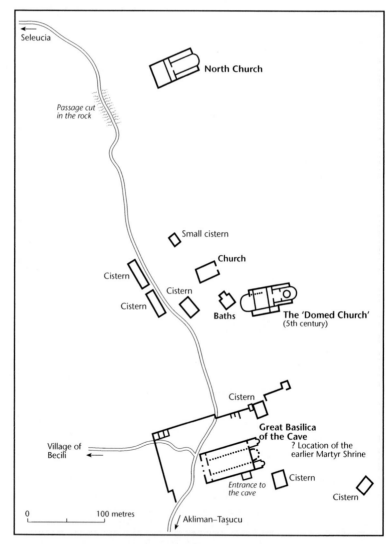

FIG. 4. Hagia Thekla, the archaeological site near Seleucia (from Dagron, *Vie et miracles*, 163; courtesy of the Société des Bollandistes).

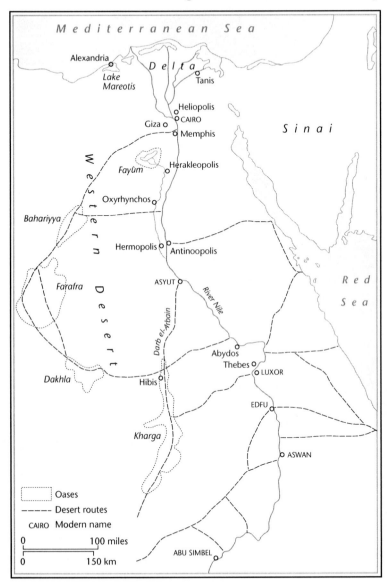

FIG. 5. Egypt: The Nile Valley and oases.

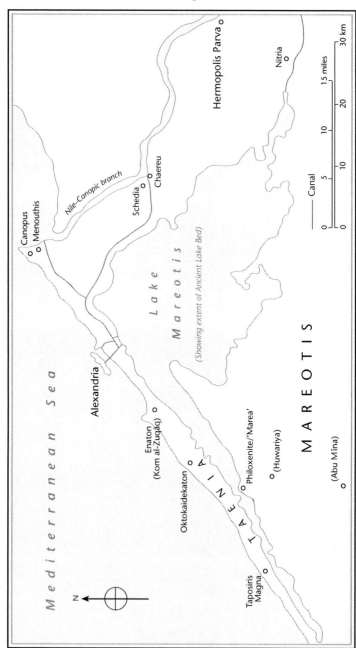

Fɪɢ. 6. Alexandria and its environs, showing the Mareotis (from C. Haas, *Alexandria in Late Antiquity: Topography and Social Conflict*, 3: © 1997, The Johns Hopkins University Press).

FIG. 7. Pilgrim flask depicting Saint Menas (obverse), diam. 17.7 cm: London, British Museum, EA 69839 (© British Museum). See Appendix A, no. 11.

FIG. 8. Pilgrim flask depicting Saint Thecla (reverse), diam. 17.7 cm. London, British Museum, EA 69839 (© British Museum). See Appendix A, no. 11.

Fɪɢ. 9. Pilgrim flask depicting Saint Menas (obverse), h. 14 cm: London, British Museum, E.C. 882 (© British Museum). See Appendix A, no. 12.

FIG. 10. Pilgrim flask depicting Saint Thecla (reverse), h. 14 cm: London, British Museum, E.C. 882 (© British Museum). See Appendix A, no. 12.

Fig. 11. Pilgrim flask depicting Saint Thecla (reverse), h. 27 cm; diam. 17.5 cm: Paris, Musée du Louvre, Département des Antiquités grecques, étrusques, et romaines, MNC 1926 (photograph by M. Chuzeville, courtesy of the Louvre). See Appendix A, no. 16.

FIG. 12. Pilgrim flask depicting Saint Menas (obverse), h. 27 cm, diam. 17.5 cm: Paris, Musée du Louvre, Département des Antiquités grecques, étrusques, et romaines, MNC 1926 (photograph by M. Chuzeville, courtesy of the Louvre). See Appendix A, no. 16.

FIG. 13. Ivory box (pyxis) depicting Saint Menas and camels, h. 8 cm, diam. 10.7 cm: London, British Museum, inv. no. 79, 19–20, 1 (from K. Weitzmann, *Age of Spirituality: Late Antique and Early Christian Art* (New York: Metropolitan Museum of Art/Princeton University Press, 1979), 575, no. 514; © British Museum). *Left*, female pilgrims approach the saint; *right*, male pilgrims approach from the opposite direction.

Fɪɢ. 14. Curtain fragment depicting Saint Thecla, h. 33.5 cm, w. 38 cm: The Textile Museum, Washington, DC, no. 71.46. *Upper right*, the final two letters of Thecla's name; *right*, lampstand with flame.

FIG. 15. Bronze cross with an inscribed petition to Saint Thecla, h. 7.7 cm, w. 6.2 cm: Byzantine Collection, Dumbarton Oaks, Washington, DC, acc. no. 52.5. The cross is embedded in lead.

FIG. 16. Moses leading the Israelites to the Promised Land, wall painting, El Bagawat, Chapel of the Exodus, north-east face of the dome (photograph by the author). *Centre*, Moses, holding a staff (his father-in-law Jethro lies on the ground behind him); *right*, the beginning of the line of Israelites; *left*, the promised Land (only partly visible).

FIG. 17. Saint Thecla in the fire, with surrounding scenes, wall painting, El Bagawat, Chapel of the Exodus, eastern arch (photograph taken before the defacement of the inscriptions in the Chapel of the Exodus, from Nauerth and Warns, *Thekla: Ihre Bilder in der Frühchristlichen Kunst*, fig. 5; courtesy of O. Harrassowitz). *Above*, Moses and the Israelites; *below left*, a procession of virgins approach a temple, and two figures lead camels in the opposite direction; *below*, an anonymous *orans*; *below right*, the Sacrifice of Isaac; *right*, a shepherd scene.

FIG. 18. Saint Thecla in the fire, with surrounding scenes, artist's sketch, El Bagawat, Chapel of the Exodus, eastern arch (sketch by C. Heginbottom, from Nauerth and Warns, *Thekla: Ihre Bilder in der Frühchristlichen Kunst*, fig. 6; courtesy of O. Harrassowitz). *Below left*, a procession of virgins approach a temple, and two figures lead camels in the opposite direction; *below*, an anonymous *orans*; *below right*, the Sacrifice of Isaac; *right*, a shepherd scene.

FIG. 19. Saint Thecla in the fire (detail), wall painting, El Bagawat, Chapel of the Exodus, eastern arch (photograph by the author). *Above*, a grey thundercloud with hail and rain.

FIG. 20. Saint Thecla with Saint Paul, wall painting, El Bagawat, Chapel of Peace, northern face of the dome (photograph by the author). *Seated on left*, Saint Thecla; *seated on right*, Saint Paul; *standing on far left*, Eve; *standing on far right*, Mary.

FIG. 21. Procession of virgins holding torches or lamps, wall painting, El Bagawat, Chapel of the Exodus, eastern arch (photograph by the author). *Below*, two figures leading camels.

FIG. 22. Anonymous *orans*, wall painting, El Bagawat, Chapel of the Exodus, eastern arch (photograph by the author).

F IG. 23. Saint Thecla and the anonymous *orans*, wall painting, El Bagawat,
Chapel of the Exodus, eastern arch (photograph by the author). *Above*, Saint
Thecla; *below*, the anonymous *orans*.

FIG. 24. Saint Thecla between two lions, wall painting, necropolis near
ancient Athribis (from de Bock, *Matériaux pour servir à l'archéologie de
l'Égypte chrétienne*, pl. 29, fig. 2; repr. Grüneisen, *Les Caractéristiques de l'art
copte*, pl. 41). *Right*, a smaller *orans* represents the deceased.

Fɪɢ. 25. Jeremiah before the Jerusalem Temple, wall painting, El Bagawat, Chapel of the Exodus, eastern arch (photograph by the author). *Below right,* Jeremiah stands before the temple; *above right,* Jonah lies in repose.

FIG. 26. The Promised Land, or the heavenly Jerusalem, wall painting, El Bagawat, Chapel of the Exodus, eastern arch (photograph by the author).

FIG. 27. Façade of a funerary chapel complex at El Bagawat, view of chapels, 23–5 from the south (photograph by the author).

FIG. 28. Wooden comb depicting Daniel and Saint Thecla among the lions, h. 23 cm: Berlin, Frühchristlich-byzantinische Sammlung, no. 3263 (from Nauerth and Warns, *Thekla: Ihre Bilder in der Frühchristlichen Kunst,* fig. 19; courtesy of O. Harrassowitz). *Left,* Daniel; *right,* Saint Thecla.

FIG. 29. Limestone roundel relief depicting Saint Thecla with lions and angels, diam. 64.7 cm: The Nelson Gallery—Atkins Museum, Kansas City, Missouri (Purchase: Nelson Trust), no. 48.10.

FIG. 30. Oil lamp depicting Saint Thecla and two lions, h. 3.4 cm, l. 11.8 cm, w. 8.8 cm: Frankfurt am Main, Liebieghaus-Museum, no. 302 (from Selesnow, *Lampen aus Ton und Bronze*, pl. 41; courtesy of the Städtische Galerie Liebieghaus).

FIG. 31. Grave stele of an Egyptian woman named Thecla, h. 22 cm, w. 20 cm: Cairo, Coptic Museum, no. 8693 (from Nauerth and Warns, *Thekla: Ihre Bilder in der Frühchristlichen Kunst*, fig. 18; courtesy of O. Harrassowitz and the Coptic Museum).

FIG. 32. Grave stele of an Egyptian woman named Thecla, with child, h. 45 cm, w. 37 cm: Cairo, Coptic Museum, no. 8703 (photograph by the author; courtesy of the Coptic Museum).

BIBLIOGRAPHY

PRIMARY SOURCES: INDIVIDUAL AUTHORS AND WORKS

Acta Andrae, ed. Jean-Marc Prieur, CCSA 6 (1989).

Acta Pauli, 2nd edn., ed. Carl Schmidt (Leipzig: J. C. Hinrichs, 1905).

Acta Pauli: Aus der heidelberger koptischen Papyrushandscrift, no. 1, ed. Carl Schmidt (Leipzig: J. C. Hinrichs, 1904).

ALEXANDER OF LYCOPOLIS, *Contra Manichaei opiniones disputatio*, ed. A. Brinkmann (Stuttgart: Teubner, 1989).

AMBROSE, *Letters*, PL 16. 913–1342.

—— *De virginibus*, PL 16. 187–234.

AMBROSIASTER, *In epistulam ad Timotheum secunda*, ed. H. Vogels, CSEL 81. 3 (1969).

ANASTASIUS THE SINAÏTE, *De sacra synaxi*, PG 89. 825–50.

Antonini Placentini Itinerarium, ed. P. Geyer, CSEL 39 (1898), 159–91.

The Apocalypse of Elijah, ed. Albert Pietersma, Susan Turner Comstock, and Harold A. Attridge, Texts and Translations, 19; Pseudepigrapha Series, 9 (Missoula, Mont.: Scholars Press, 1983).

Apophthegmata Patrum (Alphabetic collection), PG 65. 71–440.

APULEIUS, *Metamorphoses*, ed. and trans. J. Arthur Hanson, LCL (Cambridge, Mass.; London: Harvard University Press, 1989).

ARISTOTLE, *Poetics*, ed. and trans. W. Hamilton Fyfe, LCL (Cambridge, Mass.: Harvard University Press; London: Heinemann, 1973).

ASTERIUS OF AMASEA, *Description of a Painting on the Martyrdom of St. Euphemia*, ed. F. Halkin, in *Euphémie de Chalcédoine*, 4–8 (Brussels: Société des Bollandistes, 1965).

ATHANASIUS, *Contra gentes*, PG 25. 1–96.

—— *Apologia ad Constantium*, PG 25. 595–642.

—— *Apologia contra Arianos*, ed. H.-G. Opitz, in *Werke*, 2.1. 87–168.

—— *Apologia de fuga sua*, ed. H.-G. Opitz, in *Werke* 2.1. 68–86. PG 25. 643–80.

—— 'Athanasiana Syriaca I: Un Λόγος περὶ παρθενίας attribué à saint Athanase d'Alexandrie', ed. and trans. J. Lebon, *Museon*, 40 (1927), 265–92.

—— 'Athanasiana Syriaca II: Une lettre attribué à saint Athanase d'Alexandrie', ed. and trans. J. Lebon, *Museon*, 41 (1928), 169–216.

—— 'Der dem Athanasius zugeschriebene Traktat Περὶ παρθενίας', ed. R. P. Casey, *SPAW* 33 (1935), 1026–45.

ATHANASIUS, *Historia Arianorum ad monachos*, ed. H.-G. Opitz, in *Werke*, 2.1. 183–230.

—— *Lettres festales et pastorales en copte*, ed. and trans. L. Th. Lefort, 2 vols., CSCO 150–1 (Louvain: L. Durbecq, 1955).

—— *Vie d'Antoine*, ed. G. J. M. Bartelink, SC 400 (Paris: Éditions du Cerf, 1994).

—— *Werke*, ed. Hans-Georg Opitz, 3 vols. (Berlin: de Gruyter, 1935–41).

AUGUSTINE, *De beata vita*, ed. W. M. Green, CCSL 29 (1970), 65–85.

—— *Contra Faustum*, ed. J. Zycha, CSEL 25. 1 (1891), 251–797.

AVITUS, *De laude castitatis* (*Carmen* 6), PL 59. 369–82.

BASIL OF ANCYRA, *De virginitate*, PG 30. 670–810.

The Book of the Saints of the Ethiopian Church: A Translation of the Ethiopian Synaxarium, ed. E. A. Wallis Budge (Cambridge: Cambridge University Press, 1928).

Caena Cypriani, PL 4. 1007–14.

Le Calendrier d'Abou`l-Barakât, ed. Eugène Tisserant, PO 10.3 (Paris: Firmin-Didot, 1915).

CICERO, *De natura deorum*, ed. and trans. H. Rackham, LCL (Cambridge, Mass.: Harvard University Press; London: Heinemann, 1972).

CLAUDIANUS MAMERTUS, *De statu animae*, ed. A. Engelbrecht, CSEL 11 (1885), 18–197.

CLEMENT OF ALEXANDRIA, *Paidagogos*, ed. O. Stählin and U. Treu, GCS (1972), 89–292.

—— *Stromata*, ed. O. Stählin and L. Früchtel, GCS 15 (1960) and 17 (1970), 3–102.

Didascalia Apostolorum in Syriac, ed. and trans. Arthur Vööbus, CSCO 401, 402, 407, 408 (1979).

Didascalia et Constitutiones Apostolorum I, ed. F. X. Funk (Paderborn: F. Schoeningh, 1905).

DIDYMUS THE BLIND, *Kommentar zum Ecclesiastes (Tura-Papyrus)*, pt. 5, ed. M. Gronewald, Papyrologische Texte und Abhandlungen, 24 (Bonn: Rudolf Hubelt, 1979).

La Doctrine des douze apôtres (Didachè), ed. W. Rordorf and A. Tuilier, SC 248 (Paris: Éditions du Cerf, 1978).

EGERIA, *Itinerarium*, ed. E. Francheschini and R. Weber, CCSL 175 (1958), 27–90.

EPIPHANIUS, *Panarion*, ed. K. Holl, GCS 25, 31, 37 (Leipzig: Hinrichs; Berlin: Akademie, 1915–81), PG 42.

EUSEBIUS OF CAESAREA, *De martyribus Palestinae*, PG 20. 1457–520.

—— *Historia ecclesiastica*, ed. E. Schwartz, GCS 9.1 (1903) and 9.2 (1908).

EUSEBIUS OF EMESA, *Discours conservés en latin*, ed. É. M. Buytaert, OFM (Louvain: Spicilegium Sacrum Lovaniense Administration, 1953).

EUTYCHIUS (SAID IBN BATRIQ), *Annales*, ed. L. Cheikho, CSCO 50–1 (1906–9).

EVAGRIUS PONTICUS, *Epistolae*, ed. W. Frankenberg, Abhandlungen der königlichen Gesellschaft der Wissenschaften zu Göttingen, philologisch-historische Klasse, new edn. 13/2 (Berlin: Weidmannsche Buchhandlung, 1912).

—— *Nonnenspiegel und Mönchsspiegel des Evagrios Pontikos zum ersten Male in der Urschrift herausgegeben*, ed. Hugo Gressmann, TU 39.4 (Leipzig: J. C. Hinrichs, 1913).

EVAGRIUS SCHOLASTICUS, *The Ecclesiastical History of Evagrius with the Scholia*, ed. J. Bidez and L. Parmentier (London: Methuen, 1898).

GEORGE THE MONK (GEORGIUS HAMARTOLOS), *Chronicon*, PG 110. 41–1286.

GREGORY OF NAZIANZUS, *De Vita Sua*, ed. Ch. Jungck (Heidelberg, 1974), PG 37. 1029–166.

—— *Orationes*, PG 35. 395–1252 and 36. 11–664.

GREGORY OF NYSSA, *Opera Ascetica*, ed. Werner Jaeger (Leiden: E. J. Brill, 1952).

—— *In Cantica Canticorum* (*Homilia* 14), PG 44. 755–1120.

—— *Vie de Sainte Macrine*, ed. Pierre Maraval, SC 178 (Paris: Éditions du Cerf, 1971).

GREGORY OF TOURS, *Opera, Monumenta Germaniae Historica*, i. *Scriptores rerum Merovingicarum*, pt. 2 ed. W. Arndt and B. Kruesch (Hanover, 1885).

GREGORY THE GREAT, *Epistolae*, PL 77. 441–1328.

HIPPOLYTUS OF ROME, *Contre les hérésies, fragment, étude et édition critique*, ed. P. Nautin (Paris: Éditions du Cerf, 1949).

—— *The Treatise on the Apostolic Tradition*, ed. and trans. G. Dix (London: SPCK, 1937).

HOMER, *The Iliad*, ed. and trans. A. T. Murray, LCL (Cambridge, Mass.: Harvard University Press; London: Heinemann, 1924–5).

—— *The Odyssey*, ed. and trans. A. T. Murray, rev. George E. Dimock, LCL (Cambridge, Mass.: Harvard University Press, 1995).

IGNATIUS OF ANTIOCH, *Lettres*, ed. T. Camelot, SC 10, 2nd edn. (Paris: Éditions du Cerf, 1951).

IGNATIUS THE DEACON, *Vita Tarasii Archiepiscopi Constantinopolitani*, ed. I. A. Heikel, *Acta Societatis Scientificiarum Fennicae*, 17 (1891), 395–423.

ISIDORE OF PELUSIUM, *Epistolae*, PG 78. 177–1646.

JEROME, *Contra Vigilantium*, PL 23. 339–52.

—— *Epistolae*, PL 22. 235–1182.

JOHN CHRYSOSTOM, *Homiliae de statuis ad populum Antiochenum*, PG 49. 15–222.

JOHN CHRYSOSTOM, *Homiliae in epistolam primam ad Corinthios*, PG 61. 9–381.

—— *Homiliae in Matthaeum*, PG 57–8.

JOHN MOSCHUS, *Pratum Spirituale*, PL 74. 123–240.

JOHN OF DAMASCUS, *Martyrdom of St. Artemius*, PG 96. 1251–320.

JOHN OF EPHESUS, *Lives of the Eastern Saints* (excerpts), ed. and trans. S. P. Brock and S. A. Harvey, *Holy Women of the Syrian Orient* (Berkeley: University of California Press, 1987/98), 124–41.

LUCIAN, *Lucianus*, ed. N. Nilén (Lipsius: B. G. Teubner, 1906).

A Manichaean Psalm-book, pt. 2, ed. and trans. C. R. C. Allberry, Manichaean Manuscripts in the Chester Beatty Collection, vol. 2 (Stuttgart: W. Kohlhammer, 1938).

Martyrdom of Saint Menas (*Acta Sancti Menae*), ed. C. Smedt, G. van Hooff, and J. de Backer, *Analecta Bollandiana*, 3 (1884), 258–70.

METHODIUS, *Symposium*, ed. G. Nathanael Bonwetsch (Leipzig: J. C. Hinrichs, 1917).

The Miracles of St. Artemios: A Collection of Miracle Stories by an Anonymous Author of Seventh-Century Byzantium, ed. Virgil Crisafulli and John W. Nesbitt (Leiden; New York; Cologne: E. J. Brill, 1997).

NICETAS OF REMESIANA, *De lapsu virginis*, PL 16. 383–400.

ORIGEN, *In Evangelium Joannis*, ed. E. Preuschen, GCS 10 (1903), 1–574.

—— *De principis*, ed. P. Koetschau, GCS 22 (1913).

—— *In Exodum*, PG 12. 263–98.

PALLADIUS, *Dialogue sur la vie de Jean Chrysostom*, ed. and trans. Anne-Marie Malingrey and Philippe Leclercq, SC 341 (Paris: Éditions du Cerf, 1988).

—— *Historia Lausiaca*, PG 34. 995–1260.

PAULINUS OF NOLA, *Carmina*, ed. W. Hartel, CSEL 30 (1894).

—— *Letters*, ed. W. Hartel, CSEL 29 (1894).

PHILASTER OF BRESCIA, *Haereses*, ed. F. Marx, CSEL 38 (1898).

PHILO, *De Abrahamo*, ed. and trans. F. H. Colson, LCL (Cambridge, Mass.: Harvard University Press; London: Heinemann, 1935).

—— *De opificio mundi*, ed. and trans. F. H. Colson and G. H. Whitaker, LCL (London: Heinemann; New York: G. P. Putnam's Sons, 1929).

—— *Quaestiones et solutiones in Exodum*, ed. and trans. Ralph Marcus, LCL (Cambridge, Mass.: Harvard University Press; London: Heinemann, 1970).

—— *De specialibus legibus*, ed. and trans. F. H. Colson, LCL (Cambridge, Mass.: Harvard University Press; London: Heinemann, 1937).

PHILOSTORGIUS, *Historia ecclesiastica*, ed. J. Bidez, GCS 21 (1972).

PHOTIUS, *Bibliotheque*, ed. R. Henry (Paris: Belles Lettres, 1959).

—— *Homiliai (ΦΩΤΙΟΥ ΟΜΙΛΙΑΙ)*, ed. B. Laourdas, *Makedonikon Spoudon Parartema*, 12 (Thessaloniki: Hellenika periodikou syggramma, 1959).

PLATO, *The Republic*, ed. B. Jowett and Lewis Campbell (Oxford: Clarendon Press, 1894).

PLINY THE YOUNGER, *Epistles*, ed. R. A. B. Mynors, Scriptorum Classicorum Bibliotheca Oxoniensis (Oxford: Clarendon Press, 1963).

PLUTARCH, *Moralia*, ed. and trans. Frank Cole Babbitt, LCL (London: William Heinemann Ltd.; New York: G. P. Putnam's Sons, 1927).

PORPHYRY, *Ad Marcellam*, ed. W. Pötscher, Philosophia Antiqua, 15 (Leiden: E. J. Brill, 1969).

Πράξεις Παύλου: *Acta Pauli nach dem Papyrus der hamburger Staats- und Universitätsbibliothek*, ed. Carl Schmidt (Glückstadt and Hamburg: J. J. Augustin, 1936).

PSEUDO-ATHANASIUS, *Doctrina ad monachos*, PG 28. 1421–6.

—— *Vita Syncleticae*, PG 28. 1487–558.

PSEUDO-CHRYSOSTOM, *Panegyric to Thecla*, PG 50. 745–8.

PSEUDO-ISOCRATES, *Ad Demonicum*, ed. G. Mathieu and É. Brémond, i (Paris: Belles Lettres, 1928).

PSEUDO-LONGINUS, *De sublimitate*, ed. D. A. Russell (Oxford: Clarendon Press, 1968).

PSEUDO-MAXIMUS OF TURIN, *Sermones*, ed. A. Mutzenbecher, CCSL 23 (1962), PL 57. 221–760.

QUINTILLIAN, *Institutio Oratoria*, LCL (Cambridge, Mass.: Harvard University Press, 1933–6).

SENECA, *Sénèque, Lettre à Lucilius*, iv, ed. F. Préchac (Paris: Belles Lettres, 1945).

SOCRATES SCHOLASTICUS, *Historia ecclesiastica*, PG 67. 29–842.

SOPHRONIUS, *Miracles of SS. Cyrus and John*, PG 87.3. 3423–676.

SOZOMEN, *Historia ecclesiastica*, PG 67. 843–1630.

STRABO, *Geography*, ed. and trans. H. L. Jones and J. R. S. Sterrett, LCL (London: Heinemann; New York: G. P. Putnam's Sons, 1917).

SULPICIUS SEVERUS, *Dialogues*, ed. C. Halm, CSEL 1 (1867), 152–216, PL 20. 183–222.

Le Synaxaire arabe jacobite (rédaction copte), iii. *Les mois de Toubeh et d'Amchir*, ed. René Basset, PO 11. 5 (Paris: Firmin-Didot, 1916).

Le Synaxaire arabe jacobite (rédaction copte), v. *Les mois de Baounah, Abib, Mesoré et jours complémentaires*, PO 17. 3 (Paris: Firmin-Didot, 1923).

Le Synaxaire éthiopien: ii. *Mois de Hamlé*, ed. I. Guidi, PO 7. 3 (Paris: Firmin-Didot, 1911).

Synaxarium Alexandrinum, ed. J. Forget, CSCO 18–19, Scriptores Arabici (Beirut: Catholicus, 1905–12 (textus); Rome: Karolus de Luigi, 1921; Lovanio: Marcellus Istas, 1926 (versio)).

TERTULLIAN, *De baptismo*, ed. A. Reifferscheid and G. Wissowa, CSEL 20 (1890), 201 18, PL 1. 1197–224.

—— *De cultu feminarum*, ed. A. Kroymann, CSEL 70 (1942), 59–95.

TERTULLIAN, *De praescriptione haereticorum*, ed. A. Kroymann, CSEL 70 (1942), 1–58.

—— *De virginibus velandis*, PL 2. 887–914.

THEODORET OF CYRRHUS, *Haereticarum fabularum compendium*, PG 83. 335–556.

—— *Historia ecclesiastica*, ed. L. Parmentier, GCS 19 (1911).

—— *Historia religiosa*, PG 82. 1283–496.

THEODOSIUS, *De situ terrae sanctae*, ed. J. Wilkinson, in *Jerusalem Pilgrims Before the Crusades* (Warminster: Aris & Phillips, 1977).

VENANTIUS FORTUNATUS, *Carmina*, ed. F. Leo, *Monumenta Germaniae Historica*, 4.1 (Berlin: Weidmann, 1881).

Vie et miracles de Sainte Thècle, ed. Gilbert Dagron (Brussels: Société des Bollandistes, 1978).

Vie (et Récits) de l'Abbé Daniel le scétiote, ed. L. Clugnet (Paris: Librairie A. Picard et fils, 1901).

Vie de Sainte Syncletique, trans. Odile Bénédicte Bernard, *Spiritualité Orientale*, 9 (Abbaye Notre Dame de Bellefontaine, 1972).

Vita Anastasiae, in *Acta Sanctorum* (2 Mar.), 40–1.

Vita Apollonariae, ed. James Drescher, in *Three Coptic Legends* (Cairo: Imprimerie de l'Institut français d'archéologie orientale, 1947), 152–61. Also *Acta Sanctorum* (1 Jan.), 257–61.

Vita Athanasiae, in *Acta Sanctorum* (4 Oct.), 997–1000.

Vita Eugeniae, Syriac ed. and trans. Agnes Smith Lewis, in *Select Narratives* (*Studia Sinaitica*, 9–10), PL 73. 605–24 (Latin); PG 116. 609–52 (Greek). Armenian trans. and ed. F. C. Conybeare, *The Apology and Acts of Apollonius* (London: Swan Sonnenschein; New York: Macmillan, 1894), 134–89.

Vita Euphrosynes, ed. Agnes Smith Lewis, in *Select Narratives of Holy Women* (*Studia Sinaitica*, 9–10). Also *Acta Sanctorum* (2 Feb.), 533–44.

Vita Febroniae, ed. and trans. S. P. Brock and S. A. Harvey, in *Holy Women of the Syrian Orient* (Berkeley: University of California Press, 1987/98), 152–76.

Vita Hilariae, ed. J. Drescher, in *Three Coptic Legends* (Cairo: Imprimerie de l'Institut français d'archéologie orientale, 1947), 1–13, 69–82. Also PO. 624–38.

Vita Matronae (*vita prima*), in *Acta Sanctorum* (3 Nov.), 790–813.

Vita Theodorae, in *Acta Sanctorum* (3 Sept.), 788–91.

ZENO OF VERONA, *De timore*, PL 11. 322–5.

Zhitie prepodobnago Paisiia Velikago i Timofeia patriarkha aleksandri-iskago poviestvovanie o chudesakh Sv. velikomuchenika Miny (*Miracles of St. Menas*), ed. Ivan Pomialovskii (St. Peterburg: Tip. Imperatorskoi akademii nauk, 1900).

PRIMARY SOURCES: COLLECTIONS

Acta Apostolorum Apocrypha, ed. Richard A. Lipsius and M. Bonnet (Leipzig: Hermann Mendelssohn, 1891).

Acta Martyrum, i, ed. I. Balestri and H. Hyvernat, CSCO 3. 1 (Paris: Typographeo Reipublicae, 1907).

Les Actes de Paul et ses lettres apocryphes, ed. Léon Vouaux (Paris: Letouzey et Ané, 1913).

Les Actes des martyrs de l'Égypte, ed. H. Hyvernat (Paris: E. Leroux, 1886; repr. Hildesheim; New York: G. Olms, 1977).

Acts of the Christian Martyrs, ed. Herbert Musurillo (Oxford: Clarendon Press, 1972).

The Age of Spirituality: Late Antique and Early Christian Art, Third to Seventh Century, ed. Kurt Weitzmann (New York: Metropolitan Museum of Art/Princeton University Press, 1979).

Ägypten: Schätze aus dem Wüstenstand, Kunst und Kultur der Christen am Nil, Gustav-Lübcke-Museum der Stadt Namm und dem Museum für spätantike und byzantinische Kunst, Staatliche Museen zu Berlin—Preussischer Kulturbesitz (Wiesbaden: Ludwig Reichert, 1996).

Ancient Christian Magic: Coptic Texts of Ritual Power, ed. Marvin W. Meyer and R. Smith (San Francisco: Harper, 1994).

Apa Mêna: A Selection of Coptic Texts Relating to St. Menas, ed. James Drescher (Cairo: Société d'archéologie copte, 1946).

The Apocryphal New Testament: A Collection of Apocryphal Christian Literature in an English Translation, ed. and trans. J. K. Elliott. (Oxford: Clarendon Press, 1993).

The Apology and Acts of Apollonius and Other Monuments of Early Christianity, ed. F. C. Conybeare (London: Swan Sonnenschein; New York: Macmillan, 1894).

The Art of the Byzantine Empire, 312–1453, ed. Cyril Mango, Sources and Documents in the History of Art Series (Englewood Cliffs, NJ: Prentice-Hall, 1972).

Ascetic Behavior in Graeco-Roman Antiquity: A Sourcebook, ed. Vincent L. Wimbush (Minneapolis: Fortress Press, 1990).

Asclepius: Collection and Interpretation of the Testimonies, 2 vols., ed. Emma J. Edelstein and Ludwig Edelstein (Baltimore and London: Johns Hopkins University Press, 1945/98).

Ausgewählte koptische Zaubertexte, 3 vols., ed. Angelicus M. Kropp (Brussels: Fondation égyptologique reine Élisabeth, 1930–1).

Beyond the Pharaohs: Egypt and the Copts in the 2nd to 7th Centuries A.D, ed. Florence D. Friedman (Providence, RI: Museum of Art, Rhode Island School of Design, 1989).

Bildwerke aus Ton, Bein und Metall, ed. G. Kaminski-Menssen, Leibieghaus-Museum alter Plastik, Bildwerke der Sammlung Kaufmann, iii (Kassel: Verlag Gutenberg, 1996).

The Canons of Athanasius, Patriarch of Alexandria, ed. Wilhelm Riedel and W. E. Crum (London: Williams and Norgate, 1904, repr. Text and Translation Society, 9; Amsterdam: Philo Press, 1973).

Catalogue of Early Christian Antiquities and Objects from the Christian East in the Department of British and Medieval Antiquities and Ethnography of the British Museum, ed. O. M. Dalton (London: British Museum, 1901).

Catalogue of the Byzantine and Early Medieval Antiquities in the Dumbarton Oaks Collection, i. *Metalwork, Ceramics, Glass, Glyptics, Painting*, ed. Marvin C. Ross (Washington: Dumbarton Oaks, 1962).

Collections grecques de Miracles: Sainte Thècle, Saints Côme et Damien, Saints Cyr et Jean (extraits), Saint Georges, ed. A. M. J. Festugière (Paris: A. et J. Picard, 1971).

La Collezione di Lucerne del Museo di Firenze, ed. Maurizio Michelucci, Academie Toscana di scienze a lettere 'La Colombaria', 39 (Florence: Leo S. Olschki Editore, 1975).

Coptic and Greek Texts of the Christian Period from Ostraka, Stelae, etc. in the British Museum, ed. H. R. Hall (London: British Museum, 1905).

Coptic Funerary Stelae, ed. Ibrahim Kamel, Catalogue général des antiquités du Musée Copte, No. 1–253 (Cairo: Organisation égyptienne générale du livre, 1987).

Coptic Monuments, ed. W. E. Crum, Catalogue général des antiquités égyptiennes (Cairo: Imprimerie de l'Institut français d'archéologie orientale, 1902).

Coptic Ostraca from Medinet Habu, ed. Elizabeth Stefanski and Miriam Lichtheim, University of Chicago Oriental Institute Publications, vol. 71 (Chicago: University of Chicago Press, 1952).

Coptic Ostraca from the Collections of the Egypt Exploration Fund, The Cairo Museum and Others, ed. W. E. Crum (London: The Offices of the Egypt Exploration Fund; Kegan, Paul, Trench, Trübner & Co., 1902).

The Difnar of the Coptic Church, ed. De Lacy Evans O'Leary (London: Luzac & Co., 1930).

Fayûm Towns and Their Papyri, ed. B. P. Grenfell, A. S. Hunt, and D. G. Hogarth (London: Egypt Exploration Fund, 1900).

Four Martyrdoms from the Pierpont Morgan Coptic Codices, ed. E. A. E. Reymond and J. W. B. Barns (Oxford: Clarendon Press, 1973).

Die Fragmente der Vorsokratiker, ed. Hermann Diels, 6th edn., ed. Walther Kranz (Berlin: Weidmann, 1951–2).

Holy Women of Byzantium: Ten Saints' Lives in English Translation, ed. Alice-Mary Talbot (Washington: Dumbarton Oaks Research Library and Collection, 1996).

Holy Women of the Syrian Orient, ed. and trans. Sebastian P. Brock and Susan Ashbrook Harvey, updated edn. (Berkeley: University of California Press, 1987/98).

Icones du Mont Sinaï (Εἰκόνες τῆς Μονῆς Σινᾶ.), ii, ed. G. and M. Sotiriou, Collection de l'Institut français d'Athènes, 102 (Athens: Institut français d'Athènes, 1958).

The Icons, ed. Paul van Moorsel, Catalogue général du Musée Copte (Leiden: Supreme Council of Antiquities, Leiden University, Dept. of Early Christian Art, 1991).

Koptisch-gnostische Schriften, i. *Die Pistis Sophia; die beiden Bücher des Jesu; Unbekanntes altgnostisches Werk*, ed. Carl Schmidt, GCS 13 (1905).

Koptische Heiligen- und Martyrerlegenden, ed. Walter Till, Orientalia Christiana Analecta 102 and 108 (Roma: Pont. Institutum Orientalium Studiorum, 1935–6).

Koptische Rechtsurkunden des achten Jahrhunderts aus Djême (Theben), ed. W. E. Crum and G. Steindorff (Leipzig: J. C. Hinrichs, 1912).

'Die koptischen Zauberpapiere und Zauberostraka der Papyrus-Sammlung der Staatlichen Museen zu Berlin', ed. Walter Beltz, *Archiv für Papyrusforschung und verwandte Gebiete*, 31 (1985), 31–41.

Lampen aus Ton und Bronze, ed. Wolfgang Selesnow, Liebieghaus-Museum alter Plastik, Bildwerke der Sammlung Kaufmann, ii (Frankfurt am Main; Melsungen: Verlag Gutenberg, 1988).

Legends of Eastern Saints: Chiefly from Syriac Sources, ed. and partly trans. A. J. Wensinck, 2 vols. (Leiden: E. J. Brill, 1911–13).

Maenads, Martyrs, Matrons, Monastics, ed. Ross S. Kraemer (Philadelphia: Fortress Press, 1988).

Le Manuscrit de la Version copte en dialecte sahidique des 'Apophthegmata patrum', ed. Marius Chaine, Publications de l'Institut français d'archéologie orientale, Bibliotheque d'études coptes, 6 (Cairo: Institut français d'archéologie orientale, 1960).

The Monastery of Epiphanius at Thebes, pt. 2: *Coptic Ostraca and Papyri; Greek Ostraca and Papyri* (New York: Metropolitan Museum of Art, 1926).

The Monastery of Saint Catherine at Mount Sinai: The Icons, i. *From the Sixth to the Tenth Century*, ed. Kurt Weitzmann (Princeton: Princeton University Press, 1976).

Les Monuments coptes du Musée de Boulaq, ed. Albert Gayet, Mémoires publiés par les membres de la Mission archéologique français au Caire, iii, fasc. 3 (Paris: Ernest Leroux, 1889).

Moral Exhortation. A Greco-Roman Sourcebook, ed. A. J. Malherbe (Philadelphia: Westminster, 1986).

248   Bibliography

Musonius Rufus, 'The Roman Socrates', ed. and trans. Cora E. Lutz (New Haven: Yale University Press, 1947).

New Testament Apocrypha, 2 vols. rev. edn., ed. E. Hennecke and W. Schneemelcher, trans. R. McL. Wilson (Cambridge: James Clarke & Co.; Louisville, Ky.: Westminster, 1992).

P. Ant. = *The Antinoopolis Papyri*, pt. 1, 3 vols. ed. C. H. Roberts, J. W. B. Barnes, and H. Zilliacus (London: Egypt Exploration Society, 1950–67).

P. Berl. *Sarisch* = *Berliner griechische Papyri: Christliche literarische Texte und Urkunden aus dem 3.bis 8.Jh.n.Chr.*, ed. P. Sarischouli (Wiesbaden: Dr Ludwig Reichert, 1995).

P. Cair. Masp. = *Papyrus grecs d'époque byzantine*, 3 vols. ed. Jean Maspero, Catalogue général des antiquités égyptiennes du Musée du Caire (Cairo: Imprimerie de l'Institut français d'archéologie orientale, 1911–16).

P. Coll. *Youtie* = *Collectanea Papyrologica: Texts Published in Honour of H. C. Youtie*, ed. A. E. Hanson (Bonn: Habelt, 1976).

P. Grenf. 1 = *An Alexandrian Erotic Fragment and Other Greek Papyri Chiefly Ptolemaic*, ed. B. P. Grenfell (Oxford: Clarendon Press, 1896).

P. Herm. = *Papyri from Hermopolis and Other Documents of the Byzantine Period*, ed. B. R. Rees (London: Egypt Exploration Society, 1964).

P. Herm. Landl. = *Zwei Landlisten aus dem Hermopolites*, ed. P. J. Sijpesteijn and K. A. Worp (Zutphen: Terra, 1978).

P. Köln = *Kölner Papyri*, 7 vols. ed. B. Kramer, R. Hübner, et al. (Opladen: Westdeutscher Verlag, 1976–).

P. Lond. = *Greek Papyri in the British Museum*, 7 vols. ed. F. G. Kenyon, H. I. Bell, W. E. Crum, T. C. Skeat (London: British Museum, 1893–).

P. Mich. XIII = *The Aphrodite Papyri in the University of Michigan Papyrus Collection*, ed. P. J. Sijpesteijn (Zutphen: Terra, 1977).

P. Münch. = *Die Papyri der Bayerischen Staatsbibliothek München*, 3 vols. ed. A. Heisenberg, L. Wenger, et al. (Stuttgart: B. G. Teubner, 1986).

P. Oxy. = *The Oxyrhynchus Papyri*, ed. B. P. Grenfell, A. S. Hunt, et al. (London: Egypt Exploration Society, 1898–).

P. Oxy. Descr. = 'Varia Descripta Oxyrhynchita', ed. Dominic Montserrat, Georgina Fantoni, and Patrick Robinson, *Bulletin of the American Society of Papyrologists*, 31 (1994), 11–80.

P. Ryl. = *Catalogue of the Greek and Latin Papyri in the John Rylands Library of Manchester*. 4 vols, ed. A. S. Hunt, C. H. Roberts, et al. (Manchester: Manchester University Press, 1938).

PSI = *Papiri greci e latini*, ed. G. Vitelli, M. Norsa, et al. (Florence: Società Italiana per la ricerca dei papiri greci e latini in Egitto, 1912–).

P. Stras. IV–V = *Papyrus grecs de la Bibliothèque Nationale et Universitaire de Strasbourg*, Publications de la Bibliothèque Nationale et Universitaire de Strasbourg I, III, ed. J. Schwartz, *et al.* (Strasburg, 1963–73).

P. Wash. Univ. II = *Papyri from the Washington University Collection, St. Louis, Missouri*, pt. 2, ed. K. Maresch and Z. M. Packman (Opladen: Westdeutscher Verlag, 1990).

Packard Humanities Institute (PHI): Greek Documentary Texts, CD ROM no. 7 (Los Altos, Calif.: Packard Humanities Institute, 1991–6).

Pagan and Christian Egypt: Egyptian Art from the First to the Tenth Century A.D (Brooklyn: Brooklyn Museum, 1941).

I papiri copti del Museo Egizio di Torino, i, ed. F. Rossi (Turin, 1887–8).

Les Portes du désert: Recueil des inscriptions grecques d'Antinooupolis, Tentyris, Koptos, Apollonopolis Parva, et Apollonopolis Magna, ed. André Bernand (Paris: Centre national de la recherche scientifique, 1984).

O. Douch = *Les Ostraca grecs de Douch*, 3 vols. ed. H. Cuvigny and G. Wagner (Cairo: L'Institut français d'archéologie orientale, 1986–92).

Recueil des inscriptions grecques-chrétiennes d'Egypte, ed. M. Gustave Lefebvre, Service des antiquités de l'Égypte (Cairo: Imprimerie de l'Institut français d'archéologie orientale, 1907).

Religion populaire en Égypte romaine: Les terres cultes isiaques du Musées du Caire, Études préliminaires aux religions orientales dans l'empire romain, 76 (Leiden: E. J. Brill, 1979).

Roma sotterranea: Le pitture delle catacombe romane, ed. Josef (Giuseppi) Wilpert, 2 vols. (Rome: Desclée, Lefebvre, 1903).

SB = *Sammelbuch griechischer Urkunden aus Ägypten*, ed. Friedrich Preisigke, *et al.* (Strasburg: Karl J. Trübner, 1915–).

I sarcophagi cristiani antichi, i: *Tavole*, ed. Josef (Giuseppi) Wilpert (Roma: Pontificio istituto di archeologia cristiana, 1929).

Select Narratives of Holy Women from the Syro-Antiochene or Sinai Palimpsest, ed. Agnes Smith Lewis, Studia Sinaitica, 9–10 (London: C. J. Clay, 1900).

Stud. Pal. = *Studien zur Palaeographie und Papyruskunde*, ed. C. Wessely (Leipzig: Eduard Avenarius, 1901–24).

Texts Relating to Saint Mêna of Egypt and Canons of Nicaea in a Nubian Dialect, ed. E. A. Wallis Budge (London: British Museum, 1909).

Thesaurus Linguae Graecae (TLG), CD ROM no. D (Berkeley: Regents of the University of California, 1992).

Three Coptic Legends: Hilaria, Archellites, The Seven Sleepers, ed. James Drescher, Supplément aux Annales du service des antiquités de l'Égypte, cahier no. 4 (Cairo: Imprimerie de l'Institut français d'archéologie orientale, 1947).

Varia Coptica, ed. W. E. Crum (Aberdeen: Aberdeen University Press, 1939).

The Varieties of Sensory Experience: A Sourcebook in the Anthropology of the Senses, ed. David Howes (Toronto: University of Toronto Press, 1991).

Voluminum Codicumque Fragmenta Graeca cum Amuleto Christiano, ed. Ernst Schaeffer, Papyri Iandanae, Fasc. 1 (Lipsius: B. G. Teubner, 1912).

SECONDARY SOURCES

AARNE, ANTTI and THOMPSON, STITH, *The Types of the Folk-tale* (Helsinki: Academia Scientiarum Fennica, 1928/61).

ABBOTT, F. F., *Society and Politics in Ancient Rome* (New York: Scribner's Sons, 1909).

AIGRAIN, RENÉ, *L'Hagiographie: Ses sources, ses méthodes, son histoire* (Poitiers: Bloud & Gay, 1953).

ALBRECHT, RUTH, *Das Leben der heiligen Makrina auf dem Hintergrund der Thekla-Traditionen* (Göttingen: Vandenhoeck & Ruprecht, 1986).

ALCHERMES, JOSEPH, 'Cura pro mortuis and Cultis martyrum: Commemoration in Rome from the Second through the Sixth Century', Ph.D. diss., New York University, 1988.

ALLEN, PAULINE, *Evagrius Scholasticus the Church Historian*, Spicilegium Sacrum Lovaniense, Études et Documents, Fascicule 41 (Louvain: Spicilegium Sacrum Lovaniense, 1981).

ALLISON, DALE C., 'The Eye is the Lamp of the Body (Matthew 6.22–23 = Luke 11.34–36)', *New Testament Studies*, 33 (1987), 61–83.

ALPERS, S., 'Ekphrasis and Aesthetic Attitudes in Vasari's Lives', *Journal of the Warburg and Courtauld Institutes*, 23 (1960), 190–215.

AMÉLINEAU, E., *Les Actes des martyrs de l'église copte* (Paris: Ernest Leroux, 1890).

—— *La Géographie de l'Égypte à l'époque copte* (Paris: Imprimerie nationale, 1893).

—— 'Histoire des deux filles de l'empéreur Zenon', *Proceedings of the Society of Biblical Archaeology*, 4/10 (Feb. 1888), 181–206.

—— *Monuments pour servir à l'histoire de l'Égypte chrétienne: Histoire des monastères de la Basse-Egypte*, Annales du Musée Guimet, 25 (Paris: Leroux, 1894).

AMUNDSEN, LEIV, 'Christian Papyri from the Oslo Collection', *Symbolae Osloenses*, 24 (1945), 121–47.

ANASTOS, M. V., 'The Ethical Theory of Images Formulated by the Iconoclasts in 754 and 815', *Dumbarton Oaks Papers*, 8 (1954), 151–60.

ANSON, JOHN, 'The Female Transvestite in Early Monasticism: The Origin and Development of a Motif', *Viator*, 5 (1974), 1–32.

ANTONINI, LUCIANA, 'Le chiese cristiane nell'Egitto dal IV al IX secolo secondo i documenti dei papiri greci', *Aegyptus*, 20 (1940), 129–208.

ASHLEY, KATHLEEN M. (ed.), *Victor Turner and the Construction of Cultural Criticism* (Bloomington and Indianapolis: Indiana University Press, 1990).

ASPEGREN, KERSTIN, *The Male Woman: A Feminine Ideal in the Early Church*, ed., René Kieffer (Stockholm: Almqvist & Wiksell International, 1990).

ATTWATER, DONALD, *The Penguin Dictionary of Saints*, 2nd edn. (London: Penguin, 1983).

AUBINEAU, T. M., 'Les Écrits de Saint Athanase sur la Virginité', *Revue d'ascetique et de mystique*, 31 (1955), 140–73.

AUNE, DAVID, *The New Testament in its Literary Environment* (Philadelphia: Westminster, 1987).

AVRIN, LEILA, *Scribes, Script and Books: The Book Arts from Antiquity to the Renaissance* (Chicago: American Library Association, 1991).

BADAWY, ALEXANDER, *Coptic Art and Archaeology: The Art of the Christian Egyptians from the Late Antique to the Middle Ages* (Cambridge, Mass., and London: Massachusetts Institute of Technology Press, 1978).

BADGER, CARLTON M., Jr., 'The New Man Created in God: Christology, Congregation, and Asceticism in Athanasius of Alexandria', Ph.D. diss., Duke University, 1990.

BAGNALL, ROGER S., *Egypt in Late Antiquity* (Princeton: Princeton University Press, 1993).

—— 'Religious Conversion and Onomastic Change in Early Byzantine Egypt', *Bulletin of the American Society of Papyrologists*, 19/3–4 (1982), 105–24.

BALDUCCI, ANTONIO, 'Archelaide, Tecla e Susanna', *Bibliotheca Sanctorum*, 2 (1962), 375–6.

BAUER, ADOLF and STRZYGOWSKI, JOSEF, *Eine alexandrinische Weltchronik: Text und Miniaturen eines griechischen Papyrus der Sammlung W. Goleniscev*, ii: *Die Miniaturen und ihr Kunstkreis*, Denkschriften kaiserlichen Akademie der Wissenschaften in Wien, Philosophisch-historische Klasse, vol. 51 (Vienna: Carl Gerold's Sohn, 1905).

BAUMEISTER, THEOFRIED, *Martyr Invictus: Der Martyrer als Sinnbild der Erlösung in der Legende und im Kult der frühen koptischen Kirche: Zur Kontinuität des ägyptischen Denkens* (Münster: Regensberg, 1972).

BEARE, JOHN I., *Greek Theories of Elementary Cognition: From Alcmaeon to Aristotle* (Oxford: Clarendon Press, 1906).

BÉCHARD, DEAN, SJ, 'Paul Among the Rustics: A Study of Luke's Socio-Geographical Universalism in Acts 14: 8–20', Ph.D. diss., Yale University, 1997.

BECKWITH, JOHN, *Coptic Sculpture 300–1300* (London: Alec Tiranti, 1963).
—— *Early Christian and Byzantine Art*. (New York: Penguin, 1979).

BELL, CATHERINE, *Ritual Theory, Ritual Practice* (New York: Oxford University Press, 1992).

BENKO, STEPHEN, *The Virgin Goddess: Studies in the Pagan and Christian Roots of Mariology* (New York: E. J. Brill, 1993).

BENNASSER, KHALIFA, 'Gender and Sanctity in Early Byzantine Monasticism: A Study of the Phenomenon of Female Ascetics in Male Monastic Habit with a Translation of the Life of St. Matrona', Ph.D. diss., Rutgers, The State University of New Jersey, 1984.

BETZ, HANS DIETER, 'Matthew vi.22f and Ancient Greek Theories of Vision', in E. Best and R. M. Wilson (eds.), *Text and Interpretation: Studies in the New Testament Presented to Matthew Black* (Cambridge: Cambridge University Press, 1979), 43–56.

Bibliotheca Hagiographica Graeca Sociorum Bollandianorum, 3rd edn. ed. François Halkin (Brussels: Société des Bollandistes, 1957).

Bibliotheca Sanctorum, Instituto Giovanni XIII, Pontificia Universita Lateranense (Rome: Società grafica romana, 1961–70).

BOBERTZ, C. A., 'Cyprian of Carthage as Patron: A Social Historical Study of the Role of Bishop in the Ancient Christian Community of North Africa', Ph.D. diss., Yale University, 1988.

BOCK, W. DE, *Matériaux pour servir à l'archéologie de l'Égypte chrétienne* (St. Petersburg: Eugene Thiele, 1901).

BONNER, C., 'The Ship of the Soul on a Group of Grave-Stelae from Therenuthis', *Proceedings of the American Philosophical Academy*, 85 (1942), 84–91.

BONWETSCH, D. G. NATHANAEL (ed.), *Die griechischen christlichen Schriftsteller der ersten drei Jahrhunderte*, vol. 27 (Leipzig: J. C. Hinrichs, 1917).

BOUGHTON, L. C., 'From Pious Legend to Feminist Fantasy', *Journal of Religion*, 71/3 (1993), 362–83.

BOURGUET, PIERRE DU, SJ, 'Christian Subjects in Coptic Art: Saint Thecla', in *The Coptic Encyclopedia* (New York: Macmillan, 1991), ii. 541.
—— *Coptic Art*, trans. Caryll Hay-Shaw (London: Methuen, 1971).
—— *Die Kopten* (Baden-Baden: Holle, 1967).

BOUSSET, W., *Apophthegmata. Studien zur Geschichte des ältesten Mönchtums* (Tübingen: J. C. B. Mohr (Paul Siebeck), 1923).

BOWIE, EWEN, 'The Readership of Greek Novels in the Ancient World', in James Tatum (ed.), *The Search for the Ancient Novel* (Baltimore: Johns Hopkins University Press, 1994), 435–59.

Bowman, Alan K., *Egypt after the Pharaohs* (Berkeley: University of California Press, 1986).

Boyarin, Daniel, *Carnal Israel: Reading Sex in Talmudic Culture* (Berkeley: University of California Press, 1993).

Bradshaw, Paul F., *Daily Prayer in the Early Church* (New York: Oxford University Press, 1982).

Brakke, David B., *Athanasius and the Politics of Asceticism* (Oxford: Clarendon Press, 1995).

—— 'The Authenticity of the Ascetic Athanasiana', *Orientalia*, 63/2 (1994), 17–56.

—— 'St. Athanasius and Ascetic Christians', Ph.D. diss., Yale University, 1992.

Brandenburger, A. and Nalebuff, B., *Co-opetition* (New York: Doubleday, 1996).

Branigan, Keith, Hakkert, Adolf, and Zahariado, Mihail (eds.), *Lexicon of the Greek and Roman Cities and Place Names in Antiquity* (Amsterdam: Adolf M. Hakkert, 1992–).

Breccia, E. and Crum, W. E., 'D'un édifice d'époque chrétienne à El-Dekhela, et de l'emplacement du Ennaton', *Bulletin de la Société archéologique d'Alexandrie*, 9, NS (1907), 3–12.

Briére, Maurice, 'La Légende syriaque de Nestorius', *Revue de l'orient chrétien*, 15 (1910), 1–25.

Brower, Gary R., 'Ambivalent Bodies: Making Christians Eunuchs', Ph.D. diss., Duke University, 1996.

Brown, Peter, 'Arbiters of the Holy: The Christian Holy Man in Late Antiquity', in P. Brown, *Authority and the Sacred: Aspects of the Christianisation of the Roman World* (Cambridge: Cambridge University Press, 1995), 55–78, 85–7.

—— *The Body and Society: Men, Women, and Sexual Renunciation in Early Christianity* (New York: Columbia University Press, 1988).

—— *The Cult of the Saints: Its Rise and Function in Latin Christianity* (Chicago: University of Chicago Press, 1981).

—— *The Making of Late Antiquity* (Cambridge, Mass.: Harvard University Press, 1978).

—— 'The Rise and Function of the Holy Man in Late Antiquity', *Journal of Roman Studies*, 61 (1971), 80–101, repr. with updated notes in *Society and the Holy in Late Antiquity* (Berkeley: University of California Press, 1982), 103–52.

—— 'The Saint as Exemplar in Late Antiquity', *Representations*, 1/2 (1983), 1–25, repr. in J. S. Hawley (ed.), *Saints and Virtues* (Berkeley: University of California Press, 1987).

—— *Society and the Holy in Late Antiquity* (Berkeley: University of California Press, 1982).

BRUBAKER, LESLIE, 'Perception and Conception: Art Theory and Culture in Ninth-Century Byzantium', *Word and Image*, 5/1 (Jan. 1989), 19–32.

BUDGE, E. A. WALLIS, *Coptic Martyrdoms* (London: British Museum, 1914).

—— *The Paradise or Garden of the Holy Fathers*, 2 vols. (London: Chatto & Windus, 1907).

BULLIET, RICHARD W., *The Camel and the Wheel* (Cambridge, Mass.: Cambridge University Press, 1975).

BULLOUGH, VERN, 'Transvestites in the Middles Ages', *American Journal of Sociology*, 79 (1974), 1381–94.

BURKITT, F., *The Religion of the Manichees* (Cambridge: Cambridge University Press, 1925).

BURRUS, VIRGINIA, *Chastity as Autonomy: Women in the Stories of the Apocryphal Acts*, Studies in Women and Religion, 23 (Lewiston; Queenston: Edwin Mellon Press, 1987).

—— 'The Heretical Woman as Symbol in Alexander, Athanasius, Epiphanius, and Jerome', *Harvard Theological Review*, 84/3 (1991), 229–48.

BURTON-CHRISTIE, DOUGLAS, *The Word in the Desert* (Oxford: Oxford University Press, 1993).

BUSCHHAUSEN, H., 'Frühchristliches Silberreliquiar aus Isaurien', *Jahrbuch der österreichischen-byzantinischen Gesellschaft*, 11/12 (1962–3), 137–68.

BUTLER, A. J., *The Arab Conquest of Egypt and the Last Thirty Years of the Roman Dominion*, 2nd edn. (Oxford: Clarendon Press, 1978).

BUTTERWECK, CHRISTEL, *Athanasius von Alexandrien: Bibliographie*, Abhandlungen der nordrhein-westfälischen Akademie der Wissenschaften, vol. 90 (Opladen: Westdeutscher Verlag, 1995).

CABROL, FERNAND and LECLERCQ, HENRI (eds.), *Dictionnaire d'archéologie chrétienne et de liturgie* (Paris: Letouzey et Ané, 1907–53).

CALDERINI, A., *Dizionario dei nomi geografici e topgrafici dell'Egitto greco-romain* (Cairo: Società reale di geografia d'Egitto, 1935–).

CAMERON, AVERIL, *Christianity and the Rhetoric of Empire* (Berkeley: University of California Press, 1991).

—— 'Redrawing the Map: Early Christian Territory After Foucault', *Journal of Roman Studies*, 76 (1986), 266–71.

CAMPENHAUSEN, HANS VON, 'The Ascetic Idea of Exile in Ancient and Early Medieval Monasticism', in *Tradition and Life in the Church: Essays and Lectures in Church History*, trans. A. V. Littledale (Philadelphia: Fortress Press, 1968), 231–51.

—— *Die asketische Heimatlosigkeit im altkirchlichen und frühmittelalterlichen Mönchtum*, Sammlung gemeinverständlicher Vorträge und

Schriften aus dem Gebiet der Theologie und Religionsgeschichte, 149 (Tübingen: J. C. B. Mohr (Paul Siebeck), 1930).

CARROLL, MICHAEL, *'The Cult of the Virgin Mary: Psychological Origins'* (Princeton: Princeton University Press, 1986).

CARRUTHERS, MARY J., *The Book of Memory: A Study of Memory in Medieval Culture*, Cambridge Studies in Medieval Culture, 10 (Cambridge: Cambridge University Press, 1990).

CASEY, R. P., 'Armenian Manuscripts of St. Athanasius of Alexandria', *Harvard Theological Review*, 24 (1931), 43–59.

CASTELLI, ELIZABETH A., ' "I Will Make Mary Male": Pieties of the Body and Gender Transformation of Christian Women in Late Antiquity', in J. Epstein and K. Straub (eds.), *Body Guards: The Cultural Politics of Gender Ambiguity* (New York: Routledge, 1991), 29–49.

—— *Imitating Paul: A Discourse of Power*, Literary Currents in Biblical Interpretation (Louisville, Ky.: Westminster, 1991).

—— 'Mortifying the Body, Curing the Soul: Beyond Ascetic Dualism in The Life of Saint Syncletica', *Differences: A Journal of Feminist Cultural Studies*, 4/2 (Summer 1992), 134–53.

—— 'Pseudo-Athanasius: The Life and Activity of the Holy and Blessed Teacher Syncletica', in Vincent L. Wimbush (ed.), *Ascetic Behavior in Greco-Roman Antiquity: A Sourcebook* (Minneapolis: Fortress Press, 1990), 265–311.

—— 'Virginity and Its Meaning for Women's Sexuality in Early Christianity', *Journal of Feminist Studies in Religion*, 2 (1986), 61–88.

CAUWENBERGH, PAUL VAN, *Étude sur les moines d'Égypte depuis le Concile de Chalcédoine (451) jusqu'à l'invasion arabe* (Paris: Imprimerie Nationale, 1914).

Checklist of Editions of Greek and Latin Papyri, Ostraca and Tablets, 4th edn. ed. John F. Oates, Roger S. Bagnall, William H. Willis, and Klaas A. Worp, *Bulletin of the American Society of Papyrologists*, Suppl. 7 (Atlanta: Scholars Press, 1992).

CHILDESTER, DAVID, *Word and Light: Seeing, Hearing, and Religious Discourse* (Urbana and Chicago: University of Illinois Press, 1992).

CHITTY, DERWAS, *The Desert a City* (Oxford: Blackwell, 1966).

CHRISTIAN, WILLIAM A., Jr., *Local Religion in Sixteenth-Century Spain* (Princeton: Princeton University Press, 1981).

CLARK, ELIZABETH, *Ascetic Piety and Women's Faith* (Lewiston: Edwin Mellon, 1986).

—— *Jerome, Chrysostom, and Friends* (New York: Edwin Mellon, 1979).

—— 'John Chrysostom and the *Subintroductae*', *Church History*, 46 (1977), 171–85.

—— *Women in the Early Church* (Wilmington: Michael Glazier, 1983).

CLARK, GILLIAN, 'Bodies and Blood: Late Antique Debate on Martyrdom, Virginity and Resurrection', in Dominic Montserrat (ed.), *Changing Bodies, Changing Meanings: Studies on the Human Body in Antiquity* (London and New York: Routledge, 1998), 99–115.

—— *Women in Late Antiquity: Pagan and Christian Life-styles* (Oxford: Clarendon Press, 1993).

CLOKE, GILLIAN, '*This Female Man of God': Women and Spiritual Power in the Patristic Age* (London and New York: Routledge, 1995).

CLUGNET, LÉON, (ed.), *Vie (et récits) de l'Abbé Daniel le scetiote*, Bibliothéque hagiographique orientale (Paris: Librairie A. Picard et fils, 1901).

COLEMAN, SIMON and ELSNER, JOHN, *Pilgrimage: Past and Present in the World Religions* (London: British Museum Press, 1995).

COOPER, KATE, *The Virgin and the Bride: Idealized Womanhood in Late Antiquity* (Cambridge, Mass. and London: Harvard University Press, 1996).

The Coptic Encyclopedia, ed. Aziz S. Atiya, 8 vols. (New York: Macmillan, 1991).

COQUIN, RENÉ-GEORGES, 'Aphrodito', in *The Coptic Encyclopedia*, i. 153–4.

—— 'Monasteries in the Gharbiyyah Province', in *The Coptic Encyclopedia*, v. 1651–2.

—— and MARTIN, MAURICE, SJ, 'Antinoopolis, Literary and Archaeological Sources', in *The Coptic Encyclopedia*, i. 144–6.

COSSON, ANTHONY DE, *Mareotis* (London: Country Life, 1935).

COTSONIS, JOHN A., *Byzantine Figural Processional Crosses*, ed. Susan A. Boyd and Henry Maguire, Dumbarton Oaks Byzantine Collection Publications, 10 (Washington: Dumbarton Oaks Research Library and Collection, 1994).

CRUM, W. E., *A Coptic Dictionary* (Oxford: Clarendon Press, 1939, repr. 1993).

CULLER, JONATHAN, 'The Semiotics of Tourism', *American Journal of Semiotics*, 1 (1981), 127–42, repr. in *Framing the Sign: Criticism and Its Institutions* (Norman, Okla./London: University of Oklahoma Press, 1988), 153–67.

DAGRON, GILBERT, 'Le Culte des images dans le monde byzantin', in *Histoire vécue de peuple chrétien*, 2 vols. (Toulouse: Privat, 1979), i. 133–60.

—— 'Holy Images and Likeness', *Dumbarton Oaks Papers*, 45 (1991), 23–33.

DASSMANN, ERNST, *Paulus in frühchristlicher Frömmigkeit und Kunst*, Rheinisch-westfälische Akademie der Wissenschaften, Vorträge G 256 (Opladen: Westdeutscher Verlag, 1982).

DAVIES, STEVAN L., *The Revolt of the Widows: The Social World of the Apocryphal Acts* (Carbondale, Ill.: Southern Illinois University Press, 1980).

—— 'Women, Tertullian, and the *Acts of Paul*', *Semeia*, 38 (1986), 139–44.

DAVIS, STEPHEN J., 'The Cult of Saint Thecla, Apostle and Proto-martyr: A Tradition of Women's Piety in Late Antiquity', Ph.D. diss., Yale University, 1998.

—— 'Namesakes of Saint Thecla in Late Antique Egypt', *Bulletin of the American Society of Papyrologists*, 36 (1999), 71–81.

—— 'Pilgrimage and the Cult of Saint Thecla in Late Antique Egypt', in David Frankfurter (ed.), *Pilgrimage and Holy Space in Late Antique Egypt* (Leiden: Brill, 1998), 303–39.

DEICHMANN, F. W., 'Zu den Bauten der Menasstadt', *Archäologischer Anzeiger* (1932), 75–86.

DELCOURT, MARIE, 'Le complexe de Diane dans l'hagiographie chréti-enne', *Revue de l'histoire des religions*, 153 (1958), 1–33.

—— *Hermaphrodite: Myths and Rites of the Bisexual Figure in Classical Antiquity*, trans. Jennifer Nicholson (London: Studio Books, 1961).

DELEHAYE, H., *Catalogus Codicum Hagiographicorum Graecorum Regii Monasterii S. Laurentii Scorialensis*, *Analecta Bollandiana*, 28 (1909), 353–98.

—— 'L'Invention des reliques de Saint Ménas à Constantinople', *Analecta Bollandiana*, 29 (1910), 117–50.

—— *Les légendes hagiographiques* (Brussels: Bureaux de la Société des Bollandistes, 1905).

DELIA, DIANA, 'The Refreshing Water of Osiris', *Journal of the American Research Center in Egypt*, 29 (1992), 181–90.

DEUBNER, L., *De Incubatione Capita Quattuor* (Leipzig: B. G. Teubner, 1900).

—— *Kosmas und Damian* (Leipzig and Berlin: B. G. Teubner, 1907).

DIMAGGIO, PAUL J. and POWELL, WALTER W. 'The Iron Cage Revisited: Institutional Isomorphism and Collective Rationality in Organizational Fields', in W. W. Powell and P. J. DiMaggio (eds.), *The New Institutionalism in Organizational Analysis* (Chicago and London: University of Chicago Press, 1991).

DOBSCHÜTZ, ERNST VON, 'Der Roman in der alt-christlichen Literatur', *Deutsche Rundschau*, 111 (1902), 87–106.

DOW, STERLING, 'Names, Theophoric Personal', in *The Oxford Classical Dictionary*, 2nd edn., ed. N. G. L. Hammond and H. H. Scullard (Oxford: Clarendon Press, 1970).

DUTILH, J. 'Early Symbolism', *Bulletin de la Société archéologique d'Alexandrie*, 6 (1904), 61–8.

EADE, JOHN and SALLNOW, MICHAEL J. (eds.), *Contesting the Sacred: The Anthropology of Christian Pilgrimage* (London and New York: Routledge, 1991).

EFFENBERGER, ARNE, *Koptische Kunst: Ägypten in spätantiker, byzantinischer und frühislamischer Zeit* (Leipzig: Köhler und Amelang, 1975).

ELM, SUSANNA, *'Virgins of God': The Making of Asceticism in Late Antiquity* (Oxford: Clarendon Press, 1994).

EMMEL, STEPHEN L., 'Shenoute's Literary Corpus', Ph.D. diss., Yale University, 1993.

EMMETT, ALANNA M., 'An Early Fourth-Century Female Monastic Community in Egypt?', in Ann Moffatt (ed.), *Maistor: Classical, Byzantine, and Renaissance Studies for Robert Browning* (Canberra: Australian Assoc. for Byzantine Studies, 1984), 77–83.

—— 'Female Ascetics in the Greek Papyri', *Jahrbuch der österreichischen Byzantinistik*, 32/2 (1982), 507–15.

ENGEMANN, J., 'Palästinische Pilgerampullen im F. J. Dölger Institut in Bonn', *Jahrbuch für Antike und Christentum*, 16 (1973), 5–27.

EVANS, ELIZABETH CORNELIA, 'Literary Portraiture in Ancient Epic', *Harvard Studies in Classical Philology*, 58–9 (1948), 189–217.

EVELYN WHITE, HUGH G., *The Monasteries of the Wadi 'n Natrûn*, 3 vols. (New York: Metropolitan Museum of Art, 1926).

ÉVIEUX, PIERRE, *Isidore de Péluse*, Théologie Historique, 99 (Paris: Beauchesne, 1995).

FAKHRY, AHMED, *The Necropolis of El-Bagawat*, Service des antiquités de l'Égypte: The Egyptian Deserts (Cairo: Government Press, 1951).

FALK, NANCY, 'To Gaze on the Sacred Traces', *History of Religions*, 16 (1977), 281–93.

FANTHAM, ELAINE, FOLEY, HELENE PEET, KAMPEN, NATALIE BOYMEL, POMEROY, SARAH B., and SHAPIRO, H. ALAN, *Women in the Classical World* (New York and Oxford: Oxford University Press, 1994).

FARRER, CLAIRE R., 'Women and Folklore: Images and Genres', in Claire R. Farrer (ed.), *Women and Folklore* (Austin and London: University of Texas Press, 1975).

FASOLA, UMBERTO M., *Die Domitilla-Katakombe und die Basilika der Märtyrer Nereus und Achilleus*, 3rd edn., ed. Ph. Pergola, trans. into German by K. Köberl (Città del Vaticano: Pontificia Commissione di Archeologia Sacra, 1989).

—— 'Tecla', *Bibliotheca Sanctorum*, 12 (1969), 174–7, 179–81.

FELD, O., 'Bericht über eine Reise durch Kilikien', *Istanbuler Mitteilungen*, 13–14 (1963–4), 88–107.

FENOYL, MAURICE DE, *Le sanctoral copte* (Beirut: Imprimerie catholique, 1960).

FERGUSON, EVERETT (ed.), *Encyclopedia of Early Christianity* (New York and London: Garland Publishing, 1990).

FERNANDEZ MARCOS, NATALIO, *Los thaumata de Sofronio: Contribución al estudio de la incubatio cristiana* (Madrid: Instituto Antonio de Nebrija, 1975).

FITZGERALD, G. M., *Beth-Shan Excavations, 1921–1923, The Arab and Byzantine Levels*, Publications of the Palestine Section of the Museum of the University of Pennsylvania, iii (Philadelphia: University Press/University of Pennsylvania Museum, 1931).

FIYU FAQUS, JIRAR (Gérard Viaud), *Les pèlerinages coptes en Égypte, d'apres les notes du Qommos Jacob Muyser* (Cairo: Institut français d'archéologie orientale du Caire, 1979).

FORRER, ROBERT, *Die frühchristlichen Alterthümer aus dem Gräberfelde von Achmim-Panopolis* (Strassburg: F. Lohbauer, 1893).

FORSYTHE, G. H., 'Architectural Notes on a Trip through Cilicia', *Dumbarton Oaks Papers*, 11 (1957), 223–36.

FRANK, GEORGIA A., 'The Memory of the Eyes: Pilgrimage to Desert Ascetics in the Christian East During the Fourth and Fifth Centuries', Ph.D. diss., Harvard University, 1994.

FRANKFURTER, DAVID, 'The Cult of the Martyrs in Egypt before Constantine: The Evidence of the Coptic *Apocalypse of Elijah*', *Vigiliae Christianae*, 48/1 (1994), 25–47.

—— (ed.), *Pilgrimage and Holy Space in Late Antique Egypt* (Leiden: Brill, 1998).

FRAZER, RUTH, 'The Morphology of Desert Wisdom in the Apophthegmata Patrum', Ph.D. diss., University of Chicago, 1977.

FREEDBERG, DAVID, *The Power of Images: Studies in the History and Theory of Response* (Chicago: University of Chicago Press, 1989).

FREND, W. H. C., *Martyrdom and Persecution in the Early Church* (Grand Rapids, Mich.: Baker Book House, 1965).

GAMBLE, HARRY Y., *Books and Readers in the Early Church: A History of Early Christian Texts* (New Haven and London: Yale University Press, 1995).

GARRETT, SUSAN R., 'Paul's Thorn and Cultural Models of Affliction', in L. M. White and O. L. Yarbrough (eds.), *The Social World of the First Christians: Essays in Honor of Wayne A. Meeks* (Minneapolis: Fortress Press, 1995), 82–99.

GARRITTE, G., 'Un couvent de femmes au IIIᵉ siècle? Note sur un passage de la Vie grecque de saint Antoine', in E. van Cauwenbergh (ed.), *Scrinium Lovaniense: Mélanges historiques E. van Cauwenbergh* (Louvain: Éditions J. Duculot, S. A. Gembloux, 1961), 150–9.

GASCOU, JEAN, 'Enaton, The', in *The Coptic Encyclopedia*, ed. A. S. Atiya (New York: Macmillan, 1991), iii. 954–8.

—— 'Pempton', in *The Coptic Encyclopedia*, vi. 1931.

GIAMBERARDINI, GABRIELE, *Il culto mariano in Egitto*, i (Jerusalem: Franciscan Printing Press, 1974).

GIANNARELLI, ELENA, *La tipologia femminile nella biografia e nell'auto-biografia cristiana del IV° secolo* (Rome: Instituto storico italiano per il medio evo, 1980).

GIDDY, LISA L., *Egyptian Oases: Bahariya, Dakhla, Farafra and Kharga During Pharaonic Times* (Warminster: Aris & Phillips, 1986).

GLEASON, MAUD, 'The Semiotics of Gender: Physiognomy and Self-Fashioning in the Second Century, C.E.', in David Halperin, John Winkler, and Froma Zeitlin (eds.), *Before Sexuality* (Princeton: Princeton University Press, 1990), 389–415.

GOEHRING, JAMES E., 'Monastic Diversity and Ideological Boundaries in Fourth-Century Christian Egypt', *Journal of Early Christian Studies*, 5/1 (1997), 61–84.

GOLDEN, LEON, *Aristotle on Tragic and Comic Mimesis*, American Classical Studies, 29 (Atlanta: Scholars Press, 1992).

GOLDHILL, SIMON, *Foucault's Virginity: Ancient Erotic Fiction and the History of Sexuality* (Cambridge: Cambridge University Press, 1995).

GOODSPEED, E. J., 'The Book of Thekla', *American Journal of Semitic Languages and Literature*, 17 (1901), 65–95.

GOODWIN, SARAH WEBSTER and ELISABETH, BRONFEN (eds.), *Death and Representation* (Baltimore and London: Johns Hopkins University Press, 1993).

GOUGH, M., 'The Emperor Zenon and Some Cilician Churches', *Anatolian Studies*, 22 (1972), 199–212.

GOULD, GRAHAM, *The Desert Fathers on Monastic Community* (Oxford: Clarendon Press, 1993).

GRABAR, ANDRÉ, *Ampoules de Terre Sainte (Monza-Bobbio)* (Paris: Librairie C. Klincksieck, 1958).

—— 'La Fresque des saintes femmes au tombeau à Doura', *Cahiers archéologiques*, 8 (1956), 9–26.

—— *Martyrium: Recherches sur le culte des reliques et l'art chrétienne antique*, 2 vols. (Paris: Collège de France, 1946).

GRAEF, HILDA C., *Mary: A History of Doctrine and Devotion* (London: Sheed & Ward, 1985; repr. Westminster, Md.: Christian Classics, 1990).

GRANT, R. M., 'The Description of Paul in the *Acts of Paul and Thecla*', *Vigiliae Christianae*, 36 (1982), 1–4.

GRAVES, ROBERT, *The Greek Myths*, i (New York: Penguin, 1960).

GREER, ROWAN A., *Broken Lights and Mended Lives: Theology and Common Life in the Early Church* (University Park, Pa.: Pennsylvania State University Press, 1986).

—— *The Fear of Freedom: A Study of Miracles in the Roman Imperial Church* (University Park, Pa. and London: Pennsylvania State University Press, 1989).

GROHMANN, ADOLF, *Studien zur historischen Geographie und Verwaltung des frühmittelalterlichen Ägypten*, Österreichische Akademie der Wissenschaften, Philosophisch-historische Klasse, 77/2 (Vienna: R. M. Rohrer, 1959).

GROSSMANN, PETER, *Abu Mina: A Guide to the Ancient Pilgrimage Center* (Cairo: Fotiadis Press, 1986).

—— *Abu Mina I: Die Gruftkirche und die Gruft* (Mainz am Rhein: P. von Zabern, 1989).

—— 'Bagawat, Al-, Location and Architecture', in *The Coptic Encyclopedia*, ed. A. S. Atiyah (New York: Macmillan, 1991), ii. 326–7, 328 (plan).

—— 'The Gruftkirche of Abu Mina During the Fifth Century A.D.', *Bulletin de la Société d'archéologie copte*, 25 (1983), 67–71.

—— 'The Pilgrimage Center of Abû Mînâ', in David Frankfurter (ed.), *Pilgrimage and Holy Space in Late Antique Egypt* (Leiden: Brill, 1998), 281–302.

—— 'Report on the Excavations at Abu Mina in Spring 1994', *Bulletin de la Société d'archéologie copte*, 34 (1995), 149–59, pl. 9–12.

—— and DONALD S. WHITCOMB, 'Excavation in the Sanctuary of the Church in front of the Luqsur-Temple', *Annales du service des antiquités égyptiennes*, 72 (1992–3), 25–34 and pl. 1–6.

GRÜNEISEN, W. DE, *Les caractéristiques de l'art copte* (Florence: Instituto di edizioni artistiche fratelli alinari, 1922).

GUY, JEAN-CLAUDE, *Recherches sur la tradition grecque des Apophthegmata Patrum*, Subsidia Hagiographica, 36 (Brussels: Société des Bollandistes, 1962).

GWYNN, JOHN, 'Thecla (1–17)', in W. Smith and H. Wace (eds.), *A Dictionary of Christian Biography, Literature, Sects and Doctrines during the First Eight Centuries* (London: John Murray, 1887; New York: AMS Press, 1984), iv. 882–98.

HAAS, CHRISTOPHER, *Alexandria in Late Antiquity: Topography and Social Conflict* (Baltimore and London: Johns Hopkins University Press, 1997).

—— 'The Arians of Alexandria', *Vigiliae Christianae*, 47 (1993), 234–45.

HAHM, DAVID E., 'Early Hellenistic Theories of Vision and the Perception of Color', in P. K. Machamer and R. G. Turnbull (eds.), *Studies in Perception: Interrelations in the History of Philosophy and Science* (Columbus: Ohio State University Press, 1978), 60–95.

HALDON, JOHN F., 'Supplementary Essay—The Miracles of Artemios and Contemporary Attitudes: Context and Significance', in V. Crisafulli and J. W. Nesbitt (eds.), *The Miracles of St. Artemios: A Collection of Miracle Stories by an Anonymous Author of Seventh-Century Byzantium* (Leiden: E. J. Brill, 1997), 33–73.

HALLIWELL, STEPHEN, 'Aristotelian Mimesis Reevaluated', *Journal of the History of Philosophy*, 28/4 (Oct. 1990), 487–510.

HAMILTON, ANDREW, SJ, 'Athanasius and the Simile of the Mirror', *Vigiliae Christianae*, 34 (1980), 14–18.

HAMMOND, N. G. L. and SCULLARD, H. H. (eds.), *The Oxford Classical Dictionary*, 2nd edn. (Oxford: Clarendon Press, 1970).

HARPHAM, GEOFFREY GALT, *The Ascetic Imperative in Culture and Criticism* (Chicago: University of Chicago Press, 1987).

HARVEY, SUSAN ASHBROOK, 'Women in Early Byzantine Hagiography: Reversing the Story', in Lynda L. Coon, Katherine J. Haldane, and Elisabeth W. Sommer (eds.), *That Gentle Strength: Historical Perspectives on Women in Christianity* (Charlottesville, Va.: University of Virginia Press, 1990), 35–59.

HAUSER, WALTER, 'The Christian Necropolis in Khargeh Oasis', *Bulletin Metropolitan Museum of Art*, 27 (Mar. 1932), 38–50.

HAUSHERR, S. I., *Études de spiritualité orientale*, Orientalia Christiana Analecta, 183 (Rome: Pontificum Institutum Studiorum Orientalium, 1969).

HAYNE, L., 'Thecla and the Church Fathers', *Vigiliae Christianae*, 48/3 (1994), 209–18.

HEFELE, CHARLES JOSEPH, *Histoire des Conciles* (Paris: Letouzey et Ané, 1907), i. pt. 2.

HEINE, SUSANNE, *Women and Early Christianity* (London: SCM Press, 1987).

HELFRITZ, HANS, *Äthiopien-Kunst im Verborgenen: Ein Reiseführer ins Land des Löwen von Juda* (Schauberg: M. DuMont, 1972).

HERZFELD, E. and GUYER, S., *Meriamlik und Korykos: Zwei christliche Ruinenstätte des Rauhen Kilikiens*, Monumenta Asiae Minoris Antique, ii (Manchester: Manchester University Press, 1930).

HEWISON, R. NEIL, *The Fayoum: A Practical Guide* (Cairo: American University in Cairo Press, 1984).

HEYNE, HILDEGARD, *Das Gleichnis von den klugen und törichten Jungfrauen: Eine literarisch-ikonographische Studie zur altchristlichen Zeit* (Leipzig: H. Haessel, 1922).

HEYOB, SHARON KELLY, *The Cult of Isis Among Women in the Graeco-Roman World* (Leiden: E. J. Brill, 1975).

HILD, FRIEDRICH and HELLENKEMPER, H., *Kilikien und Isaurien*, Österreichische Akademie der Wissenschaften, Philosophisch-historische Klasse, Denkschriften, vol. 215 (Vienna: Österreichische Akademie der Wissenschaften, 1990).

HIRSCHFELD, YIZHAR, *The Judean Desert Monasteries in the Byzantine Period* (New Haven and London: Yale University Press, 1992).

HOBSON, D. W., 'Women as Property Owners in Roman Egypt', *Transactions of the American Philological Association*, 113 (1983), 311–21.

HOLZHEY, C., *Die Thekla-Akten: Ihre Verbreitung und Beurteilung in der Kirche*, Veröffentlichungen aus dem kirchengeschichtlichen Seminar

München 2,7. Herausgegeben von Alois Knöpfler (Munich: J. J. Lentner Buchhandlung, 1905).

HOOPER, F. A., *Funerary Stelae from Kom Abou Billou*, Kelsey Museum of Archeology, Studies, no. 1 (Ann Arbor: University of Michigan, 1961).

HORN, JÜRGEN, *Studien zu den Märtyrern des nördlichen Oberägypten I. Martyrverehrung und Märtyrerlegende im Werk des Schenute: Beiträge zur älteste ägyptischen Märtyrerüberlieferung*, Göttinger Orientforschungen, 4th series, vol. 15 (Wiesbaden: Otto Harrassowitz, 1986).

HUNT, E. D., *Holy Land Pilgrimage in the Later Roman Empire, AD 312–460* (Oxford: Clarendon Press, 1982).

JÄGER, OTTO, *Antiquities of North Ethiopia* (Stuttgart: F. A. Brockhaus K. G., 1965).

JAMES, LIZ (ed.), *Women, Men and Eunuchs: Gender in Byzantium* (London and New York: Routledge, 1997).

JANAWAY, CHRIS, 'Plato's Analogy Between Painter and Poet', *British Journal of Aesthetics*, 31/1 (1991), 1–12.

JARITZ, FELICITAS, *Die arabischen Quellen zum Heiligen Menas* (Heidelberg: Heidelberger Orientverlag, 1993).

JENSEN, ANNE, *God's Self-Confident Daughters: Early Christianity and the Liberation of Women*, trans. O. C. Dean, Jr. (Louisville, Ky.: Westminster, 1996).

—— *Thekla—die Apostolin: Ein apokrypher Text neu entdeckt* (Freiburg: Herder, 1995).

Jones, A. H. M., *Cities of the Eastern Roman Provinces*, 2nd edn., rev. Michael Avi-Yonah, *et al.* (Oxford: Clarendon Press, 1971).

—— *The Later Roman Empire 284–602*, 2 vols. (Baltimore: Johns Hopkins University Press, 1964).

JORDAN, ROSAN A., 'The Vaginal Serpent and Other Themes from Mexican-American Folklore', in Rosan A. Jordan and Susan J. Kalcik (eds.), *Women's Folklore, Women's Culture* (Philadelphia: University of Pennsylvania Press, 1985), 26–44.

—— and KALCIK, SUSAN J. (eds.), *Women's Folklore, Women's Culture* (Philadelphia: University of Pennsylvania Press, 1985).

JORGE, ANTONIO, *Competition, Cooperation, Efficiency, and Social Organization: Introduction to a Political Economy* (Rutherford, NJ: Fairleigh Dickinson University Press; London: Associated University Press, 1978).

JULLIEN, M., 'Traditions et légendes coptes sur le voyage de la sainte-famille en Égypte', *Les missions catholiques*, 19 (1887), 9–12, 20, 22–4.

JUNGMANN, JOSEF A., SJ, *The Early Liturgy: To the Time of Gregory the Great*, trans. Francis A. Brunner, C.S.S.R. (Notre Dame, Ind.: University of Notre Dame Press, 1959).

KANNENGIESSER, CHARLES, 'Athanasius of Alexandria vs. Arius: The Alexandrian Crisis', in Birger A. Pearson and James E. Goehring (eds.), *The Roots of Egyptian Christianity*, Studies in Antiquity and Christianity (Philadelphia: Fortress Press, 1986), 204–15.

KARRAS, RUTH MAZO, 'Holy Harlots: Prostitute Saints in Medieval Legend', *Journal of the History of Sexuality*, 1 (1990), 3–32.

KAUFMANN, C. M., *Ein altchristliches Pompeji in der libyschen Wüste: Die Nekropolis der 'Grossen Oase'* (Mainz: Franz Kirchheim, 1902).

—— 'Archäologische Miszellen aus Ägypten', *Oriens Christianus*, 2/3 (1913), 105–10.

—— *Die Ausgrabung der Menas-Heiligtümer in der Mareotis-Wüste* (Cairo: Finck & Baylaender, 1906–8).

—— *Die heilige Stadt der Wüste* (Kempten-München: J. Kosel & F. Pustet, 1924).

—— *Die Menastadt und das Nationalheiligtum der altchristlichen Ägypter in der westalexandrinischen Wüste* (Leipzig: K. W. Hiersemann, 1910–).

—— *Zur Ikonographie der Menasampullen* (Cairo: F. Diemer, Finck & Baylaender, 1910).

KEENAN, J. G., 'On Village and Polis in Byzantine Egypt', in *Proceedings of the XVI International Congress of Papyrology*, ed. Roger S. Bagnall, *et al.* (Chico, Calif.: Scholars Press, 1981).

KENNEDY, CHARLES ALFRED, 'The Whiting Collection of Palestinian Pottery at Yale', Ph.D. diss., Yale University, 1961.

KENNEDY, GEORGE, *The Art of Rhetoric in the Roman World 300 BC–AD 300*, A History of Rhetoric, ii. (Princeton: Princeton University Press, 1972).

KHATER, A., 'La Translation des reliques de S. Ménas à son église au Caire', *Bulletin de la Société d'archéologie copte*, 16 (1961–2), 161–81.

KILPATRICK, G. D. and ROBERTS, C. H., 'The Acta Pauli: A New Fragment', *Journal of Theological Studies*, 37 (1946), 196–9.

KIRK, G. S., RAVEN, J. E., and SCHOFIELD, M., *The Presocratic Philosophers: A Critical History with a Selection of Texts*, 2nd edn. (Cambridge: Cambridge University Press, 1983).

KISS, ZSOLT, *Les Ampoules de St. Ménas découvertes à Kôm el-Dikka (1961–1981)* (Warsaw: PWN-Éditions scientifiques de Pologne, 1989).

—— 'Les Ampoules de St. Ménas découvertes à Kôm el-Dikka (Alexandrie) en 1967', in *Travaux du Centre d'archéologie méditerranéenne de l'Académie polonaise des sciences* (Warsaw: PWN, Éditions scientifiques de Pologne, 1969), viii. 154–66.

—— 'Nouvelles ampoules de St. Ménas à Kôm el-Dikka', in *Travaux du Centre d'archéologie méditerranéenne de l'Académie polonaise des sciences* (Warsaw: PWN, Éditions scientifiques de Pologne, 1971), ii. 146–9.

KITZINGER, E., 'From Justinian to Iconoclasm: The Cult of Images in the Age Before Iconoclasm', *Dumbarton Oaks Papers*, 8 (1954), 83–150.

KLAWITER, FREDERICK C., 'The Role of Martyrdom and Persecution in Developing the Priestly Authority of Women in Early Christianity: A Case Study of Montanism', *Church History*, 49 (1980), 251–61.

KLEINER, DIANA E. E. and MATHESON, SUSAN B. (eds.), *I Claudia: Women in Ancient Rome* (Austin: University of Texas Press, 1996).

KOCH, GUNTRAM (ed.), *Studien zur frühchristlichen Kunst II*, Göttinger Orientforschungen, series 2, Studien zur spätantiken und frühchristlichen Kunst, vol. 8 (Wiesbaden: Otto Harrassowitz, 1986).

—— *Studien zur spätantiken und frühchristlichen Kunst und Kultur des Orients*, Göttinger Orientforschungen, series 2, Studien zur spätantiken und frühchristlichen Kunst, vol. 6 (Wiesbaden: Otto Harrassowitz, 1982).

KOCH, H., *Quellen zur Geschichte der Askese und des Mönchtums in der alten Kirche* (Tübingen: Mohr, 1933).

KOLLER, HANS, *Die Mimesis in der Antike: Nachahmung, Darstellung, Ausdruck*, Dissertationes Bernenses, ser. 1, fasc. 5 (Berne: A. Francke, 1954).

KÖTTING, BERNHARD, *Peregrinatio Religiosa: Wallfahrten in der Antike und das Pilgerwesen in der alten Kirche*, 2nd edn. (Münster: Antiquariat Th. Stenderhoff, 1980).

KRAELING, CARL H., *The Christian Building*, Excavations at Dura-Europos, Final Report, 8/2 (New Haven: Dura-Europos Publications, 1967).

KRAEMER, ROSS SHEPARD, *Her Share of the Blessings* (New York: Oxford University Press, 1992).

KRAUSE, MARTIN, 'Menas the Miracle Maker, Saint', in *The Coptic Encyclopedia*, ed. A. S. Atiyah (New York: Macmillan, 1991), v. 1589–90.

KRAUTHEIMER, RICHARD, *Early Christian and Byzantine Architecture*, 4th edn. (New Haven and London: Yale University Press, 1986).

KRAWIEC, REBECCA S., 'Women's Life in Shenute's White Monastery: A Study in Late Antique Egyptian Monasticism', Ph.D. diss., Yale University, 1996.

KUEFLER, MATTHEW S., 'Eunuchs and Other Men: The Crisis and Transformation of Masculinity in the Later Roman West', Ph.D. diss., Yale University, 1995.

LADNER, GERHART B., '*Homo Viator*: Mediaeval Ideas on Alienation and Order', *Speculum*, 42/2 (1967), 233–59.

LAMPE, G. W. H., *A Patristic Greek Lexicon* (Oxford: Clarendon Press, 1961).

Late Egyptian and Coptic Art: An Introduction to the Collections in the Brooklyn Museum (Brooklyn: Brooklyn Museum, 1943).

LAUSBERG, HEINRICH, *Handbuch der literarischen Rhetorik: Eine Grundlegung der Literaturwissenschaft*, 2 vols., 2nd edn. (Munich: Max Hueber, 1973).

LECLERCQ, HENRI, 'Ad bestias', DACL I, 449–62.

—— 'Oasis', DACL XII/2, 1820–33.

LEFEBVRE, M. GUSTAVE, 'Égypte chrétienne, i. Quelques inscriptions grecques', *Annales du Service des Antiquités de l'Egypte*, 9 (1908), 172–83.

LEWIS, NAPHTALI, *Life in Egypt under Roman Rule* (Oxford: Clarendon Press, 1983).

LEWIS, SUZANNE, 'The Iconography of the Coptic Horseman in Byzantine Egypt', *Journal of the American Research Center in Egypt*, 10 (1973), 27–63.

LEYERLE, BLAKE, 'John Chrysostom on the Gaze', *Journal of Early Christian Studies*, 1 (1993), 159–74.

—— 'Landscape as Cartography in Early Christian Pilgrimage Narratives', *Journal of the American Academy of Religion*, 64/1 (Spring 1996), 119–43.

LIDDELL, HENRY GEORGE and SCOTT, ROBERT, *A Greek-English Lexicon*, 9th edn. (Oxford: Clarendon Press, 1990).

LIEU, SAMUEL N. C., *Manichaeism in the Later Roman Empire and Medieval China*, 2nd edn. (Tübingen: J. C. B. Mohr (Paul Siebeck), 1992).

LINDBERG, DAVID C., *Theories of Vision from Al-Kindi to Kepler* (Chicago and London: University of Chicago Press, 1976).

LIPSIUS, RICHARD A., *Die apocryphen Apostelgeschichten und Apostellegenden* (Brunswick: C. A. Schwetschke und Sohn, 1883–7).

LOERKE, W., ' "Real Presence" in Early Christian Art', in T. G. Verdon (ed.), *Monasticism and the Arts* (Syracuse, NY: Syracuse University Press, 1984), 29–51.

LORD, A. B., *The Singer of Tales* (Cambridge, Mass.: Harvard University Press, repr. Atheneum Publishers, 1978).

MACCANNELL, DEAN, *The Tourist: A New Theory of the Leisure Class* (New York: Schocken Books, 1976).

McCLEARY, ROGER VINCENT, 'Funerary Stelae with the Orans-Motif (Workshop Traditions of Terenuthis during the Roman Occupation)', Ph.D. diss., University of Toronto, 1985.

MACCORMACK, SABINE G., *Art and Ceremony in Late Antiquity* (Berkeley: University of California Press, 1981).

MacCoull, L. S. B., 'Child Donations and Child Saints in Coptic Egypt', *East European Quarterly*, 13/4 (1979), 409–15.

MacDonald, Dennis R., *Christianizing Homer: The Odyssey, Plato, and the Acts of Andrew* (New York: Oxford University Press, 1994).

—— *The Legend and the Apostle: The Battle for Paul in Story and Canon* (Philadelphia: Westminster, 1983).

—— 'The Role of Women in the Production of the Apocryphal Acts of Apostles', *Iliff Review*, 41 (1984), 21–38.

—— and Scrimgeour, Andrew D., 'Pseudo-Chrysostom's Panegyric to Thecla: The Heroine of the *Acts of Paul* in Homily and Art', *Semeia*, 38 (1986), 151–9.

McHardy, W. D., article (untitled) in the *Expository Times*, 58 (1947), 279.

MacKay, Thomas W., 'Response to Davies', *Semeia*, 38 (1986), 145–9.

Maguire, Eunice D., Maguire, Henry P., Duncan-Flowers, Maggie J., *Art and Holy Powers in the Early Christian House*, Illinois Byzantine Studies, 2 (Urbana and Chicago: University of Illinois Press, 1989).

Maguire, Henry, *Art and Eloquence in Byzantium* (Princeton: Princeton University Press, 1981).

—— 'Garments Pleasing to God: The Significance of Domestic Textile Designs in the Early Byzantine Period', *Dumbarton Oaks Papers*, 44 (1990), 215–24.

Malherbe, Abraham J., 'God's New Family in Thessalonica', in L. M. White and O. L. Yarbrough (eds.), *The Social World of the First Christians: Essays in Honor of Wayne A. Meeks* (Minneapolis: Fortress Press, 1995), 116–25.

—— 'Hellenistic Moralists and the New Testament', *ANRW* ii. 26. 1, 267–333.

—— *Paul and the Popular Philosophers* (Philadelphia: Fortress Press, 1989).

Malone, Edward E., *The Monk and the Martyr: The Monk as the Successor of the Martyr*, The Catholic University of America Studies in Christian Antiquity, no. 12 (Washington: Catholic University of America Press, 1950).

Mancinelli, Fabrizio, *The Catacombs of Rome and the Origins of Christianity* (Florence: SCALA, 1981).

Maraval, Pierre, *Lieux saints et pèlerinages d'Orient: Histoire et géographie des origines à la conquête arabe* (Paris: Éditions du Cerf, 1985).

Markopoulos, A., 'Bios tes Autokrateiras Theodoras', *Symmeikta*, 5 (1983), 249–85.

Marrou, H. I., *A History of Education in Antiquity*, trans. G. Lamb (Madison: University of Wisconsin Press, 1982).

MATHESON, SUSAN B., *Dura-Europos: The Ancient City and the Yale Collection* (New Haven: Yale University Art Gallery, 1982).

MÉCHOULAN, ÉRIC, 'Theoria, Aisthesis, Mimesis, and Doxa', *Diogenes*, 151 (1990), 131–48.

MEEKS, WAYNE, 'The Image of the Androgyne', *History of Religions*, 13/3 (1974), 165–208.

MEER, F. VAN DER and MOHRMANN, CHRISTINE, *Atlas of the Early Christian World*, trans. and ed. Mary F. Hedlund and H. H. Rowley (London: Nelson, 1958).

MEINARDUS, OTTO, *Christian Egypt: Ancient and Modern* (Cairo: Cahiers d'histoire égyptienne, 1965).

—— *In the Steps of the Holy Family from Bethlehem to Upper Egypt* (Cairo: Dar al-Maaref, 1963).

—— *Monks and Monasteries of the Egyptian Deserts*, rev. edn. (Cairo: American University in Cairo Press, 1992).

MERKI, H., 'Ebenbildlichkeit', *RACh*, 4: 459–79.

MESKELL, L. M., 'An Archaeology of Social Relations in an Egyptian Village', *Journal of Archaeological Method and Theory*, 5/3 (1998), 209–43.

METZGER, C., *Ampoules a eulogie*, Musée du Louvre, Notes et documents des musées de France, 3 (Paris: Editions de la Réunion des musées nationaux, 1981).

MEYER, MARVIN W., 'Making Mary Male: The Categories "Male" and "Female" in the Gospel of Thomas', *New Testament Studies*, 31 (1985), 554–70.

MILES, MARGARET, ' "The Evidence of Our Eyes": Patristic Studies and Popular Christianity in the Fourth Century', in *Studia Patristica XVIII*, i. *Historica-Theologica-Gnostica-Biblica* (Kalamazoo, Mich.: Cistercian Publications, 1986), 59–63.

MILLET, G., 'Doura et El-Bagawat: La parabole des vierges', *Cahiers archéologiques*, 8 (1956), 1–8.

MILLS, MARGARET, 'Sex Role Reversals, Sex Changes, and Transvestite Disguise in the Oral Tradition of a Conservative Muslim Community in Afghanistan', in Rosan A. Jordan and Susan J. Kalcik (eds.), *Women's Folklore, Women's Culture* (Philadelphia: University of Pennsylvania Press, 1985), 187–213.

MILNE, HERBERT J. M., *The Codex Sinaiticus and the Codex Alexandrinus* (London: British Museum, 1938).

MILNE, J. GRAFTEN, 'Greek and Roman Tourists in Egypt', *Journal of Egyptian Archaeology*, 3/2 (1916), 76–80.

MIRECKI, PAUL and BEDUHN, JASON (eds.), *Emerging from Darkness: Studies in the Recovery of Manichaean Sources* (Leiden: E. J. Brill, 1997).

MONKS, G. R., 'The Church of Alexandria and the City's Economic Life in the Sixth Century', *Speculum*, 28 (1953), 349–62.

MONTSERRAT, DOMINIC, 'Pilgrimage to the Shrine of SS Cyrus and John at Menouthis in Late Antiquity', in David Frankfurter (ed.), *Pilgrimage and Holy Space in Late Antiquity* (Leiden: Brill, 1998).

—— (ed.), *Changing Bodies, Changing Meanings: Studies on the Human Body in Antiquity* (London and New York: Routledge, 1998).

MORABITO, GIUSEPPE, 'Alfio, Filadelfio, *et al.*', *Bibliotheca Sanctorum*, 1 (1961), 832–4.

MUHAMMAD, M. ABDUL-QADER, 'Preliminary Report on the Excavations Carried Out in the Temple of Luxor, Seasons 1958–1959 and 1959–1960', *Annales du service des antiquités de l'Égypte*, 60 (1968), 227–79 and pl. 1–106.

MURRAY, MARGARET A., *The Osireion at Abydos* (London: Bernard Quaritch, 1904).

NAGEL, PETER, 'Die apokryphen Apostelakten des 2. und 3. Jahrhunderts in der manichäischen Literatur', in K.-W. Tröger (ed.), *Gnosis und Neues Testament: Studien aus Religionswissenschaft und Theologie* (Gerd Mohn (Berlin): Gütersloher, 1973).

NATHON, GÉRARD, 'Tecla', *Bibliotheca Sanctorum*, 12 (1969), 173–4.

NAUERTH, CLAUDIA, 'Nachlese von Thekla-Darstellungen', in G. Koch (ed.), *Studien zur spätantiken und frühchristlichen Kunst und Kultur des Orients*, Göttinger Orientforschungen, series 2, Studien zur spätantiken und frühchristlichen Kunst, vol. 6 (Wiesbaden: Otto Harrassowitz, 1982), 14–18, tables 4–9.

—— and WARNS, RÜDIGER, *Thekla: Ihre Bilder in der frühchristlichen Kunst* (Wiesbaden: Otto Harrassowitz, 1981).

NESBITT, JOHN W., 'Introduction', in V. Crisafulli and J. W. Nesbitt (eds.), *The Miracles of St. Artemios: A Collection of Miracle Stories by an Anonymous Author of Seventh-Century Byzantium* (Leiden: E. J. Brill, 1997), 1–30.

NESTLE, E., 'Evangelien als Amulet am Hals und am Sofa', *Zeitschrift für die neutestamentliche Wissenschaft und die Kunde des Urchristentums*, 7 (1906), 96.

NEUSS, W., 'Ikonographische Studien zu den Kölner Werken der altchristlichen Kunst I', *Zeitschrift für christliche Kunst*, 38 (1915), 107–22.

NEVETT, LISA, 'Perceptions of Domestic Space in Roman Italy', in B. Rawson and P. Weaver (eds.), *The Roman Family in Italy: Status, Sentiment, Space* (Oxford: Clarendon Press, 1997), 281–98.

O'LEARY, DE LACY EVANS, *The Saints of Egypt* (New York: Macmillan, 1937; repr. Amsterdam: Philo Press, 1974).

OLRICK, ALEX, 'Epic Laws of Folk Narrative', in Alan Dundes (ed.), *The Study of Folklore* (Englewood Cliffs, NJ: Prentice-Hall, 1965), 129–41.

ONG, WALTER J., SJ, *The Presence of the Word: Some Prolegomena for Cultural and Religious History* (New Haven: Yale University Press, 1967; repr. Minneapolis: University of Minnesota Press, 1981).

ONIANS, J., 'Abstraction and Imagination in Late Antiquity', *Art History*, 3 (1980), 1–23.

OUSTERHOUT, R. (ed.), *The Blessings of Pilgrimage* (Urbana-Champaign: University of Illinois Press, 1990).

PAGELS, ELAINE, *Adam, Eve, and the Serpent* (New York: Vintage, 1988).

PATLAGEAN, EVELYN, 'L'Histoire de la femme déguisée en moine et l'évolution de la sainteté feminine à Byzance', *Studi medievalis*, 3/17 (1976), 597–623.

PAVLOVSKIS, ZOJA, 'The Life of St. Pelagia the Harlot: Hagiographic Adaptation of Pagan Romance', *Classical Folia*, 30 (1976), 138–49.

PELLAT, C., 'Ibil', in H. A. R. Gibb (ed.), *Encyclopaedia of Islam*, 2nd edn. (Leiden: E. J. Brill; London: Luzac & Co., 1971), iii. 665–8.

PERKINS, ANN, *The Art of Dura-Europos* (Oxford: Clarendon Press, 1973).

PESTMAN, P. W., *The New Papyrological Primer* (Leiden: E. J. Brill, 1994).

PHELAN, JAMES, 'Character, Progression, and the Mimetic-Didactic Distinction', *Modern Philology*, 84 (Feb. 1987), 282–99.

POLOTSKY, H. J., *Manichäische Homilien*, Manichäische Handscriften der Sammlung A. Chester Beatty, vol. 1 (Stuttgart: W. Kohlhammer, 1934).

POMEROY, SARAH B., *Goddesses, Whores, Wives, and Slaves: Women in Classical Antiquity* (New York: Schocken Books, 1975).

—— *Women in Hellenistic Egypt: From Alexander to Cleopatra* (New York: Schocken Books, 1984).

—— *Women's History and Ancient History* (Chapel Hill: University of North Carolina Press, 1991).

PREISIGKE, FRIEDRICH, *Namenbuch* (Heidelberg: Selbstverlag des Herasusgebers, 1922).

QUASTEN, JOHANNES, *Patrology*, 4 vols. (Westminster, Md.: Christian Classics, 1992).

RADERMACHER, LUDWIG, *Hippolytus und Thekla: Studien zur Geschichte von Legende und Kultus*, Kaiserliche Akademie der Wissenschaften in Wien, Philosophisch-historische Klasse, Proceedings, 182, 3 (Vienna: Alfred Hölder, 1916).

RAMSAY, W. M., 'The Acta of Paul and Thekla', in *The Church in the Roman Empire Before A.D. 170* (New York and London: G. P. Putnam's Sons, 1893), 375–428.

RASSART-DEBERGH, MARGUERITE, 'Mareotis, Coptic Paintings at', in *The Coptic Encyclopedia*, ed. A. S. Atiyah (New York: Macmillan, 1991), v. 1527–8.

REEVES, CHARLES ERIC, 'Vice Versa: Rhetorical Reflections in an Ideological Mirror', *New Literary History*, 23/1 (1992), 159–71.

REGNAULT, DOM LUCIEN, 'Introduction', to the *Vie de Sainte Syncletique*, trans. Odile Bénédicte Bernard, Spiritualité Orientale, 9 (Bégrolles-en-Mauges: Abbaye de Bellefontaine, 1972).

RIAD, HENRI, HANNA SHEHATA, YOUSSEF, and EL-GHERIANI, YOUSSEF, *Alexandria: An Archeological Guide to the City*, rev. Daoud Abdo Daoud, 2nd edn. rev. Y. El-Gheriani (Alexandria Regional Authority for Tourism Promotion, 1996).

RINGROSE, KATHRYN M., 'Living in the Shadows: Eunuchs and Gender in Byzantium', in G. Herdt (ed.), *Third Sex, Third Gender* (New York: Zone, 1994), 85–109.

ROBERTS, COLIN H., *Manuscript, Society and Belief in Early Christian Egypt* (London: Oxford University Press, 1979).

RODZIEWICZ, MIECZYSLAW, 'Alexandria and the District of Mareotis', *Graeco-Arabica*, 2 (1983), 199–216.

—— 'Remarks on the Domestic and Monastic Architecture in Alexandria and Surroundings', in E. C. M. van den Brink (ed.), *The Archaeology of the Nile Delta: Problems and Priorities* (Amsterdam: Netherlands Foundation for Archaeological Research in Egypt, 1988), 267–77.

ROHDE, ERWIN, *Der griechische Roman und seine Vorläufer*, 3rd edn. (Leipzig: Breitkopf & Hartel, 1914).

ROQUET, G., 'Bagawat, Al-, Coptic Inscriptions', in *The Coptic Encyclopedia*, ed. A. S. Atiyah (New York: Macmillan, 1991), ii. 328–9.

RORDORF, WILLY, 'Tradition and Composition in the Acts of Thecla: The State of the Question', *Semeia*, 38 (1986), 43–52.

ROSCHER, W. H. (ed.), *Ausführliches Lexikon der griechischen und römischen Mythologie* (Leipzig: B. G. Teubner, 1884–1937).

ROSTOVTZEFF, MICHAEL, *Dura-Europos and its Art* (Oxford: Clarendon Press, 1938).

ROUSSELLE, ALINE, *Porneia: On Desire and the Body in Antiquity*, trans. Felicia Pheasant (Cambridge, Mass.: Blackwell, 1988).

RUETHER, ROSEMARY RADFORD, 'Misogynism and Virginal Feminism in the Fathers of the Church', in R. R. Ruether (ed.), *Religion and Sexism: Images of Women in the Jewish and Christian Traditions* (New York: Simon and Schuster, 1974), 150–83.

SALISBURY, JOYCE E., *Church Fathers, Independent Virgins* (London: Verso, 1991).

SAMBURSKY, S., *Physics of the Stoics* (Princeton: Princeton University Press, 1987).

SAMUEL, BISHOP, and BADIE HABIB, ARCHBISHOP, *Ancient Coptic Monasteries and Churches in Delta, Sinai, and Cairo*, trans. Mina al-Shamaa. rev. Tania C. Tribe (Abbasiya (Cairo): Institute for Coptic Studies, 1996).

SANDERS, H. A., 'A Fragment of the Acta Pauli in the Michigan Collection', *Harvard Theological Review*, 31 (1938), 70–90.

SAUGET, JOSEPH-MARIA, 'Mamante, Tecla, Basilisco', *Bibliotheca Sanctorum*, 8 (1966), 612–13.

—— 'Tecla e Mugi', *Bibliotheca Sanctorum*, 12 (1969), 184–5.

SCHÄFERDIEK, KNUT, 'The Manichean Collection of Apocryphal Acts Ascribed to Leucius Charinus', in *New Testament Apocrypha*, ed. E. Hennecke and W. Schneemelcher (Cambridge: James Clarke; Louisville, Ky.: Westminster, 1992), rev. edn. ii. 87–100.

SCHMIDT, CARL, 'Bemerkungen zu einer angeblichen altkoptischen Madonnadarstellung', *Römische Quartalschrift für christliche Alterthumskunde und für Kirchengeschichte*, 11 (1897), 497–506.

—— 'Ein neues Fragment der Heidelberger Acta Pauli', *SBAW* (1909), 216 ff.

—— and POLOTSKY, H., *Ein Mani-Fund in Ägypten* (Berlin: Akademie der Wissenschaften, 1933).

SCHMITZ, ALFRED L., *Das Totenwesen der Kopten: Kritische Übersicht über die literarischen und monumentalen Quellen*, Sonderabdruck von Zeitschrift für ägyptische Sprache und Altertumskunde, 65/1 (Leipzig: J. C. Hinrichs, 1930).

SCHÜSSLER-FIORENZA, ELIZABETH, *In Memory of Her: A Feminist Reconstruction of Christian Origins* (New York: Crossroad, 1983; 10th anniversary edn. with new introduction, 1994).

SCHWARTZ, J., 'Nouvelles études sur des fresques d'El-Bagawat', *Cahiers archéologiques*, 13 (1962), 1–11.

SCHWEIKER, WILLIAM, *Mimetic Reflections: A Study in Hermeneutics, Theology, and Ethics* (New York: Fordham University Press, 1990).

SIVAN, H., 'Who Was Egeria? Piety and Pilgrimage in the Age of Gratian', *Harvard Theological Review*, 81 (1988), 59–72.

SMITH, E. BALDWIN, 'A Source of Medieval Style in France', *Art Studies*, 2 (1924), 85–112.

SÖDER, ROSA, *Die apokryphen Apostelgeschichten und die romanhafte Literatur der Antike*, Würzburger Studien zur Altertumswissenschaft 3 (Stuttgart: S. Kohlhammer, 1932; repr. Darmstadt: Wissenschaftliche Buchgesellschaft, 1969).

SÖRBOM, GÖRAN, *Mimesis and Art: Studies in the Origin and Early Development of an Aesthetic Vocabulary* (Bonniers: Svenska Bokförlaget, 1966).

SPARIOSU, MIHAI (ed.), *Mimesis in Contemporary Theory: An Interdisciplinary Approach*. i: *The Literary and Philosophical Debate* (Philadelphia and Amsterdam: John Benjamins, 1984).

ŠPIDLÍK, THOMAS, 'Bonifacio e Tecla', *Bibliotheca Sanctorum*, 3 (1969), 355–6.

STANLEY, D. M., 'Become Imitators of Me: The Pauline Conception of Apostolic Tradition', *Biblica*, 40 (1959), 859–77.

STEPHENS, SUSAN A., 'Who Read the Ancient Novels?', in James Tatum (ed.), *The Search for the Ancient Novel* (Baltimore: Johns Hopkins University Press, 1994), 405–18.

STERN, HENRI, 'Les Peintures du Mausolée "de l'exode" à El-Bagaouat', *Cahiers archéologiques*, 11 (1960), 93–119.

STEVENSON, J., *The Catacombs: Rediscovered Monuments of Early Christianity* (London: Thames and Hudson, 1978).

STEWART, RANDALL, 'Fayyûm, City of', in *The Coptic Encyclopedia*, ed. A. S. Atiyah (New York: Macmillan, 1991), iv. 1100.

—— 'Mareotis', In *The Coptic Encyclopedia*, v. 1526–7.

STRZYGOWSKI, JOSEF, *Koptische Kunst*, Catalogue général des antiquités égyptiennes du Musée du Caire (Vienna: Adolf Holzhausen, 1904).

TASKIRAN, CELÂL, *Silifke [Seleucia on Calycadnus] and Environs: Lost Cities of a Distant Past in Cilicia* (Ankara: SIM Matbaacılık, 1993).

TATUM, JAMES (ed.), *The Search for the Ancient Novel* (Baltimore: Johns Hopkins University Press, 1994).

TAUSSIG, MICHAEL, *Mimesis and Alterity: A Particular History of the Senses* (New York: Routledge, 1993).

TELSER, LESTER G., *A Theory of Efficient Cooperation and Competition* (Cambridge: Cambridge University Press, 1987).

THÉREL, M. L., 'La Composition et le symbolisme de l'iconographie du Mausolée de l'Exode à El-Bagawat', *Rivista di archeologia cristiana (Miscellaea in onore di Enrico Josi IV)*, 45 (1969), 223–70.

THIESSEN, GERD, *The Social Setting of Pauline Christianity: Essays on Corinth* (Philadelphia: Fortress Press, 1982).

—— *Sociology of Early Palestinian Christianity* (Philadelphia: Fortress Press, 1978).

THOMPSON, STITH (ed.), *Motif-Index of Folk Literature*, rev. edn. (Bloomington and London: Indiana University Press, 1955).

THURSTON, BONNIE BOWMAN, *The Widows: A Women's Ministry in the Early Church* (Minneapolis: Fortress Press, 1989).

TETZ, MARTIN, 'Athanasius von Alexandrien', *TRE* 4: 333–49.

TILL, WALTER C., *Datierung und Prosopographie der koptischen Urkunden aus Theben*, Österreichische Akademie der Wissenschaften, Philosophisch-historische Klasse, Proceedings, 240, vol. 1 (Vienna: Hermann Böhlaus, 1962).

TIMM, STEFAN, *Das christlich-koptische Ägypten in arabischer Zeit*, 6 vols. (Wiesbaden: Dr. Ludwig Reichert, 1984–92).

274   *Bibliography*

TOPPING, EVA CATAFYGIOTU, 'St. Matrona and Her Friends: Sisterhood in Byzantium', in J. Chrysostomides (ed.), *ΚΑΘΗΓΗΤΡΙΑ:
Essays presented to Joan Hussey* (Camberley: Porphyrogenitus, 1988),
211–24.

TORJESEN, KAREN JO, *When Women Were Priests* (San Francisco:
Harper, 1993).

TOUGHER, SHAUN F., 'Byzantine Eunuchs: An Overview, with Special
Reference to their Creation and Origin', in Liz James (ed.), *Women,
Men and Eunuchs: Gender in Byzantium* (London and New York:
Routledge, 1997), 168–84.

TRAN TAM TINH, V., *Isis Lactans: Corpus des monuments greco-romains
d'Isis allaitant Harpocrate*, Études préliminaires aux religions orientales dans l'empire romain, 37 (Leiden: E. J. Brill, 1973).

TREVETT, CHRISTINE, *Montanism: Gender, Authority and the New
Prophecy* (Cambridge: Cambridge University Press, 1996).

TROJE, LOUISE, *Adam und Zoe, eine Szene der altchristlichen Kunst in ihrem
religionsgeschichtlichen Zusammenhange* (Heidelberg: C. Winter, 1916).

TURNER, VICTOR, *Image and Pilgrimage in Christian Culture: Anthropological Perspectives* (New York: Columbia University Press, 1978).

—— *The Ritual Process* (Ithaca, NY: Cornell University Press, 1969).

VALANTASIS, RICHARD, 'Constructions of Power in Asceticism', *Journal
of the American Academy of Religion*, 63/4 (1995), 775–821.

VERMEULE, CORNELIUS C., 'Egyptian Contributions to Late Roman
Imperial Portraiture', *Journal of the American Research Center in
Egypt*, 1 (1962), 63–8.

VIKAN, GARY, *Byzantine Pilgrimage Art*, Dumbarton Oaks Byzantine
Collection Publications, 5 (Washington: Dumbarton Oaks, 1982).

—— 'Meaning in Coptic Funerary Sculpture', in G. Koch (ed.),
Studien zur frühchristlichen Kunst II, Göttinger Orientforschungen,
series 2, Studien zur spätantiken und frühchristlichen Kunst
(Wiesbaden: Otto Harrassowitz, 1986), viii. 15–23.

VILLIER, MARCEL, 'Le Martyre et l'ascèse', *Revue d'ascetique et de mystique*, 6 (1925), 105–42.

VIVIAN, CASSANDRA, *Islands of the Blest: A Guide to the Oases and
Western Desert of Egypt* (Maadi, Egypt: Trade Routes Enterprises/
International Publications, 1990).

VOIGT, ELLEN BRYANT, 'Image', *New England Review*, 13/3–4 (Spring,
Summer 1991), 254–68.

VOLBACH, WOLFGANG FRIEDRICH, *Late Antique Coptic and Islamic
Textiles of Egypt* (New York: E. Weyhe, 1926).

WAAL, ANTON DE, 'Vom Heiligtum des hl. Menas in der libyschen
Wüste', *Römische Quartalschrift für Kirchengeschichte*, 20 (1906),
82–92.

WAGNER, GUY, 'Bagawat, Al-, Greek Inscriptions', in *The Coptic Encyclopedia*, ed. A. S. Atiyah (New York: Macmillan, 1991), ii. 327–8.

WALLACE-HADRILL, ANDREW, 'Engendering the Roman House', in D. E. E. Kleiner and S. B. Matheson (eds.), *I Claudia: Women in Ancient Rome* (New Haven: Yale University Art Gallery, 1996).

WALSH, EFTHALIA MAKRIS, 'Wisdom as it is Manifested in the Theotokos and the Women Saints of the Byzantine Era', MA thesis, American University, 1980.

WALTER, CHRISTOPHER, 'An Iconographical Note', *REB* 38, (1980), 255–60.

WALTERS, C. C., *Monastic Archaeology in Egypt* (Westminster: Aris & Phillips, 1974).

WALTERS, ELIZABETH, *Attic Grave Reliefs That Represent Women in the Dress of Isis*, Hesperia, suppl. 22 (Princeton: American School of Classical Studies at Athens, 1988).

WARD, BENEDICTA, *The Desert Christian: Sayings of the Desert Fathers, The Alphabetic Collection* (New York: Macmillan, 1980).

—— *Harlots of the Desert: A Study of Repentance in Early Monastic Sources* (Kalamazoo, Mich.: Cistercian Publications, 1987).

—— 'Signs and Wonders: Miracles in the Desert Tradition', *Studia Patristica*, 18 (Oxford and New York: Pergamon Press, 1982).

WARD-PERKINS, J. B., 'The Shrine of St. Menas in the Maryût', *Papers of the British School at Rome*, 17 (1946), 26–71.

WARNS, RÜDIGER, 'Weitere Darstellungen der heiligen Thekla', in G. Koch (ed.), *Studien zur frühchristlichen Kunst II*, Göttinger Orientforschungen, series 2. Studien zur spätantiken und frühchristlichen Kunst, vol. 8 (Wiesbaden: Otto Harrassowitz, 1986).

WATSON, HELEN, *Women in the City of the Dead* (London: Hurst & Company, 1992).

WATTERSON, BARBARA, *Coptic Egypt* (Edinburgh: Scottish Academic Press, 1988).

WEINREICH, O., *Antike Heilungswunder: Untersuchungen zum Wunderglauben der Griechen und Romer* (Giessen: Alfred Topelmann, 1909).

WENSINCK, A. J., *Legends of Eastern Saints*, ii. *The Legend of Hilaria* (Leiden: E. J. Brill, 1913).

WESSEL, K., *Coptic Art* (New York: McGraw-Hill, 1965).

—— *Koptische Kunst: Die Spätantike in Ägypten* (Recklinghausen: Aurel Bongers, 1963).

—— *Reallexikon zur byzantinischen Kunst* (Stuttgart: Anton Hiersemann, 1966–).

WILBUR, D. N., 'The Coptic Frescoes of Saint Menas at Medinet Habu', *Art Bulletin*, 22 (1940), 36–103.

WILFONG, TERRY, 'Reading the Disjointed Body in Coptic: From Physical Modification to Textual Fragmentation', in Dominic Montserrat (ed.), *Changing Bodies, Changing Meanings: Studies on the Human Body in Antiquity* (London and New York: Routledge, 1998).

WILKINSON, C. K., 'Early Christian Paintings in the Oasis of Khargeh', *Bulletin Metropolitan Museum of Art, New York*, 23/2 (1928), 29–36.

WILKINSON, JOHN, *Egeria's Travels to the Holy Land*, rev. edn. (Jerusalem: Ariel, 1981).

—— *Jerusalem Pilgrims Before the Crusades* (Warminster: Aris & Phillips, 1977).

WILPERT, JOSEF (Giuseppi), *Die gottgeweihten Jungfrauen in den ersten Jahrhunderten der Kirche* (Freiburg am Breisgau; St. Louis, Mo.: Herder, 1892).

—— 'Menasfläschen mit der Darstellung der hl.Thekla zwischen den wilden Tieren', *Römische Quartalschrift für christliche Alterthumskunde und für Kirchengeschichte*, 20 (1906), 86–92.

WINLOCK, H. E., *The Temple of Hibis in el Khargeh Oasis*, pt. 1, *The Excavations*, Metropolitan Museum of Art Egyptian Expedition Publications, 13 (New York: Metropolitan Museum of Art, 1941).

—— and CRUM, W. E., *The Monastery of Epiphanius at Thebes*, 2 vols. (New York: Metropolitan Museum of Art, 1926).

WITHERINGTON, BEN, III, *Women and the Genesis of Christianity* (Cambridge: Cambridge University Press, 1990).

WITT, REGINALD E., 'The Importance of Isis for the Fathers', *Studia Patristica*, 8 (1966), 135–45.

—— *Isis in the Graeco-Roman World* (London: Thames and Hudson, 1971).

WOLSKA-CONUS, WANDA, 'Un programme iconographique de Patriarche Tarasios?', *REB* 38 (1980), 247–54.

WULFF, O., *Altchristliche und byzantinische Kunst*, i. *Die altchristliche Kunst* (Berlin: Akademische Verlagsgesellschaft Athenaion m.b.h., 1918).

—— *Altchristliche und mittelalterliche byzantinische und italienische Bildwerke*, iii. pt. 1, Altchristliche Bildwerke (Berlin: Georg Reimer, 1909).

—— and VOLBACH, W. F., *Spätantike und koptische Stoffe aus ägyptischen Grabfunden* (Berlin: Staatliche Museen, 1926).

YOUTIE, H. C., 'A Codex of Jonah', *Harvard Theological Review*, 38 (1945), 195–7.

ZALOSCER, HILDE, 'Gibt es eine koptische Kunst?', *Jahrbuch der österreichischen byzantinischen Gesellschaft*, 16 (1967), 225–44.

—— *Die Kunst im christlichen Ägypten* (Vienna/Munich: Anton Schroll & Co., 1974).

INDEX